ROUTLEDGE LIBRARY EDITIONS: WW2

Volume 37

VICHY FRANCE AND THE RESISTANCE

VICHY FRANCE AND THE RESISTANCE
Culture and Ideology

Edited by
RODERICK KEDWARD AND ROGER AUSTIN

LONDON AND NEW YORK

First published in 1985 by Croom Helm Ltd

This edition first published in 2022
by Routledge
2 Park Square, Milton Park, Abingdon, Oxon OX14 4RN

and by Routledge
605 Third Avenue, New York, NY 10158

Routledge is an imprint of the Taylor & Francis Group, an informa business

© 1985 Roderick Kedward and Roger Austin

All rights reserved. No part of this book may be reprinted or reproduced or utilised in any form or by any electronic, mechanical, or other means, now known or hereafter invented, including photocopying and recording, or in any information storage or retrieval system, without permission in writing from the publishers.

Trademark notice: Product or corporate names may be trademarks or registered trademarks, and are used only for identification and explanation without intent to infringe.

British Library Cataloguing in Publication Data
A catalogue record for this book is available from the British Library

ISBN: 978-1-03-201217-9 (Set)
ISBN: 978-1-00-319367-8 (Set) (ebk)
ISBN: 978-1-03-204057-8 (Volume 37) (hbk)
ISBN: 978-1-03-204058-5 (Volume 37) (pbk)
ISBN: 978-1-00-319038-7 (Volume 37) (ebk)

DOI: 10.4324/9781003190387

Publisher's Note
The publisher has gone to great lengths to ensure the quality of this reprint but points out that some imperfections in the original copies may be apparent.

Disclaimer
The publisher has made every effort to trace copyright holders and would welcome correspondence from those they have been unable to trace.

VICHY FRANCE and the RESISTANCE

CULTURE & IDEOLOGY

Edited by
RODERICK KEDWARD and ROGER AUSTIN

CROOM HELM
London & Sydney

© 1985 Roderick Kedward and Roger Austin
Croom Helm Ltd, Provident House, Burrell Row,
Beckenham, Kent BR3 1AT
Croom Helm Australia Pty Ltd, Suite 4, 6th Floor,
64-76 Kippax Street, Surry Hills, NSW 2010, Australia

British Library Cataloguing in Publication Data

Vichy France and the Resistance: culture
    and ideology.
    1. World War, 1939-1945–Underground
    movements–France
    I. Kedward, Roderick   II. Austin, Roger
    940.53'44   D802.F8

ISBN 0-7099-1562-4

Printed and bound in Great Britain
by Billing & Sons Limited, Worcester.

CONTENTS

Preface *Roderick Kedward and Roger Austin*

Introduction: Ideologies and Ambiguities *Roderick Kedward* ... 1

Part One: Vichy ... 11

1. Political Surveillance and Ideological Control in Vichy France: a Study of Teachers in the Midi, 1940-1944 *Roger Austin* ... 13
2. Women and the National Revolution *Miranda Pollard* ... 36
3. Manipulators of Vichy Propaganda: a Case Study in Personality *John Dixon* ... 48
4. Jews and Catholics *Louis Allen* ... 73

Part Two: Ambiguities ... 89

5. Saint-Exupéry's *Pilote de guerre*: Testimony, Art and Ideology *S. Beynon John* ... 91
6. The Role of Joan of Arc on the Stage of Occupied Paris *Gabriel Jacobs* ... 106
7. Ambiguities in the Film *Le Ciel est à vous* *Jeanie Semple* ... 123
8. Catholicism Under Vichy: a Study in Diversity and Ambiguity *Bill Halls* ... 133
9. Uriage: the Assault on a Reputation *Brian Darling* ... 147
10. Uriage: the Influence of Context on Content *Derek Robbins* ... 159
11. Emmanuel Mounier, *Esprit* and Vichy, 1940-1944: Ideology and Anti-ideology *John Wright* ... 171

Part Three: Resistance ... 191

12. The Resistance Experience: Teaching and Resources *Hilary Footitt and John Simmonds* ... 193
13. France, Soil and Language: Some Resistance Poems by Luc Bérimont and Jean Marcenac *Ian Higgins* ... 206
14. *Les Cahiers du Silence* *Ethel Tolanksy* ... 222
15. The Maquis and the Culture of the Outlaw (With Particular Reference to the Cévennes) *Roderick Kedward* ... 232

Contents

Outlines   253

16. Collaboration and Literary Criticism: Ramon Fernandez's
    Barrès Bill Kidd   255
17. Writing Under Vichy: Ambiguity and Literary Imagination
    in the Non-Occupied Zone *Robert Pickering*   260
18. The Cult of Joan of Arc in French Schools, 1940-1944
    Nick Atkin   265
19. Robert Brasillach: the Machismo of Impotence
    John Coombes   269

Notes on Contributors   274
Chronology   277
Index   284

PREFACE

The original idea of bringing together scholars from the UK and Ireland with an interest in Vichy France and the Resistance was conceived, appropriately enough, in France. In fact it arose in the course of a discussion between us after a long day in the Archives Départementales at Mende in the Lozère. We both owe a great deal to those archivists throughout France who have generously given time to advise us and to support our requests for access to primary sources. Without their help, many of the contributions to this book would not have been possible.

The conference we planned in Mende finally took place at the University of Sussex in April 1984 with the presentation of ten long papers and several short ones. We designed it to show the various aspects of research into Occupied France currently in progress in Britain and Ireland, but it would have been sadly impoverished without the presence of Monsieur Gilles Chouraqui, the Conseiller Culturel from the French Embassy in London, and Monsieur François Bédarida, Director of the Institut d'Histoire du Temps Présent in Paris. We were honoured and delighted that they were able to contribute in such a telling way to our discussions.

It is literally true to say that the final form in which this book appears owes a great deal to the spirit of lively and friendly discourse which characterised both the formal and informal gatherings of the conference. On behalf of the contributors to this volume, we would like to record our sincere thanks to those who attended the conference and who enlivened it with their comments and the generous criticism of the papers given. It was because all the sessions were so productive that we decided to ask for five more long papers, and to publish four of the short pieces that had originally been given as ten-minute introductions to potential research. These four are placed together as Outlines at the end of the book (Chs 16-19). We only wish we had space to publish the even shorter contributions to each discussion: had we done so, the intellectual challenge and scope of so many different aspects of Vichy France and the Resistance would have been fully apparent. As it is, we still hope that the colour, diversity and depth of the subject will be evident from these pages.

Roderick Kedward and Roger Austin

INTRODUCTION: IDEOLOGIES AND AMBIGUITIES

Roderick Kedward

The Conference at which these essays were first presented, or suggested, brought together most of the British-based scholars who are currently researching the period of the German Occupation of France. The disciplines were several and the approaches individualised and specific: there was no attempt to produce a stage-managed unity of purpose or a collective conclusion. High on empirical rummaging, whether in local archives or little known poems, the papers pleaded guilty to a selective analysis, but showed a resilient toughness in their diffused insights. Gathered together now into a book, the collection is vulnerable for its lack of an overview, but the roots are there for a landscape to develop. The research it contains coincides widely with current research in France, but it is English, or British, in most ways that the French would traditionally expect. Only the perfidy is missing.

If the book shows there to be any particular emphasis on this side of the Channel it is in the long section devoted to Ambiguities. The theme of ambiguity surfaced recurrently during the Conference, even in the papers and discussion which appeared to be dealing with unambiguous issues. In this short introduction I would like to make a few comments on this theme, prefaced by still fewer words on how I myself envisage the ideologies of Vichy and the Resistance. The comments are really little more than personal reflections, and are not intended to provide a theoretical framework to the essays which follow. They themselves have provided their own theoretical scaffolding, if any was thought to be needed.

From my own point of view I would wish to portray the ideology of Vichy, as it was contained in the Révolution Nationale and early collaboration as undoubtedly class-based, but more by reason of its open hostility to the Left and Trade Unionism than by any consistent economic measures to develop the role of private capital and property in the running of society. It is not that the Révolution Nationale had no economic rationale, but that like so many combinations of nationalism and corporatism in the twentieth century, it was full of political and cultural ideas which had little or no economic consistency. Its emphasis on provincial traditions and its doctrine of a return to the land have been seen as a willingness to play the rural role in Germany's New

Europe, but in fact the rural and provincial ideas long predate any politics of collaboration and must be seen as an embarrassment to the financiers and technocrats who were attracted to Vichy because of its determination to abolish the Trade Unions and curb the political Left, and the opportunities it gave for a directed economy.

Vichy and the Révolution Nationale were not coterminous. Vichy continued into a second stage of collaboration when the ideas of the Révolution Nationale became decidedly tarnished. We have to ask whether the various stages of collaboration, from Montoire through to Sigmaringen, have a single ideology? Whose interests did they represent? This is much more difficult, for if the interests of the economically dominant class were inconsistently represented by the Révolution Nationale and early forms of collaboration, they were hardly served at all by the collaboration in which Vichy became ultimately involved in 1943-4. The objection to this might well be that it was collaboration in its most complete form which seemed to Albert Speer in Germany and Bichelonne in France to provide a model of an efficiently planned and directed European economy, which some have seen as prefiguring the Treaty of Rome and the EEC. Surely this has an ideological dimension? Eventually, yes, when it emerges from an entirely different political source, the economic planners of the various Resistance movements in Europe. Under Vichy it was far too individualised to qualify as an ideology.

Would it not be simpler to call the whole of Vichy fascist, adding the adjective French to distinguish it from the other European varieties? It might be simpler, and it would represent the way in which the Jews and the Resisters increasingly experienced the Vichy presence, but it would still leave us with the problem of deciding what kind of an ideology French fascism actually was. In the end I would like to retain the diagnosis of fascism, but in the form that Poulantzas conceptualised.[1] I would suggest that the Révolution Nationale combined with collaboration to make Vichy in its first two years an 'exceptional state' in so far as it served the needs of the cartels and monopolies, the patronat and the financial world, which had been radically challenged by the Popular Front. But it was far more insubstantial than the 'exceptional states' which Poulantzas saw existing in the early stages of Italian Fascism and German Nazism, due to the inevitable economic disasters of being an occupied and exploited country; and it was inconsistent due to the prevalence of cultural and political ideas which stemmed only from the fringe of the dominant class and not from the centre. In the last two years, 1942-4, even this flexible definition fails to make sense, due to

Introduction

the progressive disintegration of the Vichy state, and I would venture that Vichy in its last stages was no more than the politics of opportunism, drawn towards highly derivative, Nazi-style, solutions, but with no coherent ideology, and no fundamental class basis.

What is important for many of the contributors to this book, is the role that writers and intellectuals played, and the extent to which ideas and culture were the main creative force behind the Vichy ideology rather than economic interests. This moves us away into a more free-floating conceptual world, which allows the notion that culture and economics have no predictable relationship to each other. In this perspective, ideas are not necessarily class-determined even if they become class-specific in their results and application, while the arts in the widest sense can either be dependent on class, or can establish their independence of class structures and values. Such an understanding of culture is usually combined with a definition of ideology in which class and economics play a role, but not a determining one. Ideology in this sense is a body of ideas, forming the basis of a distinct set of policies, and one which could be the projection of class interests but is not necessarily so. Within this definition it could be argued that the ideology of Action Française, which was derived from ideas about French history, culture and character, was an ideology permanently in pursuit of a class basis and an economic rationale. It appeared to have found both under Vichy, but when it lost them in the last years of the Occupation, it did not collapse as an ideology but became even more fanatically entrenched in its cultural base.

Clearly when ideology is used in this way it becomes more approximate to words like dogma and doctrine, and by and large this seems to be the way in which it is used in this book. I don't believe that this should entail a rejection of the notion that ideologies are mostly class-based, but rather it should present itself as a conceptual adjustment to do justice to the obvious limitations of relating not only collaboration but also Resistance to the interests of class. For if there are inconsistencies within the class dimension of Vichy and collaboration, there are just as many, if not more, within Resistance.

In Resistance we find a body of ideas which stemmed from a political tradition to which several economic classes were, in their different ways, attached. This was the tradition of republican patriotism, which had a revolutionary wing but a socially conservative centre. It can certainly be described as an ideology in the looser sense, but it was slow to establish itself in Resistance, and it only did so when it became fully apparent that Vichy could not protect the French nation as Pétain had so boldly claimed in July 1940. The Resistance as the *sole* embodiment of this republican patriotic tradition dates from 1942, and even then the hopes of many republicans, who had seen in the hero of Verdun the personification of their patriotism, had not been fully destroyed. Before 1942, Resistance was a notable force in the French reaction to the Occupation but it could not be said to constitute an ideology until the Resisters came to monopolise the political legacy of republican defence and the citizen at arms.

The primacy of politics in the make-up of Resistance does not mean that class interests were of little importance in its doctrines. Vichy deprived the urban working class of its bargaining strength and collaborated closely in the deportation of labour. As a result, Resistance promised much for this victimised class. Had it not been for the infighting and disarray within the politics of the Left between the victory of the Popular Front and the end of the Nazi-Soviet pact, Resistance might have started as a proletarian movement, and the exaggerated fears of the Allies and de Gaulle of a social revolution at the time of the Liberation might have been justified. Such speculative comment is only worthwhile as a way of emphasising that this did not happen: republican patriotism took ideological possession of the Resistance and never lost its hold whatever tactical concessions might have been made to ideas of radical social change.

The culture of the Resistance, unlike the culture of Vichy, is difficult to quantify. Its quality is largely found in poetry which adapted better to clandestine expression than the visual and performing arts, and demanded fewer of the scarce material resources than the novel. Like the ideology of the Révolution Nationale, the ideology of republican patriotism also had its cultural myths, sacred doctrines, heroic images of the past, and creative visions of the future. Due to the popularity of Pétainism, some of these myths overlapped for a time with the myths of Vichy, and the ambiguities were striking. They did not last, and after 1942 the ideologies have no common ground except the 'Marseillaise', and even there, as Louis Grave said in *Le Chagrin et La Pitié*, 'The evening the first arms arrived, we came to this cellar. I remember we sang the "Internationale". We weren't Communists though; it was just that Pétain sang "La Marseillaise" so we had to sing "l'Internationale".'[2] Such an anecdote is a good reminder that the ideas and cultural attitudes within the Resistance were expressed more in individual action and group behaviour than in art forms or intellectual writing. The cultural and intellectual historians of Vichy have a fairly orthodox task, with familiar forms to analyse, whereas the equivalent

Introduction

studies of Resistance must use an enlarged concept of cultural and intellectual expression. For example, we can gain a very clear picture of Vichy's attitudes to women from films, novels, plays and magazines as well as through the Government's social policies. The very few writings which the Resistance produced is poor material by comparison, but that does not make the research in that direction impossible: it will involve a search for images of women outside the cultural forms of expression, in the organisation and structures of Resistance activity. To understand the ideology of Resistance, action and expression need to become more interchangeable. There can be few better reasons for encouraging interdisciplinary research than this.

Mention of interdisciplinary work brings me back to the Conference and the recurrence of ambiguity in the papers and discussion. What are the implications, possibilities and problems of finding so many ambiguities in the history and culture of France under the German Occupation?

Several observations are possible. In the first place the empiricist will laconically remark that what has always been there will eventually be discovered, not least as the search for a viable thesis takes young researchers away from the well-trodden paths of collaboration and Resistance into the thickets of compromise, uncertainty and ambivalence. But where have the well-trodden paths run? Through the heart of the wood or only round the perimeter? Perhaps the thickets of ambiguity are really the heart of the wood, representing the very stuff of the Occupation experience, or are they no more than rebarbative clumps of undergrowth above which soar the familiar trees of collaboration and Resistance for which the wood is primarily known? The placing of the section on Ambiguities in the centre of the book may seem to have a symbolic importance, but this is really not so, for it was an unthinking, traditional (very English?) place to put ambiguities, lying between the control mechanisms of a collaborationist Vichy at one end, and the subversion of the Maquis at the other. If ambiguity was the norm of the Occupation experience and expression, then perhaps the section should come assertively at the beginning. If, however, the discovery of ambiguities is the trademark of those with a professional interest in complicating any given subject matter, then the section should come at the end, as a self-conscious admission of academic practice. The Conference only skirmished around this issue: there was no direct confrontation, and no resolution. Ambiguities remain at the centre, or should we say in the middle, *faute de mieux*.

Secondly, the fascination of ambiguities is not only that they are a whole new area for the researcher to discover and develop, but that they are also, or more so, new ways of assessing old material, sometimes as a result of new information but just as often as a result of new interests, new insights and new approaches both within and outside the academic world. Interpretations, like performances, are specific to time and place: they have their own history, their own structures, their own language. At the moment, on this side of the Channel, there is a marked preference for breaking down the polarities in French history and the French way of life. This preference values ambiguity as a force which breaks the predictability of polar opposites, and anchors both experience and expression more firmly in the complexities of their own structures. I hesitate to call it a preference for the structuralist approach, for that would be to limit its source to that particular school of thought. It derives in equal measure from a scrupulous empiricism. The result is an emphasis on links, interconnections, common sources, interchangeable language and so on, all of which make for ambiguities as soon as attempts are made to superimpose a clear-cut grid of polar opposites. The cult of Joan of Arc, the respect for Péguy, a sense of French tradition, the call to patriotism, were just some of the many ingredients in French attitudes and opinion during the Occupation, common to the cuisine of the Hôtel du Parc at Vichy, to the furtive Resistance meals in the cellars of the Croix-Rousse in Lyon, and to the long evenings round the smokeless fires of the Maquis.

Inevitably there is a certain distancing involved in this kind of emphasis, which raises controversy in France and often offends. It is easier to explore the ambiguities of patriotism under the Occupation, and even to conclude that both Vichy and the Resistance (perhaps some of the fascists in Paris also) were patriotic, if patriotism is seen as a common ingredient in all French politics, like the predilection for groupuscules. Similarly the military exploits of SOE agents, Resistance units, the SS, and the Milice can more easily be compared from a standpoint which regards war-games as endemic in masculine behaviour. What kind of patriotism and what objectives there were in the war-games, then become secondary rather than primary questions.

Such distancing suggests a lack of political commitment, or an overall cynicism about behaviour, but this is not necessarily the case. There are politics without patriotism, and human behaviour without war-games, to which the apparently distant, uncommitted researcher may be strongly tied. A preference for emphasising ambiguities, links and interconnections in Occupied France may be a step towards estab-

Introduction

lishing what the researcher feels to be wider and more important polar opposites. It is not just a current possibility. During the existence of the Nazi-Soviet pact the official opinion of the leaders of the French Communist Party was that there was little to choose between Pétain, seen as the servant of the French cartels, and de Gaulle, seen as the servant of the City of London. A larger dialectic than the struggle between Vichy and the Free French thus made de Gaulle and Pétain into confederates rather than enemies in the eyes of the PCF. The party quickly withdrew this analysis, but it surfaced again, this time among Trotskyists and other sections of the Left in the 1960s who found much to compare in the social philosophy of Gaullism and Pétainism. A class analysis of the two during the Occupation has yet to be rigorously undertaken, but it cannot be long before a full social history of all sides of the conflict introduces a host of new ambiguities, particularly if the study incorporates a feminist perspective. In a similar process, the analysis by Marrus and Paxton of attitudes and policies towards the Jews, though concentrating on the Vichy régime, nevertheless found little to recommend in the attitudes of any of the French during the first two years after the defeat. They established an area of ambiguity which cut across the traditional divide, and thereby emphasised their commitment to a larger moral perspective.[3] A destructuring of specific polar opposites is not the destructuring of all.

Thirdly, the growing research into ambiguity under the Occupation raises the problem of whether the term should be judgemental, as it has mostly been used, or whether it should become more neutrally descriptive. As a portmanteau term ambiguity has stood for bad faith, failure to choose, dishonesty, double-jeu in the Laval sense, equivocation and *attentisme*, all of which carry a derogatory flavour affecting the way we diagnose ambiguity under the Occupation and how we respond to it. Whether we intend it or not, a section called Ambiguities still carries a level of indictment within it, which is why the contributors defending the reputation of Emmanuel Mounier and the staff of the École des Cadres at Uriage do so with a discernible degree of vigour. But also discernible in the research which emerged at the Conference was the use of the term to suggest inconsistency, confusion, or the inevitable compromises involved in fulfilling the demands of everyday life under the Occupation, whether driving a train safely to its destination even though it was full of Germans, or opening an art gallery, theatre or opera to a clientele which was mainly German. François Truffaut addressed this kind of ambiguity squarely in *Le Dernier Métro* (1980) as Jean-Louis Curtis had done immediately after the war in *Les Forêts de la Nuit* (winner of the Prix Goncourt in 1947). Still further there is a widespread use of the concept of an 'ambiguous situation' as if it exists independently of the population, so that certain kinds of ambiguous behaviour and expression are seen to be unavoidable effects of something external to individual or group responsibility.

What has happened over 40 years of writing and research on the Occupation is that, inevitably, analogous periods of conflict, similar situations of occupation by a foreign power, similar liberation movements, have arisen to invite comparisons and contrasts with the French experience. Almost all researchers are also teachers, and in educational discussions and curricula there is scope for thematic observations in which the Occupation of France becomes just one in a number of linked events. Obvious examples of the comparative and generalised approach include the integration of the Paris fascists into the generic category of European, and still wider, psychological fascism; the discussion of Resistance in terms of other movements throughout the world which have been called terroristic by the prevailing forces of order; the continued debate about the quality of committed literature and the optimum role of intellectuals in a divided society; and the study of film under the Occupation less in terms of Vichy propaganda than in terms of film genres and the traditions of French film making which stretch either side of the war. An understandable interest at present lies in the comparison of Vichy, not so much with other governments in an Occupation, but with other governments in an economic recession. To what extent do these governments use a recession, as Vichy used the Occupation, to force through a sectarian political programme under the cloak of realism, the national interest and the need for sacrifice? Do similar acts of social discrimination result? or comparable methods of law enforcement? And can those who are caught between collaborating with a government's economies and resisting be studied for the same symptoms of ambiguity as were displayed in the French administration under Vichy?

Clearly, the effect of generalising the study of the Occupation may just as easily intensify the value judgements attached to ambiguity as reduce them, depending on the force of the comparisons and the subjective elements involved. The result is more to normalise the term rather than neutralise it, to make it more understandable and predictable. This is the implication of Truffaut's film and the novel by Curtis, but, excellent as they are, I feel that the scathing satire of ambiguity in Jean Dutourd's *Au Bon Beurre* (1952) should be placed alongside them to prevent the term from becoming a colourless synonym of human fallibility.

Fourthly, no one should confuse the study of ambiguity with the study of chance. They may be related but they are not the same. Chance is as often the forerunner of choice and unambiguous behaviour as it is of ambiguity. The film made by Louis Malle in 1973-4, *Lacombe Lucien*, which portrays the way in which a peasant boy in the South West of France becomes a member of the German police in the last months of the Occupation, was widely reviewed as a film about ambiguity and chance. The reviewers were not entirely wrong, but most of them failed to look carefully at the question of choice within the film. Lucien finds himself inside the collaborationist headquarters due to the chance event of a punctured bicycle tyre, but when his unintentional betrayal of his village schoolmaster leads to the arrest and torture of the schoolmaster and a realisation by Lucien of what his new-found friends are doing, he had a choice, though not an easy one, of whether to stay with them or leave. Malle does not put the choice into so many words, but the visual presentation of Lucien left to himself and wandering into the hall of the hotel where he hears the cries of the tortured schoolmaster, conveys a period of reflection and calculation during which the choice is made. He decides to stay, thereby implicating himself in the torture upstairs. Thereafter, ambiguities in his behaviour are portrayed side by side with quite unambiguous actions. There is nothing of the reluctant, accidental collaborator in his enjoyment of the power and privilege it brings, and if the suggestion of the film is that his psychological needs might just as easily have been satisfied in the Maquis, this does not invalidate the fact that what he *did* become was a willing recruit into the German police, for as long as police duty and self-interest coincided. To say that a particular collaborator might have become a Resister had circumstances been different (a claim made implicitly in the trial of Darnand), draws attention to the importance of chance, but it does not make the choice itself ambiguous. When the Resisters claimed at the trial of Laval that his double-jeu was not a defence, they were right, in so far as Laval had chosen collaboration as a way of trying to minimise the effects of Occupation, whereas they had chosen Resistance. If collaboration had won, the Germans would still be there, however skilful the *double-jeu*. Ambiguities in intention, or even the absence of intention as in the case of Lucien Lacombe, do not necessarily produce ambiguous actions.

It would be difficult, and probably foolish, to try and judge whether wider perspectives ultimately enhance or weaken our insights into the Occupation. I feel fairly sure that counter-suggestibility will always operate in discussions of this kind. A swing towards comparative or generalised perspectives will almost mechanically produce a reassertion of specificity and vice versa. It must be so, for only by creative thinking in both directions will we have anything to offer on a period in French life and culture in which huge issues were at stake and small details so determinant.

Given this assurance of a pendulum swing in research, which will swing also between the study of ambiguity and choice, one final comment comes to mind. Those who chose to resist the German Occupation, and those who chose to collaborate or wait on events, did so within a specific context as well as all the larger ones that we now recognise. All three reactions were initially based on unknown possibilities, and involved a good deal of imaginative speculation. But by 1942 there was less and less need for speculation and more and more for a decision between different sets of actualities. Some of the initial possibilities had become facts, and a choice no longer had that 'unreality' that many have diagnosed in both collaboration and Resistance in 1940-1. Throughout 1942, and still more so in 1943-4, the inhumanity of Nazism and the moral necessity of active protest impressed themselves on French society. This changing context, not outside or beyond the Occupation, but within it, gives the study of choice between collaboration and Resistance its own moral imperative. Ambiguity at that point, whether at the time or since, must surely be seen as a choice not to choose.

Notes

1. Nicos Poulantzas, *Fascisme et Dictature* (Maspero, 1970), trs. as *Fascism and Dictatorship*, Verso Edition, 1974.
2. Marcel Ophuls, *Le Chagrin et la Pitié* (Productions Télévision Rencontre, 1969), trs. as *The Sorrow and the Pity* (Paladin, 1975), p. 85.
3. M.R. Marrus and R.O. Paxton, *Vichy France and the Jews* (Basic Books, New York, 1981).

PART ONE:

VICHY

1 POLITICAL SURVEILLANCE AND IDEOLOGICAL CONTROL IN VICHY FRANCE: A STUDY OF TEACHERS IN THE MIDI, 1940-1944

Roger Austin

Recent work on Vichy France has reflected an interest in the regime's readiness to promote its ideology through propaganda[1] and through socialising young people in schools and youth movements.[2] It is now quite clear that Vichy's reforms of the educational system and its support for youth organisations were not only an attempt to overturn an allegedly republican, bookish and secular system that was held responsible for the defeat in 1940, but also a deliberate attempt to foster political integration in the new state. Work based largely on the archives of the Ministère de l'Education has shown how educational and youth policy evolved from the confused nationalist idealism of 1940 to a cynical sacrifice of the interests of young people in the face of German demands for compulsory labour in 1943-4. What has not been made clear, however, is the way in which the state developed and made use of an extensive surveillance system not only to monitor teachers as a group and as individuals but to use the intelligence that was collected to try to enforce political loyalty. The way in which this operation was conducted provides insights into how far the regime was concerned to promote ideological control, particularly among primary school teachers in state schools.

This chapter, based on hitherto classified archives, is an interpretative essay which explores how Vichy exercised political control and how effective it was. These issues are analysed and discussed by illustrating what happened in several departments in the Midi. Detailed work in the Lozère, Ardèche and Hérault, with comparable material from the Gard, Aude, Pyrénées-Orientales, Aveyron and Alpes-Maritimes, is beginning to show how widespread Vichy's political surveillance and control of teachers was. At the same time, analysis at the level of the department is starting to reveal how much latitude local officials exercised in their interpretation of national policy.

The control of teachers functioned through two main channels: firstly, through the official state apparatus of the Ministries of Education and the Interior which often relied on information sent by the Ministry of War, and secondly through populist pressure groups like

The Ministry of the Interior and the Prefecture

The responsibilities of the Ministry of the Interior and its local representative the prefect in ensuring the political loyalty of the teaching corps had a tradition which dated back to the Napoleonic era but between 1940-4 prefects not only had a far more sophisticated system of controls at this disposal but particularly strong reasons for wanting to use them. Popular belief in the role of primary school teachers in sapping the morale of the nation was widespread. Even outsiders, like Thomas Kernan, an American based in Paris, were in no doubt about where blame lay in the fall of France. In his book, *Report on France*, published in 1942, he wrote: 'If I were asked what group in France, aside from the political leaders, was chiefly responsible for the conquest of France, I'd have to answer: the school teachers.'[3] The same view was extensively promoted through the French press both nationally and in regional papers.[4] Teachers suspected of defeatism, communism or those recently naturalised were particularly likely to be disciplined either by being sacked, prematurely retired, moved to a worse post in their own or another department or temporarily suspended. The legislation to deal with these teachers was passed on 17 July 1940 and empowered prefects to take action against any teacher likely to prove 'an element of disorder, an inveterate politiciser or incompetent'.[5] But in addition to taking action against teachers for the role they were believed to have played up to the defeat, French military authorities found new reasons to keep them under surveillance. In October 1940 it was claimed that currents of opposition to the new regime were beginning to form around primary school teachers. In a report on 4 Octber 1940 the surveillance service of the Ministère de la Guerre noted: 'Left-wing extremists have not lost all hope and it is still amongst primary teachers that one discovers signs of anti-national attitudes.'[6] Within four days, a circular was transmitted to prefects ordering them to carry out a thorough investigation of the attitude of teachers[7] and later, that of inspectors.[8] Two months later, in a classified note from the Minister of the Interior to prefects in December 1940 they were reminded that it was their job to 'exercise a strict control over the loyalty of primary teachers' and to take severe sanctions where necessary.[9]

Virtually identical terms were used by the Minister of Education to regional prefects some 15 months later when Jerome Carcopino addressed them in Lyon on 20 March 1942. Prefects had not only to rally primary school teachers to the regime but 'monitor their attitude and if need be use their powers to dismiss',[10] he said. There is evidence that in some departments newly appointed prefects wanted to take extremely energetic action. In the Ardèche, where the local branch of the teacher's union the Syndicat National des Instituteurs had been both strongly pacifist and a staunch defender of teachers' rights during the 1930s, the prefect planned to take severe measures against 'antinational' teachers.[11] Indeed, as early as January 1940, several months before Vichy, the prefect had drawn up a list of teachers suspected of communism who were considered dangerous. They had enjoyed a stay of execution during the phoney war but with the defeat and the demand for a scapegoat, the prefect succeeded in taking more severe action against them than the Ministry of Education thought necessary. In at least two other departments, the Aveyron and the Alpes-Maritimes, there is no doubt that the prefects wanted to go much further than Vichy. From Rodez in the Aveyron the prefect complained in a report to the Ministry of the Interior that he had received no reply to his proposed disciplinary measures[12] while the prefect in Nice grumbled that 'some departments of central government seem more interested in putting a brake on the National Revolution than in serving it'.[13] In the Lozère it was the moderating influence of a primary school inspector that was stamped on by an unyielding prefect. The case concerned a popular and competent teacher, a recently naturalised Spaniard suspected by the police of communism. When the education inspector supported a village petition to keep the teacher the prefect commented that 'it would be dangerous to allow him to corrupt future generations with communist ideas and I am astonished that the primary school inspector does not understand this'.[14]

There is considerable evidence from other departments that this case is rather characteristic of the so-called *épuration* of the teaching profession in 1940. The schools' inspectors were mainly concerned to get rid of union leaders or incompetent teachers but were ready to take considerable risks in defending teachers against political charges provided that the teacher was respected in the community and brought credit to the state school, the école publique.[15] New prefects wanted a number of political heads to roll both to satisfy what they believed was popular demand and to give notice to the Ministry of the Interior that they were indeed exercising the 'strict control on the loyalty of teachers' that they had been instructed to do in December 1940.[16] What is clear from the way that the purge of teachers was carried out by local prefects is that it had more to do with settling old scores and providing symbolic scapegoats than any wide-scale, root and branch reform of the teaching corps. The numbers involved were extremely small, amounting to some 2-3 per cent in most departments.[17]

The political responsiveness of the prefect was, of course, subject to movement over time and space. In three departments under study, the Alpes-Maritimes, the Aveyron and Lozère, the prefects followed up the purge of teachers in 1940 by throwing their colleagues into the front line of the ideological struggle to win the population over to the National Revolution. The prefect of the Alpes-Maritimes, for example, provided the Ministry of the Interior with a quite unsolicited description of the political role that he believed teachers should play. In November 1941[18] he commented that he had once again come to realise 'the determining influence of the teaching profession on the life of the commune'. He went on to say,

> The National Revolution will never really penetrate the countryside except through the teachers: if the Government has at its disposal a body of primary school teachers who are attached to the regime and who are the leading propagandists of its doctrine, the rural masses will be all but won over.

By January 1942, the same prefect was claiming that once the core of troublemakers and agitators had been removed in 1940, the remaining teachers were now making a vital contribution to the 'work of *redressement*', and that the rural teacher was 'the best propaganda agent available to the government'.[19] In the Lozère, the prefect's endorsement of an overtly political role for teachers took the form of helping to coordinate the activities of the official 'propaganda delegate' to teachers by a thorough vetting of candidates who might be influential among their colleagues.[20] In the same report he not only signalled to his superiors a conference given by a local secondary school teacher in July 1942 on 'France, victim of anglo-bolchevik conspiracy' but commented 'I am happy to bring to your attention the excellent attitude of this teacher and his dedication to the cause of the National Revolution'.[21] At the same time the prefect in the Aveyron expressed the considered view that primary school teachers were, for the most part, 'the best artisans of the work undertaken by the Marshal'.[22] Taken together, these comments suggest that at least some prefects wanted teachers to play a dynamic role that was overtly ideological – they were to be nothing less than crusaders for the National Revolution.

In other departments, however, prefects were more concerned to direct teachers' energies to what one of them called 'social action' which involved collecting material or money either for POW parcels or for various schemes like the Secours National, or later for Parisian air-raid victims. Having set out in neat columns all the amounts of money that teachers and school children had collected for these causes, the prefect in the Pyrénées-Orientales informed the Minister of the Interior that 'this table shows better than any commentary the participation of teaching personnel in the work of national renewal'.[23] Elsewhere there is evidence that prefects sought to promote political loyalty among primary school teachers by working through the educational inspectorate. In three departments, the Gard, the Aude and the Ardèche, this meant taking steps to censure or remove the chief education officer, the Inspecteur de l'Académie, who was suspected of being lukewarm or openly hostile towards the regime.[24] But running parallel to the interest of some prefects in encouraging teachers to play a positive political role was a fear that teachers were potentially dangerous and needed to be kept under careful surveillance. To keep them under observation, Vichy's officials had a formidable network, that was both official and unofficial.

The surveillance system was, in part, the result of a long tradition that grew from the *cabinet noir* of Louis XIV,[25] through the creation of the intelligence branch of the police, the Renseignements Généraux in 1913[26] and more immediately to the inter-war surveillance organisation[27] which was substantially extended in 1939 with the outbreak of war. There is clear evidence that the system of monitoring civilian and conscript morale during the phoney war remained in the hands of the military authorities after the defeat but it was now incorporated into Vichy's apparatus for maintaining internal order.[28] To keep itself informed of the state of public opinion and, at the same time, to uncover criminal or political activities, the regime relied on both a massive interception of postal and telegraphic communications carried out by the War Ministry and the intelligence gathering activities of the 'police préventive', the Renseignements Généraux which became part of the national police structure in April 1941.[29]

The surviving archives of what was euphemistically colled the Contrôle Technique provide a remarkable picture of how the Vichy regime gathered information and pursued those suspected of criminal, political or moral deviancy. The number of letters intercepted every month in each *département* varied between 12,000 and 45,000, with a similar number of telegrams and a smaller number of phone calls.[30] For the month of January 1944 alone a total of 2,236,120 letters, 1,573,763 telegrams and 92,000 telephone calls were intercepted in metropolitan France.[31] This random sample of communications from all sections of society and all geographical areas in the southern zone was used by each departmental Président of the Contrôle Technique to write a synthesis of public opinion and to pass on copies of suspect letters for further investigation. Monthly reports on the mood of the population and the attitude of specific groups, including teachers, were sent to the local prefect, to the military commander and to a central co-ordinating bureau, the Commission de Contrôle Technique in Vichy. Interception of communications was not only intended to provide the regime with a tableau of public opinion. Its second function was 'la recherche d'indices révélateurs d'infractions, crimes et délits': indeed, each month every prefect received for his department a list of interceptions 'likely to lead to police, judicial or administrative intervention'.[32] In March 1941, Darlan complained to prefects that an inadequate number of apprehensions had been registered so far. In this aspect of the Contrôle Technique's activities it is quite clear that the system was interpreted to ensure that in their public behaviour and their private conversation, the population expressed loyalty to the ideology enshrined in the National Revolution and its chief symbol Philippe Pétain.

Teachers as a group and as individuals were of particular interest to officials in the Contrôle Technique, partly, as we have seen, through fear that they might still be attached to the ideals of the old regime, but also because they were believed to have a vital role to play in winning over the population to the new ideology. What some teachers' letters reveal is both the extent to which the system had succeeded in creating fear and uncertainty about what might be safely said or written and how wide the definition of suspect correspondence was. One teacher in Mende, for example, writing to a friend who had been forced to move to a post at Alès, in the Gard, wrote in July 1941 'you always have the impression that someone is there behind you when you are writing'.[33] Another letter, among the copies of thousands that were intercepted was sent in October 1941 from a primary school teacher in a village in the Lozère to a colleague in a neighbouring hamlet. Under the analysis 'Suspect correspondence between teachers', the archive extract reads as follows:

really the tone of your letter says more than the content: it reached me all right, but *watch yourself, indiscreet remarks can lead to a stay in Rieucros camp*, where it seems, *quite a few teachers have found a home* . . .

This reference to one of Vichy's detention camps in the Lozère where aliens and 'undesirables' were held had been underlined by an official in the Contrôle Postal, as was the conclusion of this letter which said, 'There's no point in worrying about it, *we are as temporary as the Jews so you won't have to endure your school shack mucher longer*'.[34] Other examples from the Lozère and the Ardèche suggest that the feeling of being watched was no paranoid impression. It led one young teacher to remark in October 1942, in another letter that was intercepted, 'At the moment you have to know what to say to please this regime.'[35]

It is a measure of how far Vichy had gone in determining what were considered acceptable attitudes that remarks like those described above normally led to the individuals concerned being placed on a special list of people who became the object of particular surveillance. Not only was all their outgoing and incoming correspondence now intercepted but they were likely to be investigated by the Renseignements Généraux, whose inspectors in each department wrote detailed reports on the attitude of both individual teachers and the teaching corps. In some instances their investigations led to arrest, in others, like the case of a teacher moved from the Gard to the Ardèche because of his allegedly 'subversive activity' in May 1941, the knowledge of being watched led the police to claim in December 1943 that he was no longer dangerous.[36]

The value of intercepted correspondence as a means of keeping in touch with currents of disaffection began to diminish from as early as mid-1941 when one of the officials in the Contrôle Postal noted that, at least in the Ardèche, 'communists don't use the postal services'.[37] By March 1942, clumsy efforts to trap black marketeers or profiteers with evidence from their own correspondence was felt to be counterproductive by senior inspectors in the service.[38] In May 1942, schoolchildren in Mende were warned by the Inspecteur de l'Académie in Lozère to be careful about what they said in letters. This exposure of the system of postal surveillance led the local Président of the Contrôle Postal in Lozère to complain to the prefect that there was now no further value in intercepting children's letters.[39] By early 1943 there were increasing numbers of references to people's knowledge of how the system worked: 'look and see if my letter has been steamed open, it's fairly common practice here', remarked one writer in the Ardèche on 15 January 1943.[40]

Although the effectiveness of the system was limited by the sheer volume of correspondence to be analysed and the conflicts that were provoked with other branches of the state apparatus it remained an extremely important weapon in the state's arsenal for maintaining internal security and ideological conformity. If the prefecture and the police had had to rely on the official but discreet operations of the Contrôle Technique they would only have picked up what people chose to commit to paper or said in telephone conversations. In fact, the evidence suggests that the police were kept just as busy investigating 'anti-national' activities by the floods of letters sent anonymously or by various pressure groups denouncing suspect individuals.

Populist Attacks and Denunciations

The years 1940-1 were particularly notable for the denunciation of teachers, partly because of the official campaign against them for their alleged responsibility for the defeat and also because in some departments teachers were singled out by the Church, the mayor or by the Légion as targets for populist anger. It is quite clear, for example, that in departments where there was a tradition of rivalry between state schools and confessionals ones like the Lozère and the Ardèche, political attacks on teachers in the state sector were widespread.[41] The causes for which they were denounced and the subsequent investigations by the police or by education officials provide some indication of how easy it was for teachers to fall foul of new codes of professional conduct and political outlook. For example, the primary school teacher at Préaux in the Ardèche was reported to the police for 'having let her class play noisily in front of the church' on 11 November 1940 while a commemorative service was in process. Together with three other teachers she was suspended for three months without pay.[42] This was no isolated incident: the regime's willingness to provide financial and moral support for church schools[43] rekindled old rivalries at village level to such an extent that any episode provided an opportunity for accusations and counter-accusations. In a number of cases where there were attempts to close down the state school, parents were persuaded to send their children to the church school either on the grounds that they would get a better education[44] or on the pretext that the state school teacher was immoral, incompetent, a freemason or a communist.[45]

Political Surveillance and Ideological Control 21

As late as the start of the new school year 1943/4 a state school teacher in Lozère was writing to a friend in October 1943 that 'the priest, the vicar and the church school teacher, even the mayor, are organising a massive campaign to take our kids away from school'.[46] Two further examples can be used to illustrate the intensity of feeling that this issue aroused. In July 1943 a teacher in the Lozère who was denounced by the priest in his village for having criticised the church during his lessons was put under particular surveillance when he was heard to remark 'My dream is to massacre as many priests as possible.'[47] Finally, enquiries in 1944 into the activities of those accused of collaboration threw up a large number of cases where priests were charged with having denounced state school teachers in order to close their school.[48] The threat of losing their livelihood meant that teachers had to be exceptionally careful to tow the ideological line.

Furthermore, they soon discovered that if they transgressed unwritten rules about professional behaviour they could be driven out of the village and sometimes out of a job. In one village in the Lozère, for example, the new teacher, a married women, was denounced for having an affair with a local man: what seems to have scandalised the indigenous inhabitants was, in the words of the school inspector, that 'when the school children arrived for class in the morning, they delighted in following the footprints left in the snow by M. "X" who, having spent the night at Mme. "Y"s', made his way home in the early hours'.[49] On another occasion, a teacher in Aubenas, Ardèche, was transferred from his post not because he was a bad teacher, but because, as the school inspector said, he was 'a bad husband'.[50] In addition to being good husbands or wives, state teachers had to avoid suspicion of being drinkers or too keen on fishing and ensure that they kept their classes well under control.[51] It was also essential to keep on good terms with the mayor who was not only responsible for providing the everyday but vital supplies of wood to warm the classroom but whose official position could give any complaints added weight. The nature of the complaints about teachers' morality and the way they were handled suggest that the virtues of *Famille* and *Travail* were frequently invoked and enforced both at a popular and official level. It is in this sense that one can talk about ideological penetration. In due course we shall see how educational inspectors expected teachers to conform to outward expressions of *Patrie*.

The letters which brought all the above cases to the notice of the police or the prefect in 1940 and 1941 were part of a flood that has been estimated at between three and five million for the whole period.[52]

Although this figure is certainly exaggerated, the volume of letters sent was so considerable that in January 1942 the Minister of the Interior had to write to prefects ordering them to discourage any further denunciations.[53] There is no doubt that the regime's tacit approval of informing as a legitimate and even national duty unleashed a massive and in some cases hysterical response. In December 1940, for example, an anonymous denunciation sent directly to the Minister of the Interior from an army veteran alleged that a communist cell existed at Valgorge in the Ardèche and that three local teachers were printing tracts in the school basement. The police investigation stated that the charge was 'pure fantasy'and sprang from an accusation of cheating at cards.[54] Other enquiries into complaints similar to this one were simply what a primary school inspector called 'miserable village jealousies'.[55]

While these examples were for the most part the spontaneous action of individuals who were acting from malice or a misplaced sense of patriotic duty, a far more orchestrated campaign of vengeance against teachers was mounted by some local branches of the Légion. Set up in August 1940 to act as the eyes and ears of the National Revolution, its members sometimes saw themselves as semi-official vigilantes, championing popular causes like better food supply or rooting out enemies of the state. Certainly Pétain's message to them in April 1941 appeared to give them a free rein to enlighten mayors and sub-prefects on any civic, social or moral affairs which were in contradiction to 'the Marshal's Doctrine and Instructions'.[56] In the Ardèche, it was the Légion, through a former teacher, which showed the greatest energy in carrying out a witch-hunt against teachers.[57]

After making a series of individual complaints about the attitude of particular teachers, the departmental President of the Légion sent the prefect in August 1941 the names of two primary school inspectors and 30 teachers who should be disciplined because they were allegedly disloyal or incompetent.[58] Charges against teachers included the claim that one had failed to fly the national flag in his school at Le Teil when an adjoining road had been officially renamed Boulevard Maréchal Pétain, that another had said of Pétain, 'when is he going to snuff it?', and that one of the primary school inspectors had 'an attitude that was incompatible with the new regime'.

When the prefect passed the Légion's note to the school inspector for comment, he replied that not only was there no evidence to support any of the claims made but that their 'vague and fictional nature showed how lightly teachers were being attacked'. Nevertheless, seven teachers were moved, three of whom had been denounced for being 'anti-national', 'hostile to Pétain' or 'holding advanced ideas'. These purely political offences illustrate how strongly the tide of ideological conformity was running in 1941. One other case deserves further comment: it concerned a teacher near St Jean de Muzols in the Ardèche who had been physically assaulted by two farm workers in September 1940 'simply because he was a teacher' and later denounced for anti-government propaganda.[59] When the Légion demanded his removal from office an investigation by the police recommended that no action should be taken: the Légion persisted, claiming that he was 'a notorious freemason with communist tendencies'. A further enquiry by the police revealed that behind the denunciation lay an attempt to get a relative of the Légion's secretary the teacher's job at St Jean de Muzols. Although the police commissioner and the local sub-prefect were initially prepared to have the teacher moved 'to calm things down', the local primary school inspector succeeded in getting the affair shelved. But, when the teacher in question was under threat he wrote a long letter in self-defence to the prefect in which he justified his entire career and outlook in terms of Vichy's new ideology, *Travail, Famille* and *Patrie*.[60] This case is interesting not only in showing how the Légion's insistent political denunciations could conceal purely personal intrigues but in showing how different branches of the surveillance system did not embrace the same ideological perspectives. Nevertheless, the need for teachers to fend off attacks by justifying what they did in terms of the new ideology suggests that at least in 1941 the Légion had succeeded in some areas in creating the conditions of fear and suspicion which assisted the penetration of the National Revolution.

In early 1942 there were a few spasmodic signs that the Légion was still capable of pursuing local vendettas against teachers, like a case in the Gard where a teacher was reported to the prefect because she had refused to attend a flag-saluting ceremony.[61] It is fairly clear, however, that the wave of orchestrated or spontaneous denunciations against teachers was over by mid-1942. In part this corresponded to a more general loss of confidence in the regime and the political messages that had characterised it from mid-1940 to early 1942.[62] In effect, populist vengeance against teachers belongs to that initial period of Vichy's existence which was marked first by a witch-hunt against those held responsible for defeat and then by a brief crusade to promote Pétainism. This crusade concealed an unpleasant mixture of opportunism, local intrigues and popular hysteria to which teachers were particularly vulnerable. Their fate would certainly have been far worse if the state had not become bogged down in trying to process the vast quantity of venomous and often misleading information it had unleashed from the public.

The Ministry of Education and the Inspection Académique

The direction and the various changes of national educational policy under Vichy have been well documented elsewhere[63] but the degree of ideological control exercised over teachers can only really be understood by an analysis of how local educational officials interpreted policy.

The lives of teachers in state primary schools were crucially affected by their relationship with the primary school inspector, the inspecteur primaire, and above him with the chief education officer, the Inspecteur de l'Académie. The all important inspection marks which teachers were given every year by the inspectorate often determined decisions about whether they got promotion or were able to move to a post in a better school or more congenial surroundings. The inspectorate had the most frequent, formal contact with teachers and was often asked to investigate complaints about teachers. How did these officials react to the new regime and to the idea that teachers should play a leading role in the services of the National Revolution?

There is conclusive evidence from a number of departments that the local Education Authority, the Inspection Académique, had two major preoccupations when the Vichy regime was established. The first was to reinforce their own authority over teachers which had been under attack during the 1930s by the unions: relations between the unions and the inspectorate had been severely strained during the strike called on 30 November 1938 to enforce the terms of the Matignon agreement.[64] Memories of this certainly coloured the attitude of some schools inspectors in 1940-1 whose reports on suspect teachers always indicated whether they had been 1938 strikers or not. When teachers were considered for promotion, the fact that they had gone on strike in 1938 could be held against them: indeed, when the Inspecteur de l'Académie in the Ardèche submitted a list of teachers for promotion to the prefect in 1941 he made a point of showing that no 1938 striker had been considered.[65] In the Lozère some 20 teachers who should have been promoted on grounds of seniority or excellence were held back by Vichy because of their union or political associations.[66] This is a good illustration of how local education officials were more willing to punish teachers for their past records than reward those who had

Political Surveillance and Ideological Control 25

embraced the new ideology.

Other instances show how important the reassertion of the inspectorate's authority was. When, for example, teachers were instructed by the Minister of Education to devote the first lesson of the new term in August 1940 to 'the patriotism, devotion, love of work and discipline which the Head of State shows to French people and French schoolchildren',[67] primary school inspectors in the Lozère ordered every school teacher to send in a written report on how they had taught this lesson. Teachers who failed to carry out these instructions to the letter had their previous inspection mark reduced by two.[68] In October 1940 one primary school inspector in the Lozère was written to by the Inspecteur de l'Académie in terms that made it very clear that orders were orders. In remarks that we shall return to in the context of what *patrie* meant for local officials, he wrote:

> I am surprised by the small number of teachers who have displayed the Head of State's portrait and the inscriptions which render him homage. You would do well to ensure that all teachers conform to an order that the rest of their colleagues in the department have obeyed.[69]

Further indications that the inspectorate was ready to enforce its authority in making teachers accept directives sent from Vichy can be found in the intercepted correspondence of teachers, one of whom complained to a friend in February 1942 that 'instead of demonstrating their zeal for an unthinking conformity, our superiors should consider the real interest of the class and allow teachers to adapt'.[70]

The second of the inspectorate's concerns was the defence of the state school against the claim that its teaching was unpatriotic. In order to vindicate the école publique's reputation as a vehicle for patriotism, it was vital for the Inspecteur de l'Académie to both take action against 'unpatriotic' teachers and at the same time to insist that the state school champion new forms of patriotism. In 1940-1 the local inspectorate in the Lozère perceived patriotism as identical to Pétainism and used its authority to promote the Pétain cult amongst schoolchildren. One primary school inspector in this department wrote to a head teacher in his area at the end of August 1940 in the following terms:

> Several teachers have already taken the initiative in putting up the portrait of Marshal Pétain in their classrooms. I congratulate them for having understood that children's enthusiasm needs concrete

images to develop. I therefore call upon all teachers without exception to follow the example of their colleagues . . . No excuses will be accepted. Schools are not neutral in questions of patriotism.[71]

Pétainism implied more than merely observing the exterior rituals of displaying Saint Philippe's portrait: it also meant seeing French history and French culture in a certain way. If state schools were to champion a more nationalist ethic, it was up to the inspectorate to see that the new curriculum which the regime introduced was indeed taught correctly. As Education Minister Carcopino said in a circular to each Inspecteur de l'Académie in 1941:

> The government has the will to act on children and young people through the school in order to achieve the *redressement* so necessary for the country. The reform of education, the revision and alteration of courses on Morality and Duty to the Fatherland have precisely this aim!.

He went on to say that the aims would only be achieved if instructions 'are loyally accepted and applied by all teachers and inspectors should therefore guide teachers in the interpretation of new courses'.[72]

The overall thrust of the new syllabus in history and in Education Générale et Sportive has been analysed[73] in terms of a general bias towards integral nationalism and a rehabilitation of the virtues of pre-Revolutionary France to coincide with Vichy's ideological celebration of work, family and fatherland. But how rigorously did the inspectorate monitor the way in which the regime wanted to politicise the curriculum? Teachers were usually inspected once a year, and were also required to attend conferences in their area which took place once or twice a year. In October 1940, for example, the theme in Lozère was 'The role of the primary school in the moral and civic education of the child and the awakening in him of a national and patriotic conscience.'[74] Teachers were also sent detailed instructions through the Bulletin Départemental de l'Enseignement Primaire on exactly how to handle, for example, history lessons. In 1942 the Inspecteur de l'Académie insisted that the new courses should be taught not only according to the letter, but also the spirit of new instructions which meant bringing out the 'national character'.[75]

It was one thing for the inspectorate to require teachers to display Pétain's portrait, and this was something which could be routinely checked, but it was quite another to ensure ideological commitment through the curriculum. Surveillance of this sort was impracticable and alien to the entire *formation* of most Inspecteurs de l'Académie: there were exceptions of course. One teacher in Aveyron complained to a friend in the Lozère in the spring of 1942 that the chief inspector in her department was 'absolutely pro-National Revolution and really makes us aware of our duties'.[76] Most of the evidence, however, indicates that for different reasons, the inspectorate in many departments was distancing itself from certain aspects of Vichy's educational policies.

In the Hérault, the Inspecteur de l'Académie between 1940-4 has left a remarkable picture of how Vichy's clericalism and demands for ideological conformity drove inspectors and teachers towards the Resistance.[77] In the Lozère, it was a clerical offensive designed to shut down state schools which stung the inspectorate into a rearguard defensive action of the école publique.

In other departments there were different but related causes which pushed the inspectorate into attitudes of reserve or even hostility: in a public outburst reported by the local press in Nîmes and subsequently censored, the Inspecteur de l'Académie in the Gard announced to a gathering of teachers and officials in October 1940 that the regime's decision to close the state teacher training colleges, the écoles normales, 'was the result of ignorance and injustice'.[78] To some of those who had been taught in the *écoles normales*, their closure was seen as an attack on one of the cornerstones of the French educational system. In the Ardèche it was the intrigues of the Légion that began to make the Inspecteur de l'Académie question the sort of regime that apparently legitimised populist meddling in the serious business of education. As early as December 1940, he sent a note to one of his primary school inspectors in which he warned him that one of their recent telephone conversations had been intercepted and that their criticism of a teacher, who was a prominent member of the Légion, had been reported to the teacher concerned. To stop this individual from his intention of planning to denounce the inspector for hostility to the doctrines of Marshal Pétain's government the Inspecteur de l'Académie urged his colleague to go on the offensive.[79] Further reasons for the hostility of this official to the regime were revealed in letters which were intercepted in February 1943. In them he claimed that a decision to transfer him from the Ardèche to Troyes had been motivated by his refusal to give in to the demands of certain priests for the closure of state schools and his resistance to orders to discipline certain teachers.[80] One of the difficulties that the school inspectors encountered both in the Ardèche and the Drôme was the outlook of their immediate superior in the educational hierarchy, the Recteur, who as late as December 1943 was still trying to rally schoolchildren to Pétainism. When he gave the senior pupils at Privas in the Ardèche a speech in that month he concluded with an appeal to them to shout 'Long live Pétain, Long live France'. There was an embarrassing silence from the school, according to one of the boys who was there.[81]

Indeed, the latitude of action that chief inspectors enjoyed depended to a great extent not only on the political outlook of the prefect in their department, but also that of their own superior in the educational hierarchy, the Recteur. For purposes of educational administration, France was divided into a number of Académies which grouped together five or six departments. Ardèche belonged to the Académie of Grenoble whereas Lozère was part of the Académie of Montpellier: some measure of the different political perspectives which existed between the two can be judged by comparing the incident referred to above in the Ardèche with a comparable case in the Lozère. Here, the President of the Contrôle Postal told the prefect in February 1942 that the local inspectorate was protecting if not encouraging state school teachers in an 'anti-clerical struggle' and that this could explain the 'deplorable outlook of a good number of pupils'.[82] The prefect chose to rewrite completely this comment in his report to Vichy stating that the inspectorate were working hard to discourage anti-clericalism amongst the teachers. Only two months later, the same official in the Contrôle Postal intercepted a letter from a pupil at school in Mende in which she poured scorn on the school's practice of saluting the flag. This time the letter was sent to Pétain and to the Recteur in Montpellier, presumbly to create more effect. In fact, it led the Recteur to write to all the inspecteurs in his Académie warning them to encourage pupils to be careful about what they wrote.[83] This unequivocal attempt to put his colleagues on guard against the state's surveillance agencies is entirely consistent with other evidence we have about this Recteur who was finally sacked by Vichy in June 1943 for refusing to give the authorities lists of students to be sent on the Service du Travail Obligatoire (STO).[84]

Indeed, it was this plan to send teachers and students to Germany in 1943 that placed Recteurs and Inspecteurs in a particularly invidious position since it was their responsibility to select teachers for the compulsory labour scheme. In Hérault, the action of the Inspecteur de l'Académie amounted to total sabotage of the plan to send 58 primary school teachers, since only one actually left the department.[85] But in the Lozère, a tough-minded prefect, with the co-operation of certain officials in the Inspection Académique, ensured that ten teachers left and a further seven who refused to leave were sacked.[86] These examples testify to the sort of differences that existed even between departments in the same Académie in terms of the configuration of political forces and their impact on teachers. Vichy was not a monolithic regime that stamped a uniform blueprint throughout France. Nevertheless it is now becoming clear that provided they carried out their work conscientiously, teachers could expect varying degrees of protection from the educational inspectorate in the face of a multiplicity of demands by the state. In general, Vichy failed to politicise this group of civil servants who occupied a vital tier in the educational system.

We have looked, in turn, at the various agencies, both official and unofficial, which acted as related parts of a widespread system of surveillance and control. How effective was this system in enforcing political conformity amongst teachers? The historiographical problems of answering this question are considerable. The major difficulty concerns the value that can be attached to official reports written during the Vichy period by police inspectors, prefects and school inspectors, and the problems associated with using depositions produced in 1944-5 related to enquiries about Resistance and collaboration.

Two cases can be used to illustrate these points: reports written by the Inspecteur de l'Académie in Lozère to the prefect in 1941 and 1942 on the attitude of teachers in the department both attest to their loyalty as did a report by one of the inspectors of the Renseignements Généraux in 1943.[87] In 1945, however, the same school inspector was referring to the role of teachers in the Resistance, to their patriotism, sense of civic duty and to the way they had 'maintained an ideal'.[88] When official requests for reports like these were made, it needs to be remembered that the authors' comments were neither spontaneous nor unmindful of their intended audience. Evidence about attitudes gleaned from the dossiers of those teachers accused of collaboration can be equally misleading. What is quite clear in a wide sample of cases in the Lozère and the Ardèche is that behind the charges of 'collaborationist, pro-Vichy, anti-Gaullist, anti-Allied propaganda', there frequently lay an incident in the village which had alienated the teacher from a section of parents. In the climate of liberation from August 1944 the demand for vengeance was just as strong as it had been in August 1940; where the Légion had paved the way for a flood of denunciations in 1941, a similar wave of popular clamour for justice and reparation grew from the activities of some of the locally constituted Comités Cantonaux de Libération in late 1944. Often the letters of 1944 began in exactly the same terms as those of 1941: 'Il est de notoriété publique ... ' was followed by demands that the prefect or the Inspecteur de l'Académie or the Ministry of Education take firm action 'so that the *épuration* can be seen to be done'.[89] Now that the boot was on the other foot, it was the priests and teachers in church schools who were vilified. One teacher was denounced for 'having relations with a German parachutist', another had a hand grenade thrown at her house because of remarks she made about a prominent member of the local Resistance.[90] In this case there is no doubt that the real intention was to remove an unpopular teacher who had lost the support of parents in the village.

Although caution must be taken in using this evidence about teachers' attitudes, where it has been corroborated by the intercepted correspondence of teachers, a number of conclusions can be drawn. At first, the cumulative effect of the violent press campaign unleashed against teachers after the defeat, the sanctions imposed on a minority of them and the general climate of *mea culpa* in 1940 forced most teachers into what one report described as a 'docile conformity to the new instructions'.[91] Although there were isolated individuals who refused to devote the first lesson of the new term to Pétain's 'patriotic sacrifice for the nation',[92] it was more typical to find teachers putting up his portrait.[93] But by 1941 differences between departments were beginning to become apparent: while teachers in the Ardèche were showing increasing signs of anti-clericalism,[94] and under threat from the Légion because of their views, those in the Lozère were reported to be completely loyal to Pétain.[95] In the Gard the police reported that outward conformity concealed real differences between those whose support for Vichy was genuine and others, notably around the coal-mining area at Alès who were said to be still very attached to the old regime.[96]

By 1942 there were clear indications that many of those who had rallied to Vichy were becoming increasingly irritated by the extra-curricular burdens that were being heaped on them at a time when their salaries were falling behind those of other civil servants.[97] Both in the Aveyron and the Alpes-Maritimes prefects were dismayed that teachers' loyalty to the regime should be compromised by what one of them described as a 'derisory and discouraging' salary increase.[98] Police intelligence reports from a variety of departments in the Midi in the spring of 1943[99] suggest that while teachers were extremely cool towards

Laval and the policy of collaboration they were careful not to express their views openly, and were punctilious in carrying out their duties. Even Resistance tracts specifically directed at primary school teachers urged them to break out of their shell of professional neutrality.[100] But in spite of the widespread disaffection caused by the running down of state education and the worsening effects of inflation on standards of living, the majority of teachers, like most of the population, were frozen by fear and uncertainty into a curious form of paralysis.

This was at least partly due to the effectiveness of the various branches of the surveillance network which had succeeded in creating such an atmosphere of suspicion that it was difficult to know whom to trust. Although the entire population was subject to certain forms of discreet or overt surveillance, teachers as a professional group were singled out for particular attention. Even when the state chose not to take further action against individuals whose conduct had become 'suspect', the mere knowledge that letters, phone calls or even private conversations might be monitored, was an extremely powerful weapon in ensuring internal security. This was especially true in the villages of the Midi where, as we have seen, there often existed deep-seated antagonisms between state school and church school which divided communities. The rivalry between the two schools did not simply threaten the livelihood of the state school teachers: it forced them to exercise the utmost caution in relations with the mayor, the parents and the children. The cumulative effect of this led one teacher to comment with evident *chagrin*, 'The teaching profession has been completely emasculated.'[101] A minority of teachers did play an active part in Resistance groups either because the threat of STO shook them out of what the underground paper called 'their little routine life'.[102] or because their sense of outrage at Vichy's injustices pushed them into action. The reaction of most teachers, however, was blunted by a suspicion and fear that the surveillance system had encouraged and confusion about how they should react to established authority. While many despised Vichy's ideology which ran counter to their entire training, they could not completely reject the state's authority nor ignore its cogent propaganda about the possibilities of the disorder that might accompany liberation.[103]

There is very little evidence from the departments examined in this study that teachers as an identifiable group were subject to political surveillance by the German occupying authorities. Both in terms of the ideological content of the curriculum and the surveillance of teachers, the Germans appear to have been quite satisfied with the measures taken by Vichy, and there is no indication that Vichy was acting under particular pressure from the occupying authorities in this matter. The way that Vichy developed and made use of various forms of political control over teachers indicates that, after directing this control to supporting a brief ideological crusade held together by the precepts of the National Revolution, it developed from early 1942 an obsessive concern with internal security. The major reason for this was that, while Pétainism was a sufficiently potent force for political integration until early 1942, there was nothing to replace it. As public opinion in general became increasingly disinterested in the ritualistic trappings of the National Revolution and ever more concerned with food shortage, labour demands and anxieties about liberation, teachers' identity as a group meant less and less. From April 1942 when the regime had in Abel Bonnard its most conspicuously political Education Minister, the evidence suggests that the will to enforce ideological control of teachers at local level had simply collapsed.

This conclusion serves to underline the need to look at Vichy not through the shibboleths of its ministers but through the often prosaic preoccupations of the regime's servants and subjects. It is in this way that we can see how the initial convergence of populist and official surveillance of teachers in the enforcement of Pétainist ideology began to disintegrate as early as 1941. From then on, it was precisely the gratuitous meddling of the Légion, of certain curés and officials in the Contrôle Technique that pushed civil servants like Inspecteurs de l'Académie and some prefects into a defence of the values of the Third Republic embodied in teachers and the école publique.

Notes

1. Roger Austin, 'Propaganda and Public Opinion in Vichy France, the department of Hérault 1940-1944', *European Studies Review*, October 1983.
2. W.D. Halls, *The Youth of Vichy France* (Oxford, 1981); Roger Austin, 'The Chantiers de la Jeunesse in Languedoc 1940-1944', *French Historical Studies*, Spring 1983.
3. J. Kernan, *Report on France* (London, 1942), p. 136.
4. Halls, *Vichy France* pp. 104-6; Austin, 'The Chantiers de la Jeunesse', pp. 45-51.
5. Halls, *Vichy France* p. 113.
6. Archives Nationales (hereafter AN) AJ 41 25. Report from Service des Contrôles Techniques, 4 October 1940.
7. AN FIA 3655 Circulaire No. 2822, 8 October 1940.
8. AN FIA 3655 Circulaire No. 3877, 27 October 1940.
9. Archives Départementales de l'Ardèche (hereafter ADA) CAB 895. Minister of Interior to prefects, 10 December 1940.

10. ADA CAB 897.
11. ADA CAB 895. Prefect to Education Ministry, 28 September 1940.
12. AN FIC III 1141, Report on 30 October 1940.
13. AN FIC III 1137, September 1941.
14. Archives Départementales de Lozère (hereafter ADL) T 5514, Prefect to Inspecteur de l'Académie, 13 May 1941.
15. AN F 17 13364, ADA CAB 114, ADL T 5514; Halls, *Vichy France* p. 115.
16. See note 9 above and Austin, 'The Educational and Youth Policies of the Vichy Government in the Department of Hérault, 1940-1944' (Manchester PhD, 1981), p. 89.
17. Austin, 'Educational and Youth Policies', p. 89.
18. AN FIC III 1137. Report on 6 November 1941.
19. AN FIC III 1137. Report for January 1942.
20. ADL T 5514: Correspondence in July 1941 and September 1943.
21. AN FIC III 1165. Report for July 1942.
22. AN FIC III 1141. Report for July 1942.
23. AN FIC III 1181. Prefect in the Pyrenées-Orientales, June 1942.
24. AN FIC III 1153, October 1940; AN FIC III 1141, Sept.-Oct. 1941; ADA CAB 517, February 1943.
25. Jean Tulard, 'Les Français sous surveillance', *L'Histoire*, no. 32, March 1981.
26. Marcel Le Clère, 'La naissance des Renseignements Généraux', *L'Histoire*, no. 32, March 1981.
27. Donald N. Baker, 'The Surveillance of Subversion in Inter-war France: the Carnet B in the Seine, 1922-1940', *French Historical Studies*, vol. X, no. 3, Spring 1978.
28. Archives of the Conseil Supérieur de la Defense National, 2N 263. Note from le General d'Armée, Ministre de la Guerre to Generals commanding 7th, 9th, 12th and 18th Regions, 6 July 1940.
29. Law of 23 April, 1941 quoted by Le Clère, 'La naissance', p. 84.
30. Archives Départementales du Gard (hereafter ADG) CAB 648; ADA CAB 517; ADL VI^{M2} 19, VI^{M2} 23.
31. AN F7 14929. Report on 28 January 1944.
32. ADG CAB 649. Note from Darlan on 22 March 1941.
33. ADL VI^{M2} 23, letter intercepted on 25 July 1941.
34. ADL VI^{M2} 23, letter intercepted on 16 October 1941.
35. ADL VI^{M2} 23, letters intercepted in October 1941 and October 1942.
36. ADA CAB 191. Report on 6 December 1943.
37. ADA CAB 517. Report for June 1941.
38. ADL VI^{M2} 19, note on 27 March 1942.
39. ADL VI^{M2} 23. Correspondence 21 May 1942.
40. ADA CAB 517.
41. ADA CAB 114, CAB 897.
42. ADA CAB 114, CAB 895.
43. Halls, *Vichy France*, Ch.3; Austin, 'Educational and Youth Policies', Ch. 2.
44. A number of inspectors argued that if parents were sending their children to private schools it was because the state school's curriculum was weighed down with extra curricular tasks like collecting acorns or scrap metal. Austin, 'Educational and Youth Policies', p. 197.
45. ADA CAB 897, CAB 114. ADL T 5514.
46. ADL VI^{M2} 23.
47. ADL VI^{M2} 21, 10 July 1943.

48. ADA CDL 450.
49. ADL T 5514.
50. ADA CAB 114, 18 September 1941.
51. ADA CAB 114 and CAB 895.
52. André Halimi, *La Délation sous l'Occupation* (Paris, 1983), p. 7. The author appears to have confused genuine letters of denunciation with letters that were intercepted by the Contrôle Postal.
53. ADA CAB 668. Note on 2 January 1942. This was followed by a law on 8 October 1943 threatening imprisonment and a fine to those found guilty of denunciation. AN AJ41 429.
54. ADA CAB 114, 20 December 1940.
55. ADA CAB 897, 27 March 1941.
56. AN F 41 158, 30 April 1941.
57. ADA CDL 450/2.
58. ADA CAB 114. Note on 13 August 1941.
59. ADA CAB 897.
60. ADA CAB 114, letter on 21 April 1941.
61. ADG 15^{M2} 221, 18 January 1942.
62. Austin, 'Propaganda and Public Opinion', *European Studies Review*, October 1983, p. 469.
63. Halls, *Vichy France*.
64. Austin, 'Educational and Youth Policies', p. 34, pp. 39-41.
65. ADA CAB 114, 20 February 1941.
66. ADL T 5421. Notes on 20 October 1944 and 10 April 1945.
67. ADL *Bulletin Départmental de l'Enseignement Primaire*, June-August, 1940, pp. 190-1.
68. ADL T 5438.
69. ADL T 5438, 18 October 1940.
70. ADL VI^{M2} 23, letter intercepted on 22 February 1942.
71. ADL T 5438. Note de service, 28 August 1940.
72. ADL T 5438, circular 5 December 1941.
73. Halls, *Vichy France*, Chs 7 and 8.
74. ADL BDEP Jan/Feb. 1941, pp. 90-100.
75. ADL BDEP Jan/Feb. 1942, pp. 54-5.
76. ADL VI^{M2} 23. Letter intercepted on 4 March 1942.
77. Maurice David, *Monsieur Gaeten Instituteur* (Paris, 1961).
78. AN FIC III 1165. The prefect complained to the Minister of the Interior that the IA's attitude was likely to compromise government action, 22 October 1940.
79. ADA CAB 450/2, letter on 12 December 1940
80. ADA CAB 517. Letters intercepted on 2 February 1943 were sent by the prefect in the Ardèche to Pétain as proof of the IA's outlook.
81. ADA CAB 517. Letter and enquiry on 11 December 1943.
82. ADL VI^{M2} 19, February 1942.
83. ADL VI^{M2} 23. Recteur's circular of 30 April 1942.
84. Austin, p. 133.
85. P. Delanoue, *Les Enseignants, La Lutte Syndicale du Front Populaire à la Libération* (1973), p. 284.
86. ADL T 5514, R 7251, T 5427.
87. ADL T 5516.
88. ADL T 5874. Note on 8 October 1945.
89. ADA CDL 450.
90. ADA CAB 897.
91. ADL T 5438, 21 November 1940.
92. ADL *Bulletin Départemental de l'Enseignement Primaire*, June/August

1940.
  93. ADL T 5438.
  94. ADA CAB 895, September 1940, CAB 517, April 1941, November 1941.
  95. ADL T 5438, August 1941 and T 5516, November 1941.
  96. ADG 15M 221. Report on 24 November 1941.
  97. ADL VI^{M2} 19; ADA CAB 517, July, 1942; AN FIC III 1153, March 1942.
  98. AN FIC III 1141, FIC III 1137, May/June 1942.
  99. ADL T 5516, 19 April, 1943; ADA CAB 191, 3 March 1943; AN FIC III 1141 (Aude), January 1943; FIC III 1141 (Aveyron), May 1943; FIC III 1181 (Pyrénées-Orientales), March 1943.
  100. AN AGII 609.
  101. ADL VI^{M2} 23, 13 October 1941.
  102. AN AGII 609. Tract entitled 'Aux Instituteurs'.
  103. ADA CAB 517, intercepted letters on 25 November 1943 and 19 September 1943.

2 WOMEN AND THE NATIONAL REVOLUTION
Miranda Pollard

This chapter is based on the notion that — although historians have referred to Vichy's 'femme au foyer' imperative — there has been a failure, or a reluctance, to incorporate the question of gender into interpretations of the National Revolution. Yet recent work on women and fascism underlines the significance and interpretative possibilities of this theme of sexuality and ideology.[1] Vichy itself attempted to institutionalise a paternalist and reactionary definition of women's role and status, within the family and within French society. Furthermore this definition, centred on motherhood and femininity, found expression in a wide range of antifeminist policies in education, employment and sexuality. But rather than give an account of these policies, I would like to use this opportunity to highlight the nature of Vichy's view of women and also their significance for the National Revolution, of which they constitute an integral ideological element.

Though an integral and specific element of Vichy's political culture (and hence the subject of many of the regime's tautological banalities) women were not addressed as directly or explicitly as in fascist discourse. The two predominant ideological impulses which informed Vichy's views of women were pronatalism and familialism. Both centrally concerned female sexuality and sexual divisions. The former was a preoccupation with population growth that assumed state control of fertility and reproduction; the latter an advocacy of social stability or 'rénovation' that was based on the legitimate, patriarchal family unit and required the maintenance of 'la femme au foyer'. In any analysis of government legislation and propaganda, as well as in the bulk of unofficial but supportive literature, these two themes are strikingly evident.

In order to assess the ideological originality of the National Revolution and the extent of discontinuity with its Republican progenitor, it is obviously necessary to analyse the continuity of language and symbols from the inter-war period — at greater length than I have space for here. Certainly the immediate past was crucial for both natalism and familialism, which emerged in a coherent, jointly-identified form in 1920 and had definitely entered the realm of State policy with the promulgation of the Code de la Famille in 1939. The development of both has been charted elsewhere.[2] Here it might be useful, at the risk of oversimplification, to note merely that across the political spectrum natalism and familialism had gained credence in the 1930s. Certainly among some conservative groups — the Alliance Nationale Contre la Dépopulation is the most obvious example — vigorous promotion of the French family and population growth presented a panacea to various real and perceived threats, internal or external: the civil strife of the Popular Front era, immigration, German rearmament, etc. In other words, well before Vichy, there was a conjuncture of ideas that gave prominence to certain analyses of decline and degeneracy as well as presenting specific ideological remedies. If the transition in 1940 regarding images of women and the family was not as abrupt as one might expect, it was purely because a natalist-familialist vocabulary had become commonplace in political discourse.

But this vocabulary or discourse, however pervasive, did not just progressively become amplified by 1940. Crucially, it was the crisis of military collapse and occupation, the trauma of defeat that crystallised these latent ideological trends and gave urgency to their specific perspectives. The remarkable mood of 'national self-recrimination' (Paxton) in the summer of 1940 generated a moral crusade against the institutions and mores of the Third Republic. 'Dénatalité' and 'la crise de la famille' were often highlighted as grim symptoms of pre-war decadence. Certainly the motif of this moral crusade — *'Travail, Famille, Patrie'* — was more than a convenient slogan to replace the revolutionary triptych on public buildings. These words symbolised values central to the proposed national 'rénovation'. The vision of the new moral order initiated by Pétain was firmly based in a traditional, hierarchical and organic structuring of society, antithetical to the materialism and individualism which was deemed to have characterised Republican France and which had led to national catastrophe:

> L'ancien régime n'a connu, en effet, que l'individu en face de l'Etat-Providence: l'ordre nouveau est fondé sur le groupement naturel: famille, commune, corporation et plus ces groupements sont forts, plus l'Etat l'est aussi.[3]

This social philosophy, often attributed to the influence of Le Play, gave the family a crucial public and socio-political dimension. It was not just the key area in which individual human fulfilment might be realised, although this plays an important part in later pro-family propaganda. Even more significant was the family's function as the prime unit of social organisation. The stable and fecund French family underpinned all social order; its advocacy and maintenance therefore formed a legitimate element of social policy:

> Le droit des familles est en effet antérieur et supérieur à celui des individus. La famille est la cellule essentielle; elle est l'assise même de l'édifice sociale; c'est sur elle qu'il faut bâtir, s'il elle fléchit, tout est perdu; tant qu'elle tient, tout peut être sauvé.[4]

This familial ideology was matched and complemented by intensified natalist anxieties, similarly brought centre stage by the events of 1940. Indeed they were sanctioned by Pétain himself, when he gave one of the causes of French defeat as 'Trop peu d'enfants'.

Natalist slogans of demographic panic gained currency and an array of propaganda alerted public opinion against 'un suicide collectif', comparing French demographic performance with that of her virile neighbours and melodramatically invoking the imminent demise of 'la patrie'.

This propaganda, as well as the legislation which it advertised or advocated, rested on two principal assumptions: first that the reversal of France's declining birth-rate was possible, in fact was an urgent priority; and secondly that this demographic regeneration was to be achieved by and through the French family. The campaign against social and moral decadence formed the ideological nexus between these two all-pervasive assumptions, which echoed through official publications.[5] Natalism and familialism were inextricably linked. A striking example is that of the 'Concours-Référendum sur les causes de la dénatalité française' (1941) conducted under the patronage of Maréchal Pétain, in which the public were invited to assist the authorities . . .

> à alerter l'opinion, à redresser le jugement public, afin que la France entière se préoccupe d'assurer la renaissance de la famille qui sera la renaissance de la France, condition de notre avenir meilleur.[6]

Entrants were required to choose the three most important reasons for French depopulation from a possible 15 axioms, which ranged from the availability of divorce, women's employment outside the home, fear of childbirth, to the difficulties of accommodation, etc. Given the moral bias of the sponsors (who included the Commissariat Général à la Famille and the Centre National de Coordination et d'Action des Mouvements Familiaux) and the campaign against individualism, it is perhaps unsurprising that 'absence ou insuffisance de religion' headed the poll.

The overlapping or interrelatedness of ideologies of Church and State in 1940, no less than their formal relationship, was highly complex. However, it is obvious that in this area of natalist-familialism there was an explicit identification of common interests which might be crudely schematised here as centring on support for the procreativity of French 'familles nombreuses'. It was the militants of the pre-war, predominantly Catholic, family movement who provided the message and personnel for Vichy's natalist policy. Although reference was often made to the success of fascism in this sphere, they were quick to emphasise the moral and conservative aspects of French natalism, as opposed to the racial and secular imperatives of their neighbours' policies, and were highly reticent about any undue extension of State control.[7]

None the less despite the articulation of conservative Catholic familialism, pronatalist enthusiasm often led to moral-racial ambiguities. Partially this was because the consensus which supported the idea of 'rénovation nationale' via the French family, also underpinned the broader concept of creating an exclusive national community. Although racialist paranoia had of course existed previously, it was undoubtedly war, the anti-communist purge, and the creation of a reactionary government (whose thorough anti-Semitism was one of its principal features) which gave these phenomena a more coherent socio-political form. Vichy was totally consistent in its drive to establish an exclusively French, pure national community and rid it of all foreign, degenerate elements. From the revision of recent naturalisations[8] — one of its first legislative steps — to the propaganda of its demographic instruction manuals[9], the regime pursued its specific natalist orientation.

This discussion has so far concentrated on indicating the pervasiveness of natalist-familialism and its importance for the National Revolution. I would now like to elaborate on how this perspective informed the ideological orientation of the regime towards women.

Predictably, given the preoccupation with depopulation, motherhood became the primary focus for women's social contribution:

> C'est en vertu de sa maternité même que la mère est l'ouvrière privilegiée du redressement national. Contre ce mortel ennemi du pays, la dénatalité, doit se dresser la mère française; seule sa fecondité peut assurer le salut de la race.[10]

Although Vichy did not espouse the extreme eugenicist measures of fascist regimes, the valorisation of motherhood, with its racial association, provided a common ideological dynamic. The exclusive idealisation of maternity and fecundity and the creation of separate spheres of existence and fulfilment for the sexes were fundamental to the social thinking of both. Vichy, as in other areas, did not simply act in accordance with German dictates. The regime's policies are thus not reducible to an importation of the *Kinder, Kirche, Küche* imperative. Vichy defined women's role and status by reference to an inseparable maternal and familial function:

> La famille repose essentiellement sur la mère. Or la Cité repose sur la famille. D'où le role de la mère dans la Cité ... De la famille, la mère est l'assise fondamentale ... Elle est créatrice, éducatrice, consolatrice et la conseillère et guide du foyer.[11]

The principal features of this outlook had direct antecedents in conservative and Catholic doctrine. An influential restatement, for example, had been that of Pius XI in his Encyclical 'Casti Connubii' (December 1930) which argued against any form of women's emancipation for the good of the family. But the notion of 'la femme au foyer' and the pre-eminence of women's procreative role were not solely attributable to Catholic dogma. J.F. McMillan has noted the pervasiveness of this ideology of domesticity in nineteenth-century France among republicans and anti-clericals too.[12] Crucial to this analysis, however, was the seeming interaction of such a broadly based antifeminism, with its complex but resilient roots in French traditions, and a revitalised and quite distinct natalist-familialism. There was an interesting dovetailing of paternalist images and assumptions which found expression in Vichy's policies and propaganda.

A general consensus existed as to the significance of women's domestic role. One commentator in demanding constitutional guarantees for the family as 'une unité sociale naturelle', recommended the adoption of a constitution modelled on that of the Irish Free State and in particular its article giving recognition to women's place within the home.[13] The view that the common good relied on the maintenance of a strict sexual division of labour was the basic premise for all subsequent arguments. Women's social contribution was acknowledged but delineated; her influence and fulfilment were by-products of her role in the domestic sphere. A brochure of the Commissariat Général à la Famille, destined 'Aux Educatrices' confirmed the importance of this role:

> C'est en effet autour de la préparation à la vie au foyer que doit être centré l'éducation d'une jeune fille. Ce foyer, cellule vivante de la patrie, sûr abri des enfants, bonheur à la mesure du coeur des hommes, ce foyer où tout nait, se préserve, se développe, c'est à elles qu'il appartient de défendre l'intégrité et la douceur contre les ennemis du dehors et du dedans.[14]

Thus woman was defined by her function of wife, mother and guardian of private space. The consequences of such a dichotomy between private/domestic and public/social were obviously far-reaching. Women's social existence was seen as separate and personal, the domestic ideology was reinforced. Above all the 'femme au foyer' imperative in the National Revolution involved the systematic endorsement of a specific sexual identity and the social construction of gender, within an ideology of natalist-familialism.

It is worth investigating this notion in the three key areas I mentioned earlier – education, employment and sexuality. Through each, one can detect a range of images and presumptions of gender and femininity which overlap, relate to and feed each other systematically. Sometimes these are reflected in direct relation to natalist-familialism, sometimes as the mere shadow of the National Revolution's core paternalism.

In education, for example, the primary substance of Vichy's discourse focused on 'futurs chefs', the virile cadres who would spearhead a moral regeneration. It was French male youth whose effective socialisation concerned the policy-makers and ideologues, and who were in fact mobilised into the quasi-militaristic Chantiers and Compagnons. None the less the regime's educational orientation did have certain consequences for girls' education, which in turn coincided with the change in the status and nature of female education demanded by a 'femme au foyer' principle. The egalitarian and meritocratic presumptions of Republican education were replaced by a gender-strict vocationalism. Formation, no longer mere instruction or encyclopaedic fact-cramming, was to be provided, directly fitted to future social roles and signifying therefore blatent antipathy to women's non-domestic ambitions, academic or professional. This meant for girls compulsory 'enseignement ménager', comprising hygiene, housekeeping, cooking, laundry and 'une initiation à la psychologie et à la morale familiale', and timetabled to correspond to extra hours of physical education for male students.[15]

'Enseignement ménager' was central to constructing a differentiated curriculum, underwriting women's future maternal function and domestic labour and the separateness that was to be confirmed by sexual segregation in the classroom.[16] It was claimed that equal and identical instruction led to identical qualifications ('des titres et diplômes flatteurs, n'oublions pas le vieux complexe｜d'infériorité dont souffrent encore les femmes d'aujourd'hui') which in turn incited girls, who had no need, to 'encombrer les carrières masculines'. The logical outcome of undifferentiated education for the labour market was felt to be 'l'invasion｜égoïste des jeunes filles qui voulurent se faire une situation seulement pour｜être indépendantes et se payer des toilettes coûteuses'.[17] These prejudices, though probably cultivated as hostility to the 'new' economically active female in the 1930s, were particularly misplaced and ironic in the austere France of 1940-4. But such attempts to discredit women's academic or professional ambitions, wavering between misogyny and paternalism, found clear articulation in the *Vérités et Rêveries sur l'Education* (1941) of René Benjamin – who has been called 'one of Pétain's most faithful hangers-on'.[18] Warning fathers against the costly delusion of seeking to provide a career and independence for their daughters, as well as indicating the risk of nervous debilitation from studying for the girls themselves, Benjamin concluded that he had heard from a well-informed source (probably confirmed by current rumour) that 300 qualified female lawyers 'font le trottoir à Paris'.[19]

It was not just the backdrop of German occupation that made such diatribes so pernicious. This propaganda merely amplified the National Revolution, which sought not only the educational preparedness of girls for domesticity but also the actual 'retour' of the woman, especially the married woman, to the home. From the summer of 1940 the government acted to protect male 'chefs de familles' from the rigours of demobilisation and unemployment by setting parameters to women's right to employment. A telegram of 7 July 1940 recommended a hierarchy of dismissals of women from the private sector and was followed by what Darlan was to call 'une des lois les plus importantes parmi celles qui ont été élaborées par le gouvernement du Maréchal'[20] – the Loi du 11 octobre 1940, which regulated women's employment in the public sector. Regardless of the ultimate efficacy of these measures the same paternalist ideology was being reiterated: woman's place was ideally 'au foyer' and her right to remunerative work was conditional. The exceptions permitted were when women substituted for the male breadwinner, as widows or heads of households, for example wives of prisoners of war, or else where they effectively provided no 'concurrence' for example, in traditionally 'female' industries. Similarly exempted were married women whose work was of a nature to be compatible with the fulfilment of her domestic responsibilities, that is, part time or in close proximity to her home. Above all the ideal of the dependent married woman, constrained by duty and domestic labour, was paramount.

The prominence given to the Fête des Mères under Vichy was intended to acknowledge if not compensate for this dependence, as well as providing an opportunity for eulogies on the subject of motherly virtues... 'de dévouements quotidiens, de discrets sacrifices, de vrai et pur amour'.[21] A conscious appreciation of mothers and their social function was required of the whole national community: 'Honorer la mère, c'est honorer la Patrie, Mieux encore, c'est la servir...'[22] so that familialist logic was constantly propounded:

La mère fait la famille,
La famille fait la France.[23]

The natalist imperative itself was often quite explicit as in this appeal made directly to French women:

Toi qui veut rebâtir la France
Donne-lui d'abord des enfants.[24]

Indeed one author waxed lyrical on the coincidence of benefits of maternity — for the woman and the State:

L'intérêt personnel de la femme, sa beauté physique, sa santé, son équilibre mental et surtout sa conscience morale sont devenus un facteur démographique de premier ordre... L'individu devra comprendre que ses intérêts féminins sont communs avec ceux de l'Etat. En même temps que la femme française reconnaîtra ses intérêts féminins et renaîtra à une nouvelle jeunesse par la maternité, elle servira la société, accomplira les fonctions sociales qu'on attend d'elle.[25]

Reproduction and female sexuality were constantly identified so that the natural destiny of the woman was itself continuously constructed, as in the injunction: 'il n'y a rien de plus triste qu'un jardin sans fleurs... qu'une femme sans enfant'.[26] Femininity and maternity were key attributes of this promotion of gender indentity. An official brochure entitled 'La Vie en Fleur' carried two articles extolling motherhood. One maintained that. . . 'avoir des enfants embellit la femme', the other that 'la maternité donne à la femme son équilibre'. This pervasive psycho-social approach was summed up by an illustrated slogan:

> En fondant une famille
> Elle accomplit sa destinée.[27]

It is highly significant that endorsement of this natural maternal destiny came so often from the medical profession. Of course there was an overlap, of Catholic Association militants and personnel from the medical profession or social services. But this medical orthodoxy gave the seemingly commonsensical or universalist assumptions of women's social role a fresh, quasi-scientific sanction. A consensus was formed that deemed procreation not only advantageous but essential for women, confirming again the coincidence of natalist priorities and conservative views of the female condition:

> Les découvertes scientifiques des dernières décades ont prouvé que la femme ne peut écarter systématiquement la conception sans risque de porter atteinte à son organisme. . . La maternité seule donne à la femme la plénitude de son épanouissement. Le Professeur Pinard, un des grands maîtres de l'obstétrique aimait à dire qu'il faut à une femme, en général, quatres grossesses au cours de son existence pour avoir une santé normale.[28]

The medical recommendation of at least four pregnancies, favoured unlimited procreativity and combined social, psychological and physiological arguments about the dangers of birth control. It complemented a more aggressive propaganda campaign against the 'fléau national' of abortion. On this issue a remarkably unified conservative reaction was mobilised, expressing itself in a rigorous policy of repression. Indeed the '300 Law', which established the concept of abortion as a crime against the individual (the unborn child), society and the race — and under which a woman was guillotined — was closely related to the ideological imperatives of natalism, familialism and moralism discussed above.[29] The title-page of a brochure against abortion graphically portrays this notion of personal and national 'assassination . . . L'avortement tue l'enfant, tue la femme, tue la France'.[30] Anti-abortion material, emotive and abundant as it was in this period, starkly confirmed the exclusion of a self-determined female sexuality and the primacy of militant natalism:

> Mais si l'on considère que la France perd chaque année 35,000 femmes tuées par l'avortement criminel (femmes dont chacune aurait pu donner plusieurs enfants au Pays), que les avorteurs tuent chaque année de 50,000 à 100,000 de Français, ill suffirait seulement que la France supprime l'avortement pour se retrouver au premier rang des puissances fécondes.[31]

Hopefully this brief survey has given some indication of the nature and importance of Vichy's images of women. A comprehensive analysis would obviously rely on assessing both the degree of ideological mobilisation and policy implementation involved in this 'femme au foyer' imperative. But I would argue that the significance of this imperative does not relate solely to the efficacy of individual legislative or propaganda measures. Crucially important is the articulation and amplification of these assumptions of gender and femininity as integral or dynamic elements of the National Revolution. This in turn offers two interpretative possibilities. Either these assumptions constituted a latent antifeminism, crystallised by Vichy in the natalist-familialist nexus — itself an apparently apolitical area in which the regime sought to construct a sense of national purpose and identity. Alternatively the range of images of 'la femme au foyer' may not have signified an explicit antifeminism, on the fascist model, but instead a 'shadow' or reverse of Vichy's *paternalism* — and here the term needs to be reinvested with literal meaning. The potent symbolism of the father figure in the National Revolution requires investigation. From Pétain's much-publicised encounters with women, children and peasants through to the promotion of hierarchical authority via male Chefs de Familles and Anciens Combattants, a paternalist social ideology was mobilised. This paternalism was central to the regime's efforts to project a reassuring apoliticism.[32]

Studies of particular institutions or policies (like that of Coutrot on 'La Politique Familiale de Vichy')[33] tend to confirm themes of continuity and even apoliticism. This discussion, on the other hand, suggests that with regard to sexuality and ideology the National Revolution involved discontinuity and polarisation.

Notes

1. See, for example, M.A. Macciochi, 'Female Sexuality in Fascist Ideology', *Feminist Review, I*, 1979; T. Mason, 'Women in Germany, 1925-1940', *History Workshop Journal*, 1976.
2. R. Talmy, *Histoire du Mouvement Familial en France, 1896-1939* (Paris, 1962); D.V. Glass, *Population Policies and Movements* (Oxford, 1940).
3. P. Pétain, *Principes de la Rénovation Nationale. La Doctrine et l'Action du Maréchal*, Société d'Editions Economiques et Sociales (Paris, n.d.), p. 22.
4. P. Pétain, 'La Politique Sociale de l'Avenir', *Revue des Deux Mondes 59-60*, September 1940, pp. 114-15.
5. These include tracts and brochures of the Commissariat Général à la Famille: *Aux Educatrices* (1943), *La Vie en Fleur* (1943), *Le Pharmacien et la Dénatalité* (n.d.), *L'instituteur et Son Rôle dans la Restauration de la Famille Française* (1941).
6. 'Demain que sera la France'. Exemplaire de prospectus de Concours-Référendum. AN, AGII 498.
7. G. Pernot, 'Note sur la Politique Familiale' (1940), p. 2. AN AGII 459.
8. Journal Officiel, 23 juillet 1940.
9. *Enseignement Démographique et Familiale*, Haury & Lugand, Alliance Nationale Contre la Dépopulation (Ministère de l'Information, 1944), AN F41 291.
10. *Un Fléau National: la Dénatalité*. Brochure pouvant servir pour plan aux conférences, 1942. (Services techniques de la Propagande, Vichy) AN F41 291.
11. *La Journée des Mères*. Brochure pouvant servir pour plan aux conférences, 1943. AN F41 291.
12. J.F. McMillan, *Housewife or Harlot: the Place of Women in French Society, 1870-1940* (Brighton, 1981), pp. 10-12.
13. W. Garcin, *Révolution Sociale Par la Famille*, Fédération des Associations de Familles (Service technique de la Propagande, Vichy, 1943), p. 16.
14. *Aux Educatrices*, Commissariat Général à la Famille.
15. Loi du 18 mars 1942.
16. W.D. Halls, *The Youth of Vichy France* (Oxford, 1981), p. 43.
17. *Aux Educatrices*, Commissariat Général à la Famille.
18. A. Werth, *France 1940-1955* (London, 1956), p. 67.
19. R. Benjamin, *Vérités et Rêveries sur l'Education* (1941), p. 186.
20. Letter, 7 mars 1941. AN, F60 628.
21. Poster 'Fêtes des Mères', 25 mai 1941. AN, F 41 291.
22. *La Journée des Mères*, AN, F41 291.
23. Tract 'La Maternité Embellit', AN, AG II 498.
24. A section of the tricolored triptych produced in December 1941, the others being: *Donner la vie engendre la joie; La Famille, fruit du passé, germe de l'avenir.* AN, AG II 498.
25. Dr Totis, *Santé, Beauté, Maternité* (1941).
26. AN AG II 498.
27. *La Vie en Fleur*, Commissariat Général à la Famille.
28. *Les Dangers des Pratiques Anticonceptionelles*, Alliance Nationale Contre la Dépopulation (1944). AN F41 291.
29. *Journal Officiel*, 15 février 1942. See C. Watson, 'Birth Control and Abortion in France since 1939', *Population Studies*, 5, 1952.
30. P. Lefebvre-Dibon, *La lutte contre l'avortement*, Alliance Nationale Contre la Dépopulation, 1943.
31. J.E. Roy, *L'Avortement Fléau National*, Publications de l'Université de Poitiers, no. 4, 1944.

32. H.R. Kedward, *Resistance in Vichy France* (Oxford, 1978), pp. 82-4.
33. A. Coutrot, 'La Politique Familiale de Vichy' in *Le Gouvernement de Vichy, 1940-1942*, FNSP, Paris (1972).

3 MANIPULATORS OF VICHY PROPAGANDA: A CASE STUDY IN PERSONALITY

John Dixon

The Vichy regime was an obvious failure. In four years it turned a nation of 'Quarante Millions de Pétainistes'[1] into one which, to all intents and purposes, was torn about by a bloody civil war in 1944 whose wounds have yet to heal fully, even after 40 years. Such a situation imposes severe problems for historical research.

Failure it may have been, but when the defeat occurred in 1940, it was for many French people the 'Divine surprise' for which they had been waiting and preparing for years.[2] The Vichy regime did have an ideology, however contradictory it was to prove, and, for various reasons, it was able to motivate a significant number of educated people to manipulate the vast bureaucratic machine it created to effect the restoration of France.

Dr Roger Austin has written about the propaganda machine in the Hérault *département* and how it coped with the problem of assessing public opinion.[3] There is no doubt that this vast machine was uncoordinated and to some extent chaotic; until, that is, January 1944 when rationalisation was imposed by the Milice regime of Laval and Darnand. By that time, however, many of the natural supporters of the Vichy regime had themselves been alienated.

It is to these supporters of the Vichy regime that this chapter is devoted since the success of a political machine must, to some extent, be determined by the people who inspire its development and who make it succeed — or fail.

Roderick Kedward has indicated the route towards understanding the Vichy regime: 'Above all, there is a need to see Pétainism as something which came from below, as well as from above, and to analyse its failure in those terms'.[4] This chapter is an attempt to do just that in a very small way since the two manipulators of Vichy propaganda chosen here are, in no statistical way, representative.

Marcel Paÿs, regional censor of Limoges, could be regarded as a 'professional Vichyssois', one who found compensatory employment in the new regime and one who had evident sympathy for its ideas. The demands of the Vichy regime and the proximity of his newly acquired country residence were the only reason for his three-year connection with Limoges.

'1940 is less the death of the Third Republic than the final death of the Popular Front.' This is Roderick Kedward's perspective on the nature of Vichy France.[5] He drew his conclusion from a study of prefectoral reports and a study of those written by Marcel Paÿs would not detract from that.

In the case of Me. René Farnier, *Chef de Propagande*, of the Légion Française des Combattants, this assertion would be to tell but part of the story. Because he followed Pétain without hesitation in 1940 and stayed, just like Pétain, loyally at his post until it no longer existed, Me. Farnier is here designated as an 'instinctive Pétainist'. Furthermore, a study of his life reveals a dedication to the destruction of a republican regime whose fundamental concepts were totally alien to his own culture and ideology.

My fascination for the Vichy regime lies in the conviction that it was a 'regime in waiting' for more than 45 years. Antagonism against the symbol of the Republican regime (Dreyfus) was a consistent and common theme among many supporters of Vichy and, when Maurras commenced his life sentence in prison by shouting, 'C'est la Revanche de Dreyfus' he was, for once, speaking for many more people than himself.[6]

Marcel Paÿs, Censeur Régional de Limoges: 'Vichyssois professionnel'

Weber has already penetrated Vichy incontestably, with his assertion that 'Many Frenchmen were Maurrasian without knowing it'. An occasional pre-war contributor to *Je Suis Partout* and *Gringoire*, there is no evidence that Paÿs belonged to Action Française but certainly the study of this man's three-year service as regional censor in Limoges shows both how important censorship was in the regime's control of ideology and how officials like Paÿs, brought into the regions from Vichy, carried out national policy. Marcel Paÿs was a professional in the sense that he executed his orders without regard for his personal feelings and in the sense that the Vichy regime provided him with remunerative employment when the defeat of 1940 confronted him with a future without work at the delicate age of 59.

No doubt he was then contemplating retirement at the end of what had been a flourishing career as a national journalist in Paris. In 1933 he had been promoted *Officier de la Légion d'honneur*[7] while he was diplomatic editor of *l'Excelsior*. This newspaper died with the Republican regime and, after being appointed to the censorship department of the Ministry of Information at Vichy in September 1940 he arrived, after a short period at Nîmes, in December 1941 as regional censor at Limoges. He approached this sudden and paradoxical change of direction of his career with nothing less than professional commitment. Moreover, rumour suggested that he even had ambitions for promotion in the censorship hierarchy at Vichy, staffed as it was by former Parisian colleagues.[8]

This employment was Marcel Paÿs' only connection with Limoges itself. Such a tenuous link poses very serious problems for research into his background and personality. He was also a poet but his poems and official documentation impose the onus of inference upon the reader. What does become clear is that the key to understanding Paÿs' motivation for working for Vichy and for his remaining at his post until May 1944 lies in a profound desire to earn his own living and maintain a standard of life that, by 1940, he had achieved for himself and his family by hard work and sacrifice — the sacrifice of his poetical and artistic aspirations. As he said: 'Art or Literature? Anxiety over this choice hardly taxed me; first it was necessary to live.' Marcel Regis Victor Paÿs was born in 1881, the son of the sales representative of a Lyon silk firm which failed just before his birth.[9] His father was to try, somewhat imprudently prepared, to make a living in South America. Marcel was to see his father only once before his disappearance without trace in 1899. He was accordingly reared by his mother but his education was financed by the family of the silk firm. His education was sound but, as he was a relatively poor scholar at a Catholic boarding school, he was always conscious of his own relative poverty and the need to earn his own living. He passed 'an infancy, dreamy and sad' at Le Puy, Haute Loire, a 'devout and sacred city where prayer and pleasure have the same secret ardour. Of your voluptuous fervour, the hot wax of my heart has received the secret imprint which makes me a "man of desire".' Certainly poetry, published in 1960,[10] reveals a man to whom matters of the heart were of some significance. As for religious piety, even his arch-critic, Pierre Limagne, acknowledged that he was less 'fussy' in matters religious than in matters political and military.

It is Pierre Limagne, former journalist with the Catholic newspaper, *la Croix de Paris*, who provided much intimate detail of the censor's life whilst in Limoges.[11] *La Croix* was evacuated to Limoges for the four years of the Occupation and in 1946 Limagne published a uniquely detailed diary of these years, *Les Ephémérides*.[12] Accurate as this detail is, a journalist needs a villain for his story and it is clear that the regional censor fulfils this role admirably. Relations were already strained under the regime of his predecessor, the elderly soldier Commandant Henri Peyre and as the domestic and military situation deteriorated so did relations between censor and newspapers. What makes this book dangerous as a true record of 'Marcel P.....', as he is cited, is that after the occupation of the 'free zone' in November 1942, Limagne left Limoges for active services with the Maquis in the Ardèche. Consequently information in his book is, thereafter, dependent upon documents brought to him by colleagues and upon journalists' gossip. Some of the comment on the supposed relationship between Paÿs and his German counterpart is based upon information relayed by the newspaper's cyclist-messenger boy. In an interview with me, M. Limagne admitted that he had only met Paÿs before the war and that he did not like him, because of his excessive professional zeal. The only journalist of *la Croix* who knew him personally has admitted that he is now too old and ill to remember enough to help the historian.[13] Such are the hazards which confront the historian of the 'professional Vichyssois' who was, in effect, in 'exile' from his roots.

The situation may well be remedied since, at the time of writing, the family of Marcel Paÿs has indicated that it will co-operate with my research. Conclusions outlined here must, therefore, be regarded as provisional. For the present, we must rely on his official reports, letters, poetry — and Limagne's subjective comments.

Paÿs himself was realistic enough to appreciate his predicament, now he was no longer a journalist:

> Without doubt, censors cannot pretend to be popular in the narrow world of newspapers which must be reminded of their errors. But they will |easily finish by making themselves understood, esteemed and respected... which is really the essential.[14]

Experience would frustrate these ideals since never could journalist and censor agree about 'errors'. A former journalist, however, would appear to be a more felicitous choice as a censor than a soldier as the government tried to relax the restrictions upon newspapers during 1941 and 1942.

Matters of 'information', 'propaganda' and 'censorship' were not the creation of the Vichy regime. It merely utilised and developed republican practices bequeathed to it. Introduced in haste, these services were to be chaotic and competing until rationalisation was imposed by the

Secretary of State for Information, Philippe Henriot in 1944. Censorship was an ancient practice, controlled traditionally by the military. Vichy's contribution was to staff this department by professional journalists. In the First World War, it had earned the sobriquet 'Anastasie', yet despite the best political intentions it was not until October 1936 that the government set up a commission to co-ordinate all the information services which had hitherto been operated by separate ministries. Under Camille Chautemps this commission was designed to serve the Ministry of Foreign Affairs. It was, however, fear of war in July 1938 which prompted the creation of a general service of information although another year passed before the writer Jean Giraudoux was put in charge of co-ordinating all information services. In March 1940 L.-O. Frossard became the first Minister of Information.[15]

In the provinces the role of the censor was seen to be merely that of applying *consignes* − government instructions. Soldiers, aided by civil servants were the obviously qualified staff for this limited function. Hence the arrival of Cmt. Peyre and Lt. Paul at Limoges in July 1940 along with the elderly Joseph Masson, dragged most reluctantly out of retirement since he received no extra pay for this work which was to occupy him for the whole of the Vichy era. Simon Arbellot[16] was not impressed: 'What censors! An aréopage ... of sleeping diplomats, disaffected military men, writers without inspiration.' Frossard was determined to replace these 'illiterates' and his problem was solved by the closing down of newspapers such as *l'Excelsior* in May 1940 which yielded a profusion of journalists such as Marcel Paÿs seeking to earn their living.

The Third Republic had extended the role of censorship in 1936 when the Minister of the Interior, Albert Sarraut, had instructed prefects to keep copies of all periodicals printed locally since these revealed the general state of morale and popular reaction to government ideas and acts.[17] By 1941 a weekly report on the state of public opinion as revealed by the local Press was an essential part of the censor's function.

These reports reveal that Cmt. Peyre was no illiterate − but he was ferociously anti-communist. During a feud with *la Croix* he had instigated a police phone-tap in September 1941 but the police report concentrated upon the unpopularity of the censor himself: 'numerous complaints have already been made by the local press and the removal of this personality had been requested'. Commandant Peyre had already been told by the editor of the centre-right newspaper, *le Courier du Centre*[18] that 'You know nothing of your profession and I'm beginning to have had enough of this censor.'[19] Within weeks Marcel Paÿs arrived after having completed his apprenticeship as a censor in Nîmes.

It was not, however, only in the cities that it was realised that military censorship was counter-productive. In April 1941 the government issued a circular on the role of the censor:

> Nine months after the Armistice, it is useful to revise the principles of control of the press in order to give newspapers a certain amount of liberty compatible with the general situation. . . criticisms are permitted and the press is authorised to discuss problems of the main themes of the National Revolution. Censors must meet at least weekly with editors . . . meetings of colleagues rather than administrative meetings. . . to distribute as fairly as possible praise or blame and explain necessary sanctions if need be.

Circular 30 of February 1942 went even further. Entitled 'L'Assouplissement du Régime', it made only certain communications of government obligatory for the newspapers and directed censors to have frequent contacts with prefects: 'Your task is not only to control but also to advise the press.'

On the face of it, Paÿs was well suited to the new role of the censor, envisaged by Darlan: that of 'advisor to the press'. Yet Limagne was soon complaining that Paÿs was too well suited since he claimed that Paÿs was not content to censor but wanted to rewrite the newspaper himself. Vichy backed up these complaints by reminding him that his role was to shorten and not to prolong articles![20] The censor was, accordingly, always the focus of hostilities in a regime which allowed newspapers to criticise the system, a system which quite clearly, journalists at *la Croix* were determined to undermine.

It was Paÿs' zeal which was the source of Limagne's vituperation. Paÿs own position was ultimately undermined, however, because of the indulgence shown towards newspapers by his deputy, Lt. Paul, a wounded war veteran of 58 years who arrived in Limoges as military censor in July 1940. As early as September 1942, Paÿs was expressing to Vichy his doubt about the reliability of Paul but, because of his wife and two children, he wanted to avoid a scandal. Yet it is clear that it was Paul who was in charge when articles passed the censor ultimately causing Vichy to issue a 'green' notice admonishing the censor for his laxity.[22] The ultimate crisis manifested itself on 6 December 1943 when Paul allowed *le Courier* to print a report concerning 'le préfet du Maquis' alongside one concerning Vichy's official prefect.[23] 'Le préfet du Maquis' was none other than Georges Guingouin,[24] the communist Resistance leader, 'wanted' for over two years, who was succeeding where Vichy prefects had consistently failed, in controlling food prices. This failure was a significant factor in Vichy's own defeat in the propaganda battle. Vichy reacted swiftly and ruthlessly. The *Courier* was suspended and its directors were interned – along with Lt. Paul. The President of the Légion intervened;[25] Paÿs himself defended his subordinate by claiming that the paper had 'misled' the censor[26] and, after a few weeks of genteel internment at Evaux-les-Bains,[27] all three were released but were subsequently removed from office. This crisis coincided with the arrival of Philippe Henriot as Minister of Information, and a new structure which rationalised the competing propaganda units. Lt. Paul's successor eventually succeeded Paÿs who was himself subordinated to the Regional Delegate of Propaganda and Information in March 1944.[28]

The irony of his professional demise lies in the fact that Paÿs had consistently argued for this rationalisation and unification.[29] Part of the organisational problem of French government was that such a civil servant had to satisfy two masters – central government in Vichy and the regional prefect in Limoges. If his relationship with the newspapers was disastrous, that with the préfecture was harmonious. Faced immediately in December 1941 with strife in the Dordogne between censor and prefect, he rapidly came to an agreement whereby the censor was to be the prefect's 'broadcasting and reception aerial of information' whereas the prefect was to be the censor's 'secular arm'.[30] Paÿs' relationship with prefect Lemoine was particularly close[31] but most prefects seemed content to issue censors' notices on their behalf, virtually verbatim.

Certainly the success of this relationship was based upon mutual need: the censor was an important source of comment on public opinion whose transmission to Vichy was a crucial function of the préfecture. Posterity, unlike apparently Vichy, begs the question concerning the competence of the censor in this field, especially as Paÿs claimed that his job kept him in the office day and night. However, an insight into the 'scientific' methodology was revealed by his subordinate in the Dordogne who reported:

> It goes without saying that the facts that I report here are not empty rumours and I cite my sources:
> 1. bourgeois landowners in touch with the peasant;
> 2. conversations with peasants in the hotel which I inhabit...

much visited on market days.³²

Study of the reports written by Paÿs indicate that they were read by somebody at the préfecture, because of the red and blue crayon annotations. Replacement prefect André Jean-Faure seems to have been the most assiduous. One of his suggestions caught the eyes of the historians Marrus and Paxton.³³ It concerned the paradox that Jews were excluded from the STO. It is not certain that Jean-Faure obtained the idea from the censor but certainly he read the Dordogne censor's report on 30 April 1943 which referred to 'the deep discontent from the fact that Jews escape all obligatory work'. Paÿs did not pick this up until 28 May 1943 when he suggested that the idea originated with the departmental prefect and then he was concerned that Jews were doubly prone to propaganda from London and Moscow since they were simultaneously condemned to idleness yet disposed of considerable resources. This was on 7 June, the same day on which Jean-Faure took up the theme to be marked down by posterity.³⁴

Paÿs wrote his last report in January 1944, at a time when there was a shift in authority from the prefects to the Milice.³⁵ These reports and Limagne's comments suggest that Paÿs was in no way ill at ease with the basic ideology of Vichy and its National Revolution. Interest therefore lies in the degree to which he allied himself with the regime and, ultimately, its illegitimate corollary, collaboration.

Limitations of time force the researcher to concentrate upon certain key topics. Paÿs certainly revealed himself hostile to Britain but, like many of his compatriots, this revulsion was revealed by his reaction to bombardments of French targets. He annoyed journalists by insisting upon sub-titles such as 'Indescribable British aggression' or 'Fifty-nine British aircraft shot down'.³⁶ That he was hostile at all to Britain is worthy of note since Paÿs cannot excuse xenophobia with claims of geographic isolation.

Certainly no profound understanding, born of living in Britain, emerges from his poetry which might temper traditional prejudice against 'perfidious Albion'. Marcel Paÿs had in fact lived in Britain for some three years before the Great War after his marriage to an Englishwoman, who died after a very long illness. He worked as an art critic with the magazine *Connoisseur*. He was said to have been bilingual but there is little evidence in his writing to this effect. His passport revealed that he visited England from 26 to 30 April 1938 as special correspondent of *l'Excelsior* during the visit there of Daladier and Bonnet.³⁷ One can only be disappointed, therefore, by the superficiality of his poetic references to Britain. In one entitled 'In the style of Toulouse-Lautrec,' he wrote:

> Their metallic heels,
> Pounding the parquet in step,
> The little British girls
> Dance
> Beneath the electric lights.
> ...
> Your eyes of porcelaine,
> So child like,
> Of what are they dreaming?
> What thoughts live there
> When your underwear
> Is transformed into strange corollas
> Whose pistils dance for those whom
> Lingerie excites.
> Of what are they dreaming,
> Your angel eyes?
>
> Do they see the handsome Tomy[sic]
> In Hyde Park or Kensington Gardens,
> So smart in scarlet tunic;
> Who spoke to you of marriage,
> The sweetheart who carried off
> Your life savings?[38]

Usually Paÿs was such a professional that it is difficult to know how strongly he was personally committed to the National Revolution. In February 1943 the censor reported blandly that 'a collaborationist committee has become discernible recently'.[39] A week later, he iterated his complaint of lack of co-ordination in the propaganda services when a youth conference clashed with that of the physicist, Georges Claude,[40] organised by Groupe Collaboration. In the file of this group a report dated 18 February 1943, written by the Renseignements Généraux said that 'the committee has been constituted with M. Marcel Paÿs, chief censor, and the deputy secretary of the PPF'.[41] Was this Monsieur Paÿs, dutiful censor? Or was it Marcel Paÿs, individual? There is no evidence that Paÿs belonged to any political party — nor even to the Légion Française des Combattants for which four years of service in the Great War would have entitled him. Yet it is worthy of note that it was he who was involved with this conference and not an official délégué d'information as was usual. The explanation probably lies in the maladministration of the propaganda services of which Paÿs frequently complained.

Subsequent events showed that Paÿs saw a dichotomy between his professional and private life. This is illustrated by his reporting on reaction to the STO. It had such profound impact upon public opinion that Vichy could not ignore it. On 8 March 1943 he reported 'certain bourgeois, [who] revealed themselves ulcerated at the requisition of their sons. . .'[42] That very same day Limagne noted that 'Marcel P. . . has gone to Vichy to see Laval in order to interest him in his own son, who has been designated for the deportation and he seeks his exemption'. Four days later he returned to the story: 'the son departed without waiting for the termination of steps taken to gain his exemption; upholding collaborationist sentiments, Paÿs was astounded, quite rightly, that he should be so smitten'.[43] The son rejected the preferential treatment offered by Laval. Thereafter Paÿs reveals himself a reporter with particularly detailed knowledge of the problems such 'deportees' faced.[44] There was, however, no comment of a personal nature to reveal the feelings of a father.

Nor do his reports reveal much about the German military censor, Lt. Sahm, an Austrian who arrived in Limoges on 16 January 1943. In fact Limagne is the main source of information but, as we have already emphasised, he was himself absent from Limoges during this period. The owner of *la Croix* reported meetings where Paÿs offered aperitifs and cigarettes while addressing his counterpart as 'mon cher ami' (though Limagne comments that this was a Paÿs mannerism used even with people he clearly disliked). Allegations were made that Paÿs entertained Sahm at his country residence – 'copains comme cochons' was the allegory; furthermore the two of them were alleged to have interrupted a performance of the *Barber of Seville*, which created more gossip about the closeness of Franco-German relations. M. Paÿs' family vehemently deny that Sahm stayed at their house but he did visit without invitation while he was travelling from Limoges to Châteauroux. A neighbour reported his presence. It was, however, stated that Lt. Sahm was a man of courtesy and some charm. He was also responsible for the working of the STO in Limoges yet such 'friendship' did not save Paÿs' own son from his determination.

The eventual departure of Paÿs from Limoges did not end the existence of scenes between newspapers and the new chief censor but Limagne reminds us of our theme when he paid the man the compliment that he was 'certainly anti-German'. Paÿs left Limoges, perhaps for the last time, on 3 May 1944 victim of the 'Préfet du Maquis affair' and certainly of the re-organisation of the Propaganda and Information services by Henriot which subordinated Paÿs to the Propaganda chief. Had he been any less anti-German and, therefore more collaborationist than his successor? Only the most fanatical of collaborators could have been pro-German when it was clearly obvious that German defeat was only a matter of time. It has been reported, without verification, that Paÿs was in fact on a Nazi blacklist in 1940 over articles he had written in *l'Excelsior*. A study of his signed articles reveals that the literary style of the chief of the foreign bureau became less 'diplomatic' about the Nazis after the declaration of war in 1939. Paÿs collected cuttings of his own articles which demonstrated his interest in affairs concerning Great Britain but the newspaper itself, especially in 1938, reveals that Paÿs was in the mainstream of moderate right-wing opinion in advocating Mussolini's Italy as the effective counterpoise to Nazi Germany. He, and his newspaper, were certainly *Munichois* in the sense that the agreement — and Mussolini's last minute intervention by telephone — had 'saved civilisation from a fatal experience'.[46]

Evidence therefore presents a portrait of Marcel Paÿs as an elderly man without strong political opinions or allegiance who, in the tradition of French understatement, did not 'play politics'. Like so many others he was able to accept with some enthusiasm the changes brought about by the Vichy regime and he was certainly willing to accept payment by that regime for the use of his expertise in the new circumstances. The question which has mystified even members of his own family is how a journalist could become a censor; how did he reconcile his journalistic principles of freedom of information with the censor's role of suppressing, shaping or even distorting information? The solution can only be an evident sympathy for the aims of the Vichy regime and an overriding need, which stemmed from his experience of genteel poverty during his adolescence, to earn his own living and maintain his standard of living. Along perhaps with most of the other 'quarante millions de Pétainistes' this overriding preoccupation led inevitably to the accepting of what had been hitherto unacceptable. Paÿs' co-operation with the German censor perhaps reveals no more than a logical and convenient extension of his support for a regime which, he had not yet realised, had outlived its usefulness by November 1942. It could be that Limagne would have included Paÿs in his two-edged compliment to his successor who, besides being 'anti-German' was a 'cowardly civil servant and, at the bottom, Maurrasian enough in spirit'.[47]

In December 1944 he was formally dismissed from his functions and in February 1946 he suffered the indignity of being removed from the Légion d'honneur. He was finally put on trial before the Chambre Civique de Limoges on 26 July 1946 where he was 'purely and simply' acquitted of the only charge – that of being one of Vichy's censors. He still had to wait until 20 January 1948 before being restored to the Légion. Subsequently he wrote occasional articles for *le Figaro* and other publications. Among his own document collection cuttings are found from *l'Auvergnat de Paris* where it was recalled that, before the Great War, Paÿs had been hailed as one of 16 young 'wolves' from the Auvergne who were led by Gandilhon. His last book, *Rimes Prosaïques,* published in 1960 won for him two literary prizes, le prix Gabriel Vicaire and le prix Tristan Derême. His stature at his death merited the recording of his death at the age of 82 in the 'Biography of principal French personalities who died during the year 1963'.[48] Yet it appears that Paÿs died unsure of his own reputation. In *Rimes Prosaïques* he wrote his own sad commentary in the poem, 'Resignation':

My generation wanted nothing to do with me.
Was it its fault, or mine?
Too late to call the error mine,
I have lived without knowing either how or why.[49]

His professional success was clearly eclipsed by that fateful choice he made in the desperate days of the summer of 1940, yet it is his work as a Vichy censor that has brought Marcel Paÿs to the attention of posterity. It is, therefore, somewhat ironic that this four-year aberration should finally throw the spotlight on his positive, if modest, contribution to French cultural life.

Me. René Farnier, Majoral du Félibrige, Chef de Propagande de la Légion Française des Combattants

The 'professional' Vichyssois may have been able to leave Limoges for an obscurity which, in the climate of the summer of 1944, was no doubt welcome. Me. René Farnier had no intention of leaving his home in the High Limousin. To have done so would have been an admission of self-reproach. Yet while Paÿs may have felt himself 'unwanted' by his own generation, the Liberation of Limoges on 21 August 1944 brought increasing fears that Farnier himself was very much a wanted man.[50] Three months later the denunciation came, manifesting itself at the end of a newspaper report: 'However, we have had the disagreeable surprise to report the presence at this rally of Me. Farnier, notorious legionnaire who, we are assured, is still a teacher at the Law School.'[51] Four days later the *Echo du Centre*,[52] a communist newspaper which had taken over the premises of the *Courrier du Centre* followed suit. Its tone was more strident: 'Why wait to imprison the President of the Légion? Me. Farnier [is] still a teacher at the Law School. [He] should be hunted down and interned.' That decision had been made, however, the day previously by the Comité d'Épuration in Limoges. It was to be exactly as the *Echo* had demanded but although he was interned under a regulation concerning 'denunciation of civil servants and patriots', it was significant that the Committee declared: 'The Commission repeats that no charge has been brought against [these leaders]'.[53]

Nevertheless René Farnier was interned for nearly three months in the former local Vichy concentration camp of Nexon until he was suddenly released. His reaction is best left in his own words:

> Pour du culot, c'est du culot! The Purification Commission interned me, fifty four days after which it examined my case and declared that... it did not oppose my liberation! Quel aveu! And it is signed by the hand of the [President] who assured me of the devotion of himself and his committee. These tyrants are real imbeciles!

In fact the affair was more dubious than that since he later learned that pressure was being put on his wife which kept him in prison for twelve days longer than was necessary: it was desired that he resign his job at the Law School. Fortunately when the prefect learned of this manoeuvre, he immediately ordered Farnier's release. Ironically the prefect was a communist.

The circumstances of this somewhat sordid episode, which took place in a region described by some to be in a state, initially, of political terror, illustrate alarmingly the problems of achieving objective historical research. Compared with Paÿs, René Farnier has yielded an abundance of documentation for research. Indeed he had a natural desire to rehabilitate himself and he wrote an account of the experience of Limoges from 'D-Day' until April 1945 when his son returned from the STO. It was this son who offered this account for my research, containing some 180 pages of manuscript. I have also seen a meticulous account written by Me. Farnier of his experience in the whole of the Great War, but it appears that there exists only this one volume of the

Second World War. The historian is thus faced with 'pre-selected' documentation as the author tries to justify his actions, quite naturally, and to indicate the chaos and injustice which he saw following the breakdown of the Vichy regime. It appears to be a diary, but a lapse over the execution of Brasillach[54] suggests that it was written in February 1945, *after* his release from internment. Otherwise the detail would seem, so far, to be accurate.

Nor is oral history necessarily any more reliable — indeed, concerning events of the Liberation it can be positively misleading. Having first 'encountered' Me. Farnier in an information bulletin and then, more fascinatingly, in a *Mémoire*[55] concerning the activities of the political Right in Limoges before the First World War, I included his name on a list of Vichy servants which was presented to someone who was recommended as an authority on, and survivor of, Limoges in the Vichy era. My interlocutor readily admitted they had been colleagues and that Farnier had been interned, but not as a punishment. It had been a device of his colleagues to shelter him! Months later I read in Farnier's own account a significant footnote: 'I knew later that Sieur . . . [a former civil servant] under Pétain but whom Guingouin had conserved in office, has alone among the teachers at the Law School tried to prevent my return to my post.' The job description in the footnote and corroboration of his career, leads me, and the son of Me. Farnier, to conclude that my interlocutor in 1982 may well have been, in fact, the actor in the drama of 1944. For this historian 40 years is a lifetime but for survivors and participants of this period, evidently, objectivity and even honesty is a quality that cannot be justifiably expected.

Drama concerning Me. Farnier's fate after the Liberation has perhaps over-emphasised the role that he played during the Occupation. His crime seems to have been that he was a leader of the Légion but no documents or public accusations have been found which accuse him of collaboration with either the Milice or the Germans.

As propaganda chief with the Légion he certainly launched himself into his role with gusto in 1941 but by 1942 he was beginning to label himself 'assistant commissioner for Folklore events'; by 1943 he was 'Provincial President of the National Commission on Folklore' and in 1944 he requested Vichy to let him stand down as propaganda chief. During this period his assistant was indeed complaining of rudimentary organisation and that he was running the service alone for more than a year. His assistant's claims may have had some justification since Farnier never altered his habit of going to his country home, some miles outside of Limoges, leaving others to organise that most important event of the Légion's calendar, the August anniversary.[56] The young assistant finally resigned in the Autumn of 1943 and his next appearance in Limoges was dramatic. At the Liberation he was a Lt. FFI who led a raid on the Légion headquarters and, while his men surveyed its occupants, he searched the offices for documents. Farnier reflected with some irony on this 'S.O.L. so proud of his uniform who had hunted communists' in his native and neighbouring town of St Junien.[57]

Farnier's absence in the country did not mean that he neglected what had become the inspiration of his life, his folk group called L'École du Barbichet[58] whose activities flourished in the countryside, often on the Légion's behalf, during the holiday months. It is left to the historian to deduce that Farnier increasingly diverted his energies from the Légion to regionalism. An indication that he and other Légionnaires were losing faith in the government came in a report on the invasion of the Non-Occupied Zone which he wrote in November 1942. He admitted that many of its members had 'escaped' because, among other reasons, the according of full powers to Pierre Laval had divided them since their oath was to the Marshal and not to his head of government. In addition, of course, it was evident that German victory was no longer certain.[59] Despite these misgivings, Farnier stayed at his post until it no longer existed, in the same manner as did Pétain. It was this loyalty towards and admiration of Pétain which had drawn Farnier into serving the Vichy regime as a manipulator of its propaganda. Thus he is here dubbed an 'instinctive Pétainist'. Two experiences had dominated his life before 1940: his experience as a soldier at the Front and, from an earlier stage, regionalism. Farnier had convinced himself, rightly or wrongly, that Pétain was, at heart, a Mistralian and in September 1940 he publicly advertised his position in the Légion newspaper with the headline: OUR TASK.[60]

> As in 1914, our duty is held in one word: to SERVE and to serve under the orders of that great leader whom we love and admire, whose orders will be executed eagerly and with discipline. . . our first virtue must be obedience. . .

An analysis of Farnier's service to Vichy and Pétain from 1940-4 can only be understood in the context of the first 52 years of his life, a striking example of how 1940 was seen as the apotheosis of a movement which had been life itself to Farnier and people like him, though they represented only a small part of the 'quarante millions' who had welcomed Pétain as their 'Saviour'.

Biographies of Farnier's life have already been written, but by people so close to him that they are necessarily selective.[61] What they have in common is that the life of René Farnier has a gap, unaccounted for, from 1928 until 1952, two years before his death. The aspect of his life which has been documented is his contribution to folklore. The biography written by Dr Leon Delhoume, a childhood friend, co-founder of the félibrige movement in Haute Vienne and veterans' leader from the inter-war period, fills in many of the details of the development of the culture and ideology of our subject. René Farnier was, in fact, born in exile in Savoy in 1888, the son of a railway engineer. Unlike Paÿs, he wrote of a 'delightful infancy' during which his education had religious influences. When his father retired they returned to the family estate at Bonnac la Côte from where he could attend the Lycée of Limoges. There he steeped himself in the literature and language of *Oc*, coming under the influence of Mistral. As editor of the school magazine in 1904, he reviewed poems of D'Annunzio, that 'great Italian poet'. This later turned into admiration for Mussolini's Italy combining itself with profound criticism of the Third Republic.

In 1908 he was a student in Paris at a time when students were disrupting lectures given by teachers whose political ideas were mistrusted. He then wrote to Delhoume that the end of the Republic would not come with a *coup d'état* but that its death would be its own work.[62] He condemned the regime because of its reliance on individualism which produced 'three poison fruits: Mutiny, Indiscipline and Disorder'. His sole remedy was a 'hereditary and anti-parliamentarian democracy'.

Delhoume paints a picture of this law student spending his time reading poetry, smoking a pipe and going to mass. He would seem to have been a man of conventional morality who wrote that he lived a 'solitary life' enjoying female company but was 'disgusted' by contemporary literary work in which 'everywhere the husband is deceived by his wife'. He loved the theatre and absorbed himself in 'théatre Action Française'. At this time he came to know Charles Maurras personally.[63]

By the time he had won a 'brilliant' law doctorate in 1913, he was already a journalist in Limoges for the organ of Action Française, *le Salut National*[64] where he wrote under the pseudonym of René Maison Rouge, inspired by his lovely home of that name in Bonnac. That same year he was one of the founders of the Institut Limousin de l'Action

Française at a time when this group seemed to possess a positive educational dynamic inspired by regional culture. According to his newspapers, his lectures were well received but the group itself was small in number and poorly financed.

His national service was finished just in time for him to be mobilised and despatched to the front by 8 August 1914. He participated in 'victory' on the Marne but as the war gathered in intensity in 1915 he shaved off his red beard, rose rapidly to the rank of quartermaster sergeant and started to defend soldiers on trial for their lives for disobeying orders. However his Croix de Guerre earned him an extra two days leave in Limoges in the Autumn but in these eight days, during which he realised that the 'front' and the 'rear' did not speak the same language, a disillusion set in whose engendered bitterness was to influence his subsequent writings.

His experience of the remainder of the war would seem to have been less harrowing while he exercised his talents as a barrister 'near' Verdun. Demobilised in 1920 he set up his own law office in Limoges and married in October, becoming a father in 1922. Meanwhile he had secured a post at the Law School and began writing for the new organ of Action Française.[65] His enthusiasm was consecrated, however, to the foundation of his École du Barbichet in 1923 with the climax arriving in 1928 when Limoges was the host of the félibréen festival of Ste Estelle.

Thereafter neither biographer writes of his activities. Fortunately for posterity, he assumed the task after 1931 writing, as President of a federation of Veterans' groups, in their newspapers. He retained this position until it was dissolved by Pétain in August 1940.[66] Compartmentalised as his life appears to be, it is well worth analysing themes which his writings between 1908 and 1940 tackled in order to appreciate the genesis of this 'instinctive Pétainist'.

We have already noted his criticism of the Republic, uttered at the age of 20, and the 1930s saw little change in these fundamental beliefs. The difference was that his rhetoric had been imbued with bitterness engendered by four years at the Front, followed by 20 years of frustration with the Republic. In 1938 he wrote: 'Twenty years afterwards and nothing has changed. . . lions are still led by asses.'[67] The belief that war veterans could do better had even pre-empted 6 February 1934 since a month before he had called: 'BE READY!'[68]

> It is obvious that the impotence of our politicians is irremediable . . . and if, on that day, France, disconcerted and disabused, turns

towards the *Poilu* of the Somme and Verdun in order to be saved one more time, ah well comrades, that day you will reply again: Present! and you will be ready to take power. *Poilus* who won the war are capable of winning the peace.

René Farnier was proclaimed in 1936 as the 'specialist in the question of maintaining peace'.[69] On the eve of Munich he declared that 'war is a crime' and on the morrow he was certain that 'the Munich agreement was not a misfortune'.[70] Being *Munichois* did not necessarily imply that Farnier was a potential collaborator with the Germans but he undoubtedly feared Hitler's regime greatly, blaming its rise on the 'abandonment of concessions and advances to Germany' after 1918.[71]

What was more significant was that this fear of Germany magnified his admiration of Mussolini. At Munich it was he who had 'saved millions of human lives', while in March 1939 the Duce was to go on 'to save peace and civilisation'. 'If Paris and Rome had agreed with each other', he declared, 'Hitler would be inoffensive and peace would be saved'.[72] Farnier's attachment to Italy had a curious birth, with Mistral as the Godfather. In 1932 he made a speech pleading for 'franco-latin friendship . . . the Renaissance of the Latin race and family'. He developed his thesis:[73]

> There are between us ties of family and literature . . . for if you have celebrated Mistral in Italy, we have celebrated with a profound admiration Dante and Virgil as well. Dante, poet-friend of Limousin troubadours who had the idea, it appears, of writing the 'Divine Comedy' in the Limousin language because, in the thirteenth century, Limousin was the literary language of Europe.

He went on to castigate the anti-Latin prejudice expressed in Paris and explained his lacking this prejudice by the rapid visit he had made to Italy in 1930 where he could see:

> a great country in full flight, in great vitality and in full strength. I assure you that a Frenchman can travel freely without being molested and, my faith, he can breathe as freely in Florence as in Paris.

It was this prejudice in favour of Mussolini's Italy which caused him to speak disparagingly of Britain during the Ethiopian crisis, thus displaying another essential strand of Pétainism of 1940: Anglophobia.

His antagonism lay in his belief, added to Italy's frustration with the Treaties, that 'Ethiopia is not a nation but an amalgam of tribes, barbarous and cruel'. In 1936, while ridiculing the League of Nations, 'slumbering in impotence', he claimed that it was English imperialism which 'would have French soldiers killed for the sake of pleasing the *Négus*'.[74]

This theme of spilling French blood for English gains was iterated in 1940 in the wake of Dunkirk and Mers El-Kébir. In an article entitled 'English Treachery' he declared that it was in fact Britain who had broken her word. Moreover British betrayal had not started at Oran but in 1939 when she had dragged France into an ideological war against all those people who do not love 'democracy'.[75]

Such talk of British treachery must have evoked a response in the emotionally charged atmosphere of the summer of 1940. By then Pétain was in power and, as we have seen, 'service' and 'obedience' were the watchwords. Opinions of March 1940 would therefore be interesting, at least those not obliterated by censors clumsier than Marcel Paÿs. In an article, he wrote of the 'butchers of Moscow' who wanted war. Praising 'heroic Finland', he added that 'certainly we French feel that this war is one of civilisation against Barbarism and that to defeat Germany is to defeat as well the Asiatic hordes which, under the pretext of Bolshevism, threaten the old world, heir to the Mediterranean civilisations. . .'[76] Such thoughts were to be a familiar theme of propaganda following 'Barbarossa' in 1941.

The assumption of power by Pétain caused him in September to pay homage on behalf of 5,000 regional veterans. 'The government of the Marshal has undertaken to remake France. With strict discipline we must be at his side. We can, however, collaborate in the great work of renovation.'[77]

How far did René Farnier support the National Revolution? As with Paÿs there is no doubt about his sympathy and, as with Paÿs, the only firm evidence of any political activity is based on research of departmental archives. What seems to be evident and, superficially surprising, is that after 1930 his name does not appear in documentation concerning Action Française, la Croix de Feu or the PSF.[78] One wonders if his allegiance to the first was cast in doubt by the Pope's condemnation in 1926.

Again it was the file of the PPF which cast a little light in the Autumn of 1940 when Farnier involved himself with the defence of a young man who was accused of painting anti-Jewish slogans on walls. Farnier was convinced the affair had political overtones since he criticised the police for an excess of zeal which was not manifested towards either communists or what he called 'degaullists'. He had sought the intervention of a prefect, apparently sympathetic to avoiding court action, and the matter reached Peyrouton, the Minister of the Interior himself. Correspondence on this matter reveals that the Secretary of the PPF described Farnier's attitude to them as 'very sympathetic'. No more has yet emerged.[79]

Meanwhile that same prefect had asked Farnier to undertake a task for which he had undoubted enthusiasm. On 26 November 1940 he produced a report on regionalism in which he looked forward to a 'peasant civilisation' founded by a Head of State who 'has publicly rendered homage to the memory of Mistral, founder and inspiration of the *Félibrige*'.[80]

In this way loyalty of men such as Farnier was pledged by the uniting of two crucial strands of his life; association of war veterans and regionalism. It has been shown that as the effectiveness of the Légion seemed to decline, Farnier stayed, however reluctantly, at his post yet consecrated more time and energy to regionalism and his beloved École du Barbichet. On the eve of 'D-Day' he declared to a regionalist conference: 'Folklore teaches us the history of our province; *Félibrige* makes it loved.'[81]

Evidently such love does conquer all since both the Félibrige and L'École du Barbichet survived its association with the Vichy regime and in 1983 the group celebrated its sixtieth anniversary with its founder, René Farnier, posthumously taking pride of place at the exhibition mounted in its honour. In 1952 he had, himself, become fully rehabilitated when he was elected for the second time as *batonnier* of the Limoges bar. He was by then extremely tired and he died two years later in 1954, characteristically reciting the whole of Mistral's 'Ode to the Latin race'.[82]

It appears that even the feeling of injustice felt by René Farnier could not weaken the profound fervour of the culture and ideology which he had developed during adolescence in High Limousin. It could be argued that Farnier was an 'instinctive Pétainist' without realising it until the fateful 'conjuncture' of 1940.[83] The strength of this culture and ideology is still apparent in the descendants of such men.

Marcel Paÿs' involvement with Vichy would not seem to have had such profound roots and, until proved otherwise, it would seem that he was a professional man who saw no ideological conflict in the job he was paid to perform, even though he must have felt that censorship was anathema to professional journalists such as himself.

68 Manipulators of Vichy Propaganda

The last lines that *René Maison Rouge* wrote as a youthful 26-year-old before he marched off to war were taken from Pascal:

If only man had never been corrupted ... [84]'

In 1944 both Farnier and Paÿs must have sensed themselves as being regarded as corrupt by the younger generation which had risen up to take control of liberated France. Time and the historian's perspective have both contributed, however, to the placing of the Vichy regime into the context of a fervent opposition to the very foundations of the Third Republic, a repugnance which spanned the generations and which was clearly born well before the accession to power of that hurriedly constituted Popular Front.[85] Undoubtedly Blum's government, and the workers' instinctive reaction to it, inspired the regime's opponents to greater stridency and activity in their opposition to the hated *Marianne*. The difference is merely one of emphasis.

Some 40 years later these manipulators of Vichy propaganda would seem themselves to have been misled into supporting a regime whose acts and ideas were to become increasingly unpalatable even to those who had enthused over the first changes inaugurated by Pétain in his National Revolution. Whether because of loyalty to Pétain or because of the need to earn a living, Farnier and Paÿs tied themselves inextricably to the Marshal's regime. It is interesting to contrast the reaction of these two men to coping with the unpalatable. Farnier, the youthful star of Action Française before the Great War withdrew into the relatively neutral zone of regionalism as Pétain's regime collapsed, whereas the non-political censor revealed increasing zeal, until he too lost heart at the beginning of 1944 with the professional snub administered by Henriot's reforms.

Farnier's regionalism provided an ideological bridge for his subsequent rehabilitation after Vichy, symbolised in a modern, private housing estate to the north of Limoges by the *Rue René Farnier*.[86] Paÿs, however had no such obvious avenue and his reintegration took longer and was more painful. This is some measure of the cultural and ideological gap that separated even those that Vichy was able to mobilise in its manipulation of propaganda.

Notes

I would like to thank the Foundation of Rotary International for supporting this research, Roderick Kedward of the University of Sussex and the Gloucestershire Education Authority for granting leave of absence to attend this conference.

1. H. Amouroux, *Quarante Millions de Pétainistes* (Paris, 1981).
2. M. Dank, *The French against the French* (Cassell, 1978), p. 47.
3. R. Austin, 'Propaganda and Public Opinion in Vichy France: The Department of the Hérault, 1940-44', *European Studies Review* (1983), vol. 13, pp. 455-82.
4. H.R. Kedward, 'Patriots and Patriotism in Vichy France', *Royal Historical Society*, 5th series, vol. 32 (1982), pp. 177-8.
5. Ibid.
6. Gimman-Gigandat, 'L'Accusé Procureur: Maurras', *Historia* (1975), HS 41, pp. 112-18.
7. Private Correspondence with *Grande Chancellerie de la Légion d'Honneur*, 15 June 1983.
8. P. Limagne: *Ephémérides de Quatre années tragiques, 1940-44*, 3 vols. (Paris, 1946); 23 October 1942 there was speculation about the replacement of the Head of Censorship at Vichy, Jean Dufour, who had died suddenly on 14 October 1942 at 39 years of age. He had been a journalist with *le Matin*.
9. Most of the research into Paÿs' background was gleaned from documents extracted with difficulty out of public bodies. To this end I am indebted to Mlle Liliane Delaume a professional geneologist of 28, Avenue de la Liberation, 87000 Limoges who gave her advice benevolently. In addition much professional advice was offered by Mlle Sarah Olivier, Directeur-adjoint des Archives Départmentales de la Haute-Vienne. However, almost at completion of the research stage, I at last made contact with M. Paÿs' family and in July 1984 Mme Paÿs kindly let me study her husband's papers in order to restore balance to a story strongly biased by a study based upon poetry, official documents and the subjectivity of Pierre Limagne.
10. Marcel Paÿs, *Rimes Prosaïques* (Rodez 1960). The same author also had published *Les Ailes de Cire* (Paris, 1909).
11. *La Croix de Paris* was a national pre-war Catholic newspaper which was evacuated to Limoges for the duration of the Occupation. It was a different newspaper from *La Croix de Limoges* and *La Croix de Dimanche*. In 1940 it was estimated by the prefect (Archives Nationales: F41/160) to have had a circulation of 35,000. Between 24 July and 8 August 1943 it was suspended by Laval, though Limagne claims this was after prompting by Krug von Nidda. In October 1944 it was allowed to reappear under its old title.
12. Limagne, *Ephémérides, passim*.
13. Correspondence and interview with M. Limagne, February to April 1983.
14. Archives Départementales de la Haute Vienne (hereafter ADHV), 1 PR 159, 6 June 1942.
15. Information on the confusing history of these services at government level can be obtained from the *Inventaire* to series F41 at the Archives Nationales. Further details can be found in the *Revue d'histoire de la Deuxième Guerre Mondiale*, no. 64, 1966 which is a special number devoted to 'Propaganda'.
16. Simon Arbellot, *La Presse Française sous la Francisque* (Echo de la Presse, Paris 194?). Arbellot was not a disinterested observer. A prisoner of war released in 1941 and former journalist with *le Temps* he became Head of the Information Service in the Ministry of Information in October 1941. In this capacity he was regarded by Limagne as author of the *Notes d'Orientation* by which the government expected the newspapers to follow the National Revolution. After the Nazi Occupation of France in 1942 he became the Consul in Malaga. In 1947 he was imprisoned for four months before being acquitted during

the Épuration. He was subsequently the author of several books which purport to give a subjective view of the Vichy era as he experienced it.

17. ADHV: 1 PR 157.

18. In 1939 *le Courrier du Centre* was a regional *journal d'information* which in 1936 had had a daily circulation of 68,100 with 3,200 subscribers in Limoges. By 1942 the respective figures were 95,000 and 5,000 (AN: F41/160). Pre-war its political tendency was considered to be 'moderate republican'. After the Liberation it was prosecuted before *la Cour de Justice* and all its assets were sequestered. Its premises were taken over by various newspapers, for example, *L'Echo du Centre* which is still in circulation today and *le Courrier Marseillais* whose director for a time was the deported Resistance leader, Edmond Michelet.

19. ADHV 1 PR 159; 15 November 1941. Report by Paÿs? It is thought, but not verified, that Peyre was sentenced to prison with hard labour after the Liberation.

20. ADHV: 1 PR 158 Circ. 30 of 1 February 1942. Limagne, *Ephémérides* 6 March 1942. ADHV 1 PR 16.

21. AN: F41/159 Paÿs letter to Dufour Vichy, 3 September 1942.

22. Limagne, *Ephémérides*, August 1943 in particular.

23. AN: F41/245. Cuttings of actual newspapers preserved in file.

24. M. Guingouin is the author of several books, the latest being G. Guingouin et G. Monediaire, *Georges Guingouin: Premier Maquisard de France* (Limoges, 1982).

25. ADHV: 1 PR 159; 11 February 1944.

26. ADHV: 1 PR 159; January 1944, report by Marcel Paÿs.

27. Jean Tristan, 'En 1942 les internés d'Evaux les Bains', *Le Limousin*, no. 65 (May 1972). ADHV.

28. ADHV: 1 PR 159 Law published 26 February 1944 but appeared in Circular of 10 April 1944.

29. ADHV: 1 PR 159; 17 December 1942.

30. ADHV: 1 PR 159; 20 December 1941.

31. ADHV: 1 PR 159; 29 September 1942. There was never a personal remark from the prefect.

32. ADHV: 1 PR 164; 2 August 1941.

33. M.R. Marrus and R.O. Paxton, *Vichy France and the Jews* (New York, 1981), Ch. 7, p. 325 in particular.

34. ADHV Dordogne – 1 PR 164; Paÿs – 1PR 159; Regional Prefect see AN:FICIII/ 1197 and 1200.

35. AN: F41/245 a weekly report on newspapers was sent right up until the Liberation. It was typed on a pro forma.

36. Limagne 4 March 1942.

37. Private papers of M. Paÿs.

38. Paÿs, *Rimes Prosaïques*, p. 135, author's translation.

39. ADHV 1 PR 159; 22 February 1943.

40. B. Gordon, *Collaborationism in France during World War II* (Cornell, 1980) writes that he was a patron of *La Gerbe* and a member of the Comité d'Honneur de la LVF along with Bonnard, Hermant, etc. A physicist and expert on liquid air he drew an audience described as 'assez nombreux' for his Limoges conference. Limagne reported that he was the victim of an attack at Orléans on 13 January 1944 and in 1945 he was reported to be in Fresnes prison, 'fort âgé et sourd comme un pot', C. de la Mazière, *Le Reveur Casqué* (Paris, 1972), p. 228.

41. Groupe Collaboration was formed 24 September 1940 and was larger than the RNP although it never approached its political importance (Gordon, *Collaborationism*, p. 230). Members of the LFC were allowed to adhere as individuals. On 30 January 1943 Laval wrote a circular on this group:

[It] aims to reunite all those who want to promote the restoration of relations between France and Germany, in particular that which concerns spiritual and cultural exchanges between the two countries. This group, which does not constitute a political party, is recognised by the government. (ADHV 1 PR 100)

On 26 December 1944 it was deemed 'unworthy' by the government of the day.
  42. ADHV 1 PR 159; 8 March 1943 report.
  43. Limagne, *Ephémérides*, March 1943.
  44. ADHV 1 PR 159; 15 March 1943 report.
  45. Limagne, *Ephémérides*, 16 January 1943; 14 July 1943.
  46. Bibliothèque Nationale (Sully) *L'Excelsior*, J.O. 2178, 25 September 1938.
  47. Limagne, *Ephémérides*, 3 June 1944.
  48. B.N.(S) H. Temenon, *Biographie des principales personalités françaises décédées au cours de l'année* (1963).
  49. Paÿs, 'Resignation' in *Rimes Prosaïques*, p. 74, author's translation.
  50. Cahiers Inédits par Me. René Farnier, *Petite Chronique de la Libération, Juin 1944 – Mai 1945*, lent to the writer by kind permission of his son.
  51. *Le Populaire du Centre*, 21 November 1944. In 1939 it was a *journal d'information* of tendency SFIO. On 17 January 1941 it was suspended and reappeared under the title of *L'Appel du Centre* until it was suspended in its turn on 30 August 1944 when its owners, but not its editor, were prosecuted. Since then it has continued as Limoges' leading daily newspaper under its original title. In 1936 the *Populaire* sold 12,300 copies each day and had 1,800 subscribers in Limoges. In 1942 *L'Appel* had figures respectively of 8,100 and 1,870 (AN: F41/160).
  52. *L'Echo du Centre*, 25 November 1944 (ADHV).
  53. ADHV: *Le Centre Libre, organe des Comités Départmentaux de la Libération*, 24 August 1944 onwards. This edition, 2 December 1944.
  54. Farnier, *Petite Chronique*, Chap XXVII. Brasillach was executed on 6 February 1945 and Doriot, mentioned in the same chapter, was killed on 22 February.
  55. E. Chantaraud, *Droites Nationales et Droites Populaires en Haute Vienne (1880-1914)* unpublished Mémoire de Maîtrise (Limoges, 1980).
  56. ADHV: unclassified *Fond de la LFC*. 19 November 1942.
  57. Farnier, *Petite Chronique*.
  58. The félibrige was a society of poets and prose writers formed in 1854 with the object of preserving the Provençal language. In 1893 Joseph Roux inaugurated *Lemouzie, revue régionaliste & félibréene*; revived in 1920 it is still published today at 13 Place Municipale, Tulle, Corrèze. L'École du Barbichet took its name from feminine headwear, described by Me. Farnier's widow as 'so gracious and so admired in our province'. Much information was contained in a special report written by Farnier on 25 November 1940 for the prefect. In it he wrote that the Barbichet was paralysed because of rival groups set up by politicians of the left.The neighbouring L'École du Briance ceased existence but Barbichet continued without subsidies. Consequently in 1940 they were left in debt to the tune of F4,000 (ADHV: 1 PR 152). On 14 April 1944 the LFC asked Vichy for a subsidy for the group in view of its valuable propaganda (ADHV Fond LFC).
  59. ADHV, *Fond de la Légion*, 19 November 1942.
  60. ADHV: IL 153, *Le Limousin Mutilé/Vrais Combattants*, number of September 1940 (hereafter LM).
  61. Mme Jeanne Farnier, 'Histoire du Félibrige en Limousin', *le Populaire du Centre*, 1959-60 (ADHV IJ 315).
  62. L. Delhoume, *Mon ami René Farnier* (Limoges, n.d.). Collection of

M. Farnier.

63. Farnier met Maurras whilst a student in Paris and later when passing through Paris *en route* to the front. He wrote in a letter: 'Avec Maurras toute conversation est difficile. Je me borne donc à lui crier dans l'oreille mes remerciements pour son livre . . . '

64. ADHV, *Le Salut National, organe régional de l'Action Française.* Weekly from 3 November 1912. Last edition 2 August 1914.

65. ADHV, *La Gazette du Centre: Journal Quotidien du Soir. Organe de la Défénse Sociale et des Libertés Publiques.* 1920 onwards.

66. LM July 1931 described as 'comrade'; December 1932 as 'Président du Front des Anciens Combattants'.

67. LM, December 1938.

68. LM, January 1934.

69. LM, December 1936.

70. LM, September and December 1938.

71. LM, March 1937.

72. LM, December 1932, February 1933, December 1938 and March 1939.

73. LM, December 1932.

74. LM, Ethiopia October 1935; League of Nations April 1936.

75. LM, September 1940. In this same edition Farnier wrote a letter demanding a change in the name of 'rue des Anglais'. It was not granted.

76. LM, March 1940.

77. LM, September 1940.

78. ADHV, 1M 156-9 inc.; 1 PR 121. In another veterans' newspaper, *Tribune des Amochés & Réchappés du Feu*, 20 November 1935, he commented on the aftermath of an incident which took place in Limoges on 16 November when a crowd led by 'socialists' 'attacked' a private meeting of Les Croix de Feu at l'École de Dressage. It is felt that this incident was used as the excuse by the Minister of the Interior to ban political leagues such as Les Croix. Farnier wrote then: 'we do not belong to the Croix de Feu movement'.

79. ADHV, 1 PR 101 Correspondence October 1940.

80. ADHV, 1 PR 152 Rapport de la Section Culturelle de la Commission Régionaliste Départementale, 25 November 1940.

81. 1 PR 154 Report of Renseignements Généraux, Regional Congress of Folklore, promoted on 5 June 1944 by Centre for Regional Studies at which departmental prefect was also a speaker. It is ironic that L'Ecole du Barblichet was booked to perform at Oradour-sur-Glane on Sunday, 11 June 1944 but was thwarted by the SS-Das Reich Division.

82. Delhoume, *Mon ami René Farnier*.

83. Kedward, 'Patriots and Patriotism in Vichy France', p. 180.

84. *Le Salut National* (ADHV) 2 August 1914.

85. Kedward, 'Patriots and Patriotism in Vichy France', p. 178.

86. Apparently the permission of the family was not sought, nor is it regarded particularly as an honour. Not far away is *'Cité Léon Delhoume'*.

4 JEWS AND CATHOLICS

Louis Allen

'Tout a été dit' is the natural reaction when the subject of the Jews under Vichy is in question; so my initial reaction of surprise that it did not originally figure as a topic for the Sussex conference was probably misplaced. Marrus and Paxton's *Vichy and the Jews* has dealt with it,[1] the Catholic reaction has been outlined in Pierre Pierrard's *Juifs et Catholiques français*[2], and Jacques Duquesne's *Les Catholiques français sous l'Occupation*;[3] and there is of course a vast amount of material to draw on in the Centre de Documentation juive. But there is more to a scrutiny of the topic now than a mere rehearsal of well-worn facts, however salutary the reminder may be when we see the careful crudities of Jean-Marie Le Pen taking over from the unsavoury rhetoric of Vichy politicians and intellectuals. There is a present impact to consider and there is also a picture which varies with the viewer's perspective.

It is possible to consider the four years of relations between the Catholic Church and the Jews under Vichy as one more episode in the long history of European anti-Semitism; or as an aspect of the history of Church and State relations; or as a component of the history of the massacre of European Jewry in the twentieth century. Whichever perspective we use, today is as good a time as any to look at the topic again, because we seem to be at the end of the two 40-year periods into which the history of the Catholic Church and the Jews in France can be divided: from the beginning of the century to the beginning of the German occupation shows a continuation of hostility, in the ranks of Church, Army and French bourgeoisie, derived from the Dreyfus affair and its aftermath in the Combes laws on religious education; from the Liberation to the present day is the growing awareness of the practical results of anti-Semitism on a national scale, with a realisation by the French Church, from the episcopate down, that there is theological as well as political and sociological work to be done to avoid a recurrence of the old pathological hatreds. From Dreyfus to Vichy; from Vichy to the present day when the Archbishop of Paris himself (Cardinal Lustiger) is a Jew, makes a neat segmentation and does in fact correspond to reality in the changes of feeling. And, of course, there is distressing contemporary evidence that those who suffered from the events of 1940 to 1944 have been permanently marked by it in their relations with other Frenchmen, and that the risk of recrudescence is not, now, as unthinkable as it might have appeared to be ten or twenty years ago.

As an episode in the history of European anti-Semitism, it is obvious that what happened to the Jews in France does not have the statistical dimensions of the horror inflicted on Polish and Russian Jewry, and, unlike the communities of Eastern Europe, the community left behind is now stronger and more numerous than it was in 1939, by a new immigration from French North Africa, yet at the same time ill at ease and aware of the conflict between the interests of Israel and those of French policy in the Middle East. As part of the history of French ideas, in which anti-Semitism is a constant thread on either side of the political spectrum, rationalist with Voltaire, socialist with Proudhon, chauvinist with Drumont, Barrès and Maurras, the anti-Semitism of Vichy is consciously an 'anti-judaisme d'état' claiming roots in the Catholic past of France. In this sense the visceral anti-Semitism of Céline is not typical. The Vichy laws express a view of society similar to that of Belloc's *The Jews*, hostile towards what is taken to be an intractable and irreducible minority within a sacral society. The characteristic figure is Xavier Vallat, rather than Darquier de Pellepoix. As part of the developing theology of the Catholic Church, the four years from 1940 to 1944 are the proving-ground for totally new ideas on the relations between Jews and Catholics, which, to some extent at any rate, bore fruit in the declarations of the Second Vatican Council.

What is interesting here is to find an obvious link between the theology of anti-Semitism and the theology of Occupation and Resistance. It was easy for moral theologians to indicate the reprehensible nature of support for de Gaulle from the point of view of traditional Catholic teaching. M. Lesaunier, the head of the Séminaire des Carmes, published early in 1942 a brochure entitled *La conscience catholique en face du devoir civique actuel* in which he stressed the Catholic's duty to obey the established power, which, in the case of France after 10 July 1940, was clearly Pétain. Asked by a journalist to draw conclusions about Gaullism and Anglophilia from these principles, he replied:

> Que fait de Gaulle? Il refuse de reconnaître l'autorité légitime du Chef de l'Etat, il se révolte contre cette autorité. Or, Leon XIII nous a mis en garde: 'L'Eglise a toujours réprouvé les doctrines et toujours condamné les hommes rebelles à l'autorité légitime.' Il en résulte que ceux qui se déclarent Gaullistes opposent la même résistance à l'ordre divin et encourent les mêmes peines. Chercher à susciter la

Jews and Catholics

> révolte, c'est commettre le crime de lèse-majesté humaine et divine. Sympathiser avec cette propagande, c'est participer au même égarement.

Since Germany had won the war with France, there was constituted a new situation of rights and duties on either side, based on international law:

> Pendant tout le temps que durera l'armistice, le devoir de tout Français, mais aussi de tout catholique, est la soumission à cette réglementation, et de ne rien faire pour troubler l'ordre établi.

Minds brought up on these ideas would find little difficulty in approving the early legislative measures taken against the Jews in France by a government which, after all, seemed to be providing heaven-sent opportunities for re-establishing a 'Catholic order' and taking a long overdue revenge on the Republic and its anti-clericalism. The generally piacular mood of France in the summer of 1940 found easy targets, and the idea of national repentance of a republic which was, in the eyes of the Catholic hierarchy, identified with a generalised assault on the Church since the separation of Church and State in 1906, was something to be encouraged, not deplored. The Protestant pastor, Marc Boegner, noted during a visit to Vichy as early as 26 July 1940, an almost generalised atmosphere of revenge upon French Jewry and became aware of

> l'antisémitisme déclaré de certains ministres et la menace formulée a l'égard des Juifs français, considérés comme ayant fait tant de mal au pays qu'ils avaient besoin d'un châtiment collectif.[4]

The combination of eager repentance and thirst for revenge is sufficient explanation of the fact that the Statut des Juifs of 3 October 1940 is a purely French invention, drafted and issued without any pressure from the occupying power. Theologically, the Statut des Juifs marks the end of an era in the dealings of the Catholic Church with the Jews. It is well known that the Head of State, through his ambassador, Léon Bérard, took pains to verify the acceptability of the measures, in terms of Catholic social doctrine, with the highest Vatican authorities. The identity of the Catholic official (both Monsignors Tardini and Montini were visited) who actually pronounced at some length an opinion on the issue is still a matter for speculation. But from the

Catholic point of view, what is striking about Bérard's letter to Pétain (2 September 1941) is the careful working out of a moral theology of anti-Semitic measures, none of which, of course, was intended to lead to anything like a policy of extermination, but which were clearly intended to exclude the Jews as a whole from French national life. A proviso was added that such measures should be carried out within the norms of charity (!) and without doing damage to Catholic ordinances on marriage.[5]

No clearer illustration could be asked for, to show that the moral theology of the letter is totally remote form the reality of European politics of the 1940s, let alone from the demands of Christian charity. For one thing, the Statut des Juifs, though supposedly not owing its origin to ideas of racial hatred, used racial and not religious categories in its definition of who was a Jew and who was not. The anti-judaism of Vichy's first Commissioner for Jewish Affairs, Xavier Vallat, was, in his own view, based on the Christian history of Europe; not on Nazi theories of racial superiority but on the numerous anti-Jewish decrees of the Popes and Councils and the anti-Jewish rhetoric associated with the greatest names in the history of Christian thought, St Augustine and St John Chrysostom.

A person was 'regardée comme juive issue de trois grands-parents de race juive' (a definition which permitted Simone Weil some mordant irony at the expense of the Minister of Education when her right to teach was withdrawn). There were variants, too: someone with two Jewish grandparents whose spouse had two Jewish grandparents was considered to be a Jew (October 1940); those who had two Jewish grandparents and also practised the Jewish religion were considered to be Jews (June 1941). The decrees of 2 June 1941 excluded French Jews from the magistrature, the Army (unless they happened to be war veterans) and from responsible posts in newspapers and broadcasting. Access to university education was limited by a *numerus clausus* of 3 per cent and to the liberal professions, for example the law, by one of 2 per cent. It is indicative of the mood of the French Catholic Church of the time that the Jesuit review *Confluences*, published in Algeria, not only saw nothing reprehensible in these measures, but indicated that their application to Algeria would be a useful method of 'assainissement'.[6] 'Le silence quasi absolu de la hiérarchie catholique face à la législation anti-juive de Vichy est un fait.' (Pierrard, p. 297.)

All this, of course, referred to 'juifs de nationalité française'. Foreign Jews, who had taken refuge in France by the thousand in the late 1930s, were rounded up in accordance with a decree of 4 October

1940, and interned in special camps. By the spring of 1941, 40,000 of these were interned in such camps as Gurs and Rivesaltes. Xavier Vallat's 'Commissariat Général aux questions juives' was created in March 1941 — that is, the imposition of acts of legal exclusion of the Jews was not a single measure, taken at a single moment, but a whole process, over a period of time, and was autonomous: 'Il est utile de préciser,' writes Jean-Pierre Azema, 'que la paternité du Statut des juifs revient à Vichy seul, sans que l'Allemagne nazie ait exercé la moindre pression.'[7]

Perhaps the Church, or at any rate, the higher clergy who were solidly pro-Pétain, would have continued to accept such measures without a qualm, or at any rate without public protest, had the events of July 1942 not occurred. Even when the Jewish community in Lyon protested to Cardinal Gerlier about the conditions under which Jews were interned in the camp at Gurs, he took the opportunity, while listening to their complaints, of upbraiding them for the actions of Leon Blum in the 1930s, which he deemed an 'influence néfaste' and referred to the need for 'expiation'.[8] His reaction, and the use of Blum as a scapegoat, is reflected in attitudes in the French Army at the same time. We are used to the *Boys' Own Paper* image of the prisoners of Colditz, exhibiting a gratifying and ingenious solidarity against their gaolers; but as far as the French officers were concerned, that solidarity did not include Jewish officers. In 1941, without any intervention by the German authorities, but on the orders of the senior French officer, the French mess excluded Jewish officers — Elie de Rothschild among them — who had to mess and sleep separately. When Captain Robert Blum, Leon Blum's son, arrived in Colditz as one of the *Prominente*, some of his comrades greeted him with cries of 'Blum au ghetto!' Paradoxically, those Jews who were in POW camps, under the Wehrmacht, were the only ones really safe from the SS and the Gestapo (safer than their families in France).[9]

Then 'Opération vert printanier' took place. In the Vélodrome d'Hiver, on 16/17 July 1942, 12,884 Parisian Jews, men, women and children were arrested and interned under abominable conditions; the prelude to the departure of over 75,000 Jews from France to Auschwitz, of whom 3 per cent survived.

'Il n'y a que des différences de degré et non pas de nature entre l'acceptation du *numerus clausus* et les fours crématoires, celle-là conduisant infailliblement à ceux-ci', wrote Daniel Mayer in answer to a later statement by Xavier Vallat that those who directed French anti-Jewish policy were unaware of what awaited Jews deported from

France.[10] There is no doubt that he is right; but it needed a watershed like the events of the Vélodrome d'Hiver in July 1942 to make it clear what the upshot of purely legal measures would be. There had been protests before, on the part of the French clergy, and the work of priests like Abbé Glasberg and the Amitié Chrétienne in Lyon was some indication that not all Catholic consciences had been stilled by the hierarchy's tacit acceptance of the Maurrassian 'anti-sémitisme de raison' which prevailed in Vichy. The savagery of the searches, the heart-rending separation of very young children from their parents, all this could not go unanswered. The most urgent voice was that of Monsignor Theas, Bishop of Montauban:

> Des scènes douloureuses et parfois horribles se déroulent en France, sans que la France en soit responsable. A Paris, par dizaines de milliers, des juifs ont été traités avec la plus barbare sauvagerie. Et voici que dans nos régions on assiste à un spectacle navrant: des familles disloquées, des hommes et des femmes traités comme un vil troupeau et envoyés vers une destination inconnue avec la perspective des plus graves dangers.
>
> Je fais entrendre la protestation indignée de la conscience chrétienne et je proclame que tous les hommes, quelles que soient leur race et leur religion, ont droit au respect des individuels et des Etats.
>
> Or, les mesures antisémites actuelles sont un mépris de la dignité humaine, une violation des droits les plus sacrés de la personne et de la famille.
>
> Que Dieu console et fortifie ceux qui sont indignement persécutés, qu'il accorde au monde la paix véritable et durable fondée sur la justice et la charité.

Similarly, at Toulouse on 20 August 1942, the Archbishop, Mgr. Saliège, speaking at a lunch in the diocesan seminary, declared:

> Dans notre diocèse, des scènes d'épouvante ont eu lieu dans les camps de Noé et de Récébédou. Les juifs sont des hommes, les juives sont des femmes. Tout n'est pas permis contre eux, contre ces hommes et contre ces femmes, contre ces pères et mères de famille. Ils font partie du genre humain. Ils sont nos frères comme tant d'autres. Un chrétien ne peut l'oublier. France, patrie bien-aimée, France qui porte dans la conscience de tous tes enfants, la tradition du respect de la personne humaine, France chevaleresque et gen-

éreuse, je n'en doute pas; tu n'es pas responsable de ces horreurs.[12]

The prefect, seized of the tenor of the Archbishop's speech, tried to prevent it being read from pulpits in the dioecese, as Mgr Saliège had ordered. The text was polycopied and distributed round the parishes by bicycle. Promptly, the prefect told the mayors of the communes to prevent priests reading it out loud from the pulpit on Sundays. The upshot was that some refrained, and some did not; but the Archbishop was quite clear about his own stance: 'Let them get on with it (Qu'ils la lisent!)'. And while proclaiming his loyalty to Pétain and the established order, he declared, the following month, that 'the affirmation of a Christian principle has never implied the negation of another Christian principle'. But by this time the Germans had entered the Non-Occupied Zone, and resistance to anti-Jewish measures had become infinitely more hazardous. In the event, between 75,000 and 86,000 Jews were deported from France, 24,000 being French Jews, that is, 27 per cent of the French Jewish population of 1940. The Jewish population of France stood at 290,000 in 1940, 90,000 being French Jews, the rest refugees or recent immigrants. The present population is estimated at between 600,000 and 700,000, between 1.2 per cent and 1.4 per cent of the population of France ('La population juive en France', *La Documentation catholique*, no. 1719, 1er mai, 1977, pp. 423-4)). The horrors of deportation and the extermination camps need no further chronicling here: they have become the seed of terrifying fictional portrayals on an apocalyptic scale (André Schwarz-Bart's *Le dernier des justes*) or, perhaps even more poignant because more graspable, of sober realistic depiction of intolerable fact in such autobiographies as Saul Friedländer's *Quand le printemps reviendra* ... That book, in which we see the metamorphosis of a harried Jewish child of Czech origin, Pavel, into a Christian French chrysalis, Paul (which nearly led him into the Catholic priesthood); then to a final transformation as the Israeli citizen, Saul, describes from the inside what must have been the mental odyssey of the two Finaly children.

Their relevance here is that they constitute one element of the persistence of the Vichy/Jewish theme, on one side or another, well into the post-war years. That Christian institutions, and individuals, risked their very existence to save Jewish lives, particularly Jewish children, is amply documented; but the post-war pages of, *inter alia, The Jewish Chronicle*, show that these very acts of charity, carried out at such great risk, were fraught with menace for the survival of the Jewish identity of the children involved. Not only did proselytisation occur; there were also instances of refusal to return the children to those Jewish relatives who survived.

The Finaly case is the most conspicuous and the most instructive. It split French Catholicism down the middle, and causes echoes to reverberate not of the Dreyfus case but of the kidnapping of the Mortara child in nineteenth-century Bologna, an injustice which was never reversed: a servant girl secretly baptised a Jewish child and admitted this in the confessional; the child was promptly removed from its parents by papal police and brought up as a Catholic (he ended up as a priest). Not all the considerable pressures brought on the Papacy from the outside (including that of Sir Moses Montefiore) availed to have the child restored to its parents. The Finaly case is not entirely similar, of course, in that the boys' parents had died in the extermination camps. But there was no doubt that close relatives had sought them and asked for their return in 1945, and Mlle Brun, their guardian, had put every obstacle in the way of this return. The children owed their lives to her, without a doubt; equally without a doubt, she later abused her trust.

The most soberly factual account of the affair was given in the pages of the *Cahiers sioniens* by Fr Th. Demann, who analysed the development of the doctrine of 'education after baptism' which the Mortara case had rendered necessary. The Church's Canon Law gave warnings against baptism of the children of non-Catholic families without parental consent; but it also insisted that if baptism had been administered then the children should be removed from their parents and brought up as Catholics. Mlle Brun's own phraseology about this event is instructive. 'Je les ai fait baptiser français' was how she put it. Like many such situations, intolerable in themselves, this one contained no easy solution. What is disturbing is to read the comments of leading Catholic intellectuals, people among whom one might have expected to discover an enlightened view. The historian Henri Marrou, for example, who had been involved in the Resistance and was later to play a courageous role in the defence of priests who came to the aid of Algerian rebels, weighed up the issues in what seems a judicious way but concluded with a clear wish that the children should not be returned to Jewish relatives in such a way that their Catholic upbringing might be endangered — could they not be left 'disponible' to choose at some future date? — or that their education as Frenchmen would be at risk:

> Ne peut-on envisager une solution *provisoire*, relativement équitable en face des éventualités incertaines: laisser les enfants en France, continuer à les éduquer dans un milieu français, les confier à un

Jews and Catholics

établissement d'éducation neutre; leur permettre de continuer à voir celle qu'on leur a appris d'appeler 'Maman', mais leur permettre d'autre part d'entrer en relation avec ces oncles et tantes qu'ils ignorent; les habituer à honorer cette ascendance juive qui, à nos yeux à tous, fait leur noblesse; leur permettre de continuer à pratiquer la religion catholique, la seule dans laquelle ils aient appris jusqu'ici à invoquer le Dieu d'Abraham, d'Isaac, de Jacob; tout cela jusqu'à jugement définitif, – et la date si proche de leur libre adolescence?[13]

That this solution had been put forward first by an eminent Jewish member of the Amitié Judeo-Chrétienne, Jules Isaac, as Marrou claims, is somewhat surprising; less so is Marrou's claim that 'elle ne peut pas ne pas heurter profondément la conscience religieuse juive . . . ' and his acknowledgement that it favoured the Catholic adoption at the expense of the 'natural' family. This contrast between the rights of the natural family and those of the spiritual family is the burden of the two pages devoted to the case in the journal of one of France's most eminent Catholic laymen, who had been imprisoned in Colditz. He refers to the Finaly family's attempts to gain contact with the children, and to the abusive kidnapping and removal to Franco's Spain with the collusion of French and Spanish priests and nuns, but in terms of such abstraction that they cannot lead to any firm decision. This, indeed, is where Guitton himself ends:

Alors que faire? Je ne le sais pas. Mais, qu'il y ait ici un triple problème: juridique, humain, religieux, je le vois clairement. Ce problème ne sera pas résolu par le dénouement de l'affaire présente, encore inconnu en ce premier mars où j'écris.[14]

The solution eventually arrived at – the children's settlement in Israel – was clearly at variance with that adumbrated by Marrou, and the hesitant advocacy of 'spiritual guardianship' explored by Guitton; but it was also the solution found for himself by Saul Friedländer as the answer to his own tortured search for identity.

But it would be unfair to suggest that the Finaly affair was entirely a product of conditions created by the Vichy regime: the slaughter of the Finaly parents, which underlies it, was brought about by Nazi Germany, not by Pétain's France. What matters, looking back on it, is that it was perhaps part of a general *prise de conscience* by European Catholics, the very articulate French Catholic community in particular, of the role which casually and thoughtlessly accepted items, both of religious belief and civic tradition, played in the preparation of the European mind as a sowing ground for the Holocaust. Not merely the revision of the Good Friday liturgy, with its centuries-old prayer *pro perfidis Judaeis*, and the Vatican II Declaration on the Jews, were part of this theological repentance. There was also the much more generous-spirited proclamation by the French bishops in 1973, 'Orientations épiscopales sur les relations avec le Judaïsme'. This declaration is not merely concerned with recent events. It returns to Christian theology at its earliest roots, and tries to uncumber it from the hatred and contempt to which it has undoubtedly given rise. The bishops affirm that ignorance of Jewish law in the time of Christ casts the Jews as culprits in the trial of Christ, that Christian teaching on the Pharisees is wrongheaded and based on ignorance of the true nature of Pharisee beliefs, that the Jewish roots of Christianity need to be constantly reaffirmed, that the Jewish people will continue, that they have not been deprived of the Divine election by the existence of Christianity, that the thoughtlessly accepted dichotomy between the religion of the Old Testament and that of the New as one between a religion of fear and one of love is an error, that Catholics must not seek the disappearance or absorption of the Jewish community but establish a living link with it and, most courageous of all, the bishops acknowledge the role of the State of Israel — with however many qualifications — in a way that the Second Vatican Council would never have ventured:

> Au-delà de la diversité légitime des options politiques, la conscience universelle ne peut refuser au peuple juif, qui a subi tant de vicissitudes au cours de l'histoire, le droit et les moyens d'une existence politique propre parmi les nations.[15]

In the tradition of Jules Isaac's post-war *Jésus et Israël*, asking for mutual comprehension and scrupulous examination of differences, the historian Robert Aron — appropriately, the historian of Vichy and the Liberation — gave a resounding welcome to the French bishops' initiative in his *Lettre ouverte à l'Église de France*. The moving final passage of his own highly personal introduction shows to what an extent a French Jew bathed in French traditions, both sacred and secular, could find himself at home in Christian churches as he visited Israel for the first time:

> Ces églises villageoises, ce sont elles qu'au seuil de la dernière étape,

Jews and Catholics

à l'instant où mon coeur va se délester d'un caillou, je retrouve soudain en ce monastère d'Ein-Karem, où la liturgie romaine qui baigne nos campagnes de France, s'accomplit dans la langue qui renaît en ces campagnes de Judée, dans la langue de Dieu, en hébreu.

Il me fallait donc une église pour entrer dans Jérusalem. Il me fallait le son des angélus et des vêpres de chez nous, pour aborder la ville Eternelle, où toutes les heures se confondent, où toutes les langues se mêlent, où tous les cultes s'avoisinent . . .

Merci à l'Eglise de France qui a permis au Juif français, rejoignant la terre de ses lointains ancêtres, de se sentir escorté à la fois par les souffles harmonieux de son air natal, et par les tourbillons enfiévrés et exaltants 'de la ville où peut-être l'attend Dieu, le Dieu de ses pères, de nos pères, 'Elohe avotenou'.[16]

It would be pleasing to end on such an ironic note. Pleasing, but misleading. There has been a great deal of theological rethinking of Catholic attitudes towards Jews; but some Jews are very naturally suspicious of it, and others, as the Harris-Sedouy survey of Jewish life in present-day France shows, still bear the wounds of Vichy, even if time has made them subcutaneous. A good example of the first is the essay *La Libération du Juif* (Gallimard, 1966) by the Tunisian Jewish writer settled in France, Albert Memmi. Considering two alternatives offered to the Jewish community by recent European history, left-wing socialism and absorption into the Christian community, Memmi dismisses both as specious. The continued existence of anti-Semitism in the USSR indicates that the success of the socialist revolution does not mean the end of hatred, and sooner or later the left-wing Jew discovers the disastrous alternative: 'accept finally the complete disappearance of the Jews, or stop being a communist'. The hypothetical 'acceptance' by Christians, derived from the shame and guilt for the Holocaust, is likewise dismissed. Even though we may, with the Second Vatican Council, attenuate *historically* the responsibility of the Jewish people in the passion of Christ, it still remains true, for Memmi, that *theologically* it could have happened in no other way: the Jews are needed by Christian myth. Tinkering with liturgical phrases and revising catechetical methods is irrelevant, since the whole of Christian doctrine and the whole perspective of Christian life would have to be altered to adapt to such a basic change. In spite of the hopes the Vatican Council raised, it could do nothing about this. The mere fact, too, that what took place was a volte-face carried out by command (however hesitant) of a General Council, makes it all the more suspect. Could men capable of such submission not attack again tomorrow what they accept today, on the basis of another order and another historical circumstance? Even those who pass, among Catholics, for the greatest friends of Israel – Jacques Madaule, Jacques Maritain – speak in terms which necessarily link Jewish suffering with the existence of a Jewish people. The muted violence of the Council, the hesitations, the withdrawals, the mediocrity of the final resolution, all show the depth of the Christian refusal. The close coincidence in France between a large Catholic population and virulent anti-Semitism is enough to make him sceptical. In fact a survey carried out by the magazine *Adam* at the time his book appeared seemed to confirm his views. In one-third of the French population, even after the horrors of Nazi persecution and the official change in the Church's attitude, the deeply rooted prejudice against the Jews survived. One per cent of those questioned actually approved of the Nazi exterminations; and the prejudice rose not merely, as one might expect, with the age group, but increased in north-western France and among those who declared themselves to be practising Catholics.[17]

Thirteen years after Memmi's embittered refusal of the theological olive-branch, André Harris and Alain de Sedouy's *Juifs et Français* resurrected the problem in sociological terms.[18] For many of the Jews they questioned, it was clear that the trauma of exclusion from national life was not forgotten. They noted that the interdict on anti-Semitic expression, tacitly accepted since the return of a remnant from the death camps, was now at an end, largely because a new generation of Frenchmen had no memory of it. Raymond Aron, reviewing the book in *l'Express*, pointed to de Gaulle's press conference and his reference to the 'peuple d'élite, sûr de soi et dominateur', as the signal to end the 'reprieve'. But Aron was, on the whole, not pessimistic, seeing nothing comparable to the fanaticisms of the 1930s in the occasional awkwardnesses produced by the existence of a blacklist imposed on French businesses by Middle Eastern countries with large and necessary oil reserves:

> Je puis me tromper, mais peuvent aussi se tromper ceux 'qui ont peur de la France et des Français'. Mes enfants, mes petits-enfants acceptent leur destin, ils ne veulent renier leur ascendance ni leur nationalité. Double fidélité qu'ils vivent sans déchirement.[19]

The reaction of François Furet in *le Nouvel Observateur* was different:

> Les juifs français ont donc redécouvert que les jeux ne sont jamais faits: ni par rapport au religieux, ni par rapport au national, ni par

rapport aux destins individuels'.[20]

Like Aron, Furet notes the appearance at the same time of Alfred Fabre-Luce's book *Pour en finir avec l'anti-sémitisme* (Juillard, 1979) of which a crucial feature is a reassessment of the role of Vichy in the history of French Jewry. But, of course, Fabre-Luce's way of ending anti-Semitism is to plead for the disappearance of Jewish specificity; and he accuses historians of Vichy of establishing a version of recent French history which, in his view, over-emphasises French responsibility for persecution. Paxton in particular is taken as an example of historians who have taken it upon themselves to 'présenter aux Français l'histoire de leurs années de guerre à travers un prisme juif' (Furet, op. cit., p. 72). As Furet points out, Fabre-Luce, under the pretence of ending anti-Semitism, serves as an expression of it and adds the conspiracy theory of history for good measure. Even if we accept Fabre-Luce's version of the old theory of Pétain as shield for France, and his claim that the percentage of Jews who survived in France, compared with that of Eastern Europe, demonstrates the effectiveness of Vichy in defence of its citizens, Furet replies that what characterises Vichy is its use of a familiar demon to exorcise the defeat of 1940:

> Il y a dans le statut des juifs de 1940 un acte de politique française, accompli et rédigé au nom d'une tradition nationale, par des hommes qui n'y ont pas été contraints par l'étranger. Et, si la génération juive assimilée, même de ceux qui ont été quelques mois pétainistes entre juin et l'automne, y a vu une rupture française avec la tradition de 1789, c'est que Vichy l'a claironné.[21]

On this point, he and Aron are at one, as Aron writes himself:

> les interviews de Harris et Sedouy révèlent un fait que tous les Juifs de France constatent avec tristesse. La France, pendant la guerre et depuis 1967, a déçu les Juifs, au-dedans et au-dehors. Elle passait pour la terre d'asile par excellence aux Juifs du monde entier, elle avait, la première, voté les lois d'émancipation. Elle prit un autre visage sous Vichy...[22]

The relation of the Jews to the French State and to the Catholic Church, under Vichy, and later, illustrates why the history of Vichy is still a matter of consequence. There have been a number of passionate controversies in Great Britain about the way this country conducted its war. Mostly they are on strategic issues: the policy of strategic bombing, double- or single-thrust to the Rhine in 1944, and so on. Absorbing as they are, none of these debates radically affects our view of ourselves as a nation. The opposite is true of the controversies over Occupation, Resistance and Liberation in France. They may be remote in time now, after 40 years, but they *do* affect both the way the French conceive themselves not only to have behaved, and the way they conceive themselves to *be*. Even when a much greater number of facts about the years 1940-4 have become available, it will often be a question of *tant pis pour les faits*: there will remain a confrontation, for the foreseeable future, of basic presuppositions about France as a political entity and French national life; just as, during those years, French Catholics often found the very nature of Christianity called into question.

Notes

1. M.R. Marrus and Robert O. Paxton, *Vichy France and the Jews* (Basic Books, 1981).
2. Pierre Pierrard, *Juifs et Catholiques français* (Paris, Fayard, 1970).
3. Jacques Duquesne, *Les Catholiques français sous l'Occupation* (Paris, Grasset, 1968).
4. Raymond Tournoux, 'Pétain et les Juifs', *Histoire magazine*, no. 18, Special issue on 'Histoire de l'Antisémitisme en France', juillet-août, 1981, pp. 37-8.
5. On the Bérard letter, cf. John F. Morley, *Vatican Diplomacy and the Jews during the Holocaust 1939-1943* (KTAV Publishing House, New York, 1980), pp. 49-56; Pierrard, *Juifs et Catholiques français*, p. 296; and J. Nobécourt, *'Le Vicaire' et l'Histoire* (Editions de Seuil, 1964), pp. 356-62. And cf. Xavier Vallat's use of Church history in self-exculpation: 'Toutes les mesures que contient la législation française de l'Etat nouveau et bien d'autres plus draconiennes, ont été prises jadis à la demande de ces autorités religieuses dont les juifs de 1942 prétendent aujourd'hui qu'elles désapprouvent tacitement en cette matière les actes du gouvernement du Maréchal.' Duquesne, *Les Catholiques français*, pp. 253-4. But we should remind ourselves that Gerlier's later protests earned him the virulent hatred of Brasillach in *Je Suis Partout*: 'Au nom de la France, au nom de ma patrie chérie, de la Chrétienté tout entière, je réclame la tête de Gerlier, Cardinal, talmudiste délirant, traître à sa foi, à son pays, à sa race. Gerlier, je vous hais!' Pierrard, *Juifs et Catholiques français*, p. 292.
6. Jacques Duquesne, *Les Catholiques français*, p. 252.
7. Jean-Pierre Azema, *De Munich à la Libération 1938-1944* (Seuil, 1979), p. 93.
8. Jacques Duquesne, *Les Catholiques français*, p. 254.
9. R. Tournoux, 'Pétain et les Juifs', pp. 38-9.
10. *Evidences*, déc. 1957 in Pierrard, *Juifs et Catholiques français*, p. 303.
11. Duquesne, *Les Catholiques français*, pp. 260-1.
12. Pierrard, *Juifs et Catholiques français*, p. 317.
13. Henri Marrou, 'L'affaire Finaly', *Esprit*, avril 1953, pp. 500-1.

14. Jean Guitton, *Journal*, (Plon, 1959), p. 75, entry for 1 mars 1953.
15. Text in Robert Aron, *Lettre ouverte à l'Eglise de France* (Albin Michel, 1975), p. 204.
16. Ibid., pp. 11-12.
17. Cf. L. Allen, 'Final Solutions?' (*New Blackfriars*, June 1967), p. 490.
18. André Harris and Alain de Sedouy, *Juifs et Français* (Grasset, 1979).
19. Raymond Aron, 'Les Juifs, Vichy et Israël', *L'Express*, 29 September 1979, p. 96.
20. François Furet 'Israël et les Français juifs', *Le Nouvel Observateur*, no. 775, 17-23 septembre 1979, p. 71.
21. Ibid., p. 72.
22. Raymond Aron, 'Les Juifs, Vichy et Israël', p. 96.

PART TWO:

AMBIGUITIES

5 SAINT-EXUPÉRY'S *PILOTE DE GUERRE*: TESTIMONY, ART AND IDEOLOGY

S. Beynon John

Pilote de guerre (1942)[1] is certainly an urgent and memorable work which secured for Saint-Exupéry a wartime readership well beyond the boundaries of that stricken France which forms the subject of his narrative. At the outset, I would like to emphasise that its sentiments and attitudes, like the moral, social and political ideas which lie diffused throughout it, are strikingly congruent with those of his pre-war writings: *Vol de nuit* (1931), which first brought him fame with its vivid picture of the pioneers of commercial aviation in South America; the newspaper reports on Moscow and Spain written in the 1930s; the dense, elliptical reflections committed to paper in the *Carnets* composed between 1935 and 1942; *Terre des hommes* (1939) with its brooding pages on man's destiny, sparked off by a crash-landing in the Libyan desert.

The picture of the ideal society that is implied in much of these writings is organicist, rooted in rurality and natural hierarchies. It stresses the power of the creative imagination, the importance of communal and fraternal bonds, the appeal of moral idealism, the readiness to subordinate self to the service of something greater than self, and the need for charismatic leaders capable of showing the way forward. Saint-Exupéry's preferred models of human activity tend to exemplify the virtues of creativity, nurture and disinterestedness. They are artists (whether architects, musicians or writers), scientists, priests, gardeners or shepherds. The undoctrinal and vague spirituality diffused throughout much of his writing finds its symbol in the repeated image of the cathedral which is offered as the supreme expression of the aspirations of man. Saint-Exupéry's persistent attacks on the spiritual emptiness of modern society are linked with a general disparagement of machinery and industry that is paradoxical coming from a man whose fame was associated with the technology of aviation, who loved fast cars and had a talent for mechanical invention.

The intellectual and moral consistency displayed in Saint-Exupéry's writings has its roots in the social, religious and political ambience in which he grew up. Descended on his mother's side from aristocratic stock in Aix-en-Provence and the Vivarais and, on his father's, from ancient though undistinguished gentry in Périgord and the Limousin, he was educated at religious schools by Jesuits and Marianists in a deeply Catholic and royalist tradition which produced army and naval officers.[2] He himself was originally intended for the navy and there is evidence that after the débâcle of May-June 1940 he was influenced in his attitude toward Gaullism by the hostile opinion of naval friends.[3] In a general sense, which does not imply formal political allegiances or active political involvement, it is likely that Saint-Exupéry was coloured throughout his life by the conservative nationalism that pervaded the Catholic rural gentry and which made them, like their sons in the army and navy, sympathetic to much of the ideology of Maurras's Action Française.

It is certainly significant that a number of Saint-Exupéry's associates in the 1930s were far to the right in politics. An admired colleague and friend, Jean Mermoz, was not only an ace pilot with the firm of Latécoère, but an active supporter of de La Rocque's Croix de Feu who actually became vice-president of the Parti social français during the period of the Popular Front government in 1936. Unimpressed by de La Rocque, Saint-Exupéry declined his friend's invitation to join the PSF. In the 1930s Saint-Exupéry also frequented Gaston Bergery whose newly created Front commun represented a stage in Bergery's political evolution from radicalism toward what has been called 'une forme très nette de "fascisme de gauche" . . . '[4] Bergery will subsequently turn up in Pétain's administration in 1940 and become Vichy's ambassador to Moscow before undergoing a last-minute conversion to de Gaulle (Sternhell, p. 299). So far as Saint-Exupéry is concerned, all this suggests not so much the confident possession of a radical ideology or a firm commitment to party as much as an instinctive preference for doctrines of order and authority.

Pilote de guerre represents a document of very great interest for any student of Vichy France. Part of its fascination lies in the way in which it was received by the reading public, first in the USA, and then within France itself at the time of its publication. *Pilote de guerre* originally appeared in English in New York in three successive issues of *The Atlantic Monthly* (February-April 1942) before being published in book form in both English (*Flight to Arras*) and French, the latter edition under the imprint of the Editions de la Maison française, a publishing house established in New York in September 1940 and subsequently responsible for bringing out about 120 French books in the USA between 1940 and 1945.[5] American reactions were generally very favourable, seeing the narrative as a hymn to the heroism of French pilots in wartime, a vivid record of the sufferings of the civilian population, and the expression of an idealistic faith in France. This helps to explain why *Flight to Arras* was selected by the Book of the Month Club and became a bestseller (Cate, p. 450). However, there were dissenting voices: Americans who, still outraged by the Japanese attack on Pearl Harbor on 7 December 1941, criticised Saint-Exupéry's arguments as defeatist (*Ecrits de guerre*, p. 224). Opinion of the novel in French circles in the USA was more sharply divided and included judgements that it was 'fascist' in inspiration, or 'paternalistic' and 'reactionary' (Cate, p. 459). To understand this, one has to recall the situation of French wartime exiles in the USA when Saint-Exupéry arrived in New York, via North Africa and Lisbon, on 31 December 1940.

Briefly, the French community, numbering some 20,000, was caught up in a fierce clash of political loyalties. The new Vichy emissaries to the USA (ambassador Gaston Henry-Haye and his close associates) proclaimed an aggressive Pétainism that created conflicts within the corps of French career diplomats in Washington. Apart from these, there were a number of *attentistes* among the early 'émigrés de luxe' – bankers, industrialists, businessmen, literary and other artists – who were still influenced by Pétain's great personal prestige, sympathetic to the need to 'normalise' French social and economic life, and ready to give the early policies of Vichy the benefit of the doubt. There were also figures who had been prominent in the public life of the Third Republic and who were hostile to what they saw as Pétain's usurpation of power. Such were former Prime Minister Camille Chautemps and Alexis Léger (the poet Saint-John Perse) who had been highly influential as Secretary-General of the French Foreign Office during the inter-war period, and who was to play a distinctly enigmatic role during his American exile. Like Saint-Exupéry, Alexis Léger was suspicious of de Gaulle's dictatorial tendencies but, unlike Saint-Exupéry who harboured no great love for the Third Republic, Léger, a brilliant product and beneficiary of that regime, displayed a principled if rather legalistic attachment to republican institutions and based his opposition to both Pétain and de Gaulle on the premiss that neither leader could claim constitutional warrant or democratic consent for the powers he had assumed.

Then again, there were right-wing patriots like the former deputy Henri de Kérillis whose perfervid and outdated brand of nationalism found an outlet in the weekly *Pour la victoire*. He was ardently in favour of resistance to the Germans and initially supported de Gaulle enthusiastically before transferring his loyalties to Giraud in March

1943 (Fritsch-Estrangin, p. 128). Alongside these were the unconditional supporters of de Gaulle, particularly those active in the lavishly-funded France Forever Association. These included Adrien Tixier, head of the Délégation de la France Libre in the USA, and the virulently anti-Vichy publicist, Henry Torrès, who ran the Gaullist weekly, *France-Amérique*. The aim of these men was to discredit Vichy and to establish de Gaulle as the sole legitimate representative of defeated France. It has to be said that some Gaullist activists in the USA showed a belligerence that was in inverse proportion to any risks to which they were exposed. Certainly the internecine warfare waged among these different groups seems to have been remarkable for its vehemence, pettiness and ruthless special pleading; it left little room for personalities like Saint-Exupéry who liked to think of themselves as above the battle.[6]

Given his own recent history and opinions, Saint-Exupéry could not, in any realistic sense, present himself as above the fray. In the climate of acrid controversy which prevailed among the French exiles in the USA, it was never likely that those favouring resistance to the Germans, whether they were drawn from the supporters of *Pour la victoire* or from the ranks of committed Gaullists, would judge the ideas and sentiments of *Pilote de guerre* other than in the light of what was known or rumoured of Saint-Exupéry's personal and political affiliations in wartime. It was a fact that he had made three or four trips to Vichy from Lyon between mid-August and late October 1940, that he had made contact with converts to Pétainism, like his old acquaintance Gaston Bergery who was active in implementing the policies of the National Revolution, and that he had been received by Pétain himself (Cate pp. 416-17). It was rumoured too that his name had been put forward for a post in the Vichy State Secretariat of Education which involved responsibilities for youth and sport (Cate, p. 421). It was also noted that he conspicuously failed to come out openly in favour of the Free French movement or to contribute to the pages of *Pour la victoire*; refused to condemn the Pétain government's policies; privately defended collaboration as a necessary and realistic device for saving France; and had actually been nominated in January 1941 (though without his consent) to serve on Vichy's Conseil National (*Ecrits de guerre*, p. 161). As a result, Saint-Exupéry was widely regarded in Gaullist circles in New York as a supporter, if not an agent, of Pétain, and *Pilote de guerre* seen as something of an apology for Vichy collaboration.

However, it is only when we turn to the variety of responses provoked by *Pilote de guerre* when it was authorised for publication in the Occupied Zone that we become fully aware of the degree to which interpretations of the text are largely symptoms of political divisions among the French. An edition of 2,100 copies appeared on 27 November 1942, but after favourable reviews in the Vichy press, where it was variously praised as 'beautiful', 'moving', 'perhaps the one true book about the war of 1939' (*Ecrits de guerre*, pp. 295-7), and as 'saving honour' or being 'le seul [livre] à la mesure de la France' (ibid., p. 302), or even, in the pages of the Catholic *La Croix*, as embodying Christian personalism (ibid., p. 313), it was hysterically attacked by the Paris neo-fascist P.-A. Cousteau in two successive issues of *Je suis partout* (8 and 15 January 1943). In these articles *Pilote de guerre* was criticised as 'l'apothéose du judéo-bellicisme, la justification de tous les crimes commis avant et après la guerre contre la France ...', and as legitimising the attitudes and policies of Blum, Reynaud and Mandel (*Ecrits de guerre*, pp. 300-1). In what was clearly an orchestrated campaign, these charges were subsequently taken up by other pro-fascist and anti-Semitic publications until the German Propaganda Abteilung intervened and banned the work on 8 February 1943. As a defiant reaction to this ban, *Pilote de guerre* was then taken up by the Resistance and published in Lille in a clandestine edition of 1,000 copies in December 1943. In a final irony which crowns the fascinating story of the fortunes of this text in the course of the Second World War, the Gaullists in Algiers seem deliberately to have prevented its being sold throughout North Africa (*Ecrits de guerre*, p. 467), thus punishing Saint-Exupéry both for failing to rally to de Gaulle in the USA and for supporting Giraud in Algeria after he got there in May 1943.

Pilote de guerre offers another kind of fascination, that of a work of literature that reorders the brute facts of history in such a way as to coax us into sharing the author's own moral perspective on the Fall of France. To explore this will involve some scrutiny of the narrative art of *Pilote de guerre* before discussing the nature of its formal arguments and the value of the prescriptions which the writer puts forward for the ultimate recovery of France. Finally, I shall be concerned to ask whether these ideas or moral reflections are compatible with some elements of the official ideology of the National Revolution. In putting such questions, I do not want to imply that Saint-Exupéry was ever a naïve admirer of Pétain. Nothing in what he says or writes after the summer of 1940 expresses the hysterical relief experienced by fervent supporters of the Marshal when the Armistice of June 1940 was signed. Nor is there anything to suggest that he expected marvels from the regime. In the autumn of 1940 the committed Pétainist may have hoped to see in this Methuselah the saviour of the nation, a Lazarus miraculously emerging from the grave of the Third Republic. Saint-Exupéry seems to have had more limited expectations, though he too clung to some illusions long after they should have been discarded.

Pilote de guerre represents a hybrid genre which tended to be Saint-Exupéry's preferred literary mode. The basis of the work, as in *Vol de nuit* (1931) and *Terre des hommes* (1939), is autobiographical. In a word, it is offered principally as a form of witness to the writer's own experience in the real world, though an experience that has been selected, filled out and reordered, using a modicum of fictional devices (telescoping of events, masking of real-life persons under fictitious names, introduction of minor invented episodes), in such a way as to accommodate a vein of moral discourse by which the author/narrator seeks to impose significance on his text. As a result, the freedom of the reader to interpret the action embodied in the narrative is very much reduced. There is little here of that power of invention that marks major writers of fiction, little of that capacity to create and sustain a large, autonomous imaginary world and to oblige us to take that world on trust.

I am going to argue that there is present in *Pilote de guerre* a tension, perhaps even a fissure, between the descriptive and aesthetic elements in the book and what, in the broadest sense, might be called its ideology. This ideology is sometimes explicitly presented and argued for, sometimes implicitly rendered in the choice of character, imagery and metaphor, but whatever form it takes, it tends to impose on the lived experience contained in the novel (the ordeals of wartime flying or the suffering of French civilians caught up in the panic of military defeat) a significance that does not necessarily come from the concrete experiences described as much as from the author/narrator's desire for us to share in his sensibility and in the rightness of his moral vision.

Even at its most graphic moments, *Pilote de guerre* is not the plain, unreconstructed account of an eyewitness who participated in the events described. In the first place, it is a composite picture of several of Saint-Exupéry's reconnaissance flights and not a literal recounting of the low-level sortie he made over Arras on 23 May 1940. It actually telescopes months of photoreconnaissance work and several high altitude flights into a single mission that is made emblematic of all the others. Other aspects of the narrative make it obvious that this is a fictive transposition of the real. To begin with, we cannot fail to be aware of the highly wrought language that is brought to bear on the flow of events, and which cannot possibly be mistaken for the rough notation of happenings which, in their speed, impact and multiplicity, constantly threaten to overwhelm the observer. Not that Saint-Exupéry totally neglects the mundane facts of the pilot's world. He obsessively enumerates the details of his flying equipment (belts, fasteners, zips, oxygen mask, helmet, gloves) and convincingly portrays the plane as an extension of the pilot (p. 40), as the latter runs through the range of technical functions that have to be checked: oxygen supply, machine guns, dials and controls. Here he feels himself to be a technician exercising his craft: 'En somme je fais mon métier. Je n'éprouve rien d'autre que le plaisir physique d'actes nourris de sens qui se suffisent à eux-mêmes.' (p. 43)

Elsewhere, however, one recognises the virtuosity of Saint-Exupéry's language, the way in which objects and experiences are being defamiliarised in order that they can be registered more intensely and more memorably by us as readers. I think particularly of that moment of unreal calm in Chapter X when Saint-Exupéry's plane is high enough to be safe from the anti-aircraft fire coming up from the ground, and when that unreality is captured by images whose very artificiality is exactly suited to conveying the strangeness of the experience. The pilot glances back at the slipstream trailing behind like 'l'écharpe de nacre blanche ... un voile de mariée' (p. 73) and dreamily surveys his crew: '... inaccessible comme une trop jolie femme, nous poursuivons notre destinée, traînant lentement notre robe à traîne d'étoiles de glace ...' (pp. 74-5). It could be said, and the narrator himself subsequently feels, that this precosity of language is self-indulgent and so, suspect. Yet, even if we allow that this moment tends to prettify the experience of wartime flying it might still be thought to be psychologically accurate in portraying a fleeting sense of detachment on the part of a pilot in action. More than that, this very expressive idiom strikingly confirms the distance which Saint-Exupéry the writer has placed between himself and the raw material of wartime experience. One sees the same kind of technique at work in Chapter II, at the moment when the plane is hit by gunfire from below. Here, at the very height of danger, the sense of being caught up in some terrible dream is brilliantly conveyed: 'Je vois des larmes de lumière couler vers moi à travers une huile de silence.' (p. 161) The idea of grief or suffering that we associate with tears is muffled as a result of being linked with this sense of an irresistible movement through an 'oiled' silence. Next, this haunting image is surrounded by a cluster of others which extend and intensify it. The image of a liquid world gives way to images of light or fire: projectiles coming through the air like gold stalks of wheat or a dense cluster of spears or the dizzy play of needles or a flashing web of gold threads (p. 162). These images are infinitely more suggestive of a reconnaissance plane caught in mortal danger inside a fierce concentration of anti-aircraft fire than any literal account of such disjointed and sporadic moments of action could ever be. The scene lodges in our minds as no direct report could hope to do. Such use of language throws into high relief the way in which the resources of literary art transform the raw autobiographical matter on which Saint-Exupéry draws and affects our perception of the role of the French Air Force in the military campaign of May-June 1940, encouraging us to grant to it the sympathy and admiration which the author himself feels. The war, lived out subjectively in the turmoil of events, is a bewildering and fragmented experience. It is the writer who has imposed significance on it in the act of writing about it.

In a very similar fashion, we are coaxed into seeing the stream of French refugees, driven forward by the advancing German invaders, from the same god-like point of vantage as the pilot and his crew. For much of the narrative we are not so much *with* them, sharing in their plight and subject to some degree of fellow-feeling, as poised over them, and engaged in judging the blind futility of their conduct. Our temptation to do so is shaped not only by this vertical perspective which we are obliged to adopt, but also by the language which the narrator displays. So it is that we see the choked roads below as 'endlessly flowing black syrup' (p. 110), and the creatures who move fitfully down them as 'un vol de sauterelles qui s'abat sur du macadam' (p. 12), or as a vast flock trampling the ground outside a slaughterhouse (p. 123), or, later still, in an image which obliquely evokes the Biblical massacre of the innocents, as a scattered crowd searching for the 'stable' that will provide a refuge from their calamity (p. 198). Almost imperceptibly, we have been drawn into making a negative judgement of this crowd. It has become a reluctant, bewildered, fatalistic herd, containing, no doubt, many individuals who possess distinctive qualities and skills but who are certain, in Saint-Exupéry's mind, to be reduced by war and displacement to 'parasites et vermine' (p. 115). It is true that this dark picture, consistent with much of what historians of the exodus have noted,[7] is partially offset by a few sharp vignettes of the plight of women, children and the old which excite pity (one thinks especially of the woman giving birth on the back of a cart) and which Saint-Exupéry derives from an earlier encounter with refugees on the ground when his squadron was moving its headquarters.

But the dominant image that survives is one more calculated to provoke criticism and disillusion than compassion.

There is another way in which the author attempts to structure the feeling and thinking embodied in *Pilote de guerre* and, in some degree, to control our response to them. This is his frequent use of the device of temporal elision. There is nothing unusual about this as a narrative technique and nothing innovative about the way Saint-Exupéry handles it. Characteristically, the narrator moves in memory, in a fluid and unobtrusive way, either from his active presence as a pilot to a recent incident that is located within the framework of his wartime experience, or to an episode in the remote past, usually that of childhood, which enables him conveniently to dramatise the continuity of his own life and to give us access to his private sensibility. Examples abound. *Pilote de guerre* actually opens with a moment in which the dozing narrator is dreaming about his school days, only to be recalled peremptorily to the real world by an order to appear before his superior, the commanding officer of 2/33 Reconnaisance Group. Further memories of his experiences as a schoolboy in sick-bay surface in Chapter VI when the Arras mission is already under way. In fact, several incidents from childhood are recalled in the course of the mission: his sitting silent and afraid on a table in the cold dark entrance hall of the family château as his uncles pace to and fro, oblivious to his presence (Chapter XIV); vague memories of fairy-tales and the family governess, Paula (Chapter XIX). Elsewhere it is the recollections of military life that predominate: a visit to hospital to greet the brave Sagon who had jumped from his burning plane (Chapter IX); making a fire in his freezing quarters in the village of Orconte occupied by his unit in the winter of 1939 (Chapter XI); the silent meal with the farmer and his family (Chapter XXVII).

What matters about these examples is not their psychological plausibility or lack of it. A pilot who daydreams and philosophises quite as much as the narrator of *Pilote de guerre* when he is on a dangerous mission, is a very unlikely sort of pilot. What we are dealing with here is a literary convention, a device by which essentially symbolic interludes can be introduced into the action in order that we as readers can be exposed to the values and attitudes to which the narrator attaches importance and which lie diffused, as it were, beneath the explicit moral and social arguments developed in the text and which, in some degree, prepare us for them. Almost all the narrator's memories involve families or substitute families which provide bonds of mutuality, protection and support, answering to what the narrator subsequently interprets as the fundamental need of all human beings to extend themselves through other people or through forms of art, scientific inquiry, or religion (p. 106). The Tyrolean governess, Paula, is clearly invoked as a talisman, a guarantee of protection against the perils that beset the child's world, though I personally find her introduction at a dangerous moment in the mission to be both whimsical and sentimental. In a very similar way, the narrator's bed in his spartan quarters at Orconte recalls specifically the maternal warmth and comfort known in infancy, just as the dance of the flames on the ceiling fixes, at least by implication, the memory of the nursery. Rather differently, the visit to Sagon in hospital is a ritual which reaffirms the sustaining brotherhood of arms, in much the same way as the narrator's meal with the farmer, his wife and niece is turned into a 'breaking of bread', a sacramental rite that expresses the bonds of national community. The narrator declares quite specifically: 'Mon fermier distribue le pain, dans le silence ... Il assure, pour la dernière fois peut-être, comme l'exercice d'un culte, ce partage.' (pp. 201-2) Here, it seems to me, the echo of the Last Supper strains to raise this domestic scene to the level of an allegory about the agony of the nation.

So far, I have tried to suggest, through scrutiny of certain aspects of the literary technique of *Pilote de guerre*, that it would be quite mistaken to view it simply as a piece of unvarnished testimony, though it is obvious that a large part of it originates in the experiences of an eyewitness. Nor is it, properly speaking, a piece of fiction. There is no plot and no 'characters', in the sense of autonomous fictional beings who offer the density of life and a capacity for growth and change. There are not even separate and fully realised 'voices' capable independently of entering into the reflections about war, risk, obedience and death of which *Pilote de guerre* is largely made up. There is really only *one* voice that dominates the book, that of the author/narrator. All other figures, from Paula to Commandant Alias, are simply ciphers, put there briefly to embody particular virtues or qualities (protectiveness or duty). The half-symbolic interludes which spring from the narrator's memories of the past are so handled as to persuade us to feel sympathy (and even a touch of reverence) for certain moral values and social forms: the family as focus of nurture and protection, and the group, especially the warrior group, in so far as it illustrates the unity and solidarity that comes from service to a larger purpose and acceptance of a common discipline which may require self-sacrifice.

What happens at these levels of *Pilote de guerre* is that an ideology, or fragments of it, are hinted at, implied and even, in some degree, subtly recommended. What happens elsewhere in this narrative about an aerial reconnaissance mission over Arras is that these implications are explicitly spelled out, orchestrated, it might be said, in pages of discursive prose that cease to make much pretence of springing naturally from some piece of observed action, on the ground or in the air, and which seem to have a separate existence of their own. I am not so much thinking of those substantial passages of analysis or reflection which are interpolated among scenes of the war (Chapter XVI on the chaos of the exodus, for example), although the insertion of this discursive material threatens the imaginative unity of the chapter, but of those chapters grouped toward the end of the book (most of Chapter XXIV, and Chapters XXV-XXVII). Here a kind of sermonising takes over; the pages are full of grand philosophic formulas, as if the author/ narrator were in the grip of some urgent compulsion to make us see the truth about the Fall of France, and to oblige us to take the necessary moral reforms to recover from it. What these chapters clearly demonstrate is that Saint-Exupéry is quite unwilling for us to draw our own moral conclusions from the concrete scenes and feelings so vividly conveyed in the earlier chapters. They are to be made to yield up lessons that are not simply consistent with the author's settled moral vision, as that had been elaborated in a range of pre-war writings, but also to justify retrospectively his own judgement of the Armistice of 24-25 June 1940 and of the Vichy government's early forms of collaboration.

In looking at the pages Saint-Exupéry devotes to the analysis of the causes of French defeat in the summer of 1940, and at those concluding chapters where the conditions for a kind of national 'redressement moral' are spelled out, it is important to recall that they were not dashed off in the immediate aftermath of the miltary débâcle. *Pilote de guerre* was largely written in the course of 1941 so that it necessarily represents a more detached account of events than some piece of instant reportage. In the arguments which he deploys about French military weakness and political impotence, Saint-Exupéry shows himself to be largely untouched by the important changes that had supervened in the international, as in the French domestic, situation at the time when *Pilote de guerre* was in the process of being written. There is no sense that the views it represents have been at all modified by the fact that Britain did not go down to defeat in the wake of France, that a Free French movement and an internal French Resistance have emerged, that the USSR and the USA have entered the war against Nazi Germany, or that the social, political and economic condition of France under Pétain has raised serious doubts about the vaunted independence of the Vichy régime and its capacity to defend the interests of its citizens. What we actually get is a strong sense of a rhetorical *ritual* in which deeply felt convictions are reaffirmed. Indeed, if we look beyond *Pilote de guerre*, these same arguments are rehearsed with increasing desperation, beginning with the appeal for a kind of 'union sacrée' contained in the lecture 'D'abord la France' (November 1942), continuing with the long letter sent to General Chambe (Algiers, 3 July 1943), in which the twin themes of military unpreparedness and French moral degeneration are coupled, and ending in the bitter letter written to an unidentified correspondent in November or December 1943, where dire predictions of what would have happened to France had the Armistice not been signed are juxtaposed to an outburst of fury directed against the conduct of the 'mob' in the final days of the French collapse.[8]

What precisely are the nature and force of Saint-Exupéry's arguments in *Pilote de guerre*? A first set of arguments bears quite narrowly on France's defeat in battle, and here the whole burden of Saint-Exupéry's analysis is to suggest that such a defeat was inevitable. For instance, he does not exaggerate the deplorable effects of the civilian chaos on the roads,[9] and his picture of the disparity between the French and German forces is broadly in accordance with the facts. It was certainly a fact that the Germans enjoyed vast superiority in bombers and dive-bombers, and a significant advantage in fighters because the RAF did not commit the bulk of its planes in support of the French, but even here Saint-Exupéry's determination to place the worst possible construction on events so as to prove the inevitability of France's defeat, leads him wildly to exaggerate the gap. If all types of aircraft are taken into account, the gap was much nearer a ratio of 3:1 than of 10, or 20:1, as he asserts (p. 92).[10] Equally extravagant is his claim that the Germans enjoyed a superiority of a 100:1 in tanks (p. 92). It is true that Saint-Exupéry specifies that this applies to the period after Dunkirk, but his figures are difficult to reconcile with expert estimates of the situation prior to Dunkirk when there appears to have been rough parity between French and German tanks.[11] The real issue, which is to do with the tactical use of tanks, is nowhere discussed In the same vein, Saint-Exupéry speaks of 150,000 French troops killed in a fortnight (p. 96) while military historians suggest much lower figures for the whole of the campaign.[12]

There is no need to labour the point. Such statistics are highly subjective and impressionistic. They speak of a state of mind, a predisposition to find the worst so as to account for the French collapse and so as to justify the Armistice. After retailing this order of facts, it comes as no surprise to find Saint-Exupéry reaching very pessimistic conclusions: 'Aucun sacrifice, jamais, nulle part, n'est susceptible de ralentir l'avance allemande' (p. 92), a view at variance with cooler professional assessments.[13] This, it is implied, is the natural and inevitable result of a clash between a nation of 40 million farmers and another of 80 million industrial workers (p. 92). In this fanciful figure of speech the France of 1939 is pictured as a nation without industry and so manifestly incapable of meeting the challenge from across the Rhine. The fatalism implicit in this is the necessary prelude to Saint-Exupéry's subsequent interpretation of the true significance of the French defeat.

Just as the retreat and the chaotic exodus down the roads of France are seen not so much as evidence of military dislocation resulting from errors of strategy and tactics or from lack of competence in the French High Command, but as a form of moral disintegration, a loss of the 'organic' wholeness of the nation (p. 136), so the Armistice is viewed by Saint-Exupéry as an act of abnegation. France, it is argued, is to be judged by her readiness to sacrifice herself. If France continued to fight in the face of overwhelming odds, it was because she had a spiritual mission: 'L'Esprit chez nous a dominé l'Intelligence' (p. 138). The defeat of France was a necessary stage in preparing the conditions that would make effective resistance to Germany possible: 'La France a joué son rôle. Il consistait pour elle *à se proposer à l'écrasement* (my italics) ... et à se voir ensevelir pour un temps dans le silence.' (p. 138) There is something breathtaking about this specious attempt to draw an ethical position from the facts of defeat and armistice. It attributes to France a clear-sighted resolve to sacrifice herself for the good of Europe and the future of freedom. As such, it is a piece of special pleading, an *ex post facto* attempt to justify what has happened by an appeal to a higher tribunal, a grand mystical design in which France emerges as the chosen instrument of an abstraction called History. This is the language of religion, not politics: here we see expressed the escape from history into the realm of eschatology. Nowhere is *Pilote de guerre* more in tune with the official Vichy gospel of contrition and spiritual regeneration.

The prescriptions that conclude *Pilote de guerre* are wholly consistent with such a vision. By insisting on the common guilt and responsibility of all Frenchmen for the defeat of 1940, they effectively move the argument on to a purely moral plane and so enable Saint-Exupéry conveniently to avoid having to discriminate between the relative responsibilities of social or political groups within France: 'La défaite divise . . . je ne contribuerai pas à ces divisions, en rejetant la responsabilité du désastre sur ceux des miens qui pensent autrement que moi . . . ' (p. 211) The same failure to engage with concrete realities manifests itself when Saint-Exupéry urges his readers to make the gift of self in order to create a truly human community (p. 233). The sentiments are unexceptionable but they take us no nearer to an understanding of how fraternity is to be established within the French community, or toward any clearer perception of that common ideal of sacrifice to which we can all subscribe (pp. 240-1). Faced (at the moment when *Pilote de guerre* appears in the Spring of 1942) with the problem of how to act when one finds oneself occupied by a foreign power that is involved in the spoliation of one's country and the persecution of one's fellow citizens, it hardly helps to be told that 'le culte de l'Universel exalte et noue les richesses particulières' (p. 242) or that the 'primacy of Man' is the only proper foundation for liberty and equality (p. 243). Confronted with the cruel realities of 1942, these vague gestures in the direction of spirituality strike one as the last remnants of an archaic and discredited rhetoric.

Notes

1. All subsequent references to this text are to: *Pilote de guerre* (Paris, Le Livre de poche, 1963).
2. As late as 1943 he could still write: 'Je ne suis pas royaliste mais je respecte profondément le vieux gentilhomme royaliste.' See: Saint-Exupéry, *Ecrits de guerre*, ed. Louis Evrard (Paris, Gallimard, 1982), p. 366.
3. Curtis Cate, *Antoine de Saint-Exupéry. His Life and Times* (London, Heinemann, 1970), p. 415.
4. Zeev Sternhell, *Ni droite ni gauche: L'Idéologie fasciste en France* (Paris, Editions du Seuil, 1983), p. 28.
5. Guy Fritsch-Estrangin, *New York entre de Gaulle et Pétain* (Paris, La Table Ronde, 1969).
6. A very partial but lively account of this infighting is given in Fritsch-Estrangin, *passim*.
7. E.g., Nicole Ollier, *L'Exode sur les routes de l'an 40* (Paris, Laffont, 1970).
8. All three texts can be consulted in *Ecrits de guerre*, pp. 265-70; 389-91; 427-31.
9. Indeed, Nicole Ollier argues that official estimates of the number of refugees in the Free Zone on 13 August 1940 (2,486,500) were far too low.
10. Alistair Horne, *To Lose a Battle. France 1940* (Harmondsworth, Penguin Books, 1979), p. 220, gives a comparative table.
11. Horne (pp. 217-18) gives 2,400-3,000 German tanks to 3,100 French; J.-B. Duroselle, *L'Abîme 1939-1945* (Paris, Imprimerie Nationale, 1982), p. 136 gives 3,000-4,000 German tanks to 3,300 French. It may be that Saint-Exupéry had heard of the Deuxième Bureau's 'vastly inflated' (Horne, p. 217) estimate of

7,000-7,500 German tanks.

12. Horne (p. 650) gives 90,000; Jeffery A. Gunsburg, *Divided and Conquered: The French High Command and the Defeat of the West, 1940* (London, Greenwood Press, 1979), p. 275 gives 120,000.

13. E.g. A. Goutard, *1940. La Guerre des occasions perdues* (Paris, Hachette, 1956).

6 THE ROLE OF JOAN OF ARC ON THE STAGE OF OCCUPIED PARIS[1]

Gabriel Jacobs

By 1920, when the upsurge of interest in Joan of Arc in the second half of the last century and the early years of our own had resulted in her canonisation, Joan had already long represented in France a wide spectrum of nationalistic and religious ideals. In the 1920s, she symbolised the determination of a great victorious nation, and one of the forces which had made possible the flowering of its culture and genius. She was not overlooked in the 1930s when, for instance, the banners of the extreme Left proclaimed her '[la] fille du peuple, vendue par son roi, brûlée per ses prêtres'.[2] Her story was nevertheless perceived at that time as rather too equivocal to be taken up with much gusto by the majority of intellectuals, even when events in Spain prompted left-wing pacifists to embrace the notion of the Just War, and right-wing Catholics to support Franco's cause as a crusade against Godless communism. Being identified universally as an upholder of the doctrine of non-intervention in the affairs of other nations, unless those nations tried to annex one's own, she was probably too blurred a symbol to be of decisive benefit to either faction. But given on the one hand the strength and depth of Anglophobia in many sections of pre-war French society, soon to be sharpened by Dunkirk and Mers-el-Kébir, and on the other the reality of occupation by a foreign power, it was inevitable from the outset that Joan would be an important double figure in France between 1940 and 1944.

During the Occupation, potential comparisons between the fifteenth-century France of Joan of Arc and France's predicament after the débâcle of 1940 were too striking to be disregarded even by the most unpolitical of commentators. Chanoine Glorieux, in the preface to his carefully neutral biography of Joan which appeared in 1941, was at pains to point out that although his work had been all but completed before the War, the advent of the new regime had served only to enhance the importance of its subject.[3] Marcel Vioux's 1942 *Jeanne d'Arc*, intended for popular consumption, while in no way didactic, nevertheless incorporated on its title-page Pétain's pronouncement: 'Martyre de l'Unité Nationale, Jeanne d'Arc est le symbole de la France'. In more highly-coloured Vichy-orientated propaganda, from political histories to posters, the full range of possible analogies was explored. The headlines of *le Petit Parisien* of 11 May 1941 — 'La France célèbre aujourd'hui la fête nationale de Jeanne d'Arc, brûlée vive par les Anglais . . .'[4] — illustrates the way in which charged language was used to arouse feelings of revenge against the English for an event separated in time from the mid-twentieth century by half a millennium. In both zones Joan was made the epitome of the Vichy ideal. 'Comme la Romée serait fière de sa fille qui s'entendait si bien aux soins du ménage!' wrote René Jeanneret in 1942 in his life of Joan officially approved for use in schools,[5] appearing to forget for a moment the rather small role played by 'les soins du ménage' in the life of the real Joan. Joan's peasant upbringing was generally extolled as an example of the solid vigour of rural virtues, while the militant partisan in her was for the most part ignored in favour of a picture of humility and obedience. But above all she was presented as the forger of political unity at a time of grave national crisis: 'Eternel sujet d'émerveillement', exlaimed Henri de Sarrau, adding, with what now seems remarkable credulity, 'comme celui qui a placé le Maréchal Pétain à la tête de l'Etat français'.[6] Some writers presented her less as the precursor of Vichy than as the embodiment of heroic grandeur, and saw her story as the Triumph of the Will. Jean Jacoby, the author of works whose titles did not hide his political colours — *Le Front Populaire en France et les égarements du socialisme moderne, Le Déclin des grandes démocraties et le retour à l'autorité, La Race* — was drawn to a Jeanne in whom he saw a manifestation of iron resolution and fascist vitality. In his *Scènes de la vie de Jeanne d'Arc* of 1941 he rejected Anatole France's *magnum opus* on the life of Joan on account of its author's 'sordide sectarisme' (p. 16). For him, Anatole France had hidden the true Joan, whose heart had indeed been full of charity, but who in no way had sought reform or so-called social justice: 'Elle ne se plonge pas dans les masses', Jacoby insisted, 'ne spécule pas sur leurs sentiments' (p. 223).

Clandestine propaganda naturally concentrated on Joan the freedom fighter, the solitary visionary who, surrounded by the lies and deceit of her own countrymen, had in the midst of defeat liberated France from foreign occupation. In such a context, the very fact that Thomas Pugey's 1943 history of Joan was published in Switzerland by the Editions de la Baconnière,[7] whose list has already included works by Eluard, Aragon and Louis Parrot, was enough to indicate that this work was to be taken as a Resistance text, despite the fact that its content was almost wholly confined to a treatise on mystical Catholicism. It seemed natural for the Resistance to adopt the Cross of Lorraine as the emblem of Free France, and parallels were frequently drawn between De Gaulle and Joan. Was not Joan, like De Gaulle, the very opposite of the *défaitistes*, who, at best, were men who had ignominiously accepted occupation in order to salvage a small corner of French existence, while the very essence of France was being dissipated? How could one fail to see in the Armistice of 1940 an image of the Treaty of Troyes, at which defeat and occupation had been legalised? 'Aux yeux de tous les défaitistes', proclaimed an anonymous pamphlet published in Brazil, 'Jeanne est une protestation violente, acharnée . . . Jeanne *nie* la défaite.'[8] But the Resistance was also obliged to diminish the fact that Joan of Arc had been burned by the English. And here, the French service of the BBC in London was in an especially sensitive position. Its broadcasters chose either to overlook this feature of the story, or to meet the problem at a tangent by arguing that England was an island outpost of Free France, like Orleans when Joan had raised her standard.[9]

Though Joan maintained a high status, then, in most forms of propaganda, particularly during the first half of the Occupation, her fate as a theatrical character was not quite as illustrious as might have been expected. It may seem surprising, and especially so given the French dramatists' predilection for myth and legend during this period (Sartre's *Les Mouches* and Anouilh's *Antigone* spring immediately to mind), but it is a fact that no Joan of Arc play written between 1940 and 1944 was produced on the stage of occupied Paris, nor, as far as professional theatre is concerned, in the provinces. Probably the most important published play on the theme of Joan of Arc written under German occupation was *Portique pour une fille de France* by Pierre Schaeffer and Pierre Barbier. Performed by amateurs in Lyons and Marseilles in the spring of 1941,[10] it was nothing more than a stylised piece of propaganda intended for use in the *Camps de Jeunesse*. It had recourse to lines like the one used – repeatedly – by an anonymous Englishman in the play: 'Les Français sont pourris, pourris, pourris', and the published version included an appendix containing chants recommended by the authors for communal performance by an entire camp: 'Comme Jeanne, nous croyons en la résurrection de la France' (p. 111), and the like. The play's importance as theatre, even in the eyes of its own creators, may be judged from the following extraordinary (if eminently practical) directive: 'Il y a lieu de supprimer entièrement le personnage de Jeanne qui pourrait être grotesque, tenu par un garçon.' (p. 107)

In Paris, given the ever-increasing popularity of legitimate theatre, the importance of Joan as a symbol, and the wide choice of available pre-war plays extolling her, it might have seemed that only glitter and stardom awaited her on stage for the foreseeable future. She made her début in occupied Paris in Shaw's *Sainte Jeanne* in December 1940. This was followed six months later by an appearance in Péguy's *Jeanne d'Arc*, then in Vermorel's *Jeanne avec nous*, which opened in January 1942. But the final performance of this play in August of that year was also virtually the end of Joan as a character in Parisian theatres for the rest of the Occupation.

With Ludmilla Pitoëff in the title role, Shaw's *Saint Joan* had had its French première in 1925, in the translation by Augustin and Henriette Hamon. The same text was used by Raymond Rouleau's company, with Jany Holt as Jeanne, for the production at the Théâtre de l'Avenue which ran from 24 December 1940 to the end of January 1941. Even with the play's illustrious past, and its potential dramatic impact (theatrically it is far superior to the efforts of either Péguy or Vermorel), it attracted relatively little critical attention. This may have been the result of various factors difficult or impossible to evaluate: the quality of the acting, costumes and sets, even the temperature inside the theatre in the middle of that first winter of the Occupation. Be that as it may, the fact that reviews are comparatively few and far between is certainly a measure of the lack of serious interest, at this early period, in Joan of Arc as a symbolic character, particularly since the play closed well before the first Occupation Joan of Arc Day of May 1941, which was to mark the beginning of the *Pucelle* as a true cult figure. No doubt, therefore, the performances of the play were neither deliberately didactic, nor deliberately contentious, nor deliberately ambiguous. Historians of propaganda (censorship boards too) are of course faced with a peculiar difficulty when it comes to the interpretative art of theatre, since generally only the plain text is available for examination, while it is obvious that all manner of signals and messages can be made to appear when actors garnish it on the stage. And, at a distance of nearly half a century from that period of chaos and hardship, when the last thing in a theatre director's mind was the importance of preserving the prompter's copies of a script, the problem is compounded by the impossibility of discovering which material was deleted, or even inserted, and at which performance. However, in the case of Rouleau's production of Shaw's *Sainte Jeanne*, it may reasonably be assumed, at least, that few cuts were made. Shaw's play is not inordinately long, and with the possible exception of the Epilogue, is sufficiently compact as it stands to sustain dramatic intensity. Moreover, its strong anti-English flavour (and the fact that Shaw was Irish was emphasised in a number of reviews of the play) had considerable appeal at the end of 1940, when Albion was still exceptionally perfidious for a part of the French bourgeois theatre-going public. Shaw's numerous references to the English probably remained intact, and indeed among the few reviewers who chose to deal specifically with what they saw as the play's contemporary significance, there was unanimous agreement that its punch came from its biting and cynical treatmnt of British attitudes and policies. An anonymous reviewer in *Paris Soir* (24 December 1941) contended that the original 1924 London production had flopped because English audiences had preferred the Joan of Arc of Shakespeare's *Henry VI*, 'Pièce qui se termine par d'affreuses grossièretés à l'égard de Jeanne et dont le public anglais s'est fort réjoui', and Armory in *Les Nouveaux Temps* (6 January 1941) recommended the play as a cure for Anglophilia.

The vast majority of critics, however, concentrated virtually exclusively on the literary and dramatic qualities of Shaw's play. Indeed, of all the major reviewers, only the theatre critic of *l'Illustration* (R. de B., 14 January 1941) was sufficiently jostled by it as a *pièce de circonstance* to comment on its enormous latent value as propaganda beyond that of its conspicuous anti-British ethos. For him, Shaw's Joan clearly represented on stage the creation of French nationalism; for him, she was 'miraculeuse dans la mesure où elle a galvanisé pour un idéal un pays aveuli par la défaite'. And the play does truly abound in what might have been taken as allusions to contemporary circumstances. 'Nous avons besoin de quelques fous maintenant . . . Voyez où nous ont menés les sages' says Poulangy to Baudricourt (p. 20)[11] — a line briefly noted in some reviews;[12] 'Un nouvel esprit commence à se développer chez les hommes', comments l'Archevêque (p. 49); 'Si j'étais le maître', thunders Le Chapelain, 'je ne laisserais pas un Juif vivant dans toute la chrétienté' (p. 86). Some remarks, such as Jeanne's 'rien ne comptant, en dehors de Dieu, que la France libre et française' (p. 216), may have sounded too much like a call to arms not to have caught the attention of the censor, but little of the play would have remained if all possible topical allusions had been removed. Shaw's Joan, in the words of Ingvald Raknem is 'a sort of intractable, intolerable, sexless suffragette',[13] but she is also plainly an apostle of national unity and a severe critic of French attitudes, both political and military. Warwick, the only important English character in the play not portrayed as a nincompoop, is quick to see the dangers inherent in Jeanne's idea that the rule of the king should be absolute, since a fragmented country makes occupation and exploitation a relatively simple matter, while for

The Role of Joan of Arc

Jeanne, says Cauchon, 'les gens qui parlent français constituent ce que les Saintes Ecritures décrivent comme une nation. Appelez ce côté de son hérésie Nationalisme, si vous voulez . . . ' (p. 110) Shaw's Joan understands that the cause of France's defeat has been its moral and military unpreparedness. 'Notre ennemi est à nos portes et nous sommes là sans rien faire' she exlaims (p. 73). 'Nous faisons les imbéciles', she says to Charles, 'tandis que les godons, eux, prenaient la guerre au sérieux'(p. 122), (. . .)'A quoi sert l'armure contre la poudre à canon?' (p. 129). Could the audiences of the winter of 1940 have been insensitive to such patent implications, heavy with overtones of pre-war hesitation, infighting, self-indulgence and low military morale, in the face of order, discipline and blitzkrieg tactics? It would seem that Jeanne's symbolic role was as yet too ill-defined in the national consciousness, or the critics unsure of how far it was appropriate to press the point home – after all, the Hero of Verdun had not yet been pronounced the equal of the Heroine of Orleans.

By 1941, however, Pétain had crowned Joan Queen of the New Order, and her Day was commemorated in a burst of nationalistic enthusiasm, 'comme le signe de la réconciliation et de l'unité nationale retrouvées', as *L'Oeuvre* (11 May 1941) put it. De Gaulle retaliated with the idea that between 3.00 and 4.00 p.m. on Sunday 11 May, the French should take to the streets, simply to look at each other in silence as a gesture of solidarity with Joan and the Resistance. According to the clandestine *Libération* (18 May 1941), the demonstration was a magnificent success, the people of Paris pouring into the streets at the appointed time watched by terrified and dismayed German soldiers who did not dare to intervene – such is the stuff of propaganda. The collaborationist press, on the other hand, did not need to exaggerate. In the domain of the theatre alone, Joan of Arc Day was the signal for a salvo of special occasions throughout the provinces, while in Paris the Palais de la Mutualité and the stage of the Comédie Française saw star-studded casts in scenes from the major *Pucelle* plays.[14] Perhaps it was this theatrical fervour which prompted Robert Brasillach to work on his *Procès de Jeanne d'Arc*, written in dialogue form, and published in July, and Jacques Hébertot with the Compagnie du Rideau des Jeunes to produce Péguy's *Jeanne d'Arc* at the Théâtre Hébertot (formerly the Théâtre des Arts). It opened on 23 June, with Juliette Faber in the title role.

The 1941 production of Péguy's play presents a textual problem far greater than that of Shaw's *Sainte Jeanne*. A complete performance of Péguy's *Jeanne d'Arc*, in fact three plays in one, would have lasted more than eight hours. This was cut to well under three hours —'avec le respect qu'on devine' commented *Les Nouveaux Temps* (25 June 1941) — by the author's son, Marcel Péguy, but it is today impossible to know which extracts were selected for inclusion. It is certain, at least, that the production was based primarily on the original three plays of 1897: Péguy's shorter *Mystère de la charité de Jeanne d'Arc* of 1910 consists basically of a new version of two dialogues taken from only the first play of the trilogy, but most critics in 1941 give all three plays equal weight in their reviews. It is likely that Marcel Péguy's adaptation included parts of the later version, sometimes called the 'Christian Joan' as opposed to the earlier 'Socialist Joan'. But whatever his sources, after the Liberation the uncertainty led to some mystification, to which I shall return.

Partly for his numerous writings on Joan of Arc, Péguy had been seen as a luminary by the collaborationist establishment. Alexandre Marc may well have been right in his view, expressed just before the defeat of 1940, that Péguy's Jeanne was a character alien to the followers of the Führer, for whom, as he put it, 'seule la santé importe, non la sainteté'.[15] Péguy himself was nevertheless soon to become, in the words of the collaborationist author and critic Maurice Rostand (*Paris Midi*, 25 June 1941), a 'grand inspiré en qui la France s'est exprimée comme en son héroïne'. Péguy was recommended reading in the youth camps of Vichy France, and schools and *Chantiers de Jeunesse* were named after him.[16] Those who before the War had seen in his portrayal of Joan anything other than the future vindication of the Vichy ideal were vigorously denounced. 'Il est fâcheux', exlaimed Comeau in 1942, 'que les passions politiques aient pour un temps rendu suspect ... le message de l'héroïne chantée par Péguy.[17] Not all commentators forgot that Péguy had once espoused the cause of socialism, nor that he had been Dreyfusard, but the very fact that by 1943 Jean Variot, in a general eulogy of *Jeanne d'Arc*, felt that it was necessary to point out that the play's author had not himself been a saint, tainted as he had been by *démocratisme* and *philosémitisme*, is in itself some indication of the heights to which Péguy had been elevated by Vichy.[18]

It may safely be assumed that Marcel Péguy's 1941 adaptation of *Jeanne d'Arc* was a cento reflecting this official exaltation of his father. And it is evident that the play could with little difficulty be made to fit the circumstances. Despite the fact that it differs from nearly all other *Pucelle* dramas in ending on an unheroic and fundamentally pessimistic note; despite the fact that Péguy was less interested in Joan as a maker of history and the forger of a new France than as a

The Role of Joan of Arc

victim of 'le Mal universel', his heroine is of spotless moral rectitude, and wages an exemplary war against the forces of social and political disorder. And the critics, who for the most part received the 1941 production enthusiastically, were not slow to take note of what they saw as its contemporary significance. 'Certes, cet ouvrage vient, ou jamais, à son heure', wrote Armory in *le Matin* (20 June 1941); '... si présent, si actuel', cried Jacques Berland with astonishment (*Paris Soir*, 27 June 1941); Claude Véré (*Semaine à Paris*, 23 June 1941) thought the success of the play assured, since the performers were so obviously driven by the idea of a new France embodied in the combination of Péguy and Joan of Arc. Above all, Péguy's heroine was taken as a symbol of strong leadership emerging from simple Christian virtues. Didier Gex (*le Matin*, 28 June 1941) saw in her 'ce génie des gens simples et droits', and Armory, in his piece for *Les Nouveaux Temps* (1 July 1941), was struck by Péguy's desire to produce a heroic character who remained essentially *paysanne*. But no critic dealt with one of the basic themes of Péguy's play, that charity by itself is worthless and that one is helpless in the face of human misery unless some effort is made to understand and eradicate its cause, in this case the imposition of the will of one nation on another. Jeanne comes to realise that a new war must be waged, since the peace of occupation has resulted in only the semblance of order, which cannot be the will of God. With so much to cut, Marcel Péguy was perhaps able to manipulate this theme of armed revolution, or even to purge the text of it entirely, but this would have been difficult, and it is more likely that it remained, and that audiences associated it with the ideals of Pétain's National Revolution.

Now a word on the mystification I mentioned earlier. In 1947 a different three-hour abridgement by Marcel Péguy (how different we are not sure) began a run at the Théâtre Hébertot to mark the post-war reopening of the theatre. It generated a proliferation of previews and reviews, and attracted the attention of the major critics of the day,[19] but nowhere is any mention to be found of the 1941 production. *Samedi Soir* (27 September 1947) devoted several columns to a history of the Théâtre Hébertot, based on an interview with Jacques Hébertot himself, but for the period of the Occupation noted only that Giraudoux, Cocteau, Passeur and Crommelynk had been produced. Marc Beigbeder (*le Parisien Libéré*, 25 September 1947) was so impressed by Péguy's play that he thought the delay in bringing the 1897 version for the first time ever to the Paris stage was scandalous. Marcel Péguy himself, in a piece written for the 1947 programme, commented, with a certain *équivoque*, that it was surely the length of his father's original *Jeanne d'Arc* which had prevented it from ever being performed commercially.[20] The fact that the so-called première of 18 September 1947 was a charity affair for the benefit of La Fédération des Maquis[21] prompted P(ol) Gaillard in *l'Humanité* (26 September 1947) to point out that Marcel Péguy's past was not without stain, since the latter had contributed to *la Gerbe* and other collaborationist newspapers, and in *Les Lettres Françaises* (25 September 1947) Gaillard remembered that this ex-collaborator had for four years promoted his father as the guiding light of the 'régime hitléro-vichyssois'. One may imagine how Gaillard might have reacted if he had known of the special performance given at the Comédie Française in June 1941 'au profit des Ecrivains Combattants',[22] but he appears to have been as unaware of the first Hébertot production as his fellow critics. It is hard not to conclude that there had been a conspiracy of silence. Was Marcel Péguy's original 1941 adaptation so obviously pro-Vichy that in 1947 he thought it best forgotten? Did Jacques Hébertot simply erase the fact of the 1941 run from his memory? Did certain critics deliberately refrain from mentioning it? If such is the case, then it was perhaps in the desire to see the rapid rehabilitation of Charles Péguy.[23]

Be that as it may, the momentum created by Shaw and Péguy in 1940 and 1941 was boosted by Claudel. In July 1941, his oratorio *Jeanne d'Arc au bûcher*, with music by Honegger, began a two-month Tour de France, taking in 30 towns, covering 3,000 kilometres, and involving a special train for the actors and musicians, lorries loaded with instruments, costumes and sets, and an advance guard of administrators to organise board and lodging – all in the desire to bring to the provinces, as the author himself put it, a vision of Joan of Arc surrounded by a united France.[24] Meanwhile, rehearsals were beginning in Paris for the next production on the theme of the *Pucelle*, Vermorel's *Jeanne avec nous*.[25] The venture was rather meagrely funded, and the actors of the Compagnie du Théâtre d'Essais worked without pay during the rehearsal period; but their obvious enthusiasm carried them through, and the play opened to a warm reception at the Théâtre des Champs-Élysées on 10 January 1942. Towards the end of February, it moved to the Théâtre de l'Ambigu, and on 26 June to the Théâtre Pigalle, where it ran until August. Berthe Tissen, a formerly unknown actress, played Jeanne, and in doing so made her name.[26]

Almost nothing written about *Jeanne avec nous* during the Occupation could lead one to conclude that it was taken by audiences to be anti-Nazi or anti-Vichy. However, in contrast to the fate of Péguy's *Jeanne d'Arc*, the post-war *reprise* of Vermorel's play (in December

1945) prompted reviewers to deal almost exclusively with the impact and meaning it had had for occupied audiences, and moreover to brand it the first Resistance play to be performed in Paris. Before returning, therefore, to its 1942 reception, it is worth examining this retrospective reaction, unconstrained as it was by the German presence.

Only the unqualified post-war acknowledgement of the clandestine message of *Les Mouches* is comparable with that accorded to *Jeanne avec nous*. The vast majority of critics present at the 1945 staging saw the play as having been, in 1942, as magnificently subordinate as Joan herself. For them, the earlier production had been 'la révolte . . . contre l'ennemi de l'extérieur', 'un beau travail de pied-de-nez', '*à la barbe des Allemands, le procès de la collboration*'.[27] They marvelled at the apparent stupidity of the German censors. 'Comment [ont-ils] su se méprendre', asked J. Van den Esch incredulously (*Pays*, 22 December 1945), 'ignorer le danger de ces répliques capables d'arracher les pavés des rues?' Jacques Mauchemps of *Spectateur* (2 January 1946) offered his own version of what he imagined to have been the German censors' reasoning: 'ça, très bonne pièce. Pièce contre Anglais. Une pièce pour Jeanne d'Arc, c'est forcément une pièce pour Allemands.'

But if the Germans were dull-witted, it seems the French were not. A large number of reviewers, though with no unbiased evidence to back their claims, affirmed with remarkable assuredness that the 1942 audiences had easily discerned Vermorel's real message, the only possible message, according to Thierry Maulnier (*Essor*, 19 January 1946), in an occupied country: an indictment of the occupying power. Maurice Delarue, one of the few 1945 critics who had seen the original production, maintained that audiences had strained to see allusions to the Occupation and Vichy in every line delivered, and that they had unmistakably recognised Pétain and Déat in Jeanne's contemptible judges (*Terre des Hommes*, 19 January 1946). And Simone de Beauvoir informs us that each burst of applause was an unequivocal demonstration against Nazi rule,[28] though Vermorel himself (*Opéra*, 19 December 1945), talks of the shiver that had run down his spine each time the *silence* of the audience had highlighted a daring allusion, such as his English officers clicking their heels, or his men of the Church referring to each other as 'camarade'.

Yet some 1945 voices were not quite in harmony with the chorus. François de Roux (*Minerve*, 4 January 1946) thought that the censors must have given *Jeanne avec nous* its visa not only because Joan had been burned by the English, but also because of a certain cynicism Vermorel had put in the mouths of those judging his heroine at her trial.

Jean Sauvenay (*Témoignage Chrétien*, 4 January 1946) considered that one of the distinct themes of the play was the problem of the relative merits of, on the one hand, peace bought with bloodshed, and, on the other, its less costly counterpart, that of collaboration – a problem on which, in his opinion, Vermorel had rightly declined to give guidance. And Marc Beigbeder (*les Etoiles*, 1 January 1946), while recognising that it was no doubt possible in 1942 to see Vermorel's Englishmen as Germans, and his Inquisition as Vichy, thought the textual clues to these transpositions far from obvious.

How, then, is one to decide how the 1942 audiences reacted to *Jeanne avec nous?* To begin with, by this date any play treating the Joan of Arc theme, whatever the intentions of the dramatist, would have been seen in the light of pressing contemporary concerns, so that surprise at the implications of Shaw's *Sainte Jeanne* and Péguy's *Jeanne d'Arc* had now been replaced by a sense of expectation. For *les Nouveaux Temps* (20 January 1942) Vermorel's play was 'une preuve nouvelle de l'intérêt que les auteurs de la génération présente trouvent, au lendemain de nos revers, à remonter le cours de notre histoire'. What is more, the title *Jeanne avec nous*, as Michel Florisoone and Raymond Cogniat noted in their survey of the 1941-2 season, was proof that the play had been written as a comment on contemporary problems.[29] In that hard and disheartening winter of 1941-2, it was also to be anticipated that the critical emphasis would be firmly on heroic grandeur. In the words of André Castelot of *la Gerbe* (15 January 1942), *Jeanne avec nous* was 'une pièce écrite dans le sens de la vraie grandeur, voie dans laquelle nous aimerions tant, en cette noire époque, voir le théâtre de France s'engager'. Absent are the references to Joan's simplicity. Gone is the spate of negative Anglophobic comments: only one major reviewer, Charles Quinel (*le Matin*, 21 January 1942), thought it worth mentioning that the *Pucelle* had been burned by the English. Rather, for the 1942 critics, Vermorel's Jeanne is the incarnation of positive glory and majesty, and his play has, as Georges Pioch (*l'Oeuvre*, 13 January 1942) put it, 'cet accent sobre et fort ... lequel vaut pour toutes les époques du monde, et singulièrement pour celle où nous purgeons notre peine et le morne destin qu'elle nous fait'.

In the case of *Jeanne avec nous* it is possible to ascertain precisely the relationship between this critical reaction and the text of the play, since the first published version, dated October 1942,[30] is for all practical purposes a prompter's script, with those lines which had been excluded from the Rideau des Jeunes production clearly indicated. And it is plain from this text that Vermorel's heroine does indeed symbolise self-respect, fortitude and lionheartedness.[31] 'La France, c'est l'audace, l'orgueil, la sainte brutalité, l'héroïsme', she cries to Bedfort, [sic, p. 99], a line which epitomises her outlook. Bedfort himself, a mature, pragmatic and perceptive character, is the mouthpiece for moderation, and thus collaboration. It was to be expected, he explains in a self-conscious passage about the role of Joan of Arc, that a people defeated morally and physically would snatch desperately at a symbol of hope for the future (pp. 58-9), while the *reality* of that hope was there for all to see: peace and order in the unification of two great nations. 'Allons-nous vivre encore pour des générations dans cet état de guerre, de crime passionel, à nous entretuer tous les vingt ans . . . ?', he asks with pacifist wordly wisdom (p. 141). The 1942 audiences cannot have been insensitive to such remarks, but since they came from the mouth of one of Jeanne's oppressors, the critics seem to have been at a loss as to how they should be received, and abstained from discussing them. Only Morvan Lebesque (*le Petit Parisien*, 12 January 1942) showed any willingness to come to terms with the problem, and concluded that Jeanne's opponents 'se trompent, mais de bonne foi'. In his review, Lebesque had already made his right-wing affiliations clear by disparaging the 1936 May Day celebrations, when 'Jeanne avec nous!' had been one of the rallying cries of the Front Populaire, but had commented that Vermorel's play belied the implication of its title. The 1942 critics generally ignored aspects of the play which were manifestly an incitement to revolt against imposed order. 'Ce peuple sait encore descendre dans la rue, s'ameuter contre l'injustice' says the kindly Lohier (p. 81); and Jeanne's response to those who argue that her cause will throw France into chaos, is pointedly explicit: 'La terre n'est pas là pour les peuples lâches, ou fatigués. Et le mien tout entier n'en voulait pas de votre paix de honte.' (p. 40) *Jeanne contre nous?*

It is clear that much of the play could have been interpreted to suit one's own prejudices and preoccupations. Many of Jeanne's heroic, patriotic lines could have been interpreted equally as justifying the National Revolution or the cause of the Resistance. Vermorel's postwar claim (*Opéra*, 19 December 1945) that Jeanne's remark about her sovereign – 'Sa France sera grande' – had had a special impact in 1942 since the King of Bourges and General de Gaulle by coincidence shared the same Christian name, may well have been true, but Vermorel's Charles is also a buffoon. In 1945, Pol Gaillard (*les Lettres Françaises*, 11 January 1946) was to deride 'le triste Alain Laubreaux de *Je Suis Partout* [qui] prétendait même découvrir dans la pièce des allusions anti-soviétiques et s'étonnait avec joie de voir les juges de Jeanne s'appeler inexplicablement "camarades"!' But Laubreaux's view (*Je Suis Partout*, 21 February 1942) is perfectly understandable, even justifiable, given the black picture Vermorel paints of the Church and the Inquisition, whose members use this term in addressing one another. Patrick Marsh has argued that *Jeanne avec nous* was one of only two wartime French plays (the other being Sartre's *Bariona*) unquestionably written with the specific aim of encouraging the Resistance.[32] Yet the author of *Jeanne avec nous* himself pointed out both during and after the Occupation that he put the finishing touches to it in 1938.[33] Nor must it be forgotten that Vermorel had contributed articles to the pro-Nazi newspaper *la Gerbe*, not only as a preview to the opening of his play in 1942, but also as a critic who, the year before, had strongly attacked surrealist and avant-garde theatre.[34]

Nevertheless, if it must be accepted that the claims made by critics in 1945 and 1946, though exaggerated, contained more than a germ of truth, the scales are tipped from the point of view of the text not by the confrontation of Jeanne and her judges, and even less so by that of Jeanne and Befort (a forerunner of the equilibrium maintained by Anouilh in the contest between Antigone and Créon), but by the character of Jeanne's most dangerous enemy, the Inquisitor Lemaître. Jacques Berland's attempt (in 1942) to classify Lemaître's position as 'l'entêtement partisan' (*Paris-Soir*, 16 January 1942) was patently strained. Lemaître's long and detailed accounts of the physical torture inflicted by the Inquisition (pp. 60-1, 149), little of which was cut from the 1942 production, and which read like a synopsis of Sartre's *Morts sans sépulture*, were too close to reality not to have been taken as an indictment of the methods of the Gestapo or the Milice.

Jeanne is not tortured (nor was the real Joan, though Vermorel breaks with historical accuracy in having her raped by English soldiers in her cell), but she is nevertheless very clearly the victim of a system capable of bloodcurdling atrocities carried out in the name of expediency. In effect, therefore, her role has changed, partly in the way she herself is presented, but equally within the wider symbol of the unjust and sometimes brutal treatment of innocent individuals by the State, in this case itself a puppet of a ruthless foreign regime. *Jeanne avec nous* cannot have had the immediate impact as a Resistance play implied by post-war critics, since it ran almost continuously for nearly eight months without being banned by the Propaganda-staffel or its French theatrical equivalent, the Comité d'Organisation des Entreprises de Spectacle. But the fact that it was the last major theatrical Joan of Arc venture in Paris suggests either that the censors did finally consider that the subject itself had become weighted in favour of resistance to occupation as such, or that playwrights and theatre directors suspected that the censors had come to this conclusion.[35] The double meaning of *Jeanne avec nous* did not of course prevent it from being used as collaborationist propaganda. In March 1942, for example, excerpts were performed on the stage of the Théâtre de la Madeleine after Pierre Champion's lecture in the series 'De Jeanne d'Arc à Philippe Pétain',[36] and the play figured prominently in the 1942 Joan of Arc Day celebrations. Fragments of it, together with other texts on the same theme, were used as interludes for a radio broadcast entitled *Noblesse musicale de Jeanne d'Arc*,[37] and it joined the *Pucelle* plays of Schiller, Péguy, Shaw, René Bruyez, Jean Loisy, André Villiers, François Porché and Saint-Georges de Bouhélier, from all of which works scenes were performed in a gala matinée organised in honour of Joan by the Théâtre National Populaire on 10 May 1942 at the Palais de Chaillot.[38] But while Gaston Denizot of *la Gerbe* (14 May 1942), in his account of yet another celebration held at the Salle Pleyel, did not hesitate almost to echo the title of Vermorel's play in exclaiming 'Jamais la grande Lorraine n'a été plus près de nous', a curt note which appeared inconspicuously in a number of newspapers[39] signified the concern of the authorities over what Joan might have come to symbolise despite their efforts. It announced that on Joan of Arc Day, celebratory rallies or meetings of any kind were strictly forbidden. To what extent did Vermorel's *Jeanne avec nous* influence official reasoning? Since the play's message was determined largely by the preformed attitudes of its audience, Vermorel's own objectives are probably rather beside the point. But *Jeanne avec nous* caught the mood of the times, and thus no doubt contributed to the growing feeling among those in power that Joan could no longer by relied upon to be a clear symbol of the New Order.

By the middle of 1942, then, Joan had little future as a theatrical character. From then until the end of the War, her sole appearance on the Parisian stage was in a *reprise* of Claudel's *Jeanne au bûcher* on 9 May 1943. This single performance at the Salle Pleyel, with the celebrated Mary Marquet reading the part of Jeanne, and Honegger himself conducting the Orchestre National, was given to a packed house, and broadcast live on radio.[40] But Claudel's oratorio belongs, if anything, more to the world of music than to that of theatre, in any case left little room for any variable interpretation of its message either by performers or audience, and its 1943 production was nothing more than a last flicker of limelight for Saint Joan.

120 The Role of Joan of Arc

Her disappearance from the stage was not wholly reflected in other forms of communication during the second two years of occupation. As late as 1944, for example, as Allied bombings increased and preparations for invasion were known to be under way, a poster showing her manacled, behind the devastated churches and cathedral of Rouen, declared: 'Les assassins reviennent toujours sur les lieux de leur crime'.[41] But posters are not live theatre, nor, like live theatre, rich in possible ambivalence. It is perfectly understandable not only that Joan's stage career should have been the first to suffer once the tide had turned, but also that in that little Golden Age of French theatre which the Occupation produced, when one might have expected her to dominate the stage, her role appears to have been somewhat restricted. Hindsight is of course of doubtful validity: in the final account we cannot know what she truly represented for individual audiences. The very fact, for instance, that virtually all theatre critics were men must certainly have distorted for us the effect she had on the women who watched her on stage. Yet it is clear that her theatrical role changed between 1940 and 1942 in a discernible way. Always a potentially fickle symbol for those who wished to promote her as the defender of the New Order, she soon became an image of the tradition of resistance. It is only natural that it should have been the theatre, as a living happening with its close dependence on the moods and emotions of the public, that paved the way for Joan's new role after the Liberation as the champion of *l'esprit de la Résistance*.

Notes

1. I wish to acknowledge with gratitude the help of Stuart Ferguson, a postgraduate student currently researching on the theatre of the Occupation. Mr Ferguson did a good part of the primary work for this chapter in various libraries in Paris.
2. See Henri Guillemin, *Jeanne dite 'Jeanne d'Arc'* (1970), p. 240. For all references in text and in notes, the place of publication is Paris unless otherwise specified.
 3. Chanoine P. Glorieux, *Jeanne d'Arc, fille de Dieu* (1941), p. 5.
 4. Joan of Arc Day (8 May) is celebrated on the first Sunday following 7 May.
 5. *Le Miracle de Jeanne* (Tours, 1942), p. 59.
 6. *La Leçon de Jeanne d'Arc*, no publisher, no date [1941].
 7. *Traité de l'étonnement*, 'Les Cahiers du Rhône' (Neuchâtel, 1943)
 8. *A Jeanne d'Arc, sainte héroïne de France inspiratrice de la Résistance française*, Comité Centrale de la France Combattante au Brésil (Rio de Janeiro, 1941), pp. 5, 6. The words are those of Paul Doncoeur, and taken from his pamphlet, *Qui a brûlé Jeanne d'Arc?* (1931).
 9. See the text of the broadcast made by Maurice Schumann on 10 May

1941, *La Voix de la Liberté: Ici Londres, 1940-1944* (1975), p. 228.
  10. See the title page of the published edition, 1941.
  11. Page numbers refer to the 1925 edition of *Sainte Jeanne*.
  12. For example in *Le Matin*, 22 decembre 1940 and *Les Nouveaux Temps*, 6 janvier 1941.
  13. *Joan of Arc in History, Legend and Literature* (Oslo, 1971), p. 195.
  14. See, *inter alia, le Petit Parisien*, 11 mai 1941; *l'Oeuvre*, 11 mai 1941; and *le Matin*, 12 mai 1941.
  15. 'Héroïsme et sainteté dans le message de Péguy', *Temps Présent*, 24 mai 1940.
  16. See, for example, W.D. Halls, *The Youth of Vichy France* (Oxford, 1981), p. 225, and Jean Baudéan, 'Un hérétique: Charles Péguy', *La France Socialiste*, 23 octobre 1943.
  17. 'Péguy et l'âme populaire', *Les Cahiers de Neuilly*, 1st *cahier*, 1942.
  18. Péguy was not a saint, but his wartime fate was curiously akin to that of Joan of Arc, for he was claimed as a champion by both sides: for example, it was during the Vichy adulation of Péguy that the Editions de Minuit produced the booklet *Péguy-Péri* (1944).
  19. For example, Thierry Maulnier, *Spectateur*, 20 septembre 1947; Robert Kemp, *le Monde* 22 septembre 1947 and *Une Semaine dans le Monde*, 27 septembre 1947; Francis Ambrière, *Opéra*, 24 septembre 1947; and Gabriel Marcel, *les Nouvelles Littéraires*, 25 septembre 1947.
  20. The programme is in the Bibliothèque de l'Arsenal, R. Supp. 2290.
  21. See J.M., *Spectateur*, 9 septembre 1947.
  22. See *Paris Soir*, 27 juin 1941.
  23. Whatever the explanation, the misunderstanding has persisted. As recently as 1975, in the important exhibition *Jeanne au Théâtre* held in Orleans, the first performance of Péguy's play, apart from some excerpts briefly seen at the Comédie Française in June 1942, was given as the post-war Hébertot adaptation; see the *Catalogue* of the exhibition, published by the Centre Jeanne d'Arc d'Orléans (Orleans, 1976), Exhibit 88. In Hervé Le Boterf's, *La Vie parisienne sous l'occupation*, II, *Paris la nuit* (1975), pp. 167-8, and in Patrick Marsh's 'Le Théâtre à Paris sous l'occupation allemande', *Revue d'Histoire du Théâtre*, III, 1981 (the entire issue), pp. 287-8, the 1941 production is given as that of the *Mystère* of 1910.
  24. *Comoedia*, 12 juillet 1941.
  25. See Vermorel, 'Avant *Jeanne avec nous*', *la Gerbe*, 8 janvier 1942 and *Comoedia*, 10 janvier 1942.
  26. Vermorel reported on the difficulties encountered in putting on the play, and of finding an actress for the role of Jeanne, in *Comoedia*, 10 janvier 1941. See also the issues of 28 février 1942 and 20 juillet 1942 for information concerning the successive theatres involved in the production.
  27. Quotations taken respectively from Georges Grégory, *Front National*, 28 decembre 1945; J. G.-R., *Arts*, and André Alter, *l'Actualité Théâtrale*, 30 decembre 1945.
  28. *La Force de l'âge* (1960), p. 470.
  29. *Un an de théâtre: 1941-1942* (1942), p. 8.
  30. The *achevé d'imprimer* is 26 octobre 1942. Page numbers refer to this first edition.
  31. This despite Le Boterf's view of Vermorel's Jeanne as, principally, 'une fille des champs, naïve . . . véritable reflet de la paysannerie française', *La Vie parisienne*, II, 194.
  32. Marsh, 'Le Théâtre à Paris', p. 362.
  33. See *la Gerbe*, 8 janvier 1942; *Comoedia*, 10 janvier 1942; and *Opéra*,

19 decembre 1945.

34. See *la Gerbe*, 8 janvier 1942 and 2 février 1941.

35. Marsh, 'Le Théâtre à Paris', p. 292, suggests that the play's run was limited to only three months (*sic*) because the censors had by then understood its real message, and in the *Catalogue* of the 1975 Orleans exhibition (see note 23) the play is described as '[une pièce] qui soulignait au temps de l'occupation allemande le caractère "résistant" de la mission de Jeanne, et qui fut, de ce fait, rapidement interdite' (Exhibit 124).

36. See *le Petit Parisien*, 14 mars 1942.

37. See *Paris Midi*, 7 mai 1942, and the review by Honegger in *Comoedia*, 9 mai 1942.

38. For details of the gala see the preview in *l'Oeuvre*, 6 mai 1942.

39. See, for example, *le Petit Parisien*, 9 mai 1942.

40. See *Comoedia*, 15 mai 1943. There were also single radio broadcasts of René Bruyez's, *Jeanne et la vie des autres*, on 8 May, and a new play on the Joan of Arc theme by Marcelle Mauriette, *La Servante*, on 10 May; see the previews in *Comoedia*, 8 mai 1943.

41. See Pierre Bourget and Charles de Lacretelle, *Sur les murs de Paris et de France, 1939-1945* (1980), p. 166.

7 AMBIGUITIES IN THE FILM *LE CIEL EST A VOUS*

Jeanie Semple

' . . . tu décolles, et puis tu te promènes dans le ciel comme dans un jardin.' Thus Thérèse Gauthier, the middle-aged, provincial housewife who is the heroine of Jean Grémillon's film, *Le Ciel est à vous*,[1] describes her impression of ease and pleasure during her first aeroplane flight. French cinema audiences who saw the film early in 1944 may have envied Thérèse's ability to move freely in the skies above France, and the title does hint at hope, confidence, and even freedom. Nevertheless, no film-maker would have risked any but the most oblique reference to the actual historical situation. On the contrary, the film's ideological credibility was such that it received the honour of a gala performance before Mme Pétain and various government ministers in the town of Vichy on 8 February 1944.[2] That the film's director was suspected of left-wing sympathies, and was in fact a member of the clandestine *Comité de Libération du Cinéma Français*,[3] is only one of the many ambiguities about this film.

Made in 1943, it has as many affinities with the France of the Popular Front as with Vichy France; it was praised highly, even extravagantly, in both the pro-Vichy and the clandestine press (and still arouses strong feeling among film historians): it shows an exemplary Vichy-style wife and mother who is ready to sacrifice her own life and the happiness of her family to a personal ambition which has become an obsession; in the fourth year of the German occupation, it showed French crowds cheering the arrival of a French plane (a Caudron) at an aerodrome bedecked with tricolour flags; it even played a tiny part in the war, since the unusual activities of the hundreds of extras engaged for the scene at Le Bourget airport attracted the attention of the RAF, who subsequently bombed the airport. (The flying sequences were eventually shot at Lyon-Bron airport.)[4]

Even the word 'ciel' is open to more interpretations than already indicated: the film is effectively framed by opening and closing shots of a priest with a group of orphans. A reminder that heaven is attainable by all? A warning that Thérèse's foolhardy exploit may leave her children motherless? And what to make of the shepherd and his flock of sheep who pass the orphans? Another ambiguous symbol, or simply an interesting visual contrast in black and white? In short, the film offers a number of ambiguities, anomalies, inconsistencies, contradictions and paradoxes, that are worth examining more closely.

In many ways, *Le Ciel est à vous* is reminiscent of the France of the mid-1930s, of the Popular Front. To begin with, the title itself would remind the politically aware film-goer of *La Vie est à nous*, the title of the film commissioned by the French Communist party for the election campaign of 1936.[5] Then, the Popular Front Government had emphasised the new opportunities available for sport and leisure, and one of its ministers, Pierre Cot, had been keen to promote aviation as a popular sport.

This promise of aviation for all is echoed in the film itself: Pierre Gauthier offers '*baptêmes de l'air*' to the townspeople; Dr Maulette, president of the aéroclub, asks the Conseil Municipal to vote 50,000 francs for '*propagande aérienne*', while the expression '*aviation populaire*' occurs two or three times during the aéroclub sequences. Even Maulette's rather patronising remark to Pierre that '*une chose comme l'aviation n'a pas besoin que de superchampions. Il faut aussi des obscurs, des sans-grade*' implies that aviation is no longer the privilege of a minority.

Le Ciel est à vous also shares a common theme with Frontist films such as *Le Crime de Monsieur Lange*[6] and *La Belle Équipe*.[7] In the first, workers take over the printing house where they work as a cooperative; and in the second, a group of unemployed friends win 100,000 francs in a lottery and decide to turn a tumbledown riverside house into an open-air café. In both, ordinary people achieve independence and success through hard work, directed towards a common goal, and in both, the characters are seen rooted in their environment, especially their working environment. In the same way, Pierre and Thérèse, an ordinary lower-middle-class couple are fired with enthusiasm for an ideal, and with mutually supportive devotion and loyalty, triumph over all obstacles.

A final link with the 1930s is that the film is based on the story of a real-life woman pilot — Andrée Duyperon, wife of a garage owner from Mont-de-Marsan, who did break a similar solo flight record in 1937, and her achievement was widely circulated in the magazine *Marie-Claire*. And the aviatrix Lucienne Ivry who is portrayed in the film was another record-breaking pilot of that time.

When the film was first shown, reaction in the pro-Vichy press was predictable. Other films had taken different aspects of Vichy ideology, such as the 'return to the land' (*Monsieur des Lourdines*,[8] or the self-sacrificing mother (*Le Voile Bleu*)[9] or the glorious French heritage (*Symphonie Fantastique*).[10] None had managed to synthesise so many as had this story of a hard-working, enterprising, provincial artisan and his wife, portrayed sympathetically and realistically, which ends in a blaze of patriotism and glory.

The tone was set by *Le Film*,[11] which called it the best film made since the armistice ('le film nous apporte un souffle bienfaisant d'idéal et de santé morale; c'est une oeuvre exaltante et émouvante qui . . . montre . . . le rôle de la femme dans un foyer et la beauté de la famille'). Similar sentiments were expressed in *Aujourd'hui*[12] ('véritable épopée de l'esprit d'entreprise, de l'effort persévérant . . . un film exaltant'); in *la Gerbe*[13] 'il faudra être privé de toute sensibilité, de toute chaleur humaine, pour n'être point ému') and in *l'Atelier*[14] ('c'est pur, c'est sain, et ça exalte l'énergie individuelle').

The most interesting comment, however, came from a totally unexpected quarter. François Vinneuil,[15] writing in *Je Suis Partout*,[16] praised Grémillon's fine observation and warm sympathy in a film that was sentimental in the best sense, but went on to spell out a paradox that lies at the heart of this film – that the most 'Vichy' film was made by a man wholly out of sympathy with Vichy ideology ('le piquant de la chose est que ce film des vertus françaises, dont nous n'avons vu depuis trois ans que les absurdes caricatures, ait été réussi par un homme qui se situe, sans aucun doute, aux antipodes de Vichy, parmi les "réfractaires de tempérament" '). Journalists in the clandestine press, often utilising the same expression ('santé morale') found other reasons to praise the film. For *l'Écran Français*,[17] it was a film 'qui sauve l'honneur du cinéma français, qui réussit à faire entendre un cri dont la résonance ne s'éteindra pas . . . des personnages pleines de sève française, de courage authentique, de santé morale, où nous retrouvons une vérité nationale qui ne veut pas et ne peut pas mourir . . .'

The staunchest defender of the film as a call to resistance was Georges Sadoul, who first wrote about it in *Confluences*.[18] He describes Pierre Gauthier as a typical 'French' hero ('un brave type, bricoleur et débrouillard, frondeur surtout à la manière de Gavroche ou d'Artagnan. Cette fronde veut d'abord dire indépendance . . . ') and he praises the genuine patriotism of the film itself ('L'amour de notre patrie bat dans ses simples images, et le spectateur qui le sait sincère et profond, se sent les larmes aux yeux.' After the war, in his *Histoire Générale du Cinéma*, Sadoul quotes part of this review, and adds that ' . . . *Le Ciel est à vous* sonnait alors pour nous comme un appel aux armes',[19] and again in *le Cinéma Français*, he writes that for the cinema audiences on the eve of the Liberation, the Gauthiers had become a symbol of those ordinary middle-class French people who risked their lives 'pour soutenir la résistance armée à l'intérieur du pays . . . cette peinture réaliste d'un certain aspect de l'héroïsme français sonna comme un appel aux armes pour ceux qui comprirent le message'.[20]

To what extent this interpretation was widely accepted by those in the Resistance is less certain, and here it is interesting to compare the vigorous rebuttal by Raymond Borde,[21] in his introduction to Francis Courtade's *Les Malédictions du Cinéma Français.*[22] Nothing, he writes, could be further from the truth:

> Rien n'est plus faux. J'étais à l'époque militant communiste et j'affirme ici solonnellement, qu'il fut ressenti comme un acte de propagande de l'ennemi de classe. Objectivement, il servait les intérêts du Maréchal et toute la Révolution Nationale s'y retrouvait: l'artisan rouspéteur, bien de chez nous, avec son zinc de quatre sous, qui donnait une leçon à l'aviation industrielle; sa femme, pure héroïne dans le ciel de gloire, qui avait les humbles vertus de notre sol immémorial; le travail de fourmi qui magnifiait le métier d'homme . . .

By the early 1970s French attitudes to the Occupation had modified, especially after the watershed of the television film, *Le Chagrin et la Pitié*,[23] in 1971. Attitudes to the cinema of the Occupation were also examined at the conference held at the Cinémathèque de Toulouse in July 1972, which resulted in various papers and articles on Vichy cinema. Jean-Pierre Jeancolas in *Jeune Cinéma*[24] linked the cinema of 1940-4 to traditional French conservative thought ('travail-famille-église-patrie') rather than the 'Parisian' ideology of Brasillach[25] and Rebatet, and denied that *Le Ciel est à vous* could be considered a call to arms.

> Plus personne ne lit dans *Le Ciel est à vous* un 'appel aux armes, mais bien plutôt le ronron d'une France perpetuellement satisfaite. Car enfin ce grand frémissement de drapeaux tricolores à la fin du film évoque autant la France du Maréchal que celle du Tripartisme de 1946 . . .

On the other hand, in an article entitled 'Une société malade de moralite,[26] Jean A. Gili declared that Thérèse Gauthier was not in the least a 'Vichy' heroine ('une femme qui refuse de rester au foyer, qui ne sacrifie pas tout à l'éducation de ses enfants, qui, avec l'aide de son mari, ose affirmer sa personnalité et accomplir l'exploit dont elle se sent capable') and that her real victory was . . . d'avoir vaincu la sottise d'une société qui ne voit dans la femme que l'épouse et la mère entre les quatre murs de son foyer'.

It is at this time that Joseph Daniel, in *Guerre et Cinéma*[27], uses *Le Ciel est à vous* to illustrate how the same film can appeal to opposing ideologies: 'les adversaires du régime . . . monopoliseront à leur profit cette oeuvre au titre prometteur: *Le Ciel est à vous*. Dans le même temps, les partisans de la Révolution nationale ne peuvent que se louer de cette discrète exaltation de valeurs dont ils se veulent les champions'. He adds that this was not an uncommon phenomenon at the time 'pour des raisons opposées, ils applaudissent parfois les mêmes héros, comme ils le font ailleurs pour Jeanne d'Arc ou pour Péguy'.

It should perhaps be pointed out that the appeal of this film remained largely theoretical, for the one point on which film historians agree is that it was not a commercial success. The film's reputation was made in ciné-clubs after the war.

Over the next decade, if one excepts the comments of Raymond Borde, the analysis of possible Vichy elements in this particular film has received decreasing attention in books about the cinema.[28] By the 1980s, a degree of ambiguity is considered both acceptable and inevitable. Jacques Siclier, however, in *La France de Pétain et son Cinéma*, firmly places any ambiguity outside the film itself, in its historical context: 'L'ambiguïté morale de "valeurs nationales" revendiquées à la fois par le pétainisme et par la Résistance vint des circonstances et non – on ne le dira jamais assez – du film lui-même'.[29] While Jean-Pierre Jeancolas, in *Le Cinéma des Français 1929-1944*,[30] states that since film-makers were obliged to walk a tightrope between opposing worlds, a theme like that of human endeavour would be 'récupérable' by both camps. Incidentally, this aura of ambiguity seems to have extended across the Channel to those who wrote about the film in the immediate post-war period.

Roy Fuller, in *The Film in France*,[31] notes that the film was considered 'a glorification of the French spirit and genius', but adds, 'Even if that is debatable, it may be that the public did not care to be reminded of their past glories at a time when they were so helpless.' For *Penguin Film Review*,[32] *Le Ciel est à vous* was 'dull, very solid, and rich in moving emotional scenes', and continues 'one does not know whether the moral of this story is that this mechanic . . . ought to have been content to stay in his own middling station or whether he is a symbol for the popular hero who ought to be allowed to rise as high as he wants to'.

Sight and Sound,[33] however, did opt for the 'pro-Resistance' theory. 'The film exercised a great resistance influence because it illustrates how determination and hard work can attain the seemingly impossible.' This comment is doubly interesting, since the same journalist interviewed Grémillon in Paris a year later, and wrote[34] 'he refused to accept the dictatorship of subject imposed by the German censorship and found his own way of presenting to the French people a picture of their fellow-countrymen which was honest, touching and inspiring', and this might just possibly be a clue as to Grémillon's original intention.

Nevertheless, making a film is a group enterprise, and it is unusual for any one person, even the director, to exert a total influence over the final result. Here again, a closer look at the personalities involved in making this film, reveals the same contradictions and anomalies to be found in the critical attitudes towards the film. To begin with the director, whereas *Le Ciel est à vous* had received accolades from the Vichy regime, his previous film, *Lumière d'Eté*,[35] had, according to Sadoul,[36] almost been banned by that same regime for its pro-communist sympathies. There may have been some justification for their suspicion, since the Catholic 'analyse morale' published by the CCR[37] does describe the film as 'une belle opposition de milieu de travail à un milieu malsain . . . jeune ingénieur vu sympathiquement . . . châtelain sadique'. Immediately after the war, Grémillon went on to make a semi-documentary about the Normandy landings called *Le Six Juin à l'Aube*, which he started in the autumn of 1944. Before the war, however, he had directed three films for ACE, the section of UFA which produced French films with German capital.[38-40]

There was of course nothing reprehensible about working on individual films for ACE/UFA — some of the most talented French directors, writers and actors had done so in the late 1930s. But in the case of Raoul Ploquin, producer of *Le Ciel est à vous*, his involvement with the Nazi state film organisation went deeper; he was director of French production for ACE between 1934 and 1939. Later, in December 1940, he became the first director of COIC,[41] whose objective was to reorganise the entire French cinema industry along corporatist lines.

One of the scriptwriters, Albert Valentin, had also worked for ACE before the war and during the occupation in 1943 had directed *Vie de Plaisir* for Continental, the Paris-based French subsidiary of UFA, which produced 30 films during this period. The other scriptwriter, Charles Spaak had been associated with the pro-communist *Ciné-*

Liberté[42] in the mid-1930s, and had scripted *La Belle Équipe* for Julien Duvivier in 1936. Then, before the war, he too had worked (with Grémillon) on two films for ACE.[43] During the occupation, he wrote scripts for eight films, three of them for Continental (*L'Assassinat du Pere Noël*, *Péchés de Jeunesse* and *Les Caves du Majestic*). He actually completed the script for this last-named while in Fresnes prison. The reason for his arrest early in 1944 remains obscure. Francis Courtade[44] mentions an interesting hypothesis -- that Spaak chose to seek shelter at a time when his activities for Continental might have risked the charge of collaboration later. This would account for the fact that he received preferential treatment during his imprisonment. However, Courtade adds 'mais selon sa veuve, il avait été inquieté pour n'avoir pas dénoncé son frère Claude, actif résistant'.

The cameraman, Louis Page, had worked with Grémillon both before and after *Le Ciel est à vous*, and was known for the characteristic grainy documentary effect he could bring to what were in fact feature films (an ambiguity in itself). He had used this talent to great purpose in 1938, in Spain, working as cameraman for André Malraux, when the latter was making the film version of his novel *Espoir*.

Finally, among the performers, the actor Léonce Corne (Dr Maulette) also appeared in two of the most virulent propaganda films of the occupation period – *Les Corrupteurs*,[45] and *Forces Occultes*[46]; Charles Vanel was openly pro-Vichy[47] while Madeleine Renaud, in a television programme in 1975[48] affirmed that *Le Ciel est à vous* had meant to her 'foi', 'espoir' and 'liberté'.

There are also some ambiguities contained within the character of Thérèse. In 1944, she was seen, both by those for and against the regime, as exalting the role of wife and mother ('pure héroïne dans le ciel de gloire'); since then she is more often seen as having transcended this role and having found fulfilment by breaking free of the confines of home and family. Is she then an anti-heroine, or perhaps even a feminist one?

In dress and general appearance and behaviour, Thérèse is a realistic portrayal of a lower-middle-class provincial housewife and mother of two teenage children, a woman who helps her garage-owner husband in his business, and at one time takes on a temporary job to help with the family budget. This portrayal is in contrast to the real-life aviatrix, Lucienne Ivry, since the actress who plays this role is younger, slimmer and more glamorous. But the very ordinariness of Thérèse would allow audience identification with a new kind of heroine who had begun to appear in the cinema – an ordinary woman, often left on her own, coping with domestic difficulties, or, as a member of one of the caring professions, dealing with other people's problems. Earlier in 1943, Madeleine Renaud had played such a woman, a welfare worker, in Georges Lacombe's, *L'Escalier Sans Fin*. The most popular film of 1942 had been *Le Voile Bleu*, starring Gaby Morlay as a First World War widow who devotes the rest of her life to caring for other people's children. Robert Bresson's first feature film, *Les Anges du Péché* is about the rehabilitation of delinquent girls. Such portrayals mesh with certain aspects of Vichy ideology (motherhood, sef-sacrifice, redemption) but at the same time they mirrored the historical realities of this period, when women had to shoulder additional domestic and other responsibilities, when family life had been disrupted, and when young people were growing up in an atmosphere of insecurity and tension.

The strength and originality of Thérèse is that she demonstrably reconciles the 'domestic' and the 'adventurous' sides of her nature, although, just occasionally, her display of domestic virtues borders on parody. For instance, in the role of conscientious mother, she sets the alarm to wake her every two hours through the night so that she can give her son his cough medecine ('il ne tousse plus, mais enfin le docteur a dit toutes les deux heures, alors je continue'). Or again, when, having safely landed at a French army post in the desert, she accepts a cup of coffee, and the model housekeeper in her can't resist commenting 'Vous direz au cuisinier que son eau n'était pas assez chaude, et le café a perdu un peu de son parfum'. There are good reasons, then, for considering Thérèse as a Vichy heroine (or even a Vichy anti-heroine) since her actions are governed by the words *Travail-Famille-Patrie*, even if she doesn't always give them that order of priority.

For her courage, independence and success, can she also be considered a feminist heroine? There is an illuminating passage half-way through the film. The elder child, Jacqueline, is a gifted pianist, and her music teacher, Monsieur Larchet, tries to persuade the family to let the girl study at the Conservatoire. Thérèse is outraged: 'Monsieur, vous encouragez Jacqueline à abandonner ses études sérieuses pour suivre, Dieu sait dans quelles conditions, une carrière insensée! Vous voyez Jacqueline vivre seule, à Paris? A Montmartre?' and with this she locks the piano – which is sold later to raise funds for Thérèse's flight.

Apart from indicating excessive maternal concern, this highlights another aspect of Thérèse, her attitude to the passionately held ambitions of another person. For Thérèse, independence and fulfilment remain a private matter, a personal issue, and not related to any wider freedom of action for women in general or for her own daughter in particular.

Notes

1. *Le Ciel est à vous*: synopsis and credits.

Pierre and Thérèse Gauthier, who own a garage in the provincial town of Villeneuve, are forced to move when the site of their business is wanted for the construction of an aerodrome. Pierre, who served as mechanic to the French flyer Guynemer during the First World War, becomes more and more fascinated with flying and spends most of his free time at the aeroclub, to the exasperation of his wife. One day, the president of the club dares her to take her 'baptême de l'air', and she is won over. She learns to fly, and the couple use all their savings to buy a plane of their own. Next, Thérèse decides to attempt the world record for a long-distance, non-stop flight by a woman pilot. She breaks the record, and returns in triumph to Villeneuve and her family.

Producer	Raoul Ploquin
Director	Jean Grémillon
Story	Albert Valentin
Adaptation	Charles Spaak
Photography	Louis Page
Thérèse Gauthier	Madeleine Renaud
Pierre Gauthier	Charles Vanel
Monsieur Larchet	Jean Debucourt
Madame Brissard	Raymonde Vernay
Dr Maulette	Léonce Corne
Jacqueline	Anne-Marie Labaye
Claudinet	Michel Francois
Lucienne Ivry	Anne Vandénne

The film was begun on 31 May 1943 and first shown, in Paris, on 2 February 1944. Quotations from the dialogue are from the script, published by L'Avant-Scène du Cinéma, November 1981.

2. *Le Film*, 19 février 1944.
3. George Sadoul, *Histoire Générale du Cinéma* (Denoel, 1954). vol. 6, p. 56.
4. Henri Agel, *Jean Grémillon* (Seghers, 1969), p. 70.
5. Directed by Jean Renoir, with script supervision by Paul Vaillant-Couturier.
6. 1935. Directed by Jean Renoir, script by Jacques Prévert. Many actors from the left-wing October Group appeared in the film.
7. 1936. Directed by Julien Duvivier, script by Charles Spaak.
8. 1942. Directed by Pierre de Hérain, Pétain's stepson; from the novel by Alphonse de Châteaubriant.
9. 1942. Directed by Jean Stelli. One of the most popular and successful films of this period.
10. 1941. Directed by Christian-Jaque, for Continental. The film starred Jean-Louis Barrault as Hector Berlioz, and other characters were Victor Hugo, Eugène Delacroix, Prosper Merimée and Alexandre Dumas.
11. *Le Film*, 5 février 1944.
12. *Aujourd'hui*, 27 janvier 1944.
13. *La Gerbe*, 3 février 1944.
14. *L'Atelier* 5 février 1944.
15. Pseudonym of Lucien Rebatet, journalist and film critic, imprisoned after the Liberation for his collaborationist activities.
16. February 1944. Rebatet-Vinneuil devoted two articles to this film.
17. Supplement to the clandestine *Lettres Françaises*.

18. *Confluences* March/April 1944, under the pseudonym Claude Jacquier.
19. Sadoul, *Histoire Générale du Cinéma*, pp. 51-3.
20. Georges Sadoul, *Le Cinéma français* (Flammarion, 1962), p. 99.
21. Director of the Cinémathèque de Toulouse.
22. Francis Courtade, *Les Malédictions du Cinéma Français* (Moreau, 1978) p. 14.
23. Directed by Marcel Ophuls, produced by André Harris and Alain de Sédouy. The film is subtitled 'Chronique d'une ville Française sous l'Occupation'.
24. *Jeune Cinéma*, no. 65, October 1972, p. 40.
25. Film historian, and editor of *Je Suis partout*, executed after the Liberation for collaborationist activities.
26. *Ecran 72*, no. 8, 1972, p. 9.
27. Joseph Daniel, *Guerre et Cinéma* (Armand Colin, 1972), pp. 200-1.
28. Hervé Leboterf, *La Vie Parisienne sous l'Occupation* (France-Empire, 1974-5); Paul Léglise, *Histoire de la Politique du Cinéma Français* (Pierre L'Herminier, 1977).
29. Jacques Siclier, *La France de Pétain et son Cinéma* (Henri Veyrier, 1981), pp. 202-7.
30. Jean-Pierre Jeancolas, *Le Cinéma des Français 1929-1944* (Stock, 1983), p. 331.
31. *The Film in France*, Pendulum Publications, 1946, p. 12.
32. *Penguin Film Review*, no. 8, January 1949, p. 67.
33. *Sight and Sound*, Spring 1946, French Cinema during the Occupation, by Hazel Hackett, p. 2.
34. *Sight and Sound*, Summer 1947.
35. *Lumière d'Eté*, 1942, script by Jacques Prévert, photography by Louis Page. The October/November 1984 National Film Theatre brochure calls the film 'a probing study of society in dissolution, centring on a collection of decadent, lost souls holed up in a mountain hotel, with the silence broken only by massive blastings from a nearby dam construction'.
36. Sadoul, *Histoire Générale du Cinéma*, p. 53.
37. Centrale Catholique du Cinéma et de la Radio.
38. 1936 *Pattes de Mouche;* 1937 *Gueule d'Amour;* 1938 *L'Etrange Monsieur Victor*.
39. Alliance Cinématographique Européenne.
40. Universum Film Aktiengesellschaft.
41. Comité d'Organisation de l'Industrie Cinématographique.
42. Created in 1936, *Ciné-Liberté* grouped together people working in all branches of the cinema industry, as well as left-wing intellectuals. It had close links with the French Communist Party. Charles Spaak had given lectures to members.
43. *Gueule d'Amour* and *L'Etrange Monsieur Victor*.
44. Francis Courtade, *Les Malédictions du Cinéma français* (Alain Moreau, 1978), p. 225.
45. *Les Corrupteurs*, 1942, directed by Pierre Ramelot. According to *Le Film*, 12 septembre 1942, the film showed 'le rôle néfaste que les Juifs exerçaient en France, avant cette guerre, grâce à la presse, la radio et le cinéma, dont ils tenaient toutes les rênes'.
46. *Forces Occultes*, 1943, directed by Jean Mamy. The film is both anti-Freemason and anti-Semitic. Jean Mamy was executed after the Liberation.
47. Claude Beylie, 'Réévaluations', *Ecran 72*, no. 8, p. 4.
48. *Le Cinéma Français par ceux qui l'ont fait*, directed by Armand Panigel for France-Région-3, Episode 8, 5 May 1975.

8 CATHOLICISM UNDER VICHY: A STUDY IN DIVERSITY AND AMBIGUITY

Bill Halls

Catholicism under Vichy was not a monolithic phenomenon. It represented a wide variety of views that evolved over time, or failed to do so, and that were often equivocal. This chapter highlights the strong initial position of the Church and the decline in its influence, and then indicates the diversity and ambiguity in the attitudes of what might be described as 'official' Catholicism.

Alone among the institutions of pre-war France the Catholic Church survived the defeat of 1940 virtually intact. In the coming months politically and socially, culturally and spiritually, it was to demonstrate its power. The armed forces had been beaten or immobilised; the nation's political fabric had been torn asunder, and Parliament was quickly rendered impotent; trade unions were in disarray; the state education system was thrown into confusion. Yet the institutional framework of the Church had survived, perhaps even strengthened by the débâcle, if only because generally the clergy had not fled before the invader. Small wonder, therefore, that the Germans were apprehensive of Catholicism. For the future police overseers of France, the SS, Catholicism represented an ideological adversary in the same way as Freemasonry and Jewry. It was a force to be reckoned with, sustained by a creed far more venerable than Nazism, run by a Hierarchy commanding an absolute obedience and with world-wide contacts. The Church controlled by far the largest proportion of organised French youth; among 'Black France', the industrial and provincial bourgeoisie, it wielded massive influence; peasants and workers alike were aware of its power. Throughout the Occupation its activities were under constant German surveillance.

As in 1870, defeat in battle had brought about an upsurge of religious feeling among Frenchmen. The churches had not been so full for years; sin, retribution and repentance were the themes of many sermons. Prayer was in fashion — for families to be reunited, for the million and a half prisoners of war to be swiftly released; later, women prayed for their menfolk deported to Germany and even for husbands who fought under the wrong flag on the Eastern front. Processions, pilgrimages and retreats became the vogue. Such revivalism had political overtones. In 1940 most Catholics — and many Frenchmen — believed that the Third Republic had failed because it was corrupt; socialists and communists had promoted materialism; democratic institutions had not been able to withstand the crisis. The Church could redress the balance. France had lost the war, but could yet achieve salvation through the Marshal. Cardinal Gerlier's remark, which he lived to regret, that 'today France is Pétain and Pétain is France', epitomised a national sentiment.

Thus Catholic leaders took the initiative in acknowledging the authoritarian power of the Marshal. They rejected arguments against the validity of the regime. How could it be invalid when there was a Papal Nuncio at Vichy and a duly accredited French ambassador to the Vatican? Vichy constituted the 'pouvoir établi'. Some went further: a dozen bishops shared the view of archbishop Chollet of Cambrai that Pétain was the 'autorité légitime'. In any case the usual practice of the Church was to recognise any *de facto* government. 'Nous referons chrétiens nos frères': when in July 1940 Cardinals Gerlier and Suhard met in Paris their agenda was the regeneration of France, beginning with education.[1]

Reciprocally, the regime eagerly accepted Catholic political and social support. The new 'doctrine' of *travail, famille, patrie* on which Vichy based its policies accorded admirably with views the Church had long expounded: 'ces trois mots sont les nôtres', declared Gerlier in another injudicious remark.[2] Thus the higher clergy advised on legislation on the family, youth, education and employment.

At the same time prominent Catholic laymen were drawn into the political and administrative machine. Two ardent believers, Alibert and Chevalier achieved ministerial rank, and measures not displeasing to the higher clergy followed quickly. As Minister of Justice, Alibert, a recent convert, instituted a review of all naturalisations since 1927, which made stateless some 15,000 people, including 6,000 Jews. In October he promulgated the first Statut des Juifs, which excluded Jews from certain civil service posts and presaged action against those in the liberal professions. The very broad categorisation of a Jew — later to include anyone with at least two Jewish grandparents — swept many into the net. There is no evidence that this legislation was introduced at German instigation. Those Catholics who rationalised their anti-Semitism by 'the guilt for the death of Christ argument' approved the inhumane laws by their silence. Nor did they protest at the other target of Alibert, Freemasonry, where bitterness between the Church and the Lodges was long-standing, and the law of August 1940 abolishing secret organisations was welcomed. A devout Catholic, Bernard Fay, administrator of the Bibliothèque Nationale, aided by the no less Catholic Vallery-Radot, was given the task of rooting out from public life some 15,000 masonic dignitaries. These new tribunes vetted all public appointments and, according to one Resistance organisation that threatened reprisals, the posts declared vacant were reallocated so as to 'favoriser certains catholiques, traîtres à la patrie'.[4] Fay moved in collaborationist circles, a somewhat rare occurrence for Catholics in 1940.

Jacques Chevalier was a man of a different stamp from Alibert – he never faltered, for example, in his allegiance as a philosopher to his master Henri Bergson, a Jew. An academic, dean of the faculty of letters at Grenoble, he was also the godson of Pétain. He was placed in charge of education. Devoutly Catholic, variously described as 'a proselyte, a sort of Knight Templar, a Leaguing monk,' and more ironically as 'a great believer, a predestined creature', in a short while he pushed through a number of measures favourable to the Church: subsidies, through the communes, for Catholic schools, and the reintroduction of the 'devoirs envers Dieu' into the State school curriculum and of religious education as an optional subject. However, neither of these key Catholics who ventured into politics lasted for long in their two ministries.

Other notable Catholics who implemented policies favourable to the Church took up administrative posts, although eventually most were ousted or resigned as the regime willy-nilly became more favourable to the Germans. They were particularly prominent in youth affairs. Dunoyer de Segonzac, the Catholic cavalry officer who had created the École des Cadres at Uriage, took to the *maquis* at the end of 1942. Lamirand, the enthusiastic but politically naïve Secretary General for Youth, who had sought to protect Jewish scouts and in November 1942 had urged Pétain to flee to North Africa, resigned in February 1943. General de La Porte du Theil, a Catholic ex-scout commissioner, who had founded the Chantiers de la Jeunesse, was arrested and deported by the Germans in January 1944. Likewise Valentin, director of the Ligue des Anciens Combattants, onetime president of the Association Catholique de la Jeunesse Française (ACJF) in Lorraine and an intimate of Cardinal Gerlier, had finally broken with Vichy in June 1943. On the contrary, Robert Garric, the Catholic founder of the Équipes Sociales after the First World War, held his post as head of the Secours National throughout the Occupation and even continued after the Liberation.

Nevertheless, there were other Catholics who, like Alibert, played a more sinister role. Xavier Vallat, a strong Catholic, became the first head of the Commissariat Général aux Questions juives. He it was who told the SS officer Dannecker, charged with the execution of the 'final solution' in France, 'I am an older anti-Semite than you; I could be your grandfather in that respect.' However, by February 1942 Vallat could no longer hide his hostility to the Germans and resigned.

Appraisal of such a cross-section of lay Catholic notables who achieved high political or administrative office and who carried out policies favourable to the Church thus reveals their diminishing direct influence as Vichy became increasingly enmeshed in the German war effort.

The same decline in the power to influence events, but perhaps with greater compliance in pro-German policies, is noticeable in those cultural and spiritual forces embodied in the higher clergy and particularly in the Hierarchy, as indeed they become more political. Among the clerical intelligentsia, both academic and theological, the rift deepens. Likewise, as the bishops are led inexorably into positions incompatible with their pastoral and spiritual role, there is disarray, although a majority, including three out of the four diocesan cardinals, cling desperately to loyalty to Pétain as their rock of salvation, and in so doing lose pastoral authority.

The 'official' Catholic higher culture was represented in the Instituts Catholiques, the Church's 'universities'. Like Catholic schools, these institutions of higher education had eventually been granted subsidies. A detailed study of what influence they exerted and the stance they maintained towards Vichy has yet to be made, but certain indications are already clear, from the actions of those that ran them.

Thus the rector of the Institut Catholique of Toulouse, Bruno de Solages, was as outspoken as his diocesan, Cardinal Saliège. Never *persona grata* at Vichy, he had been forbidden to lecture at Uriage, a prohibition he disobeyed.[5] His attitude was uncompromising. In June 1942 speaking at Montauban before the mass Jewish deportations had begun, he asserted that racism and communism were both unacceptable and that drawing a distinction between Jews and 'Aryans' was, and always had been, contrary to Christian teaching.[6] His speech inaugurating the academic year 1943-4 contained a clear allusion to the Service du Travail Obligatoire (STO). God rather than man must be obeyed, and the moral law had precedence over man-made laws. It would appear that the library of the Institut became a centre of intellectual resistance both to Vichy and the Germans.

About the Institut at Lyon there is little information. However, in June 1941 a group located in the theology faculty of the Institut are reported as having drafted a document opposing a second Statut des Juifs.[7] This document was cited by Mgr Guerry in his post-war apologia for the Church (*L'Église sous l'Occupation*, Paris, 1947) who gives the impression that this written protest was made public. In fact, the original has never been discovered.

The Institut Catholique at Lille – 'la Catho', as it was known – comprised 1,400 students, some of whom became deeply involved in the Resistance. There were links with the pre-war Parti Démocrate Populaire, the advocate of social Catholicism and industrial harmony, which seized the opportunity through the Resistance to re-enter the political arena, and refused to accept the Marshal's 'new order'. Indeed, at Lille the rift between Pétainists and the rest ran deep. On the one side were ranged Cardinal Liénart, bishop of Lille, and, within the Institut itself Eugène Duthoit, a theologian of note, then president of the Catholic organisation Semaines sociales; both remained implacably loyal to the Marshal to the bitter end. On the other side were ranged teachers at the Institut such as Louis Blanckaert, who became active in the Resistance network, La Voix du Nord. In 1941 a group of law professors at the Institut wrote to Mgr Dutoit, archbishop of Arras, stating how deeply their consciences had been troubled by his pastoral letter (22 December 1941) in which, after Montoire, he had advocated collaboration on the basis of a 'free and fair desire for understanding'. This they followed up in October 1942 by a note to Liénart euphemistically termed 'some technical considerations concerning the problems of government'. It asked whether Christians owed a duty of obedience to a government 'which must be considered without legitimacy'.[8] Liénart contented himself with replying somewhat tartly that their implied proposition was unacceptable.

There is no indication that the attitude of the Institut Catholique at Angers was anything other than acceptance of the *status quo*, and even perhaps with a nuance of collaboration. One instance may perhaps exemplify the official viewpoint. By November 1942 the unsavoury moral reputation of Bonnard, then Minister of Education, and his pro-German views were widely known. Nevertheless on 24 November the rector of the Institut wrote thanking him for the subsidies that had been granted, incidentally illegally styling his institution as 'L'Université catholique de l'Ouest'. After a ritual obeisance to Pétain as the 'vénéré chef de l'Etat' and to Laval as head of the government, he assured Bonnard that 'the University of Angers is, in this great moment in our history [the Germans had just occupied the whole of France], as faithful and devoted as before to its legitimate leaders'. He ended with a flourish, 'You know, Minister, how much I personally like and admire your work, following the example of Cardinal Baudrillart, my master.'[9]

The evocation of Baudrillart, rector of the Institut Catholique in Paris, the largest Catholic institution of higher education, is significant. The almost senile cardinal was a fervent anti-communist, a devoted admirer of Pétain, having even published a book about him, *La Voix du Chef*. But he had also gone further than anyone down the road to collaboration, on which he had published articles in *La Gerbe* (21 novembre 1940), the virulently anti-Semitic and pro-Nazi organ of Alphonse de Chateaubriant, and in *Le Nouvelliste* (Lyon, 10 août 1941). Chateaubriant and Baudrillart were also associated together in the Groupe Collaboration. The cardinal also gave his patronage to the Légion Antibolchévique. When Déat launched this 'legion of the damned' this prelate turned crusader is alleged to have exclaimed, 'Cette chevalerie délivrera le tombeau du Christ' — presumably by capturing Moscow.[10] He was aided and abetted by a friend and colleague in the Institut, Paul Lesourd, who founded the Catholic collaborationist journal, *Voix françaises*.

After Baudrillart's death in late 1942 Mgr Beaussart, auxiliary bishop to Cardinal Suhard in Paris, who for a while had liaised on the Church's behalf with Bonnard at the Ministry of Education, was canvassed as a possible successor. Although wide of the mark, the president of the Comité Antibolchévique wrote to Bonnard signifying that the staff at the Institut Catholique wanted none of Beaussart, whom they stigmatised as 'Anglophile, Gaullist and anti-collaborationist'.[11] Bonnard, whose esteem for Beaussart was great,[12] did not accept this assessment but nevertheless agreed to the appointment of another, Mgr Calvet.

From the foregoing it is clear that one important segment of 'official' Catholic culture, as represented by its faculties of higher education, was deeply divided. What is remarkable is the extremes represented in it, ranging from active Resistance to committed pro-Nazism.

The spectrum of attitudes was not so broad among those Frenchmen who wielded ultimate spiritual and pastoral authority in the Church.[13] The prelate who most consistently spoke out against certain more extreme measures of the Germans and Vichy, such as the persecution of the Jews and the compulsory conscription of youth for work in Germany was undoubtedly Cardinal Saliège, archbishop of Toulouse. It

Catholicism Under Vichy

is said that only his parlous state of health prevented the Germans from deporting him. On the other hand, the diocesan bishops included none who sought a total German victory. Indeed at the Liberation, from the 87 dioceses spread over the 17 ecclesiastical provinces or archbishoprics of which France was made up, only four of the Hierarchy were deposed from their sees because of their conduct during the Occupation: Villerabel, archbishop of Aix; Dutoit, archbishop of Arras; Auvity, bishop of Mende; and Beaussart, auxiliary bishop of Paris.

Yet the Hierarchy was undoubtedly responsible for the disarray in which the Church found itself in 1944. A large share of that responsibility must be borne by the three other pastoral cardinals: Suhard (Paris), Liénart (Lille), and Gerlier (Lyon). All had incurred the hostility of the Gaullists and the Resistance. Suhard had welcomed Pétain to Paris when the Marshal officially visited the capital after the bombings of 1944; he had later officiated at the funeral of the assassinated collaborator, Philippe Henriot. Thus he was told in no uncertain terms that he would not be welcome at the Te Deum attended by de Gaulle sung in Notre-Dame after the Liberation. Likewise, when the general visited his native Lille and attended a service, Liénart, very cavalierly, had not greeted him at the church door, on the pretext that he was only the head of a *provisional* government. The personal coolness was mutual. As for Gerlier, he complained that he was being persecuted by the liberators for his sins of omission. How 'Resistance-minded' they were is a matter of dispute: French Catholics have found justification for both their action and inaction. The outsider would tend to agree that all three suffered from 'compromis, attentisme, mutisme'. A tract circulating in Northern France in mid-1942 on 'what Christian workers expect in vain from the cardinals and bishops of France' sums up the situation: they 'approve of everything by their silence'.

Collectively all prelates shunned extremes because of their unswerving devotion to Pétain. But as the hapless Marshal became increasingly a tool in German hands they failed, with some honourable exceptions, to disengage themselves. Their view of the world was naturally authoritarian. Thus Mgr Harzcouet, bishop of Chartres, wrote to congratulate Bonnard on being appointed minister of education: 'I have reason to be assured that the Education ministry will be in good hands, which will preserve us not only from the sectarianism of former times, *but also from democratic weaknesses*.'[14] (My emphasis.)

All bishops supported the abolition of Freemasonry, from whose members they had suffered under the Third Republic; many tolerated the persecution of the Jews, from whom they had not directly suffered at all. Thus Mgr Caillot, bishop of Grenoble, preaching an Easter sermon in 1941, condemned not only the Lodges but 'that other, equally harmful power, the *métèques*, of which the Jews are a particularly conspicuous specimen'. Two years later his Easter homily exhorted his seminarists – and indeed all young Frenchmen – to accept the STO. Mgr Auvity of Mende forbade his priests to act as chaplains to the Resistance and likewise cajoled his seminarists to depart for Germany. Mgr Dutoit of Arras protested in January 1944 against the 'bandits' (sc. maquisards) 'terrorising' the countryside and issued a solemn warning against propaganda that might lead to civil war.

The conduct of other ecclesiastics was not consistent. Mgr Delay of Marseille, who spoke out against the anti-Jewish measures in 1942, nevertheless later officiated at a memorial service for Henriot. As late as 1943 Serrand, bishop of St-Brieuc and Tréguier, an 'ancien combattant' mentioned five times in despatches, published a pastoral letter restating the regime's legitimacy and condemning those who asserted the Marshal was playing a double game – such duplicity would be unworthy of the Head of State.

In one respect the patriotism of at least half the bishops should have been beyond suspicion. Out of the 96 prelates no less than 51 were veterans of the First world war. Liénart and Gerlier held the Médaille Militaire. Nevertheless, it was estimated that the extreme Gaullists had a 'hit list' of 23 bishops marked out for 'épuration' on grounds of lack of patriotism. This sprang from the declaration by the Assembly of Cardinals and Archbishops of 24 July 1941, which promised 'loyalisme sans inféodation' to the 'pouvoir établi'.

The same declaration had enjoined Catholics not to indulge in politics: the watchword was to be national unity. There followed a honeymoon period for the Church, in which it notched up solid advantages. However after the return of Laval in April 1942 it faced hard choices. That summer the Hierarchy was forced to take up a position on racism. The following spring the problem of the STO arose, and what should be the attitude towards the Resistance. The injunction to the rank and file to avoid politics became an impossible condition: they were faced with many quasi-political choices every day. It was at this point that the princes of the Church failed to give an unambiguous lead. Instead they apportioned blame. The declaration of the Assembly of Cardinals and Archbishops of 12 February 1943 was not pastoral but political. The Germans were condemned for conscripting young Frenchmen; the Allies were castigated for the harsh bombing of French cities;

and the Resistance for the continued acts of 'terrorism'. For the first time the authority of Pétain was not invoked, but the theme was rather unity in the common suffering.

Such negativism began to cause the Hierarchy to lose all credibility. Catholics, like other young Frenchmen, turned towards de Gaulle and the Resistance: this was where unity and salvation lay. How the problems that arose were tackled can best be studied through the personality and actions of the three cardinals.

Suhard, archbishop of Paris, was perhaps the least complex character.[15] A man of humble origins, lacking the diplomatic finesse of Gerlier and the charisma of Liénart, in 1940 he had only newly taken over the see of Paris. His interests were indeed largely pastoral, and if he compromised himself it was for the sake of others. One of his main concerns was to secure the future of Catholic schools. He shunned politics: he hesitated to sit on the Conseil National on the grounds that this would be a political act. He was not averse to negotiating with Abetz to secure the release of priests in the Occupied Zone who had fallen foul of the Germans. Through Rhodain, Chaplain General for prisoners and Frenchmen working in Germany, he wrung some advantages for those so exiled. The secret mission of the priests he sent to minister to them as fellow-workers was the genesis of the post-war worker-priest movement.[16]

Gerlier was a man of a different stamp. Given his unswerving loyalty to Pétain, he did not deserve the reputation the Germans gave him, that he was not the 'Primat des Gaulles' but the 'Primat de de Gaulle'. The cross he had to bear was the persecution of the Jews, and what measures he should and could have taken to mitigate their suffering. His failing was his credulity: he could not believe the Marshal would be a party to atrocities. A lawyer by training, he remained for a long time insensitive to the moral standpoint. Before the war he had condemned the Nuremberg racial laws, but had nevertheless maintained that there was a 'Jewish question' in France. Indeed he had raised the problem on 31 August 1940, long before Alibert's Statut des Juifs, at a meeting of the Hierarchy — perhaps an indication that he anticipated measures being taken against the Jews. He nevertheless protested against the living conditions for foreign Jews in the Gurs internment camp; he also urged his friend, Valentin, to see that Jewish ex-servicemen were not stripped of their rights. He may have protested to Pétain in September 1941, when the Marshal visited Lyon, against the manner in which the second Statut des Juifs was being applied. In January 1942 he warned Christians not to harbour animosity against the Jews, although, he went on, 'in certain respects the Jewish problem concerns the State'. The reading of the fourth and fifth *Cahiers du Témoignage Chrétien*,[17] published clandestinely in the spring of 1942 (which are devoted to a condemnation of racism and anti-Semitism) does not appear to have aroused his conscience.

However, the round-up of Jews in Paris and Lyon that summer did summon up action. Gerlier intervened to help Jews in the Lyon area, although as Abbé Glasberg makes clear with some acerbity, he was initially less than helpful in that priest's efforts to save Jewish children from deportation. It is likely that at this stage Gerlier remained ignorant of, or blind to, the horrible fate that awaited Jews at the end of their journey into darkness.

By then, however, other Christian voices had been raised. On 22 July 1942 the Assembly of Cardinals and Archbishops in the occupied zone spoke out. On 23 August Saliège issued his solemn protest: 'Jews are men and women. Everything is not permitted against them . . . They are our brothers.' Théas, bishop of Montauban, followed: 'All men, Aryan or non-Aryan, are brothers because they have been created by God.' On 6 September, it was Gerlier's turn. In a markedly restrained manner he defended the 'inalienable rights of the human person', but added, excusing the regime, 'We do not forget that for the French authorities a problem has to be resolved and we gauge the difficulties the government has to face.' Although he partly redeemed himself in subsequent months by urging priests and nuns to hide as many Jews as possible, unfortunately his intervention was too modest and too late. Ambiguity and indecisiveness, coupled with a modicum of blindness and prejudice, appear to characterise his comportment. He acted more as a local archdeacon might have done, rather than as the good pastor, the spiritual leader of all Frenchmen.

Cardinal Liénart of Lille was the natural interlocutor for the other great issue of conscience that confronted leaders in the Church, the deportation of young men for forced labour.[18] It posed questions of patriotism as well as of the right Christian course of conduct. It was from the Northern industrial areas that many young men would be conscripted. Trade-union leaders and the young Catholic workers, the Jocistes, looked to Liénart for guidance.

The STO had been formally imposed in September 1942, but it was not until February 1943, when various year-groups began to be called up, that matters came to a head. Théas, bishop of Montauban, and Gerlier had already condemned the violation of natural rights when Liénart gave his first advice to young people at Roubaix on 15 March

1943. The text of his message has not been discovered, although the collaborationist press reported it as an injunction to obey the law. The incensed Jocistes demanded an audience of the cardinal. According to one member of the delegation, Roger Bailleul, they did not mince their words: 'Vous savez ce que l'on pense de vous dans les entreprises; on dit que "le Cardinal, c'est un vendu" . . . Liénart fait son petit Baudrillart.'[19]

The reproach may have induced Liénart to speak out again in Lille a week later. This time his message has been preserved, but for many it remained ambiguous. For the first time Christians were to be allowed to follow the dictates of their own conscience. It would be no sin to disobey the call-up, but, if they felt it their duty to share the fate of their fellows, esteeming that theirs was an apostolic mission that they had to fulfil by going, they should comply. Liénart, whilst allowing disobedience, showed extreme reluctance to dissent from what he still conceived of as Pétain's good pleasure. Many, reading between the lines, found it difficult to believe the cardinal was advocating more than spiritual resistance to the STO. However, for a while his words were well received in London.

Liénart, who was also Président of the Assembly of Cardinals and Archbishops, did not settle the argument among Catholics. Not only Catholic workers but also the Catholic bourgeoisie, who saw their sons snatched away from them, were involved. Albert Gortais, of the ACJF, came out against compliance, as did Catholic students generally: for him, rendering unto Caesar what was Caesar's was all very well, he declared, but Caesar was not Vichy, which was a mere transmission belt for the Germans. Jocistes were divided: some complied, and alleviated materially the fate of their comrades in Germany; others went into hiding or joined the Resistance. The Catholic scouts were for passive acceptance, influenced by their chaplain general, Father Forestier. Those in the Catholic student movement, such as Domenach and Dru, set up in Lyon a Comité Interfacultés to help student 'draft-dodgers', the so-called 'réfractaires'.

In their Easter message of 1943 the bishops said nothing of the theology of resistance to oppressive and unjust laws, but gave the impression that compliance was the laudable course, although the advice they had requested from a Jesuit theologian, Mgr Courbe, ran counter to this. Later Mgr Caillot of Grenoble (in the *Semaine religieuse*, Grenoble, 12 August 1943) was even more categorical:

There is a clear-cut attitude to be taken, one that is really manly,

French, Christian . . . in imitating Christ himself as he took up his cross to carry it to the very end, a means of personal sanctification, of apostolate for others, of reparation and redemption for France.

Later, when there was question of extending the scope of STO laws to women and girls, the cardinals and archbishops issued another statement criticising the proposed measure. But the fact that it criticised the proposal not on any grounds of justice, but on the moral dangers that might arise, aroused the wrath of Saliège who wrote to Liénart complaining that references in the document to Allied 'terrorism' were one-sided, the question of conscience was not tackled, and, although allusion was made to 'injustices' there was no mention made of the low wages earned by workers, the evils of the black market and the depredations of war profiteers. Liénart brushed aside these reproaches and fastened on a procedural point in his reply.[20]

Since by then the Church was the only institution, apart from the Resistance itself, that could stand up to the exactions of Laval and the Germans, Liénart's failure to give the young, Christian and non-Christian, a clear lead was disastrous. Evasion, ambiguity and weak compromise characterised his attitude.

What may one conclude regarding the 'official' forces of Catholicism, political and social, cultural and spiritual during four tumultuous years? That they were poorly represented by their protagonists appears self-evident. It cannot be emphasised enough that attitudes among the lower clergy and the rank-and-file laity were vastly different from those of their leaders. By and large those of the latter failed to evolve because they were rooted in prejudices that harked back to the separation of Church and State and Dreyfus, and perhaps even to the great Revolution itself. The grievances of the inter-war period still rankled. In the new Ralliement that Vichy stood for, the leading figures mainly sought advantages for the Church, blind to the fact that in the event of a German victory, all such advances would be swept away, and they with them. As the war took a course, from about mid-1942 onwards, that turned away from a German victory and thus against the possibility of Vichy's own survival, Catholic opinion began to diverge, with its leaders either renouncing power or becoming ever more isolated from their flock. If, in particular, the prelates had been typical of all Catholics, at the Liberation the very credibility of the Church in France as a great religious institution might well have been at stake.

Notes

NB: AN = Archives Nationales; AD = Archives Départementales. The following basic texts should be consulted:

1. *Eglises et chrétiens dans la Deuxième Guerre mondiale. La région Rhône-Alpes*. Actes du Colloque de Grenoble, 1976, publiés sous la direction de Xavier de Montclos, Lyon, 1978. (Henceforth, *Actes: Grenoble*.)
2. *Eglises et chrétiens pendant la Seconde Guerre mondiale dans le Nord-Pas de Calais*. Actes du Colloque de Lille, 1977, publiés dans *La Revue du Nord*, nos. 237 et 238, avril-juin et juillet-septembre 1978, Lille (Henceforth, *Actes: Lille*.)
3. *Eglises et chrétiens dans la Deuxième Guerre mondiale. La France*. Actes du Colloque de Lyon, 1978, publiés sous la direction de Xavier de Montclos, Lyon, 1982. (Henceforth: *Actes: Lyon*.)

1. For a discussion of the legitimacy of Vichy, cf. Renée Bédarida, *Les Armes de l'Esprit. Témoignage Chrétien, 1941-1944* (Paris, 1977), pp. 15-16.
2. Quoted in J. Duquesne, *Les Catholiques français sous l'Occupation* (Paris, 1966), p. 44. Although superseded by works that have appeared since, Duquesne's work is still the best volume on Catholicism over the period.
3. Cf. M.R. Marrus and R.O. Paxton, *Vichy France and the Jews* (New York, 1981), *passim*.
4. AN F. 17. 13346.
5. H.R. Kedward, *Resistance in Vichy France* (Oxford, 1978), p. 25.
6. Marrus and Paxton, *Vichy France*, p. 275 note.
7. *Actes: Lyon*, p. 288.
8. *Actes: Lille*, p. 594.
9. AN F. 17. 13342. Letter from François Vincent, recteur, to Bonnard, Angers, 24 November 1942.
10. He also declared that it was 'the time of a new crusade'. Cf. Duquesne, *Les Catholiques français*, p. 169.
11. AN F. 17. 13344. Letter from the Président du Comité d'Action anti-bolchévique to Bonnard, Minister of Education, Paris, 18 July 1942.
12. When Mgr Beaussart gave up his post as liaison between the Ministry of Education and the Church, Bonnard thought it worth the trouble to write to Cardinal Liénart, as President of the Assembly of Cardinals and Archbishops, on 16 December 1942, regretting Beaussart's displacement by Mgr Chappoulie. Cf. AN F. 17. 13390. File: Enseignement libre. After the Liberation the view officially taken of Beaussart was that he had been too favourable to Doriot's PPF. Cf. A. Latreille, *De Gaulle, la Libération et l'Eglise catholique* (Paris, 1978). This book has many illuminating sidelights on the comportment of the bishops during the Occupation.
13. For much of what follows I am deeply indebted to the three Colloquia cited above.
14. AN F. 17. 13344. Letter to Bonnard dated Chartres, 19 April, 1942.
15. For an appreciation of Suhard, cf. Cardinal Suhard, *Vers une Eglise en état de mission*, présenté par Olivier de la Brosse OP, (Paris, 1965).
16. Cf. E. Poulat, *Naissance des Prêtres-Ouvriers* (Tournai (Belgium), 1965), *passim*.
17. Now republished in facsimile, Paris, 1980. The issues referred to are: Cahiers IV & V. Les racistes peints par eux-mêmes, February-March 1942. Cahiers VI & VII. Antisémites. April-May 1942.

18. Cf. AD du Nord, Lille, File R2457: Cardinal Liénart.
19. Cf. 'Témoignage' of Roger Bailleul, cited in *Actes: Lille*, pp. 687-8.
20. Cf. F. Delpech, 'Les Chrétiens et le STO' in *Actes: Lyon*, pp. 347-54. Correspondance Saliège-Liénart.

9 URIAGE: THE ASSAULT ON A REPUTATION
Brian Darling

This is the story of a small group of Frenchmen whose experience during the war and Resistance equipped a number of them to exert a disproportionate influence on post-war France. It is also the story of an attempt, by others, to reinterpret and belittle the experience, and in some cases to denounce the influence.

The difficulty for students of the question comes from the paucity of sources and of evidence but, more importantly, from the interpretation of intentions. Historians are familiar with the problem of conflicting accounts and interpretations left by figures in the past, but here we are dealing with a generation which survived the event, and has exercised some degree of control of the sources.

We shall therefore seek to present what we characterise as the 'house view' before examining the various 'revisionist' assaults upon it. The 'house' in this instance is an impressive one, both from the standpoint of the estate agent and for the historian. The *École Nationale des Cadres d'Uriage*, functioned from late in 1940 to the end of 1942. The 'house view' of its activities comes to us largely through two scholarly articles, the first by Janine Bourdin in 1959[1] was as an example of the political involvement of intellectuals. The second was by an historian, Raymond Josse[2] and was published in a historical journal. However, though tackling Uriage from different points of view, both were based for the most part on common sources. Briefly these comprise a collection of the letters and diaries of Emmanuel Mounier which appeared in 1956[3] six years after his death, and two publications which emerged from the École but were not actually published until after the Liberation. These were a 'summa' of the École's project for the post-war reconstruction of France, and an account of the École's pedagogical views based upon a six-month training programme[4].

These printed sources were supplemented by conversations with Gilles Ferry, author of the École's pedagogical manual referred to above and, equally importantly, with Jean-Marie Domenach who was a 'stagiaire' at Uriage and, subsequently, editorial secretary and then editorial director of the monthly review, *Esprit*. The published sources and the 'témoignages', as relayed by Bourdin and Josse, form what one might call the kernel of the house view.

The story, briefly, is as follows. A young cavalry officer, Captain Pierre Dunoyer de Segonzac, graduate of Saint Cyr, demobilised in the defeat of 1940 had the idea that one of the major reasons for the débâcle was poor leadership, and particularly in the case of young people – no leadership at all. Thanks to military contacts he had at Vichy he was able to convince the Secrétariat Général à la Jeunesse to provide funds and a commission to found an École des Cadres, initially to form cadres for the Chantiers de la Jeunesse. His first was at the Château de la Faulconnière close to Gannat (only 19 km from Vichy). In September 1940 he received his first stagiaires from the Chantiers, but after a visit from Pétain, Segonzac decided to look for somewhere further away and less accessible. His new location met that criterion, and many others. His choice was a château of the family of Bayard, 'chevalier sans peur et sans reproche', which overlooks Uriage (just south-west of Grenoble, on the slopes of the Belledonne). About as far away as he could be, and in as impressive a site as one could imagine.

The move to Uriage prompted a change in personnel and a change in orientation. Though Segonzac's military career had left him with a personal loyalty to Pétain, it is clear through the quality of the team he now recruited that this loyalty coexisted with a very strong element of nonconformism as well as a patriotism which would not countenance collaboration. The style of life at Uriage has often been characterised as 'Spartan' with its diet of intellectual activity, manual work, physical training, its group singing, and its marching from one activity to another.

Under the influence of its new team, and particularly that of the Abbé de Naurois, Hubert Beuve-Méry, and Emmanuel Mounier the École developed as a centre of analysis of the present and particularly of the future. Its standard courses were of three weeks duration, with only one being of six months, but they were all *intensive*. The teaching came from people in all walks of life but most notably from such figures as the RP Maydieu, de Lubac, Fraisse, Mgr de Solages, Mgr Guerry, Jean Lacroix, abbé de Naurois, Paul-Henry Chombart de Lauwe, Robert Mossé, Joffre Dumazedier and, of course, Mounier and Beuve-Méry. Lectures and study sessions on economic and political questions were interspersed with reflections on the spiritual crisis. This effort to rethink Christianity at Uriage and in the pages of *Esprit* before it was closed down was of considerable importance especially given the support which so much of the hierarchy had given to the Vichy regime.

From its beginnings as an institution recognised and funded by Vichy, Uriage became in the space of two years a provider of cadres for the Resistance. Indeed throughout the two years it had been in close touch with the local Resistance, and Segonzac was a close friend of Henri Frenay, the leader of Combat, who had been hidden on a number of occasions at the school. After its closure at the end of 1942, and the warrant issued for Segonzac's arrest, virtually the entire staff of Uriage joined the Maquis. The school operated clandestinely for a time from the Château de Murinet near St Marcellin, between Grenoble and Valence, providing 'équipes volantes' for the Resistance, and assembling its collective wisdom in its 'summa', *Vers le Style du XXe Siècle*, until it was discovered and blown up by the SS and the Milice. Uriage itself had the unhappy destiny to be subsequently occupied by the Milice.

Uriage's contribution to the future reconstruction of France went far. Beuve-Méry was to become Director of *Le Monde* and bring it to a position where it was perhaps the most influential daily newspaper in the world. Emmanuel Mounier relaunched *Esprit* in December 1944, with Lacroix, and later Domenach. To Dumazedier and Benigno Cacérès, we owe the movement Peuple et Culture; Simon Nora became one of the central figures in French economic planning; Paul Delouvrier, after being de Gaulle's civil délégué général in Algeria, became the author of the overall Plan (schéma directeur) for Paris in 1961 and later Préfet of the Ile de France region. Many of the priests and theologians who were at Uriage were later to be found in the preparatory commissions for the Second Vatican Council.

But despite its contribution to the future, Uriage itself must be seen very much in the context of its time. Its values, or at least the school's way of expressing them, are not necessarily either universal nor eternal. But it must never be forgotten that France's army had been swept aside by the invading army from across the Rhine, and that the victorious Wehrmacht now occupied Europe from Brest to Brest-Litovsk. The defeat had not been due simply to a superiority in armaments, and the values of Uriage, l'honneur, la fidélité, le discipline, le service de la collectivité, are the response of Dunoyer de Segonzac to this crisis.

This abridged account of the Uriage experience, what has been called the 'house view' because of the nature of its sources, is reproduced, though not always uncritically, in such works as Winock's *Histoire politique de la revue Esprit 1932-1950*, Julliard and Jeanneney's *Le Monde de Beuve-Méry*, Kedward's *Resistance in Vichy France*, and Halls' *The Youth of Vichy France*.[5] It is the view developed in great detail and with great authority by Bernard Comte whose thesis will one day become available.

The original 'revisionist' salvo was hinted at by Robert Paxton in his study of *Vichy France*[6] which appeared in 1972 in New York and in a French edition two years later. The work has much to recommend it, particularly in Paxton's use of the German archives to demonstrate the eagerness of some sectors at Vichy to offer more than the occupant had originally demanded in the way of collaboration. His widely accepted analysis of Vichy's ideas and intentions has been influential among those we intend to call the 'revisionists'. Concerning Uriage he is quite clear. Though quoting Bourdin as the major source of his analysis, he promotes Segonzac to Major, 'under whose leadership the cream of young civil servants and intellectuals camped and studied in an exalted atmosphere strongly coloured by Emmanuel Mounier's "Personalism"'. He goes on to observe that 'The Uriage school went underground in a body when France was totally occupied in November 1942, but it had been no less committed to its version of the National Revolution.'[7] These two assertions were to be taken up and developed in their turn by Hellman and Lévy, as seen below.

In 1976, the assault came in an article in the periodical *Actes de la Recherche en Sciences Sociales*[8] Pierre Bourdieu and Luc Boltanski sought to show links between Uriage and Vichy and to find the origin of both in the Third Force movements of the 1930s. In addition, by means of a similar 'fishing' in a large number of books concerned with the modernisation of France in the 1960s and 1970s they succeeded in compiling a glossary of terms which, with quotations being used as definitions enabled them to confound the genuine reformers with liberal conservatives such as the then President Giscard d'Estaing and his close associate Michel Poniatowski.

> cette recherche d'une troisième voie, qui mène souvent aux portes du fascisme, parfois pourtant refusé, du cote d'un élitisme de la compétence, associé à un populisme pastoral, anticipe jusque dans le détail, l'effort collectif des commissions du plan: l'avant-garde de classe, qui inspire l'entreprise de reconversion idéologique de l'après-guerre, met en pratique, consciemment ou inconsciemment, les schèmes déjà éprouvés dans les débats de l'avant-guerre et dans les tables rondes d'Uriage qui, à la faveur de l'ambiguité des 'humanismes' associés au 'planisme', ont assuré la continuité entre la gauche de la Révolution nationale et la droite de la Résistance.'[9]

Firing back from the 'house'[10], Domenach was prepared to admit that there was some correspondence between 'une certaine inspiration

Uriage: The Assault on a Reputation   151

de la Révolution nationale et une certaine théorisation de la Résistance'. However, it was not because of 'planning' or of 'humanism' that people chose which side to be on, but rather in response to concrete events such as the handing over of political refugees to the Germans, or the deportation of the Jews.

> J'assure Bourdieu et Boltanski que nous prenions ces idéologies beaucoup moins au sérieux qu'ils le font. Il s'agissait alors non pas de servir le pouvoir, comme ils disent, mais de le prendre. Et non pas dans l'Université ou dans les commissions du C.N.R.S., mais dans la nation. A coups de fusil.

This ahistorical approach, ignoring events and responses to them in favour of an analysis of the written word is all the more surprising in Bourdieu and Boltanski, given that they insist in their theoretical introduction[11] that their research dialectic has thrown up questions which can only be resolved by an analysis of the social conditions in which this literary 'product' was produced. As Domenach points out, it is absurd to write the history of an ideology from 1930 to 1970 without taking account of Nazism in Germany or the Resistance in France.[12]

It is of course true that at Uriage almost all viewpoints were permitted to be expressed on condition that they were open to contradiction and analysis. It is also true that, for example, in Charles Péguy, who was perhaps the most important reference point for Uriage, one can find both the pious Catholic and the socialist patriot. This is why he was published as inspirational literature by both Vichy and the Resistance.[13] But an analysis of discourse which pays no attention to action and intention, which seeks to study content with no reference to context, and which nevertheless feels able to draw political conclusions, is an arid and indeed arrogant exercise.

However, these were the works of scholars, albeit with axes to grind. Bernard-Henri Lévy's *L'Idéologie française*[14], published in 1981, was a different animal entirely. The search for 'fascists' has taken some interesting turns in twentieth-century France. In the late 1920s and early 1930s the Left as a whole found them in the ex-servicemen's 'leagues' which had attempted an assault on Parliament on 6 February 1934. A few years later institutionalised fascism was to surround France – in Portugal and Spain, in Italy and in Nazi Germany – and French 'fascists' came out in open support of all or some of the neighbouring regimes. Post-war 'fascists' kept a very low profile, but by the 1960s young people were identifying almost any overt exercise of authority as 'fascist', and in 1968 de Gaulle was equated with Hitler, and the riot police with the SS (CRS = SS). The only common thread in this tortuous story is that attacks on 'fascism' had always been mounted from within the 'Left'.

The originality of Lévy, which gave him a lot of his notoriety and access to the media, was that here was a 'transfuge' from the extreme left of 1968 who had now arrived in the new Right and was prepared to take on and discredit the sacred myths of the Left; defence of the Republic, and the Resistance, by finding 'fascism' within *them*.

L'Idéologie française is a virulent pamphlet − mounted with a phenomenal publicity operation. 'Le fascisme aux couleurs de la France', anounced *l'Express*[15] as it ran prepublication extracts adorned with a photograph of the château at Uriage displaying a banner of the Milice. No reference was made to the picture having been taken after the École had been closed down and the château taken over by the Milice! Lévy has no real thesis unless it is that with scissors and paste and racy headlines one can swamp the superficial weeklies and the media, and assume with safety that no one will bother to check where your scissors chopped your sources. In a book published two years earlier, Régis Debray had outlined the rationale when he asked rhetorically,

> Pourquoi investir dix années de sa vie dans la rédaction d'une thèse d'État qui vous fera docteur ès lettres emprisonné à vie dans une faculté de province . . . alors qu'il suffit d'un mois de travail pour vitrioler un pamphlet idéologique sur le sujet du jour [Goulag et Destin], qui me donnera un nom dans la grande presse, d'une heure de verve à la télévision pour devenir un héros national?[16-17]

Lévy's pamphlet is a theatrical attempt to show that France has a fascist tradition within the Left and Centre, and that this is the skeleton in the cupboard, or the smell on the landing, which has only been hidden by a conspiracy of silence. Lévy, who puts himself forward (the book is written in the first person active) as a cross between Saint George and the avenging angel, is determined to rescue France from its guilty secret, by revelation and denunciation.

His whole argument, which moves back and forth between the Dreyfus Affair and the 1970s, hinges upon the fact that he has two definitions, which allows him to accuse anyone of anything. His first definition of fascism quite reasonably includes anti-Semitism, collaboration and compulsory labour service in Germany (STO). But in order to take in many people who could not possibly be included in this maximal classification there is a minimal definition, according to which fascism comprises a concern for national unity, a critique of parliamentarism and the parties of the Third Republic, an emphasis on youth, and the need for national renewal. Armed with this all-encompassing definition, Lévy can say of Uriage that it was 'le style du pétainisme achevé', 'la quintéssence du pétainisme', while at the same time being fiercely nationalistic and denouncing collaboration.[18] The minimal definition is thus used to indict not only Uriage as fascist, but also *Esprit* and Mounier, and it could easily have included much of the Resistance.[19]

To move on to John Hellman's doctoral thesis, described as 'well-researched' by the reviewer in the *Times Literary Supplement*, who ventured himself further to assure his readers that 'Mr Hellman's book is by far the best guide to personalism we have had and his knowledge of French intellectual history is impressive'[20] should be to move into a less heady atmosphere. If only . . .

Hellman's view on Uriage is coloured by a desire to relate it to the German Ordensburg which is the subject of a 750-word footnote. Though he quotes from Josse, and from Winock, Hellman confuses Murinet with Uriage, and talks of the Château de Murinet being *at* Uriage[21]. (He also claims that La Fauconnière was lent to Segonzac 'by Philippe Lamour a former director of the review *Plans*'[22] — thus making a tenuous connection with Mounier's associations in the 1930s). In fact, according to the same Josse article the chateau belonged to an advocate, Me Raymond Hubert, Lamour was merely starting his own personal 'retour à la terre' in the environs[23].

But the really disturbing feature of Hellman is the vertiginious path he treads between an orthodox account of the establishment of the École, listing the staff involved, indicating some of their conflicts with the Vichy authorities, and a brooding mystical preoccupation with heady German ideas. One example must suffice:

> The Uriage school alumni later maintained that it was a peculiar 'island of freedom' in a more and more authoritarian régime. In 1940-1, however, Uriage sometimes seemed to be fulfilling Paul Nizan's prophecy: Mounier was distilling the thick foreign currents into the spiritualized national socialism of a French Ordensburg above Grenoble. Precisely where, according to German ethnologists, the Nordic Alleman family had maintained their aerie centuries earlier . . .[24]

Nizan's prophecy? It comes some 120 pages earlier as Hellman relates the story of the famous *Cahier de Revendications*, published by the

NRF in December 1932. This collection of a dozen essays by spokesmen of the various young political tendencies, assembled by Denis de Rougement[25], included an article by Nizan. At the last minute he attempted in vain to withdraw it under pressure from the Party. Writing the following month in *Europe*, Nizan did the hatchet job required of him[26] and denounced the call for a 'spiritual revolution' with which Mounier had been associated in the *Cahier*:

> they criticize fascism to the degree that it is weakened by certain survivals of outmoded bourgeois positions: the French are much more 'intelligent' than the Italians and the Germans. We know very well that they decant, purify, and perfect the thick foreign currents; they bring the experiences to fruition: French national socialism will simply be more artful than the others . . .[27]

Hellman has made it clear that he found this text totally convincing and that it served as a signpost for the remainder of his thesis.[28] But is it not Hellman who is in danger of catching a whiff of the vapours?

> Uriage was, in a sense, a noble, romantic enterprise which played a role in freeing France from Nazi domination. It was also an imprudent and dangerous venture under the circumstances. Some miles to the north at the École de Cadres in the occupied zone, young Frenchmen were walking on broken glass, bloodletting, and engaging in a whole set of pagan rites that recalled Heinrich Himmler's black order.[29]

To turn from Hellman to Zeev Sternhell's *Ni droite ni gauche* is to become almost punch-drunk. Sternhell, an academic historian, has made something of a speciality of defending a largely non-existent liberal-democratic tradition of thought in France, against assaults from both Left and Right.[30]

His demonstration in *Maurice Barrès et le Nationalisme français*, and *La Droite révolutionaire, 1885-1914; Les origines françaises du fascisme* that nearly all ideas found in fascism and national socialism had first surfaced in France, is completed in this third volume. In *Ni droite ni gauche: L'idéologie fasciste en France*, a book of 300 pages with a further 65 pages of footnotes, Sternhell looks for fascists among socialists, syndicalists, left-wing Catholics, indeed anyone who was critical of democracy as it was practised by the Third Republic, and inevitably he arrives at the nonconformist writings of Mounier in the 1930s. Uriage is mentioned only once, but Sternhell has room for two of its major figures, Beuve-Méry, and especially Mounier. Indeed the

Uriage: The Assault on a Reputation

whole structure of the book, and indeed of the series, seems to be organised to demonstrate that since France delivered herself up to Pétain in 1940 it must all have been the fault of Mounier and everything that happened before was merely a prelude to Mounier's accouchement of the Vichy regime.

Curiously enough, though in Sternhell's eyes largely a child of Mounier's nonconformist youth, Vichy is not seen as a fascist institution: 'Certes, le fascisme en France n'est parvenu à s'emparer du pouvoir . . . ' (p. 20), and 'Le fascisme . . . n'y a jamais dépassé le stade de la théorie . . . ' (p. 293). Vichy disappointed the fascists, as indeed would Mounier, since as Sternhell himself recognises:

> dans les années qui précèdent la guerre, Mounier a toujours fait des choix politiques conformes à sa philosophie. Fin 1935 la sympathie d'*Esprit* au Rassemblement populaire est acquise, et la revue de Mounier se démarque en cela des autres 'non-conformistes' des années trente. Elle preserve certes sa liberté de critique et ne se prive pas d'exprimer ses craintes, notamment en ce qui concerne la politique extérieure et une éventuelle alliance anti-allemande. Mais la revue ne fait surtout aucune concession au stalinisme et, en juin 1936, elle reçoit les premières contributions volontaires de Victor Serge qui vient d'être libéré d'Union Soviétique et dénonce les atrocités du régime. Quelque mois plus tard, Mounier s'engage contre le franquisme et entreprend sur la guerre d'Espagne un remarquable travail d'information. *Esprit* combat la vision manichéenne de l'opinion catholique selon laquelle la guerre est un affrontement entre communisme et catholicisme. Prouver, ainsi que le montre Michel Winock, que des catholiques, que des prêtres, ont pris parti pour la République, comme ce fut notamment le cas de la nation et du clergé basques, tel est l'un des objectifs d'*Esprit*. Finalement, en octobre 1938, Mounier publie un vibrant éditorial contre la politique munichoise: il dénonce la démission de la France qui ne peut qu'encourager l'expansion des fascismes.[31]

The evidence is clear. Someone who, on Sternhell's own evidence, fought fascism in his writing as well as in his 'prises de position' thoughout the 1930s, can hardly be accused of giving birth to Vichy. But Sternhell works at another level, in which books count for more than actions in politics. It is for that reason that so much of his book is taken up with literary analysis, seeking the political message where a Leavis may distil the moral element. Within Sternhell's 'great tradition' of fascism, Barrès, De Man, Drieu la Rochelle, Juvenal, Maulnier, Sorel and Mounier, are all given an infinitely larger part in the history of fascist ideas than the overtly fascist activists Doriot, Déat and Darnand, all of whom collaborated with Nazism. And, as if that was not tendentious enough, to leave collaborationist Vichy out of his 'great tradition' altogether suggests a wilful refusal to look for any fascist movement *on the ground*. The history of ideas, as with the analysis of discourse, becomes a very arid exercise when it is detached from history and from 'le vécu des gens'. It may give some satisfaction, that the inhumanities, the tragedies, the betrayals, of the twentieth century can be explained by the writings of a handful of not excessively gifted writers. But what really is the importance of a dozen books in shaping the political life of a society? How many fascists did they make, and were they really made by reading books? And what did they *do*?

So much of real political life consists in trying to wrest concepts and vocabulary from the dominant class and give them a genuinely democratic and popular content. This is what Republican and workers' movements have been engaged in for more than a century. It is a task which Uriage took upon itself, in discussion and, eventually, in armed struggle. They deserve a better history than that into which our 'revisionists' seek to integrate them.

Notes

1. J. Bourdin, 'Des intellectuels à la recherche d'un style de vie – l'École Nationale des Cadres d'Uriage', *Revue française de Science Politique*, no. 4 (Décembre, 1959).

2. R. Josse, 'L'École des Cadres d'Uriage', *Revue d'Histoire de la Deuxième Guerre Mondiale*, no. 61 (1966).

3. E. Mounier, *Mounier et sa génération* (Editions du Seuil, coll. Esprit, 1956).

4. Equipe d'Uriage (sous la direction de Gilbert Gadoffre), *Vers le style du XXe siècle* (Editions du Seuil, 1945; G. Ferry, *Une expérience de formation des chefs* (*Editions du Seuil*, 1945).

5. M. Winock, *Histoire politique de la revue Esprit 1932-1950* (Editions du Seuil, 1975); J. Julliard and J.-N. Jeanneney, *Le Monde de Beuve-Méry* (Editions du Seuil, 1970); H.R. Kedward, *Resistance in Vichy France* (Oxford University Press, 1978); W.R. Halls, *The Youth of Vichy France* (Clarendon Press, Oxford, 1981).

On Uriage, Bernard Comte has published 'L'Expérience d'Uriage' in *Eglises et Chrétiens dans la Deuxième Guerre mondiale; la Région Rhône-Alpes*, sous la direction d'Xavier de Montclos (Presses Universitaires de Lyon, 1978), pp. 251-67.

6. R. Paxton, *Vichy France: Old Guard and New Order, 1940-44*, (Alfred Knopf, New York, 1972).

7. Ibid., p. 165.

8. P. Bourdieu, and L. Boltanski, 'La production de l'idéologie dominante' in

Actes de la Recherche en sciences sociales, nos. 2-3 (1976).
  9. Ibid., p. 8.
  10. In *Esprit*, nos. 7-8 (1976), pp. 99-101.
  11. Bourdieu and Boltanski, 'La production de l'idéologie', pp. 9-10.
  12. In *Esprit*, nos. 7-8 (1976), p. 100.
  13. An edition of Charles Péguy coupled with the Communist writer Gabriel Péri was published by Les Editions de Minuit (aux dépens de quelques lettrés patriotes . . . achevé d'imprimer sous l'Oppression à Paris le 22 juin 1944), as *Deux voix françaises – Péguy/Péri*. It contains (p. 39) this superbly apposite passage from Péguy's *L'Argent suite* of 1913:

Du Gouvernement des Vieillards
On me dit: C'est un vieillard. Je dis pardon. Les vieillards ont droit au respect. Ils n'ont pas droit au commandement. Ils ont droit au commandement s'ils savent commander, s'ils sont bons pour commander. Mais ils n'ont pas droit au commandement par cela seul qu'ils sont de vieillards.

Les vieillards, comme tels, parce qui'ils sont vieillards, ont peut-etre droit au respect, aux honneurs; ils n'ont, comme tels et en cela même, aucun droit au commandement. Autrement il suffirait de devenir suprêmement vieux, dans n'importe quel ordre, pour parvenir, dans cet ordre, au commandement suprême. On admet bien, dans le militaire, et tout le monde admet, pour les militaires, que rien n'est dangereux comme les généraux fatigués. Et loin de donner aux généraux vieillis les commandements suprêmes on a créé la *limite d'âge*. Et on ne parle que de rajeunir les cadres. Et on croit avoir bien fait, et on se félicite, et on croit presque avoir remporté une victoire quand on a réussi à rejeunir les cadres, quand on a réussi à abaisser les limites d'âge. Et on a raison.

  14. B.-H. Lévy, *L'Idéologie française* (Grasset, 1981).
  15. L'Express, no. 1540, 17 janvier 1981, pp. 82-90. The photograph is on p. 86.
  16. R. Debray, *Le pouvoir intellectuel en France* (Editions Ramsay, 1979). p. 182.
  17. Ibid.,
  18. Lévy, *L'Idéologie française*, p. 52.
  19. C.f. Kedward, *Resistance in Vichy France*, p. 157 and Chapter VII, *passim*.
  20. Patrick McCarthy in *Times Literary Supplement*, 12 February 1982.
  21. J. Hellman, *Emmanuel Mounier and the new Catholic left 1930-1950* (University of Toronto Press, 1981) see p. 175. The 750-word footnote is on pp. 316-18.
  22. Ibid., pp. 174-5.
  23. Josse, 'L'Ecole des Cadres', p. 52.
  24. Hellman, *Emmanuel Mounier*, p. 177.
  25. *La Nouvelle Revue Française* (Décembre, 1932).
  26. This account of the incident was given by Denis de Rougement at a congress to mark the 50th anniversary of the founding of *Esprit*. Dourdan, December 1982.

The context in which Nizan found himself *vis à vis* the PCF in 1932-3 is related in Ariel Ginsbourg, 'Une promenade politique avec Paul Nizan' in *Atoll*, no. 1, numéro spécial sur Nizan, Nov.-Déc. 1967-Jan. 1968.

  27. In *Europe* (Janvier, 1933) quoted by Hellman, *Emmanuel Mounier*, p. 55. Hellman's translation.
  28. Speaking at the *Congrès pour le cinquantenaire d'Esprit*, Dourdan, Décembre 1982.

29. Hellman, *Emmanuel Mounier*, p. 178.
30. Z. Sternhell, *Maurice Barrès et le Nationalisme français* (Armand Colin, 1972); *La Droite révolutionnaire, 1885-1914. Les origines françaises du fascisme* (Editions du Seuil, 1978); *Ni droite ni gauche; L'idéologie fasciste en France* (Editions du Seuil, 1983).

Zeev Sternhell is Director of the Centre for European Studies at the Hebrew University in Jerusalem.

31. Z. Sternhell, *Ni droite ni gauche. L'idéologie fasciste en France*, pp. 309-10.

10 URIAGE: THE INFLUENCE OF CONTEXT ON CONTENT

Derek Robbins

My texts for an interpretation of L'École des Cadres à Uriage are derived from the collection of documents held at the Bureau des archives of the Département de l'Isère at Grenoble which I was able to study in two visits in 1977 and 1982.[1] These texts can be divided into three categories: *working papers* used within L'École; *pamphlets* published by L'École; and *Journalism* produced by L'École. These are texts of the period from 1940 until 1944. They are different from those which have hitherto dominated the secondary interpretations of L'École as offered by Janine Bourdin and Raymond Josse[2] which, for subsequent discussion, have assumed the status of primary sources – *Vers le style du XXe siecle* by 'l'équipe d'Uriage', edited by Gilbert Gadoffre, and *Une expérience de formation de chefs*, by Gilles Ferry. These were both publications of 1945.

The development of L'École's ideological position from 1940, culminating in the texts of 1945, is a theme of interest in itself, as is that of the historiography of accounts of L'École offered elsewhere in this volume by Brian Darling. My purpose, however, is to consider the extent to which the thinking of two authors of *pamphlets* of L'École – Jean-Jacques Chevallier and Paul-Henry Chombart de Lauwe – can both be said to have been influenced by the social context provided by L'École, but in different directions.

That context can best be indicated by reference to an early number of *Jeunesse-France* – the 'Journal des Chefs de la Jeunesse' which was issued bi-monthly by L'École. No. 21 of 22 September 1941 carried a four-page analysis of the first year of L'École's existence. An article by F. Ducruy offered a 'Historique de l'École'. It describes how Dunoyer de Segonzac, a military captain, had in September 1940 gathered together a group of about a dozen young men who were committed to the task of reviving the morale of French youth by re-emphasising a sense of discipline. This group chose to attach themselves to the 'Chantiers de la Jeunesse' movement which had been organised by General de la Porte du Theil. About 100 volunteers met for a first session at the Château de la Faulconnière near to Gannat – not far from Vichy itself. These first 'stagiaires' mainly comprised young

159

soldiers who had only been mobilised in June and belonged to a regiment which was stationed at Vichy. The first session lasted from September 16th until October 1st. For the second session, which began on October 5th, the character of the 'stagiaires' was already substantially altered. L'École was now to be used by the Vichy government as part of its policy for finding activity for unemployed youth. L'École was to be partly a work camp and partly an institution for education and training and was seen to be part of a plan to constitute groups for the 'Entr'aide nationale des Jeunes'. L'École was honoured by the presence of Pétain himself for the last day of the second sesson – 20 October 1940.

It was at this point – already having shaken off the military orientation of the Chantiers de la Jeunesse – that L'École moved to the Château d'Uriage, just outside Grenoble. The third session of L'École – the first at Uriage – took place from the 4th until the 19th November with 111 stagiaires. For all sessions held at Uriage, the statistical analysis offered in *Jeunesse-France*, no. 21, provides a detailed breakdown of the occupations of stagiaires. At the date of going to press, there had been a total of 10 sessions of L'École, and Ducruy concludes that

> Après un an d'efforts, le résultat acquis n'est pas contestable: plus de 1,000 jeunes hommes ont suivi les stages normaux, près de 600 autres y ont fait des séjours plus ou moins longs.'[3]

Another article in the same number of *Jeunesse-France* gives an account of the normal pattern of a 'stage'. On arrival 'stagiaires' were placed in teams of between 15 and 20 'dans lesquelles sont autant que possible dosées les diverses catégories sociales'. The purpose of the communal experience was to establish in microcosm in a small-group situation the basis of national reintegration:

> Tout le temps de son stage, le futur chef vivra en équipe, apprenant à connaître au sein de ce groupe élémentaire les éléments divers de la communauté nationale, prenant ainsi une conscience plus nette à la fois de sa personnalité propre et de son insertion dans l'effort commun.[4]

For the period of two weeks, the rough timetable for each day was as follows:

> une heure et demie à deux heures d'éducation physique et de

sport, deux heures de travail manuel, trois à quatre heures de travail intellectuel. Chaque soir a lieu une 'veillée' par équipe, soit commune à tous.[5]

To offer a break to this daily routine

> deux journées sont consacrées l'une à une promenade d'exploration régionale, au cours de laquelle l'équipe va prendre contact avec la vie d'une agglomération rurale ou industrielle, l'autre à la visite d'un chantier de jeunes.[6]

The intellectual component of each day consisted of a programme of 'conférences' – given either by a University professor or by people with professional experience; a series of 'témoignages' in which stagiaires shared their own practical experiences; and a series of 'cercles d'étude' initiated by the instructor of each group.

Finally, each 'stage' culminated in a ceremony of dedication:

> Le couronnement du stage est le serment solennel de tous ceux qui veulent s'engager à servir et à commander pour la France, de toutes leurs forces, de tout leur coeur. Cet engagement est prononcé, après le baptême de la promotion, devant le drapeau que chaque matin les équipes formées en carré ont regardé monter dans le soleil levant, en assurant plus ferme la résolution qui désormais tracera leur voie au service du pays.[7]

The intellectual life of L'École, as represented in this one of its journalistic texts, was an integral part of a total experience which was organised for 'stagiaires'. L'École quickly moved into a new phase. By the end of 1941, much consideration was being given to the organisation of L'École's alumni, and, therefore, to an 'encadrement' of the whole of society. Series 22.J.8 in the Bureau des archives départementales de l'Isère contains 20 documents which allow us to trace the development of an 'Équipe Nationale d'Uriage' (ENU) which was mainly made up of former stagiaires of L'École. In November, 1941, members of the Association des Anciens d'Uriage were invited to offer themselves as candidates for membership of the ENU. In order to ensure that the ENU remained an 'équipe', the chefs d'écoles in the regions were invited to attend periodic reunions at Uriage, the first of which took place on 10 and 11 January 1942. Thus L'École sought to enlarge its sphere of influence. It was no longer content to offer transient instruction to a series of stagiaires. It sought, instead, to maintain control of a national organisation exercised through the activity in the regions of ex-stagiaires and to retain central authority at Uriage. It was as part of this extended ambition that, on 5 December 1941, it was agreed at Uriage that there should be created 'une série de Cahiers de l'Équipe Nationale d'Uriage permettant de diffuser, lorsque cela sera nécessaire, tout document donnant des renseignements utiles aux membres de l'Association'.[8]

The series of pamphlets issued by L'École in 1942 under the title of *Le Chef et ses Jeunes* must be seen as one manifestation of L'École's policy of communicating to a wider audience than simply those in attendance at the Château d'Uriage. The bureau des archives holds twelve pamphlets. The first three 'fascicules' were quickly withdrawn, never re-published, and are missing; several announced pamphlets are missing; and several projected pamphlets did not materialise. The advertisement for the series makes it clear that the purpose of the collection was to make the thinking of L'École, as it had developed during the early 'stages', available to instructors and chefs who were seeking to establish similar institutions in the regions. The advertisement reads:

> Composée de courtes brochures, d'un format pratique, cette collection est l'instrument indispensable aux jeunes chefs qui désirent perfectionner leurs méthodes de commandement, poursuivre leur formation personnelle, augmenter leurs moyens de rayonnement et développer leur action sociale dans leur milieu ou dans leur profession.
>
> Publiée par l'École Nationale des Cadres . . . elle est le résultat d'un travail par équipe représentatif de l'enseignement d'Uriage. Elle sera en outre, pour tous les jeunes Français, un moyen sûr de comprendre l'esprit de la révolution nationale.[9]

Throughout 1942, therefore, L'École issued pamphlets which manifested the spirit of the discussions which had occurred in the conférences and cercles d'étude of the *stages* and which sought to support the emphasis of the Révolution Nationale. In considering these pamphlets, therefore, we are looking at texts which were themselves removed from the pedagogical situation which had generated them. By the second half of 1942, new emphases were emerging at Uriage itself. One of the working papers of Uriage, dated September, 1942 entitled 'Le Prolétariat: Justes Aspirations Révolutionnaires' by Joffre Dumazedier (an instructor at L'École) begins with the sentence

> La Révolution annoncée dans les messages du Maréchal est à peine amorcée dans les faits.[10]

whilst a working paper of October, 1942 states categorically that a new initiative of radical thought is now necessary:

> En Octobre 1942 il semble que jamais l'opinion française n'ait été plus affaissée et plus absorbée dans des préoccupations immédiates. Un mouvement politique avorté, la Révolution Nationale a laissé les Français indifférents à tout grand mouvement révolutionnaire. Or, nous croyons à la nécessité d'une vraie révolution, dont le bouleversement de l'univers nous montre l'étendue.[11]

It is this initiative which was continued after the closure of L'École in December, 1942 and culminated in the production of *Vers le style du XXe siècle* after the Liberation.

In focusing attention on two of L'École's pamphlets, I am considering two texts which were expressions of 'la vie d'école' of 1941. Even though, through 1942, these texts became increasingly at odds with new intellectual initiatives at Uriage, the context of the 'vie d'école' of 1941 which I have described did influence the content of the contributions made by the two authors.

Various articles of the late 1920s and early 1930s suggest that there were seen to be two opposed sociological tendencies in France between the Wars. The Durkheimian tradition was dominant and had successfully captured some university chairs. More generally, there was thought to be a consonance between Durkheimian social science and the ideal of the social function of universities embraced by French educational reformers from the 1890s onwards. Non-Durkheimian sociology could not easily find a home within institutions which shared Durkheimian assumptions.[12]

An alternative tendency which had failed to establish itself within university institutions was that associated with the followers of Frédéric Le Play. In his survey of *Contemporary Sociological Theories* of 1928, Pitirim Sorokin had asserted that 'Le Play deserves to be put on the level with such masters of social science as Comte and Spencer'[13] and had outlined the five main contributions of the Le Play School – notably the production of family monographs. The approach employed by Le Play and his followers was closely associated with developments in 'human geography' which Claude Lévi-Strauss was to acknowledge in his review of French Sociology of 1945.[14] In particular, Vidal de la Blache — a major figure in French human geography — is listed by Sorokin as a pupil and collaborator of Le Play. It was with this aspect of the non-Durkheimian tradition of sociological thinking that P.H. Chombart de Lauwe explicitly associated himself in the early pages of his pamphlet for l'École entitled *Pour retrourver la France. Enquêtes sociales en équipes*. In his introduction, he immediately locates himself as a 'human geographer' — quoting, particularly, Vidal de la Blache. But he also cites the benefits to be derived from other disciplines in conducting social enquiries, and he refers to: '*monographies sociales* en sociologie (Le Play), étude du travail en *géographie économique*; tableaux de *géographie politique* (tels qu'en a tracés, par exemple, M. André Siegfried)'.[15] The kind of study which is to be described is not a dry-as-dust study: 'L'exploration régionale consiste moins, pour nous, en une étude de géographie humaine qu'en une enquête sociale.'[16] Regional geography study is seen, therefore, as a means rather than an end — as a means to discovery in action of a new sense of national identity and unity for France. Social observation is not the goal but, rather, the development of sympathy with different kinds of people.

The pamphlet continued by claiming that engagement with real problems and the problems as perceived by those experiencing them, is a prerequisite for developing new social solutions. Working in groups is seen as the best way to achieve such involvement with real problems, and the first part of the pamphlet gives detailed advice. Chombart de Lauwe here illustrates the way in which groups should marshal and maximise the capacities of their members:

> Le Chef d'équipe doit initier ses collaborateurs à sa méthode au course d'une ou plusieurs discussions en commun. Puis, suivant les goûts et les compétences, il les divise en petits groupes indépendants chargés chacun d'une tâche précise. Chaque groupe a lui-même son Chef qui répartit le travail entre ses camarades. Par exemple, un ouvrier et un ingénieur étudient les industries de la région, tandis qu'un paysan se charge de l'agriculture et un étudiant en droit des échanges et des problèmes plus généraux de la vie économique. Pendant que ce groupe fait son travail, un autre groupe, dans le même village, étudie la vie familiale, la vie politique, les traditions sociales . . . Un architecte étudie habitat et un géographe le cadre physique, etc . . .[17]

Chombart de Lauwe also emphasises that groups should not only observe; they must participate in the life of the community in which they are situated:

> L'enquête approfondie doit permettre d'entrer plus intimement dans la vie d'un groupe social. Les équipiers doivent peu à peu s'intégrer au pays, participer aux activités des habitants, comprendre leurs préoccupations, et essayer de les aider à les résoudre. Il faut prendre parti, s'attacher à la nature et surtout aux hommes.[18]

A form of community action is envisaged: 'Parfois on profite de ces visites pour participer à des travaux, rendre service à des familles qui sont en difficulté,'[19] and, by these means, groups can secure an *entrée* to village social occasions. These provide an opportunity to 'enseigner des chants et d'en apprendre, de faire connaître les organisations de Jeunesse, de poser des problèmes ayant trait à la Révolution Nationale, à la situation de la France, de suggérer des mesures à prendre sur le plan local'.[20]

Chombart de Lauwe's groups are clearly 'task-oriented'. The mode of analysis and activity which he advocates is meant to generate national unity by stimulating mutual respect among all social participants. The groups are seen as agents of change in a context of community development. Members of the groups acquire knowledge but it is knowledge which is not detached from the process of securing social integration. Members collaborate in groups in order to relate more comprehensively to the larger social group which is the object of their analysis. It is clear, therefore, that the context of l'École reinforced the 'action-research' orientation of Chombart de Lauwe's sociological approach. His pamphlet was conceived as a working document for particular use on those days of each 'stage' in which 'stagiaires' embarked on exploratory forays into the surrounding communities. The process of conducting an enquiry was itself intellectually in accord with the ideological intentions of the institution whether or not the investigative groups achieved an accurate understanding of the social situations which they encountered. Chombart de Lauwe sought to transmit a method of enquiry rather than a body of knowledge and the emphasis of l'École enabled him to sustain a commitment to practice and activity.

Jean-Jacques Chevallier's contribution to the series *Le Chef et ses Jeunes* was very different. Whereas Chombart de Lauwe was a young instructor without, I think, any experience in university teaching,

Chevallier was already 40 years old in 1940 and was established with an academic reputation. His two main early works show the extent to which legal knowledge was becoming sociologised in the period between the Wars. His first book, published in 1930, was entitled *L'Évolution de l'Empire britannique*. It was in two volumes and was clearly the product of work which had commenced in the early 1920s. The phenomenon which fascinated Chevallier was that, 'De petites colonies, Canada, Australie, Afrique du Sud, Nouvelle-Zélande ont grandi, sont devenues des nations libres, sans rompre avec la métropole comme avaient rompu les Treize Colonies d'Amérique...'[21] and that, and here is the crux, 'cela s'est fait sans que le Droit strict fût modifié, sans qu'une Constitution impériale écrite intervînt.'[22]

He was fascinated by the way in which the British Empire seemed to cohere without reference to the strict imposition of law. In short, his interest in charting the legal and constitutional changes from 1776 until 1926 was to demonstrate the social and political impotence of law in achieving social solidarity. His concern, in other words, was the fundamentally sociological concern with the problem of what makes societies cohere. The British success, he argues, arises precisely from their disinclination to be tied down to the letter of any law, or as Chevallier puts it, from 'Incertitude, équivoque, contradictions, combien tout cela répugne à notre esprit français logique et unitaire...'[23]

Chevallier quotes Boutmy's description of the evolution of the English constitution as based on a *'parti pris d'optimisme* et de confiance' and, in conclusion, Chevallier gives expression to his belief that a spiritual regeneration is necessary for France to learn from English successes. He writes:

> Confiance dans la vie qui guérit les blessures, qui cicatrise et qui fait croître, qui crée même avec de la mort. Confiance dans la vie de la race britannique et dans ses destinées! Confiance dans la vie, à quoi correspond une vive méfiance à l'égard des constructions de l'esprit, parce qu'elles prétendent emprisonner la vie dans les mailles de la logique...[24]

Although this outburst in favour of the heroic spirit is isolated in the whole work, my point is that Chevallier's critical attitude towards the social value of law, in comparison with other spiritual forces, could not readily be expressed within his university context. The sociological law professor needed the opportunity offered by an alternative educational institution to develop his thinking. This he did in the Uriage pamphlet,

L'Ordre Viril et l'efficacité dans l'action.

This pamphlet consists of two separate sections. The first is devoted to a consideration of 'L'Ordre Viril'. Chevallier argues that French people need an internalised order: and proposes four principal aspects which constitute 'L'ordre viril' – 'sens de la responsabilité, sens de l'honneur, sens de la qualité, sens de la force'. His elaboration of the 'sens de la force' provides, first of all, a rationale for concentration upon physical education – 'force du corps' and, then, an opportunity to launch an attack on intellectuality which is detached from action.

It is this overriding concern for action which is developed in the second part of the pamphlet – 'L'Efficacité dans l'action'. The loss of the capacity to act is offered as a major explanatory cause of French failure in the fighting before the armistice:

> pendant cette guerre, surtout pendant les jours noirs de juin, il a paru que de haut en bas de notre peuple plein de tant de qualités, composé de tant d'hommes intelligents, ingénieux, d'esprit raffiné au sommet et à la base, de tant de 'braves types' faciles à vivre, doués de bon sens, de finesse et d'humanité, un certain sens de l'action était perdu.[25]

The specific tactics for encouraging 'efficacité' are all subsumed by operating within a team. Chevallier's view of l'équipe is of an introverted group which exists for personal and moral purposes:

> Une équipe digne de ce nom est une société parfaite... Isolés, individus attelés à notre seul destin personnel, il nous est parfois si difficile de ramener à la surface cette bonne part dont j'ai parlé. C'est si facile quand nous sommes attelés ensemble en équipe, à une tâche qui dépasse chacun de nous, quand il s'agit de servir l'équipe et de ne pas la trahir – car nous sentons que ce serait trahir gravement nous-mêmes ce qu'il y a de meilleur en nous. Ainsi: l'équipe et son sens vivant en chacun de nous sont éminemment propres à susciter cet élan actif, cette allégresse dans le travail, cette impatience du résultat, ce goût de la perfection, qui font l'action efficace.[26]

Chevallier finally responds to the charge that 'efficacité' may be incompatible with respect for the individual or the person by asserting that 'Toute communauté inefficace qui respecte la personne sera écrasée et absorbée par une communauté efficace qui ne la respecte pas.'[27] The seeds of this extremism are there in Chevallier's academically respectable analysis of the development of the British Empire. The scepticism of the professor of International Law about its value in international relations is reinforced by the opportunity provided by Uriage to glorify physical force and activity and to denigrate judicious rationality. Mirroring his own development, Chevallier's introduction to the Uriage pamphlet shows how, within the 'vie d'école', it was possible to move from rational debate to assertive propaganda. It also shows how the integration of Chevallier's text into the 'vie d'école' necessarily diminished the scope for liberal enquiry or debate:

> Ces deux conférences ont pour origine un exposé fait par l'auteur, professeur de Droit Public, aux Journées d'études d'Uriage de décembre 1940, sur le thème suivant: 'Démocraties libérales et régimes totalitaires.' L'auteur fut amené à dire que les régimes totalitaires, abstraction faite de toutes différences de nature ou d'inspiration, avaient démontré une plus grande efficacité que les régimes démocratiques. Un débat intéressant s'ouvrit alors sur le sens exact et la portée de cette notion. L'auteur fut invité à préciser ce qu'il entendait par 'efficacité,' non plus seulement dans le cadre politique, mais dans le cadre général de l'action, et notamment, puisque Uriage est une 'école de chefs', de l'action du Chef. De là cette conférence, reproduite en seconde place dans le présent fascicule, et qui fut répétée à chaque session de l'École, avant le départ des élèves, comme une sorte de 'consigne d'action.'[28]

If we visualise the presentation of Chevallier's 'L'Efficacité dans l'action' as part of the ceremony of dedication terminating each stage of l'École des Cadres, we can see the extent to which his ideas were influenced by a context other than that of the Faculté de Droit of the University of Grenoble. Equally, if we visualise teams of stagiaires involving themselves in the *veillées* of local communities in pursuit of an experience of La Patrie, we can see the way in which the Le Playist tradition of social scientific enquiry was influenced by a context that pre-eminently sought to encourage group action.

Accounts of Uriage in recent years have tended to be partisan. Bourdin's article of 1959[29] appeared in a number of the *Revue française de science politique* devoted to a consideration of 'Les Intellectuels dans la Société Française Contemporaine' and its orientation – reflected in its title – was towards an analysis of the attempts of the contributors to *Vers le style du XXe siécle* to devise a new style of intellectuality. Although Bourdin offered information about the

Uriage context, her intention was to present the thinking of 'l'équipe d'Uriage'. The thought became disembodied. By contrast, in his account of Uriage in *L'Idéologie Française*,[30] Bernard-Henri Lévy was determined to regard such an extrapolation of thought from events as part of the French nation's self-deceit about its continuing Fascist inclinations. Consideration of the thought of the Uriage participants without reference to the Uriage context reinforces the conspiracy of silence about what actually happened between 1940 and 1944. What Uriage stood for has, for Lévy, tarnished the thought which was generated there.

The study of Uriage seems to attract those who wish to be 'apologists' for its participants or to 'expose' its activities. To take refuge in this polarisation is to lose awareness of the complex nature of the present reception of past thought. I have tried to suggest that the ideological stance of Uriage as an institution was partly constitutive of the thinking of J-J. Chevallier and P.H. Chombart de Lauwe whilst, equally, their thinking helped to reinforce the practice of l'École. A balanced account of Uriage must do justice to the 'autonomous' thought, the context, and the interrelationships between the two. Our value judgement must follow from our assessment of how far any thinker, or speaker, or writer, has a moral responsibility to evaluate the intrinsic meaning of the context within which he or she communicates.

In conclusion, the different influence of the 'vie d'école' on these two thinkers, clearly shows the ambiguity within the ideology of Vichy to which Uriage contributed. On the one hand there was an involvement in local *veillées*, with a wish to learn from participation in the communities, and on the other hand suggestions of a respect for totalitarian action which could easily negate this empathetic concern. It is small wonder that an institution which could stimulate such contrasting developments should itself be seen as the epitome of ambiguity.

Notes

1. I am grateful for grants from the British Academy and the Centre National de la Recherche Scientifique; to the staff of the Bureau des archives départementales de l'Isère; and to Judy and Erik Geissler for their kindness on both occasions.

2. See Janine Bourdin, 'Des intellectuels à la recherche d'un style de vie, l'Ecole nationale des Cadres d'Uriage' in *Revue française de science politique*, 201 ix, no. 4, décembre 1959; and Raymond Josse: 'L'école des cadres d'Uriage' in *Revue d'histoire de la Seconde Guerre mondiale*, 1966, no. 61

3. Jeunesse – France, no. 21, 22 septembre 1941. Bureau des archives de l'Isère, 22 J43, p. 8.

4. Ibid., p. 6.
5. Ibid., p. 6.
6. Ibid., p. 7.
7. Ibid., p. 7.
8. See Bureau des archives de l'Isère, 22J8.
9. See, for instance, Jean-Jacques Chevallier, 'L'Ordre Viril et l'Efficacité dans l'Action. Le Chef et ses Jeunes', no. 7, Uriage 1942. Bureau des archives de l'Isere, 22J29, p. 49.
10. See Bureau des archives de l'Isère, 22J26.
11. See Bureau des archives de l'Isère, 22J4, 'Directives Générales de notre pensée et de notre action'.
12. For a full discussion of these issues, see both T.N. Clark, *Prophets and Patrons. The French University and the Emergence of the Social Sciences* (Harvard University Press, 1973) and George Weisz, *The Emergence of Modern Universities in France. 1863-1914* (Princeton University Press, 1983).
13. Pitirim Sorokin, *Contemporary Sociological Theories* (New York, Harper, 1928), p. 92.
14. See C. Lévy-Strauss: 'French Sociology' in G. Gurvitch and W.E. Moore, (eds.) *Twentieth Century Sociology* (The Philosophical Library, New York, 1945).
15. Paul-Henry Chombart de Lauwe, 'Pour retrouver la France. Le Chef et ses Jeunes', no. 6 (Uriage, 1942), Bureau des archives de l'Isère, 22J28, p. 6.
16. Ibid., p. 3.
17. Ibid., p. 17.
18. Ibid., p. 19.
19. Ibid., p. 21.
20. Ibid., p. 22.
21. Jean-Jacques Chevallier, *L'Évolution de l'Empire britannique* (Paris, 1930), p. 7.
22. Ibid., p. 7.
23. Ibid., p. 1050.
24. Ibid., p. 1051.
25. Jean-Jacques Chevallier, 'L'Ordre Viril et l'Efficacité dans l'Action. Le Chef et ses Jeunes', no. 7 (Uriage, 1942), Bureau des archives de l'Isère, 22J29, p. 37.
26. Ibid., p. 45.
27. Ibid., p. 47.
28. Ibid., Introduction.
29. Janine Bourdin, 'Des intellectuels à la recherche'.
30. Bernard-Henri Lévy, *L'Idéologie Française* (Paris, 1981).

11 EMMANUEL MOUNIER, *ESPRIT* AND VICHY, 1940-1944: IDEOLOGY AND ANTI-IDEOLOGY

John Wright

By the time of the Fall of France in June 1940 Emmanuel Mounier (1905-50), the founder, managing editor and *spiritus rector* of the monthly review *Esprit*, had written some 250 items, Through some 90 numbers of *Esprit* and through his numerous contacts, he had contributed to the ideological ferment of the 1930s.[1] Did the turmoil of 1940 enable 'an esoteric and marginal set of ideas' with its 'high-sounding phrases' to be applied practically? Was it the case that 'personalists were catapulted from obscurity into positions of influence and importance'? Did Mounier emerge 'from his relative obscurity to notoriety as the chief theorist of several ambitious projects to transform the youth of his country'? Why have recent revisionist interpretations of Mounier's ideological development, in concentrating on his seemingly compliant attitude to Vichy in 1940-1, generated such a vigorous polemical reaction in France?

There are two main primary sources for an analysis of Mounier's ideological development during the period 1940-4. Firstly, Mounier's own writings, and particularly his substantial, if sporadic, private Diaries ('Entretiens'), together with his weighty correspondence, published in 1956 as 'Mounier et sa génération' and republished, in 1963, with amendments, under the same title, in *Oeuvres*, IV, Editions du Seuil. However, neither published version includes his 'Journal de Dieulefit' of June-August 1944 which has been published in the *Bulletin des Amis d'E. Mounier*, Nos. 7-8, December 1955 (61 *Bulletins* have been published to date and constitute a rich source of unpublished or inaccessible material).[2]

Unpublished correspondence, available for consultation in the Bibliothèque Mounier,[3] is an essential supplement to that published both in *Oeuvres*, IV, and the memorial volume of *Esprit*, December 1950, which also contains Mounier's 'Journaux de Prison' ('Prison de Clermont janvier-février 1942', 'Journal d'un acte fragile [grève de la faim]' and 'Prison Saint-Paul Lyon, 7 juillet 1942 – octobre 1942'), an embryonic 'Mounier et sa génération' and important testimonies and commentaries by close associates. The second major source on Mounier are those numbers of *Esprit* (no. 94, November 1940 – no. 103, August

1941) published during what Mounier later referred to as 'l'aventure lyonnaise' or 'la clandestinité ouverte'. These should not, however, be analysed in isolation: they include only a relatively small amount of Mounier's total output (24 items out of almost 700). For a balanced analysis they should be related to the broader sweep of his ideological development from both 1932-40 and from 1944-50. Finally, it should be mentioned that Madame Mounier has recently stressed to the present writer that there is no additional correspondence to that available in the Bibliothèque Mounier likely to lend a more radical dimension or interpretation to the 1940-4 period (numerous items of correspondence, particularly Mounier's letters to his parents, having been lost in 1949). Plans to publish Mounier's private writings during the war years under the title 'Journal de l'Occupation' have been recently abandoned.

In addition to the *témoignages* referred to above, two works are of special interest in an analysis of Mounier's contacts during the period 1940-4: Henri Frenay (the leader of the Resistance mouvement, *Combat*), *La nuit finira* (Laffont, 1973), and Pierre Dunoyer de Segonzac (the Director of the *Ecole Nationale des Cadres d'Uriage*), *Le Vieux Chef* (Editions du Seuil, 1971). The testimonies of two active participants in Mounier's activities in 1940-1, Roger Leenhardt and Marc Beigbeder (whose 'Supplément aux *Mémoires d'un âne*', *Esprit*, no. 102, July 1941, led directly to the review's suppression) are to be found in *Esprit*, no. 53, May 1981, and no. 73, January 1983. Beigbeder's privately circulated 'La bouteille à la mer' (particularly January 1981 and February 1983), communicated to the present writer, in addition to presenting personal commentaries on the period 1940-1, reproduce the text of the 'Supplément' and respond to B.-H. Levy's accusations in *L'idéologie française* (see below). An autobiographical novel *Prelude choral et fugue*, Flammarion, 1983, by Pierre Schaeffer, the Director of the cultural movement *Jeune France*, despite its disclaimer to biographical exactitude, contains not only explicit references to Mounier and his influence, but usefully reconstructs the ambiance of the late 1930s and the war years. Finally, valuable information will become available with the imminent publication of the texts of the papers and testimonies of the *Colloque du Cinquantenaire* held in October-November 1982, which brought together surviving associates of *Esprit* from the period of Mounier's editorship.

Two recent radical interpretations of Mounier's ideological stance during 1940-4 – B.-H. Lévy, *L'idéologie française* (Grasset, 1981) and John Hellman, *Emmanuel Mounier and the New Catholic Left 1932-50* (University of Toronto Press, 1981) – allege not only his sympathy with Vichy during 1940-1 but his more general sympathy with fascism. Lévy's book generated a vigorous debate, notably in *Le Monde*, January 1981 and *L'Express*, February 1981. It taxes Mounier with lending intellectual support to Vichy in his 'exaltation devant cette grande révolution culturelle et populaire que lui propose l'époque' (p. 48) and in his opportunistic desire to ensure the insertion of personalist values into Vichy youth organisations. In Lévy's view, it was Mounier's conviction that with the defeat of France a new era was beginning that prompted him to take up his staff of 'pèlerin philosophique' with the aim of evangelising the *Chantiers, Compagnons* and *Uriage* (p. 49).

He was fired by 'cette euphorie réformatrice qui enfiévra les élites françaises en ces temps de confusion' (p. 50). His decision to republish *Esprit* is regarded by Lévy as 'une obligée compromission' and his personalist viewpoint made him an active participant (alongside Proudhon, Barrès, Maurras, Sorel, Péguy and Bernanos) in 'le fascisme aux couleurs de la France' (pp. 194-291). Responses from Mounier's associates during 1940-1 published in *Le Monde*, together with the views expressed in *L'Express*, referred to above, sought to put the record straight. *Esprit* responded with further testimonies (see above) and Paul Thibaud's article 'Du sel sur nos plaies' (*Esprit*, no. 53, May 1981, pp. 18-26) responded not only to *L'idéologie française* but to such views as that expressed by J-F. Revel – 'On n'anime pas pendant deux ans un centre subventionné par le gouvernement de Vichy sans une certaine équivoque, même si l'on a souvent maille à partir avec l'orthodoxie de Vichy' (*L'Express*, 14 février 1981, p. 22).[4] Also of interest is the response to Lévy by Denis de Rougemont 'Un falsificateur vu de près', Geneva, Cadmos, Summer 1982, which insists that through *Uriage* Mounier passed openly into the Resistance (p. 80).

Hellman's major, highly documented analysis – acknowledged in Mounier circles as the most detailed biographical study to date (Paul Fraisse, *Bulletin des Amis d'E. Mounier*, no. 59, pp. 20-1) – arrives at a similar, if more nuanced, interpretation. For Hellman, Mounier's activities during 1940-1, and even beyond, remain 'a subject of passionate controversy' (p. 187). Having flirted with fascism and anarchism in the late 1930s, Mounier became an important figure in the National Revolution. In Chapter 8, entitled 'Personalism in Power', Hellman states that by the end of 1940 *Esprit* had become 'a key publication in an effort to transform all French youth' (p. 163) and its associates 'intellectual architects of the metamorphosis of France' (p. 163). He sees a close proximity between the rhetoric of the National Revolution and *Esprit*'s appeal for a spiritual regeneration among French youth.

174 *Emmanuel Mounier*, Esprit *and Vichy*

The republication of *Esprit* under Vichy is regarded by Hellman as part of a double game in which Mounier, despite his private misgivings, adopted an active role in the new order (to the extent of becoming the chief theorist of Vichy's youth projects). His ideological success brought hostility from supporters of collaboration. In common with many of his generation, Hellman contends, he refused to admit later that his hopes for a new order in Europe had contributed to the confusion surrounding Vichy, despite his rude awakening after his arrest to the realisation that his personalist ideals were being prostituted by Vichy. Between 1942 and 1944 he sought an answer to this in an attempt 'to recreate Christian spirituality in its radiant purity and simplicity' (p. 190). Not only should he have admitted that his slogans had been 'profitably used by a corrupt and dishonourable regime' but that the personalist movement had promoted 'complacency towards nazism' (p. 200). Hellman concludes that the war period served to divide the personalist movement into those 'self-consciously Catholic' members – Mounier, Lacroix and Perroux – who chose to work within the National Revolution and Maritain and De Rougemont who chose the Resistance. He concedes that 'it is understandable that for a time Catholics should have been seduced by forces or ideologies which promised to reverse the tide of history' (p. 201) thereby dispelling their innate fear of a progressive secularisation of Europe, and a decline in hierarchy and authority with its threat to the Catholic Church. According to Hellman, Mounier should have acknowledged this instead of choosing to reconstruct and simplify the history of his role within Vichy and refusing to accept his compromise with both Vichy and Catholicism (p. 258).

Finally, in this brief survey of radical interpretations, mention must be made of the analysis of Mounier expressed in Zeev Sternhell, *Ni droite ni gauche, L'idéologie fasciste en France* (Editions du Seuil, 1983) (see Raymond Aron's review, with its reference to Mounier and Vichy, 'L'imprégnation fasciste', *L'Express*, 11 February 1983, pp. 22-4). He states: 'Les positions prises par Mounier immédiatement après la défaite s'expliquent par les jugements qu'il portait sur le "désordre établi", en d'autres termes sur la démocratie libérale.' (p. 24) He adds – 'Ce qui répandit la confusion dans les esprits et favorisa la Révolution nationale, ce fut moins la poésie du fascisme – l'esprit simple dans un corps sain – que la dénonciation permanente, excessive, obsessionelle de la démocratie par les litterateurs en quête de rénovation.' (p. 24) Without previous mention, Mounier figures prominently in Sternhell's 'Conclusion'. Having stated that political phenomena are best comprehended during their incubation period and that 'le seul critère authentique pour percevoir le comportement des hommes est la période comprise entre juin 1940 et juin 1941' (p. 298), he adds that Mounier's case is 'sans doute le plus intéressant, tout d'abord parce qui'il s'agit d'une personnalité hors pair, d'une droiture morale sans failles et dont l'influence fut considérable dans l'immédiat après-guerre' (p. 299). For Sternhell, Mounier's complex reaction to the defeat of France and the installation of Vichy is very characteristic of the period in its illustration of 'la profondeur du malaise moral, le dégoût de régime et la volonté de changement' (p. 299). Mounier's willingness to work within the framework of Vichy is an indication that anything was preferable to a return to the Third Republic. He is representative of the 'intellectuels contestataires' of the 1930s and, although he rejected fascism, his critical rejection of the 'désordre établi' led him to share common ground with fascism, while his rejection of bourgeois liberalism and his desire for a new world led to 'une forme d'acceptation ambiguë de la légitimité de Vichy' (p. 299).

Sternhell suggests that in the 1930s Mounier saw a tragic significance in the weakness and insufficiency of liberal democracy compared to the dynamic resolve of Nazism and fascism, a view which explains his involvement in 'l'effort de rénovation intellectuelle et spirituelle entrepris dans le régime' (p. 301). Although never the *jeune-turc* or *hussard* of fascism suggested by Lévy, Mounier contributed with the *Esprit* team to create intellectual confusion, an involvement which must not be minimised: 'dans la constitution du climat intellectuel qui rend possible la révolution nationale et qui contribuera à la poussée du fascisme, les hommes de cette équipe ont incontestablement leur part' (p. 303). The numbers of *Esprit* from 1940-1 are seen as an encouragement to participate in the National Revolution and not at all a call to resistance. Sternhell draws a general conclusion:

> Si un homme qui a consacré son existence à la défense des valeurs de l'esprit décide que, entre un passé qu'il méprise et une réalité qu'il abhorre, la balance penche quand même en faveur de ce qui est en train de se construire, cela signifie que le malaise est vraiment très général. (p. 309)

Moreover, the ambiguity and lack of clarity prevalent in the inter-war years and displayed in the fight against materialism by movements such as *Esprit*, helped create a favourable environment for the diffusion of fascism.[5]

The radical interpretations referred to above reject more popular interpretations, among which figure, in Hellman's view, the vast majority of studies of Mounier, with the notable exceptions of the works of Etienne Borne (*Mounier ou le combat pour l'homme*, Seghers, 1972) and Jean-Marie Domenach (*Emmanuel Mounier*, Editions du Seuil, 1972) although even these, despite their more subtle treatment, are designed 'to turn people on to Mounier' (Hellman, op. cit., p. 332, Note 6). Hellman shares the view, expressed some ten years earlier, of Michael Kelly ('The fate of Emmanuel Mounier: a bibliograhical essay', *Journal of European Studies*, 2, 1972, p. 257) that critical works sympathetic to Mounier constitute 'a kind of unofficial orthodoxy'. It is also worth noting that in a later, more substantial study, *Emmanuel Mounier, Pioneer of the Catholic Revival* (Sheed and Ward, 1979) Kelly assesses Mounier's activities under Vichy as comprising a force for anti-totalitarian opposition at a time before Resistance had become organised. In so doing *Esprit* became the most dissident of the non-clandestine reviews. Of particular interest is Kelly's conclusion that in view of Mounier's contribution to the development of Catholicism 'from a virtually monolithic right-wing stance to a pluralistic and increasingly left-wing position' (p. viii) it is not surprising that he should still arouse right-wing opposition. Also excepted from Hellman's 'hagiographical exposition category' (despite his association with *Esprit* in the 1960s and 1970s) is Michel Winock's *Histoire politique de la revue 'Esprit' 1930-50*, (Editions du Seuil, 1975). For Winock, the political aspect of the review is 'le plus problématique, c'est-à-dire le plus révélateur de la tension permanente vécue intimement par l'intellectuel entre la volonté de témoignage et la volonté d'efficacité' (p. 7). Chapter 7, entitled 'Quarantaines: 1939-44' (pp. 198-238) presents an analysis of the difficulties facing Mounier during this period: personal problems, the dilemma of republishing *Esprit*, his rejection of *attentisme* and involvement in Vichy organisations, his activities in Lyon including links with *Combat*, the *Esprit* numbers of 1940-1 regarded by Winock as expressions of 'combat' and 'une pensée libre' (p. 235), arrest, trial and preparation for the post-war situation.

The analyses of Bernard Comte, although less substantial than the above, are of no less interest.[6] In addition to his contributions to *Églises et chrétiens dans la IIe guerre mondiale. La Région Rhone-Alpes* (Presses Universitaires de Lyon, 1978), an unpublished paper of September 1983, 'A propos de l'action d'Emmanuel Mounier dans les organisations de jeunesse aux débuts du régime de Vichy 1940-41' stresses Mounier's influence in challenging 'le conformisme Vichyssois'

(p. 7), and his doctrinal deviation which led to his exclusion from Vichy organisations on the grounds of his pernicious influence. Comte argues that his provisional involvement in Vichy ensured 'la présence d'une pensée engagée' (p. 10) and demonstrated 'le choix d'une présence active et combattante sur le terrain miné où se jouait à ses yeux une partie décisive, pour y affirmer dans un langage renouvelé, au risque de l'ambiguité et de l'approximation, la permanence des valeurs défendues depuis l'origine d'*Esprit*' (p. 10). Comte also refers to W.D. Halls', *The Youth of Vichy France* (Oxford, The Clarendon Press, 1981) (for an analysis of this work see the present writer's review in *Bulletin des Amis d'E. Mounier*, no. 59, February, 1983, pp. 22-3). In this solidly documented work Halls draws the conclusion that in lending an original, intellectual component to the National Revolution Mounier contributed significantly to maintain a plurality of ideas within Vichy. Personalism, however, with its stress on the need for a radical restructuring of society went beyond the National Revolution and its potential political implications rendered it unacceptable to Vichy.

If considerable space has been devoted to a survey of recent interpretations of Mounier's ideological involvement during 1940-4, it is to show that, despite drawing upon common sources, analyses of Mounier's ideological positions arrive at fundamentally divergent interpretations. It seems important that any analysis of Mounier's attitudes during 1940-4 should seek to understand the objectives and methods of both Mounier and personalism as delineated during the 1930s. Moreover, his actions should not be judged with the benefit of hindsight. It should be borne in mind that despite his considerable network of wide-ranging contacts he did not have at his disposal the instant availability of information provided by today's mass communication systems. His judgements risked, therefore, being either hasty or overcautious; as has been seen, he has been criticised on both scores.

The *Prospectus* of January 1932 announcing the publication of *Esprit* stated that the review's aim would be: 'retrouver la vraie notion de l'homme' through 'une révolution permanente contre les tyrannies de cette époque' (6 January 1932, *Bulletin*, no. 57, April, 1982, p. 14). The ideological reality of statements such as 'nous entreprenons une oeuvre pour un monde neuf' (ibid., p. 15) only become apparent through the publication of *Esprit* with its increasing reaction to the historical reality of the 1930s. The review came to be, for Mounier, 'une revue de combat' (*Bulletin*, no. 15, March, p. 4), committed to sensitive opinions, to the need to oppose 'le désordre établi' with a social dynamic which would allow self-realisation and self-fulfilment within an organic society: *le personnalisme communautaire*. Mounier's first editorial of October, 1932, entitled 'Refaire la Renaissance', revealed not only the common attitude to life held by the review's contributors but urged the rejection of a decadent society. The bourgeois ethic should be broken, the capitalist system based on wealth opposed, and liberal individualism rejected in favour of a truly democratic society with an economy based on the service of Man. Superficially a reaction to the economic crisis precipitated by the Wall Street crash, Mounier's militant critique was the passionate expression of his feeling of Western society's spiritual bankruptcy: 'une crise de civilisation'. This spiritual disorder had led, in Mounier's estimation, to the negation of Man's fundamental sociability (*homo faber*) and to the promotion of materialism at the expense of humanism: 'Il n'est pas de pays, pas de forme de la pensée ou de l'activité, qui ne soient pas asservis à un matérialisme propre' (*Prospectus, Bulletin*, no. 57, p. 14). Moreover, the human alienation produced by the machine age was compounded by the reactionary attitude of the Church, locked in solidarity with established values and, in its inertia, unable to face the modern world (see *Esprit*, March 1933, 'Rupture entre l'ordre chrétien et le désordre établi'). Within this expression of revolutionary sentiment (which from today's viewpoint appears tame) *Esprit's* aim became, for Mounier, 'Rendre révolutionnaires les Spirituels' (*Bulletin*, no. 29, p. 22).

Mounier's attempt to reconcile a utopian vision of life with material reality, to the enrichment of both personal and community life, was developed in the review's 'période doctrinaire' and 'période d'engagement' (Mounier's own, later expressions, see *Bulletin*, no. 29, March 1967, pp. 9-25). The apparently naïve fulminations of a group of young nonconformists were challenged by the tensions of the period from 1932-9. Responding to events, the review rejected the 1934 riots, opposed any form of hegemony or totalitarianism, the actions of the Spanish Nationalists and Munich. However, Mounier avoided direct political action in the belief, shared with his ideological mentor Péguy, that it debased and diluted spiritual action: 'Tout commence en mystique et finit en politique' (Péguy, *Notre Jeunesse, Oeuvres en prose, 1909-1914*, Gallimard, 1961, p. 518). With its insistence that 'la révolution sera morale ou elle ne sera pas', the review succeeded in increasing the number of its subscribers from 500 in 1933 to 1500 in 1936 (see Winock, op. cit., pp. 161 and 164) and in becoming, in Mounier's own view, 'un circuit d'amitiés agissantes, tournées selon la vocation, vers une collaboration intellectuelle ou vers l'action sur l'opinion' (*Oeuvres*, IV, p. 494). In addition, the publication of Mounier's *Révolution personnaliste et communautaire* (Aubier, 1935) and *Manifeste au Service du personnalisme* (Aubier, 1936) had brought personalism to the attention of a wider audience than that of *Esprit*.

In its assertion of Man's spiritual dimension and in seeking the rehabilitation of human values in a dehumanised world, Mounier's social project, infused with his deep faith — the basis of his *vocation* (see 'Personnalisme et Christianisme', *Oeuvres*, I, pp. 751-2) — had become by 1939 more than an audacious, naïve criticism of bourgeois materialism. Its appeal for social regeneration in a society ruled by self-interest was accompanied by a growing disillusionment with the debilitated world, social and political, of the Third Republic. As an amalgam of social perception, human concern and Christian inspiration, personalism was set to offer a new model for an organic society. From the time of the launching of *Esprit* Mounier stressed that the movement's attitudes did not constitute 'un système fermé' ('Chronique du Mouvement', October, 1932, *Bulletin*, no. 57, April 1982, p. 9). This stemmed, above all, from the review's declared independence: 'libre de tout parti intellectuel, politique ou littéraire, [il] se gardera de dicter des disciplines' (ibid., p. 9). When faced in 1936 with scrutiny by Rome, Mounier stressed that while the contributors to the review shared 'certains carrefours communs' (*Oeuvres*, IV, p. 586) *Esprit* was not a Catholic review but rather 'une revue de rassemblement, donc de confrontation entre croyants et incroyants' (ibid., p. 588). He reiterated that '*Esprit* n'est pas une école' but 'une revue de recherche et de confrontation' (ibid., p. 589). Its aim was 'la recherche de nouvelles forces temporelles qui ne soient ni capitalistes ni marxistes' (ibid., p. 587) and through its spiritual influence it hoped to 'affranchir le sens de la personne des erreurs individualistes et le sens de la communion des erreurs collectivistes' (ibid., p. 589).

In seeking a permanent dialogue, Mounier believed that *Esprit* could open up the world of the unbeliever to the Catholic, thereby freeing the Catholic from his ghetto complex. Just as Mounier's desire for dialogue with Vichy has led to accusations that he was sympathetic to the regime, his later dialogue with communism led to accusations of crypto-communism, despite his references to 'ce discours dur et fraternel' ('Débat à haute voix', 1946, *Oeuvres*, IV, p. 137). Mounier shared the view expressed by his close associate, Jean Lacroix, that 'Tout dialogue est affrontement' (Roger Garaudy, *Perspectives de l'Homme*, PUF, 1969, p. 168).

By the end of the 1930s personalism had emerged, not as a doctrinaire ideology with political ambitions, but as an attitude to life, 'un style de vie' in conflict with the predominant values of the age. The non-ideological nature of personalism, with its stress on Man's spiritual dimension, is underlined in two works by close associates of Mounier: in *Le personnalisme comme anti-idéologie*, PUF, 1972, Jean Lacroix affirms that 'une inspiration n'est pas une doctrine' (p. 8) while Etienne Borne in *Les nouveaux inquisiteurs*, PUF, 1983, defines the person as 'cette idée de l'homme non-systématique et anti-idéologique capable de nourrir et d'animer toute une philosophie' (p. 127). Personalism was 'un combat pour l'homme' (ibid., p. 128).

After the experience of the war years Mounier reiterated that personalism was 'ce terme commode pour désigner une certaine perspective des problèmes humains, et pour accentuer, dans la solution de la crise du XXe siècle, certaines exigences qui ne sont pas toujours mises en valeur' (*Qu'est-ce que le personnalisme, Oeuvres*, III, p. 179). More than ever, it needed to realise 'le sens total de l'homme' (ibid.). However, his basic principle remained unchanged: 'Le 'personnalisme', tant qu'il dépendra de moi, ne sera jamais un système ni une machine politique' (ibid.). He was aware of the difficulties posed by personalism: 'Ce qui rend à certains le personnalisme insaisissable, c'est qu'ils y cherchent un système, alors qu'il est perspective, méthode, exigence' (ibid., p. 179). It was this seeming lack of precise definition which has led in the view of Mounier's critics to the ambiguity of his ideological position within the National Revolution. He did, however, offer a new definition – 'cet optimisme tragique' (ibid., p. 242) – but insisted that in the new ideological situation of the post-war period the power of human agency would be called even more into play: 'les idées ne sont rien sans les hommes qui seuls peuvent les nourrir' (ibid., p. 245). These statements may well be the expressions of his wartime experiences which, although colouring his aims, did not divert them.

Mounier faced the outbreak of war with a philosophy of life based on three principles: *ouverture* (a readiness to engage in ideological debate), *affrontement* (the confrontation of historical reality) and *engagement* (commitment to a number of spiritual values). In September 1939 he stressed that *Esprit* would seek to defend 'le maximum d'humanité au milieu des forces déchaînées'. Mobilised, he was obliged to hand over the management of the review to P-A. Touchard. In the Spring of 1940 his personal burdens were increased with the news that his daughter's illness was incurable. In January 1940 Mounier felt that in the event of war *Esprit* should act as 'un éducateur de la sensibilité publique' (*Esprit*, January, 1940) and bridge the gap between an undesirable past and an uncertain future. The June 1940 issue aimed to awaken 'les jeunes forces qui peuvent apporter à notre pays et à notre civilisation un sang neuf, des idées vraies'.

After captivity and demobilisation Mounier, preoccupied with the welfare of his family (an often understated aspect of his preoccupations), moved to Lyon and initiated a series of meetings with a wide range of contacts in an attempt to sense the mood of France. His meeting with the Christian Democrat, Charles Blondel, led to the belief that

> un nouveau visage est imposé à l'histoire qui nous attend, un visage autoritaire; nous ne pouvons éluder ces oscillations à grande amplitude de l'histoire, ni travailler à contre-courant de ses données élémentaires;. il ne reste qu'à assurer les mêmes fidélités, avec des gestes et des formes nouvelles, dans la nouvelle matière. (Entretiens X, 4 August 1940, *Oeuvres*, IV, p. 668)

He was attracted to Blondel's formula – 'faire de l'armement spirituel clandestin' – by which was meant 'profiter des similitudes de noms entre nos valeurs et les valeurs publiquement proclamées pour y introduire, à la faveur de cette coïncidence, le contenu désirable' (ibid.).

Barely six weeks after the Armistice Mounier was seeking means of future action in a conscious attempt to capitalise on the situation and ensure the penetration of personalist values.[7] His decision to return to writing a Diary shows his awareness of potential difficulties: 'nous entrons dans une période clandestine, où toute pensée ne pourra s'afficher, tout fait se publier, tout dessein s'affirmer' (26 August 1940, *Oeuvres*, IV, p. 670). He had also decided to remain in Lyon ('Toute activité en zone occupée s'avère impossible') and to republish *Esprit*. He confided his mixed reaction: 'Je suis à la fois pessimiste, car je crois que les épreuves commencent seulement, et qe nous verrons pire, – et optimiste, parce que nous entrons dans une époque ardente' (6 September 1940, *Oeuvres*, IV, p. 672). He was convinced of the need of 'des gestes créateurs, si modestes soient-ils' (ibid.). His activities were to take three forms: participation in certain Vichy youth organisations, the republication of *Esprit* and contact with certain Resistance groups. The relationship between his thought and his activities was to lead to misgivings but, by March 1941, he had assessed his role and contribution:

> Je suis un homme de conversation, de méditation, de dialogue, qui sent l'étroite responsabilité de sa méditation parmi les hommes, ne veut la poursuivre que dans une communication et un service permanents. C'est en ce sens que je fais de l'action. (30 March 1941, Entretiens XI, *Oeuvres IV*, p. 701)

It is crucial to understand his motivation. In his own opinion he lacked those qualities necessary for direct political action ('une action offensive de style politique') but felt that he could bring an influence to bear on other areas:

> Je me vois aisément travaillant sur toutes les pentes politiques dans ce qu'elles gardent d'ouvert pour les maintenir ouvertes. Dans une régime subnazi ou communiste, non. Mais dans un régime communisant ou hors Vichy, si, dans la mesure où les jeux ne sont pas faits, où l'on peut pousser de toutes ses forces encore dans le sens de l'homme, si. (ibid.)

He concluded that 'Je pense bien peser dans *le sens d'une efficacité mais dont le point d'insertion est autre que politique*' (ibid.).

By October 1940 he had made contact with the fledgling youth movements set up by Vichy as a means of ideological education for the National Revolution. He wrote later of the dangers of the inculcation of Vichy ideas – 'Pour la première fois, le jeunesse avait un ministère, des institutions de plein air, un rôle dirigeant. Ces éléments de séduction jouèrent.' ('Le complexe Pétain', August 1945, *Bulletin*, no. 56, October 1981, p. 8) He agreed to contribute to the weekly magazine of the Compagnons in the light of his assessment that 'A Vichy "la Jeunesse" (Ministère et "Compagnons") est certainement ce qu'il y a de mieux là-bas, bien que peu lourde d'idées mais avec des volontés nettes et saines.' (15 October 1940, *Oeuvres*, IV, p. 674) For Mounier, as for Vichy, youth was a symbol of renewal and presented the opportunity to shape spiritually a new generation. Yet, while there seemed to be a direct correspondence in the stress placed by both Vichy and *Esprit* on personal and community values, Mounier sought to avoid 'cette déformation des consciences' which might be produced by Vichy's policy of collective self-condemnation. In what he regarded as a situation of 'open expression' (see R. Kedward, *Resistance in Vichy France*, OUP, 1978, pp. 185-209) – 'une situation publique plurivalente' – he sought 'de multiples activités de présence' (having contacts with the Compagnons, Chantiers, École des Cadres d'Uriage and Jeune

France).

In October, 1940 he referred in his Diary to 'le honteux *statut des Juifs*' (*Oeuvres*, IV, p. 675) but found some consolation in the fact that there was a muted opposition to it within the Compagnons. By December he concluded that the Compagnons' ideological positions were not 'franchement totalitaires, ni même complaisantes avec le nazisme, mais indéterminées et violentes sur un fond d'ambition illimitée, ce qui est le climat exact pour qu'elles s'engagent sur les pentes les plus dangereuses . . . ' (*Oeuvres*, IV, p. 682). Only one of his articles had been published and by November his contribution was no longer sought – 'l'Etatisme menaçant' was making progress, and Mounier was aware of this fact (*Oeuvres*, IV, p. 692).

His prospection of youth movements led to an invitation to join the cultural movement Jeune France.[8] He questioned its degree of independence from Vichy and refused to become a committee member prefering to maintain 'une situation plus libre, et, tout en travaillant, collaborer tangentiellement à 'Jeune France', à Uriage, etc., de manière à n'être ni l'homme d'un seul régime ni d'un seul organisme' (January 1941, *Oeuvres*, IV, p. 621). Schaeffer has referred to his encounter with Mounier: 'Rassurant de trouver dans ce bazar de Vichy, quelqu'un d'aussi ferme que lui, qui sait quoi penser. Très en garde bien entendu contre les mouvements de jeunesse' (Schaeffer, op. cit., p. 342). In February, 1941 he responded to Borne's serious misgivings about the republication of *Esprit* ('tout ou rien') with his belief that he had brought fresh air to 'des îlots réels de santé, des coins de France vraiment libre, l'Ecole d'Uriage, Jeune France' (22 February 1941, *Oeuvres*, IV, p. 695). In March 1941 he wrote to G. Zérapha – 'A *Esprit*, hors *Esprit*, je pense pouvoir armer l'âme française contre la contamination nazie' (9 March 1941, *Oeuvres*, IV, p. 697) and in his Diary stressed the legitimacy of 'une action de présence', underlined that his actions were non-political and insisted in March 1941 'Nous, nous sommes dans une situation encore très ouverte, nous jouons à l'ouvrir de plus en plus, et pesons dans ce sens par l'écrit et la parole' (*Oeuvres*, IV, p. 702). By April, however, he noted that as part of what he saw as an ideological counter-offensive Vichy had dispensed with his services at Uriage. Vichy had become aware of the School's opposition to collaboration and Mounier's role in fostering a spirit of free enquiry within Uriage which led to many of its students joining the Resistance. Dunoyer de Segonzac has declared Uriage's aim to be 'la recherche d'un homme nouveau, capable de s'imposer dans le monde nouveau' (op cit., p. 85) and has commented on 'cet étonnant rassemblement, dans une unité presque oecuménique d'hommes venus de tous les horizons et de tous les milieux' (ibid., p. 13). In August 1941 Mounier was excluded from all Vichy youth organisations, a decision which corresponded with the proscription of *Esprit*. However, his attention had already turned to other forms of activity – creative writing and a clandestine study centre to draw up a 'Déclaration des droits de la personne'.

How effective was Mounier's activity within the youth organisations? At a time of national disgrace he was able to offer an alternative, in the form of a optimistic social ethic, to a disillusioned section of the French Nation. Yet he was unable to stave off the hardening orthodoxy of Vichy. His public pronouncements were necessarily guarded and even some of his close associates found it difficult not to see apparent complicity and compromise in his activities. At a time of ideological hesitation he was able to offer a form of spiritual opposition but it was clear by March-April 1941 that an increasingly vigilant State found his ideological nonconformism unacceptable, preferring to leave the ideological training of its youth in more orthodox hands.

In March 1941 Mounier felt that his action within the youth movements was more important than that of *Esprit*; it had served to stem the spread of totalitarianism among French youth. This action is, however, closely interwoven with the issues of *Esprit* published during what Mounier came to refer to as 'la clandestinité ouverte' (*Bulletin*, no. 29, p. 20). As has been seen above, the decision to republish was not an easy one. He rejected the view that to publish was to risk compromise, arguing that not to publish was to concede in advance the unknown orientation of the new régime – pure abstentionism. He was aware of the need to 'armer clandestinement les mots' (12 November 1940, *Oeuvres*, IV, p. 678) and he recorded his pleasure in avoiding the censor's vigilance regarding the first issue of November 1940. Equally he was aware of the need for circumspection in his declarations: 'La question est de savoir s'il faut se faire tuer tout de suite' (he had been advised not to publish a proposed article on the Jews) (17 November 1940, Entretiens X, *Oeuvres*, IV, p. 679). Despite this awareness, his proposed second issue with its implicit disapproval of the Occupation met with the censor's disapproval. Among Mounier's associates, particularly in the Occupied Zone, the initial reaction to *Esprit*'s republication was that 'des demi-vérités' might be interpreted as 'des contre-vérités' (*Oeuvres*, IV, p. 683): duplicity might be taken as complicity. From correspondence he had received, however, he concluded that the vast majority of his readers accepted the first reissue 'sans contresens' (ibid.).

In January, 1941 Mounier reacted strongly in private to the Vichy formula of 'Dieu à l'école', promoted by his former teacher Jacques Chevalier, and to the pro-German attitude of the Church hierarchy. Moved by Bergson's death and news of Jewish refugee camps, he noted: 'Nous mettons au point toute une série de projets destinés à donner aux notes un tonus d'indépendance, de résistance au conformisme.' (18 January 1941, *Oeuvres*, IV, p. 689) He felt that his readers would be aware of 'ce jeu d'intelligence' (ibid., IV, p. 690) and by March, 1941 he had achieved, to his own satisfaction, despite the tightening grip of the censor, 'un succès d'indépendance' (8 March 1941, *Oeuvres*, IV, p. 696). He was also aware that in welcoming the transfer from the Third Republic to Vichy France he risked the accusation of ambiguity but insisted that 'Nous ne participons pas à la guerre des fusils, mais nous n'avons pas signé l'armistice de la guerre spirituelle, que nous avons commencée en 1932' (Letter to Contributors, March 1941, *Oeuvres*, IV, p. 698). He wished, though, to continue to benefit from the open situation in the conviction that *Esprit* would be read as 'l'organe de l'indépendance et da la résistance' (*Oeuvres*, IV, p. 703).

Although he wrote in April 1941 that duplicity was still possible, he felt increasingly that given Vichy's hardening ideological positions, he could no longer continue to practise subterfuge: 'chaque mois je tire un peu plus sur la corde. Elle cassera un jour.' (15 June 1941, *Oeuvres*, IV, p. 710.) By July 1941 he had tersely dismissed Vichy as 'senilité et manque de foi' (25 July 1941, ibid.), adding to his condemnation in April 1941 that 'la Révolution nationale est pour les deux tiers de ses chefs une révolution de parti et de classe, sous la réalité d'une démission nationale' (*Oeuvres*, IV, p. 704). He was in no way surprised by the review's suppression in August 1941 'en raison des tendances générales qu'elle manifeste' and was convinced that it had achieved 'le freinage net de la poussée totalitaire' and ensured 'la suture entre notre génération et les jeunes' (10 September 1941, *Oeuvres*, IV, p. 714).

Are Mounier's private reflections consistent with *Esprit*'s public expressions during this period of 'open expression'? Was his gamble in republishing the review justified? The indications are that from the outset Mounier knew that republication would lead to suppression. He felt that he must maintain a fidelity to his readers and by publishing they would be made aware not only of the censor's blindness but Vichy's ideological position. His readers had been alerted to the review's circumspection: 'si certaines limitations de notre champ de vision, si certains durs silences, si la mise en veilleuse d'une certaine critique font partie des disciplines aujourd'hui nécessaires, nous les consentirons volontiers' (*Esprit*, no. 94, November 1940, p. 7). They knew that a review which had spent the previous eight years affirming its independence did not readily and naturally volunteer its conformism. They realised that this transparent compliance did not imply automatic political obedience to Vichy or an advocacy of *maréchalisme*. Where the censor insisted on cuts Mounier indicated these by leaving blanks, including a whole page in December 1940, a practice soon forbidden and which indicated the refusal of free expression. He hoped also to contribute to the process of social regeneration but in line with the views expressed in the 1930s. His participation in 'cet accouchement du monde nouveau' would be a continuation of 'une révolution au service de l'homme' ('D'une France à l'autre', *Esprit*, November 1940). Lacroix's article on 'Nation et Révolution' (November 1940) suggested that current events would enable *Esprit* to pass from theory to practice and 'incarner nos idées en de multiples expériences'. The initial reissues reveal Mounier's ready condemnation of the Third Republic for its individualism, capitalism and sterile, liberal democracy and the coincidence of *Esprit*'s values with those of the National Revolution in its emphasis on respect for the person, corporatism and Catholic values. His appeal to *Esprit*'s readers to reject 'une mauvaise conscience morbide' contained the seeds of opposition to a currently tolerant regime but it was inevitable that any sign of acquiescence, even that required by expediency, should evaporate completely, for any hopes Mounier may have entertained of social renovation by Vichy were certainly betrayed within some six months. Any semblance of approval for Vichy gave way to nonconformism, increasing temerity and dissidence. *Esprit*'s disapproval of Vichy's education policy and mystique of *le chef* was reinforced by the review's implied support of Jews (and condemnation of 'Le Juif Süss' in June 1941) and by Beigbeder's lampoon of Pétain in July 1941 — 'Supplément aux *Mémoires d'un âne*,' regarded by Mounier as 'tout le procès du collaborationisme des démissionaires' (15 June 1941, *Oeuvres*, IV, p. 710). According to Mounier the number of *Esprit*'s readers had at least doubled in the Occupied Zone (see *Oeuvres*, IV, p. 720) but its suppression by Vichy was an unambiguous recognition that it had become a serious opponent in the battle for hearts and minds.

From November 1940 Mounier had stressed that the review was an organ of communication aimed principally at 'la création culturelle et les problèmes de civilisation'. Within this perspective he offered French youth 'le sens d'une communauté' (January 1941) in order to avoid its becoming 'étatisée et politisée', asserted that '*Jeune France* ne veut pas être une école artistique, encore moins une académie officielle, un mouvement d'Etat' (February 1941) and stressed Uriage's desire to 'faire des hommes complets' (April 1941). Confronted by such statements it was inevitable that Vichy should pronounce it 'une doctrine néfaste' and 'une conception philosophique de l'homme qui fait partie de ces mensonges qui nous ont fait tant de mal'. Mounier learned via the censor that the suppression was due to the combined efforts of Massis, the maurrasiens and a vigilant Propaganda Ministry resolved to promote 'un Etat totalitaire acceptant un minimum d'humanisme chrétien' (*Oeuvres*, IV, p. 718). He appealed to his readers to continue 'ce relèvement spirituel français auquel nous travaillons ensemble depuis neuf ans' (2 September 1941, *Oeuvres*, IV, p. 714).

Mounier's third area of spiritual activity, his links with Résistance movements, had begun as early as November 1940 with the creation of clandestine study groups. Frenay confirms his meeting with Mounier and Stanislas Fumet which led to Combat's contacts with many of Mounier's associates (Frenay, p. 87). Mounier's links with *Témoignage Chrétien* led to pressure being put on him to abandon his continued publication of *Esprit* in order to avoid any suspicion of pro-Vichy activity. By January 1942 with *Esprit* suppressed as an organ of dissidence, Mounier was arrested in a general round-up of Combat suspects (see M. Granet and H. Michel, *Combat*, PUF, 1957). After three months imprisonment in Clermont-Ferrand, provisional release, re-arrest and subjection to 'un internement administratif' he was removed to prison in Lyon where he remained from July until October. During his 12-day hunger strike in June 1942, in protest against what he saw as unjustifiably prolonged internment, he suffered the spiritual anguish of being refused Communion: 'j'étais un peu ému de ce contact vigoureux avec mon Eglise' (*Esprit*, December 1950, p. 744). Further pressure from the Church to abandon his hunger strike met with no success and brought from him the passionate comment – ' . . . mon Eglise, hélas mêlée à tout cela' (ibid., p. 746). His abandonment by his Church resulted, he was informed, from 'le caractère de rébellion contre le pouvoir établi' (ibid., p. 739). The *Procès Combat* held in October 1942 failed to produce sufficient evidence for his conviction. (Frenay claims to have minimised Mounier's role in Combat to Pucheu, op. cit., p. 161.) Later, Mounier prefaced his *Journaux de Prison* with his belief that 'Il manque à un homme de n'avoir pas connu la maladie ou la prison' (ibid., p. 721) – the war years had provided him with a further 'expérience vécue'.[9]

During his imprisonment Mounier had worked on his *Traité du Caractère*, a long, reflective study and *L'Affrontement chrétien* which continued his analysis of the necessity to restore Christianity as a community reality (the theme of discussions with Father Montuclard in November 1940). His Preface to the *Traité* reveals his preoccupations between 1942-4: 'Nous sommes entrés dans une des crises périodiques de l'homme, où l'homme cherche dans l'angoisse à retenir les traits d'un viage qui se défait, ou à se reconnaître figure d'homme dans un visage qui se défait.' Faced by a confusion of values each individual must choose: 'Nous avons choisi. Nous n'avons pas seulement, dans notre recherche, voulu traiter de l'homme, mais combattre pour l'homme.' This spiritual activity, exemplary for his associates, served to triple the review's circulation in the post-war years, thereby offering a doctrinal alternative to Existentialism and Marxism and becoming a barometer of opinion for progressive Catholics. *Esprit* had achieved recognition as 'un poste de combat spirituel' (*Bulletin*, no. 15, March 1960, p. 45), fulfilling Mounier's desire, that the review should be 'la pointe et le cadran d'une activité spirituelle multiple' (*Oeuvres*, IV, p. 491). Mounier had become an intellectual figure not to be ignored.

It is difficult to quantify Mounier's contribution to the provision of an alternative to Vichy ideology. He acted as a focus for a section of French ideological opinion, from diverse creeds, and by his various activities helped avoid the imposition of a single ideology by Vichy, at least in the initial phase of its ideological development. For an influential section of the Resistance he was a spiritual guide. For Mounier himself his experiences had served to confirm him in his long-term global project, in his faith and in therealisation that 'Nous ne nous engageons jamais que dans des combats discutables sur des causes imparfaites. Refuser pour autant l'engagement, c'est refuser la condition humaine' (*Le personnalisme*, PUF, 1949, p. 111).

Notes

1. See J.-L. Loubet del Bayle, *Les non-conformistes des années 30* (Editions du Seuil, 1969).
2. Of particular interest are nos. 56 (October 1981), 59 (February 1983), 60 (October 1983) and 61 (March 1984).
3. 19 rue Henri-Marrou, 92290 Châtenay-Malabry.
4. See also Raymond Aron, *Mémoires*, Julliard, 1983, pp. 705-9.
5. See J.-M. Domenach's response in *Lettre à mes ennemis de classe* (Editions du Seuil, 1984), p. 12 and pp. 125-7.
6. In his review of Sternhell's, *Ni droite ni gauche* (*Bulletin*, no. 61, p. 18) he

stresses that Mounier was not an 'idéologue élaborant un système idéal, mais témoin de valeurs affirmées au contact de l'événement'.

7. According to Madame P. Mounier, Mounier firmly believed that the Occupation would last far longer than it did. This belief was at the basis of his actions during 1940-1.

8. In Schaeffer's view there was room for 'un mouvement de culture populaire' between 'la politique et les bonnes oeuvres' (*Prélude choral et fugue*, pp. 34-2).

9. See also *L'Affrontement chrétien* (*Oeuvres*, III, p. 9): 'Un catholique français imaginait-il volontiers, dans les cent dernières années, que les prisons pussent être une place plus normale pour lui que la bienveillance rassurante des discours officiels? Les faits en ont jugé.'

PART THREE:

RESISTANCE

12 THE RESISTANCE EXPERIENCE: TEACHING AND RESOURCES

Hilary Footitt and John Simmonds

The 'ideology and culture' of the Resistance is contained in the verbal and written utterances of participants, and in the visual testimonies of attitudes and stance which remain to us. Experience in teaching a course on the Resistance has led us away from what was in effect a joint-disciplinary approach – historical survey of the Resistance, illustrated by novels, essays and poetry – towards a concentration on the textual analysis of a variety of documents. The focus has narrowed and the scope of what we term a 'text' has widened. In this sense, the archive that we have collected has been a product of our changing attitudes and emphases as teachers.

The Modern Languages degree at our College is composed roughly of 60 per cent languages and 40 per cent history, which replaces the traditional literature in a language degree, and attempts are made during the four years of the degree to make the two disciplines combine; we would not, I think, make the ambitions claim 'integrate'. The final year seminar entitled 'Writers and the Resistance' is a course in which the two teachers – a linguist and a historian – treat the same documents from two points of view: stylistic analysis and historical investigation. With the prospect of an hourly seminar for 20 weeks, we set about trying to examine the whole of the wartime period and the whole of the Resistance movement, which proved to be a far too ambitious project.

To use the somewhat hermetic vocabulary beloved of CNAA submissions: the early objectives of the course were first to 'provide an understanding of the beginnings and development of the Resistance', and secondly to offer an insight into the 'perceptions and motivations of Resisters as seen through literature and press material'. At the planning stage, these two objectives were intended to be complementary – the historical study of the Resistance would be enhanced by a study of the literature, and the literature would be given greater depth by an appreciation of its historical environment.

Looking back on the way the course has developed over ten years, it is clear that in practice our early approach was to treat history and literature as two separate compartments, with the emphasis on the latter illustrative material. The historical survey of the Resistance was considered as contextual, providing a framework for analysis of the literature. It should be said that the frame was skeletal. We largely expected students to develop an understanding of the period themselves via reading from a general bibliography and the provision of maps, tables and the inevitable 'organigrammes' of Resistance organisation. Our class time was concerned with discussing the novels, poetry and essays, with students either answering specific questions given in advance, or presenting an exposé in French. The programme included Sartre, *Paris sous l'occupation*; Camus, *La Peste*; Vercors, *Le Silence de la Mer*; Triolet, *Les Amants d'Avignon*; Vaillanà, *Drôle de Jeu*; Anouilh, *Antigone*; selections from the poems of Eluard and Aragon, copies of *Lettres Françaises, L'Humanité, Franc-Tireur, Libération* and Sartre, *Qu'est-ce qu'un collaborateur?*

Several problems in this approach became apparent. Most obviously, students, asked to roam through an ample bibliography, as well as prepare a novel for class discussion, opted for the latter and seldom did the former. It was evident that their understanding of, for example, the political development of the Resistance was, in terms of the objectives set, embarrassingly slender. In an attempt to meet the difficulty we added three introductory lectures to our programme. We were in effect tacitly accepting the fact that the historical context would have to be almost totally provided in these three lectures, which rapidly assumed the form of last-ditch stands to stem the tide of ignorance by injecting massive amounts of relevant information into one hour. It need hardly be said that this proved to be no solution at all.

In terms of the other objective set, providing an appreciation of 'perceptions and motivations of resisters' we were perhaps slightly more successful. However, judged by the admittedly rough-and-ready criterion of 'Does the student feel confident enough to answer an exam. essay question on this?', the course could not be described as a triumph. The verdict appeared to be that whilst they found the course enjoyable, they were wary about where it 'fitted in', or what they were 'supposed to be looking for'. This reaction could partly be ascribed to the initial reluctance of history students to handle mainly literary material. More likely, however, it was a just reflection of the problems of the course itself: perceptions and motivations existing in a vacuum of discrete literature and press texts, apparently unrelated to the historical context. We limped back to the drawing-board.

In common with many others in this situation we had fallen victim to the academic respectability trap — that is to say, we had felt that the course had to 'pass muster' as a coherent history course taken out of a history degree, and a coherent French course taken from a traditional French degree. The result was unsatisfactory. Accordingly we revised our objectives and hence our materials and approach. If the aim of the course was to provide an understanding of the culture and ideology of the Resistance, the emphasis should fall primarily on what the participants said themselves, rather than what later observers inferred about them. The text itself, closely analysed, was therefore of major importance. This had certain implications.

Firstly, since the course was no longer a general history of the Resistance with the usual nods towards historiography, lectures on the background to the Resistance became purely contextual; not designed to give a fulsome background, but tailored to make the texts intelligible. Students were still given synopses of particular topics, maps, diagrams and assorted aids, and, as the course was not designed to be a 'gobbet' class, each document had concise notes about its origin, authorship, time period, allusions, names and references. Even with all this help we have found that we can still only tackle a relatively small number of documents, but we do examine them very thoroughly.

Secondly, our choice of material widened, whilst the focus narrowed. We turned away from the use of novels (although we occasionally used extracts from them), and included more clandestine newspaper material, as well as pamphlets and posters. We played short excerpts of taped material, songs, speeches and interviews that we had recorded ourselves. In all cases the approach used was close textual analysis, the texts grouped around themes: the fall of France, the Occupation, the beginning of the Resistance, the political development of the Resistance and the Liberation.

For the historian, the study of such documents provides, as do other sources, concrete examples of Resistance, including the strength and development of movements, and general statements of intent and policy. Thus a comparison of the southern Resistance in early 1943 shows a variety of clearly-stated objectives, from *Combat*'s 'Révolution nécessaire'[1], to *Libération*'s 'victoire du peuple'[2] and *Témoignage Chrétien*'s 'transformation des âmes et des institutions'.[3] Apart from these direct statements of intent, a textual examination reveals indirect evidence – what Marwick, quoting Guerlac, likes to call 'unwitting' evidence[4] – of other objectives . . . or the lack of them. An absence of objectives can be seen in De Gaulle's famous radio broadcast of the 18 June 1940, the anti-climactic language of the call to arms and the absence of a concrete aim underline his problems at the time. He could insist that the war was not over and that the flame of resistance would never die, but he could not risk a rallying cry that might be superseded by events. Similarly, the French Communist Party (PCF), surprised by the Germano-Soviet Pact in late August of 1939, could only throw together a garbled propaganda tract, whose remarkable variety of language and styles betrayed the work of many hands and many 'editors', none of whom was sure of which line to take. As evidence of the strength and peaceful intentions of the USSR, for example, the statement: 'Le Japon en sait quelque chose!' has baffled our students for many a year.[6] But one can go a stage further than this with the Resistance documentation along the path of indirect internal evidence.

Whilst in this 'new' course the history student may appear to have lost out on the traditional narrative and historiography — which in any case is supplied in other areas of the degree — he or she gains from the interesting and more unconventional areas of detailed social history. Studying a broad spread of comments from the Resistance in detail can take the historian into the difficult areas of assessing the reactions, attitudes and motivations of individuals and groups. We are in some ways following the spirit of the 'Annales' school without its typical material or long time-periods, but even the 'Annales' approach, with its illustrious pedigree, still provokes strident debates over the merits and drawbacks of the 'histoire des mentalités'. As Bailyn recently noted:

> The characterisation of a community's interior life, even when its members stand alive before me, available for interviewing, polling and participant observation, is problematic for the anthropologists, sociologists and psychologists who design methods precisely for such studies. For historians, lacking living subjects and dependent on random documentation, all of the difficulties are compounded.[7]

Whilst noting these warnings, and not wishing to claim that we are working in the 'total' sense that the 'Annales' label often implies, we feel that our detailed textual study does allow our students to make more solidly founded analyses of small areas within the period, from which broader generalisations can be drawn.

Similarly, the recent trend of studies in modern history towards a view of society 'from below' has made historians aware of the difficulties involved in collecting and analysing evidence of popular social and political attitudes. This evidence is often seen as less reliable and of an inferior quality to that provided by formal institutions, but perhaps one way to enhance its quality is by careful study of its language and expression.[8] The documents available for the Resistance come from all levels of the 'hierarchy of evidence', but even the less valuable can reveal — through their language — a great deal more than one might at first glance suppose.

It is the advantage of a close textual study that the historian can focus on the individual and group responses to events. Without beginning to analyse the language, one can already find individual and group reactions in a host of documents. In Sartre's *Paris sous l'Occupation* the student can begin to understand the psychological and emotional reaction of the individual to the banal daytime of Occupation and the terrifying night of the German repression. It is an admittedly intellectual impression of occupied Paris, but through its image the student can transpose him, or herself, into the mind of the occupied Frenchman. For the reactions of individuals and social groups in a whole society one can turn to Camus' *La Peste*, with its insights on social solidarity and disintegration. As if carefully studying a good diary, the students can judge the actions of these authors from their own emotional and psychological points of view.

The next step is to go behind these *post-facto* accounts — even if written by actors in the drama — to the contemporary impressions, concerns and problems of the Resisters at the time. One of the overwhelming problems for the French in the war, as seen through the material produced by the Resistance, was that of identity. The identity of the individual Resister became blurred, and Juliette Noël in Triolet's *Les Amants d'Avignon*, although only on the fringes of the Resistance, had a moment of panic when she could not remember whether her real or assumed identity was the one borne out by the documents she had in her bag. This serves as a metaphor for the larger problems of individual identity within Resistance movements.

For the Resistance group there was the problem of establishing an identity which was clearly its own, but also at one with the broader movement led by de Gaulle. For an organisation like Témoignage Chrétien there was the even more difficult task of establishing an identity which was Christian, but not associated with the Catholic church establishment in France, which was linked with Vichy. The means they used were to associate themselves in metaphor and parable with the clandestine church of early Christianity and the persecuted Christ. The identification of the *whole* movement was also a constant concern of the Resistance, and although calls for unity were frequently made around concepts of identity — Aragon's 'Celui qui croyait au ciel, celui qui n'y croyait pas'[9] — the political colour of the movement more often shone through in its vocabulary. Thus for *Combat* the movement was one of patriots – 'français digne de ce nom'[10] – rallying behind De Gaulle, and for the PCF a 'mobilisation des masses pour l'insurrection nationale': both predictable identities. But for *Libération*, the diversity of its politics produced a front page in February 1943, which described the Resisters as 'bons Français' in one article and 'le peuple' – 'les Français sans carnets de chèque – in a neighbouring one.

The identity of Vichy was even more important to the Resistance, particularly after the liberation of French North Africa when, to their horror and amazement, the Resistance saw Vichy personalities appearing as potential leaders of the new France. Laval was always clearly associated with the Nazis, but Pétain was rarely slandered and the common identification, 'vieillard', was indicative of a reluctance on the part of the Resistance to attack such a venerable national figure. Vichy sympathisers in North Africa were another matter. *Combat* gave a public warning; 'prenons garde. Ne nous laissons pas berner par les félons qui jouent aux traîtres repentis' and *Libération*, with more sarcasm than hate, identified them as insects and declared 'Chacun à son tour. Passez à la queue messieurs.'[14] With the image of Vichy – French but yet not France – came the problem of identifying France, and in particular combatting the effects of collaborationist propaganda. For Texcier it was quite easy. The published expression of French views no longer existed; 'La lecture des journaux de chez nous n'a jamais été conseillée à ceux qui voulaient apprendre à s'exprimer correctement en français. Aujourd'hui, c'est mieux encore, les quotidiens de Paris ne sont même plus pensés en français.'[15] For *Les Lettres Françaises* it was a more serious matter, and to combat the flood of banality and distortion published by the collaborators and occupiers, they declared that the duty of the Resistance was to 'Crier la Vérité'.[16] *Les Lettres Françaises* and the work of the Comité National des Ecrivains is replete with references from France's cultural and historical heritage, and to a lesser extent these references occur in other works, binding the writer and readers together in a cultural union against the alien and barbarian influences of the occupier and his collaborating allies. Thus culture, language and style not only identify the enemy and the true France, but they band the resisting French together in a cultural conspiracy against the occupier.

The historian can, with relative ease, determine the motivation of political and activist groups who declare their intentions and their arguments clearly in their propaganda, but there remains the level of 'hidden' motivations for the Resistance. In a document like Texcier's

Conseils à l'Occupé the humour indicated the author's desire to resist by means of re-establishing individual and national pride at a moment of dark tragedy:

> C'est entendu. Ils [the German Occupiers] savent chanter en choeur et d'une voix juste. Mais c'est au commandement, comme pour un exercise respiratoire. Chez nous, le soldat chante faux et rarement en mesure; mais il ignore la corvée du chant. Il chante quand ça lui chante.
>
> Tu grognes parce qu'ils t'obligent à être rentré chez toi à 23 heures précises. Innocent, tu n'a pas compris que c'est pour te permettre d'écouter la radio anglaise?[17]

The slight schoolbook references to French history and culture, the play on words and the gently mocking humour draw the reader and writer together, and thus we see the more subtle motivation behind resistance; to rebuild social solidarity and individual self-esteem. Texcier is attempting to gather the French into a cultural conspiracy against the Germans; a conspiracy which will distance the individual from the 'ordinary German' and help him develop a resistance attitude.

Vercors' *Le Silence de la Mer* is an example of individual resistance not to be found in the 'documents', but the silence itself, so tense and disturbing, is the attitude that Vercors wants the French to adopt, because he wants them to be always aware of the evil behind the 'ordinary German'. The pauses and the halting dialogue of the German denote the skirmishes of a battle that Vercors wants the French to fight every day, so as to maintain their rejection of Nazism and the brutality hidden behind the propaganda for the New Europe. He has some sympathy for the German and for the unspoken love which develops between him and the daughter, but he counsels silence as the only attitude in the long run.

In a sense of course, the whole approach outlined so far assumes that language is an adjunct of history – the application of linguistics to history. One is still implicitly examining and elucidating the content of a text, what is said or implied, rather than studying the means by which it is said. It is accepted in many quarters, however, that discourse itself, the way in which people define themselves and their world, is as useful and valid a subject of study for the historian as say institutions or social groups. The questions that J.P. Faye[18] raises on the relationship between language and change lie at the centre of this debate. In addition, Régine Robin and her colleagues[19] have analysed a variety of political discourse to see what ideologies determine them — she prefers 'ideology' incidentally to 'mentalités'. From this viewpoint, a history of ideologies can only be attempted through an understanding of discourse strategies.

This has several implications for a study of the ideology of the Resistance. King has pointed out that 'Language is the last line of defence of a defeated country'.[20] In occupied and Vichy France, language was more than just a weapon, it was itself a permanent battlefield. Debû-Bridel, faced with the speeches and writings of the new authorities, spoke of, 'une contrée où les mots les plus essentiels auraient perdu dans l'expression courante leur signification'.[21] Language, before being used as an offensive weapon had first to be clarified, almost remade, in relation to its usage by Vichy and the Germans. It is no surprise that one way of doing this was by reusing methods of discourse which had been tried and established in previous situations. The classic example is *Père Duchesne*. The paper of 1942 consciously imitates the original Hébertiste version. The introduction of the April 1942 issue is virtually an extract from the revolutionary model, the absence of verbs adding to the temporal disorientation. Vocabulary of the revolutionary period is immediately quoted at the reader: 'affamés et pillés' 'le tyran des peuples, ses hordes, ses suppôts', 'bougrement en colère', 'tremblez, canailles'. The 'Marseillaise' is added, and the opposition is described in Hébertiste terms as: 'une réaction de sabre et de goupillon . . . les uns regrettant Capet.[22] All this becomes of considerably more interest in the light of Guilhaumou's[23] painstaking analysis of the language of the original *Père Duchesne*. His conclusions were that Hébert's strategy was one of simulation. He was attempting to 'véhiculer, dans les masses sans-culottes, une conception bourgeoise de la démocratie à l'aide d'un processus de camouflage du contenu au niveau de la forme'. In short a 'camouflage . . . du contenu politique de l'idéologie du Père Duchesne par la forme', the objective being to link the people with the Jacobins, the popular masses with the more radical members of the bourgeoisie. The fact that some members of the Resistance have opted for the same linguistic strategy prompts several questions: is Hébert's 'camouflage trick' understood and accepted by readers in 1942, becoming merely one of those shared cultural references which exclude outsiders? Is it rather a replaying of the same device, albeit with somewhat 'recherché' materials? — the anachronistic populist form carries a general message of unremarkable loyalty to the long-established republican tradition: 'la Grande Révolution, la vraie, la Nôtre'. Only a Guilhaumou-type analysis of the way in which the

The Resistance Experience

parody is achieved and presented would allow firm conclusions on this. It seems indeed that there is a great deal of scope for this systematic discourse analysis on the whole corpus of Resistance material. In the confines of our present undergraduate course, we do not, needless to say, follow more than a comparative stylistic approach, attempting to appreciate varieties of language and hence the breadth of experience and ideology that they define in the Resistance.

To summarise then, our teaching experience has led us to a greater reliance on the text itself, and an increasingly eclectic approach to what constitutes a legitimate text. We were fortunate to receive funding from the Nuffield Foundation to start a teaching archive which could be used not only by us, but potentially by teachers at different levels in departments of History, French or European Studies. In awarding the grant, the trustees pointed out that they had some doubt about the educational value of the proposed literary sources, such as poems and songs about the Resistance experience. They felt that the quality of these was not likely to be particularly high and that the consequent benefit for students' foreign language skill was likely to be limited. They suggested that the acquisition of historical material might well deserve a greater share of the effort. Without in any way wishing to, 'bite the hand that has fed us', it should be said that we have found this implicit differentiation between literary and historical material difficult to sustain and unhelpful as a guide to selecting material.

Since the collection was intended as a teaching archive to serve a variety of courses, range and representativeness were clearly key factors in selection of material. We understood the latter in two ways. Firstly we aimed to establish an archive which would illustrate a gamut of political/ideological persuasions, and also attempt to represent the attitudes of various social and occupational groups. In addition we wanted, by selecting material relating to different areas of France to provide an indication of the variety of experience in the whole country. We also took note of the need to provide examples of what one might term 'special cases': early resistance documents, tracts or editions which had a particular function, and copies of fake tracts and newspapers produced by the authorities. Secondly, the collection took account of key points in time (and we produced an obvious check-list of the most important of these) which would, as far as possible, represent the development of the war, and thus, when taken with political/functional/regional criteria, suggest the changing attitudes of groups towards these events.

A third approach to selection of material was less concerned with representativeness and more with the possible educational uses to which the particular resources could be put. Here again we accepted that variety and range were essential. Linguistically sophisticated documents, which degree students of French and French History could profitably read and listen to, should be complemented by less complex and shorter pieces (tracts, *papillons*, posters), a limited amount of relevant material in English, and a considerable body of visual material (photographs, slides, maps) which would interest all students, from degree level specialists to school children who had barely studied French. The collection incidentally has something in the order of 270 photographs of a generally very high quality.

Every researcher has an individual tale of the 'agony and the ecstasy' of locating documents. It would perhaps be better to acknowledge briefly the institutions that we found particularly helpful in assembling the archive. We received indispensable help from Roderick Kedward, whose enthusiasm and generosity were crucial at the outset of the project. In England, the Imperial War Museum and the British Museum (Colindale) were helpful, but had relatively little relevant material. In France, the then Comité d'Histoire de la Deuxième Guerre Mondiale was a mine of information, providing copies of photographs, *témoignages*, maps and invaluable contacts, addresses and advice. The bulk of our clandestine newspapers was obtained from the Bibliothèque Nationale, and we also received valuable assistance from the Bibliothèque de Documentation Internationale Contemporaine, the Institut Charles de Gaulle, the Musée de la Résistance in Lyon, the Archives Départementales des Bouches-du-Rhône, the Musée de l'Histoire Vivante at Montreuil, and the Association pour la création d'un Musée de la Résistance at Ivry. We have, regretfully, to report our failure over several years to obtain from the ORTF a set of what appear to be very useful recordings from the period.

One important aspect of the work was selecting and locating suitable people to interview. Again the rather crude criteria outlined above served as a rough guide. Contacts were given us by the Comité, the Institut Charles de Gaulle, Roderick Kedward, the UNADIF (Union Nationale des Associations de Déportés, Internés et Familles de Disparus), the Féderation des Amicales de Réseaux Renseignement et Evasion de la France Combattante, the Comité d'Action de la Résistance, the ANCVR (Association Nationale des Combattants Volontaires de la Résistance), and the ANACR (Association Nationale des Anciens Combattants de la Résistance). In all there are around 25 interviews with survivors, ranging from intellectuals like Debû-Bridel and leaders of movements like Jean-Pierre Lévy through to participants at grassroots and observers in a variety of situations. The interviews were intended to follow a questionnaire which the listener could be given as an explanatory guide before playing the tape. In practice of course, some interviews were hijacked by the subject and went their own interesting way.

Once collected, the material would clearly only be of use if it was catalogued in a way which permitted different types of approach. In a situation of reduced educational expenditure, the process took some little time, but thanks to the initiative and work of the College catalogue librarian, Jeremy Miettinen, the archive is now computer catalogued, each item given a unique number and then indexed by code numbers related to a list of descriptors. The latter presently stands at some 400 subjects.

Does it however actually *work*? If one imagines two potential readers with rather different requirements: firstly a teacher in an institution of higher education, who is setting up a history course on 'Women in the Resistance' and would like some illustrative material. The descriptor list has 'women' as one heading, but others are probably of relevance too: 'Casanova', 'Triolet', various papers with titles like: *Jeanne de la Lorraine, Femmes Françaises* and *Jeunes Filles de France.* Suppose the teacher starts with the descriptor 'women'. The result is that four broad groups of documents are listed in a random order. Firstly, there are documents and other materials relating directly to individual Resistance women from the famous like Bertie Albrecht, Danièle Casanova and Germaine Tillon to the less well-known like Mme Diebolt, Mme Wagner and Mme Merlat. The second group of documents are those journals and tracts produced by women's Resistance groups: *Jeanne de la Lorraine, La Voix des Femmes, Patriote Parisienne, Femmes Françaises, Femmes Patriotes, Femmes Comtoises, L'Humanité (Edition Féminine)* and so on, representing a wide variety of womens' groups and several different geographical locations. The third group of documents are those from groups who are not directly involved with resistance, but are clandestine and associated with the Resistance movement. Typical of this group are *Comité Femmes de Prisonniers, Comités Féminins de Montceau-les-Mines, Comité Populaire des Femmes de Marseilles* and *Ménagère.* Lastly the descriptor turns out a long list of journals, from the famous to the obscure in which there are major references to women, their groups and Resistance activities. All in all such a descriptor applied to the collection produces a quite comprehensive selection of groups, individuals, types of action, time periods and locations. It also has some unusual and perhaps evocative contributions such as *Le Cri d'Alarme, L'Eveil du XXe Arrondissement*, and one document simply entitled 'Maison Française d'Oxford'.

The second imaginary reader is a schoolteacher who would like some illustrative material to complement an 'O' level history course. The material should be general, to provide a series of impressions, and should be suitable for students with little or no knowledge of French. A profitable approach might be to run through the list of photograph and poster material, bringing together a mini-exhibition, complemented by some of the *papillons*. A similar run through the tape listing would isolate any interviews in English which might be of use to him, as well as broadcast speeches/songs in English which could be played to introduce the display.

The Resistance archive has been a product of our experience as teachers, and has fed back into that experience. It is happily not a static thing, since particular contacts continue to send us relevant documents as they become available. Most importantly, we hope that as other teachers come and consult the collection and use material from it, they will be able to add copies of their own resources which they have found useful in teaching courses on the Resistance. In this way, the collection, established with Nuffield money, can become the nucleus of a growing archive which will reflect the interest and approaches of many other teachers and feed back into the work that is done on this subject at different levels in colleges, schools and universities.

Notes

1. *Combat* (Supplément Local pour Lyon), no. 1, décembre 1942.
2. *Libération*, no. 23, 1 février 1943.
3. *Témoignage Chrétien* no. 8, n.d.
4. A. Marwick, *The Nature of History* (Macmillan, London, 1970), p. 136; 'Archive Film as Source Material' *Archive Film Compilation Booklet* (Milton Keynes, 1973).
5. De Gaulle, 'Appel du Général De Gaulle lancé à la radio de Londres dans la soirée du 18 juin 1940'.
6. 'Moscou montre la voie de la PAIX' (PCF pamphlet), n.d. (possibly 25 August 1939).
7. B. Bailyn, 'The Challenge of Modern Historiography', *American Historical Review*, vol. 87 (1), February 1982, p. 21. See also Kedward's discussion of the 'Opinion event' as evidence in 'Behind the Polemics: the French Communists and the Resistance' in S. Hawes and R. White (eds), *Resistance in Europe 1939-1945*, Allen Lane, London, 1975; F. Furet, Beyond the *Annales*', *Journal of Modern History*, vol. 55, September 1983 and J. Webb, Foucault for Historians', *History Workshop Journal*, vol. 14, Autumn 1982.

The Resistance Experience

8. See T.V. Rabb, 'Towards the Future; Coherence, Synthesis and Quality in History', *Journal of Interdisciplinary History*, vol. 12 (2), Autumn 1981.
9. L. Aragon – 'La Rose et le Réséda' in *La Diane Française* (Paris, 1946).
10. *Combat*, Supplément Locale pour Lyon.
11. *L'Humanité*, no. 293, mai 1944.
12. *Libération*, 1 février 1943.
13. *Combat*, Supplément local, décembre 1943.
14. *Libération*, 1 février 1943.
15. J. Texcier, *Les Conseils à l'Occupé*, juillet 1940.
16. *Les Lettres Françaises* no. 2, octobre 1942.
17. J. Texcier, *Les Conseils*.
18. See, for example, J.P. Faye in *Change* 'Hypothèses' (Editions Seghers/Laffont, Paris, 1972).
19. R. Robin in the collection of articles *Le Mouvement Social*, Oct./Dec. 1973, no. 85. See also, R. Robin, *Histoire et Linguistique* (Armand Colin, Paris, 1973).
20. J. King, 'Language and Silence: Some Aspects of French Writing and the French Resistance', *European Studies Review*, vol. 2, no. 3, 1972.
21. J. Debû-Bridel, *La Résistance Intellectuelle*, Juillard, Paris, 1970, p. 38.
22. *Le Père Duchesne*, avril 1942.
23. J. Guilhaumou, 'l'idéologie du Père Duchesne' in *Le Mouvement Social*, op. cit.

13 FRANCE, SOIL AND LANGUAGE: SOME RESISTANCE POEMS BY LUC BERIMONT AND JEAN MARCENAC

Ian Higgins

This chapter was written after the conference, in response to a generous invitation from the organisers to add a contribution on Resistance poetry. The main problem is to avoid the trap of generalisation, into which most work on the subject has fallen. Encouraged by the view of Hilary Footitt and Don Simmonds that discourse analysis is essential to an *histoire des mentalités* (let alone for any assessment of poetry), I shall limit myself to a relatively detailed discussion of one poem by Luc Bérimont and two by Jean Marcenac.

There are four reasons for this. First, I want to exemplify kinds of textual analysis which might be useful in tackling Resistance poetry. Second, I want to show some of the characteristic themes in that poetry, some of the ways in which they are manifested, and some of the possible relations between them. There can be no question of complete coverage. The study is just a suggestion as to what the yet-to-be-written typology of Resistance poetry might include. Third, while plenty of other poems would have suited my purpose equally well, analysing these three is an economical way of showing a relation between the three themes of France, the soil and language. Finally, the discussion partially complements the chapters of Roderick Kedward and S. Beynon John. Marcenac was active in the FTP du Lot, and his poems are typical of the militant outlaw poetry of *L'Honneur des poètes*. Bérimont's poem is an example of the other extreme of Resistance poetry, so-called *contrebande*.[1] Indeed, taken on its own, it might well not seem to be any kind of Resistance poem at all. Its emphasis on the soil and natural cycles could even, at first sight, be seen as sympathetic to Vichy. Such an ambiguity is perhaps similar to the one seen by S. Beynon John in *Pilote de guerre*. Yet if the circumstances of publication are taken into account, what the soil produces in Bérimont's poem seems to me as unambiguous as the 'Produits du sol' in the painting mentioned by Roderick Kedward. In short, these three poems are good examples of an area where historical and literary concerns are one.

France, Soil and Language   207

Luc Bérimont: 'Le temps du beau plaisir...'

Written in 1942 and published in 1943, this is the tenth of a series of 15 consecutive pieces in verse in *La Huche à pain*:[2]

    Le temps du beau plaisir serpente par des plaines
    Où les blés vont rugir avec leurs lions roux.
    Les enfants couleront de ces toisons oisives:
    Un peuple est à mûrir dans les caves de l'août
5   Des lèvres, par milliers, sucent la terre ouverte.

    C'est le cargo du blé, c'est l'océan du sang
    On entend s'élever des vivats à la lune
    Les morts sont à nourrir la bouche des vivants
    Un étendard de vent bat à la grande hune.

10 Les couchés dresseront leurs poings d'épis luisants
    De leurs ventres fendus jailliront des armées
    Tout retourne à l'été, tout rentre dans le rang
    Le boulanger pétrit des neiges explosées.

I am going to confine myself to the four main themes: time and the seasons; the cycle of life and death, with the dead materially resurrecting through the soil; language; and, by implication, France.

The theme of time and the seasons appears in the first line. 'Serpente' suggests a winding river, so that the 'beau plaisir' might be summertime boating parties or riverside picnics. Summer is also implied in the ripening wheat, and it is explicit in 'août' and 'tout retourne à l'été'. This last phrase implies a cyclical succession, which is also suggested in two other ways: in 'neiges explosées' (winter exploding into summer, and eventually becoming bread); and in the overall contrast between the sunlit first stanza and the moonlit second stanza. The theme of passing time is reinforced by the three future tenses, and by the use of 'est à mûrir' and 'sont à nourrir' instead of 'mûrit' and 'nourrissent', the infinitive construction emphasising the idea of continuous process.

The imagery of cyclical process is what links the theme of time to that of the dead resurrecting. The dead become wheat and feed the living. There are three key expressions of this. First, the people maturing underground. There is a basic ambiguity here: is this 'people' the children of line 3 maturing in the womb before being born, or is it the dead, slowly dissolving into the soil before springing up as shoots of wheat? In the end, it comes to the same thing: the living live off the dead. This ambiguity is structurally analogous to the theme of cycle. The second example is in line 5. Are the lips the children underground suckling at the earth (perhaps where the rainwater (or melted snow – cf. line 13) drains into it), or are they the wheat-roots drinking at the earth? Again, it comes to the same thing, and again, the ambiguity is analogous to the theme of cycle. The third example is in lines 10-11, where the age-old idea of the body resurrecting in different physical form is given new treatment. The dead are a whole collective people (line 4), and they are going to raise their fists. Every stalk of wheat will carry a clenched fist, rising up in their thousands, like whole armies.

This image helps to crystallise the theme of language and give it political significance. New life is given to the dead metaphor in 'tout rentre dans le rang'. This phrase has a regular figurative meaning of 'return to normal, settle down', or 'come to heel after misbehaving'. On its own, it would sound like resignation, acceptance of the wisdom of ages – 'it'll all be the same in a hundred years', 'things'll settle down again'. But of course it is not on its own. It comes immediately after the unexpected image of the armies springing up, and therefore inevitably connotes the expression *rentrer dans les rangs*. The implication is paradoxical, but unmistakable. 'Settling down again' does not mean fatalism or *attentisme*, coming to heel and resigning oneself to defeat and death. It means forming ranks again and preparing to fight. The norm is not death, but life. This is where the theme of language acquires decisive importance. It is hinted at in the image of roaring lions, and then again in the use of 'lèvres', instead of, say, 'bébés' or 'nourrissons'. It is taken up in the image of cheers (by implication eerily silent), and clinched when Bérimont writes 'nourrir *la bouche* des vivants', instead of the more usual 'nourrir les vivants'. Because of the close semantic, phonetic and contextual associations of 'vivats', 'bouche' and 'vivants', the reader is reminded that the mouth is used for speaking as well as for eating, and that living people are people who – among other things – speak: the living are being fed partly in order to speak. And they will speak partly in order that people should live (Latin *vivat* = French *vive*).

So the poem is not a piece of materialist monism. The utterly physical transformation of a dead body into water and wheat is transformed into values. There is no explicit statement of these values – at best, a reference to new armies arising from violent death, but with no statement of what they would fight for. They could even be an Armistice army. However, the poem contains a number of *contrebande* allusions which would be clear to readers in 1943. First, no one in 1943 is going to see the dead and the ocean of blood as anything but a reference — albeit an ideologically neutral one — to the war and the Occupation. Even this neutrality evaporates if one considers the circumstances of publication. *La Huche à pain* was published by Les Amis de Rochefort. Rochefort, which was a well-known centre for poetry, stands on the Loire, near Angers. The first line of the poem then might well suggest the castles of the Loire, a time-honoured glory of French civilisation in stark contrast with contemporary alien barbarity (a regular theme in Resistance writing). The Loire is in any case explicitly named in the third poem of the suite from which this one is taken, so that the allusion is more or less transparent. There may be another allusion, as well. The Loire flows down to Nantes, passing to the south of Châteaubriant. There is a strong chance that the reader in 1943 would be reminded of the execution of hostages from Châteaubriant and Nantes.[3] This allusion strengthens, and is strengthened by, the connotation in 'beau plaisir' of the authoritarian 'bon plaisir' (as in *le bon plaisir du roi*). Other allusions would confirm the poem's ideological stance. The image of new life flowing from lying lions (the tawny rolling plains) may suggest Samson; and in 1943, the reader would think immediately of Samson the Jewish resistance-worker fighting the Philistines (Judges, 13-16). The invisible banner would very likely suggest the tricolour, initially forbidden in the Occupied Zone. Just as the cheers are silent, the flag is invisible, but the values it represents are still alive, audible in the wind. The plural 'neiges' implies vast continental snows. In 1943, exploding snows would connote the plains of the USSR (cf. the raised fists), where the Soviet army was fighting the Germans.

An essential conclusion is that this poem is itself an example of what it is talking about, a defiant *vivat*: a new generation of children will only rise from the soil of France in so far as they are willed and created through language. That is the sense in which the dead nourish the living — through being talked about in a particular manner. In this case, it is a metaphorical and allusive manner.[4] And how else might the bakers of Anjou knead Russian snows?

Jean Marcenac: 'Mort à nos ennemis' and 'L'agent de liaison'

Mort à nos ennemis

Ils ont un dos pour le couteau
Ils ont des yeux pour ne pas voir

Une tête pour oublier
Tout ce qui fait notre misère

5 Rien ne se lève quand ils parlent
Leurs mots sont perclus Et leur souffle
Ternit nos miroirs nos images

Ce qu'ils ont de vivant en eux
S'est élevé contre la vie
10 Les signes qu'ils essaient de faire
Comme ils n'ont servi que la mort
Elle seule peut les comprendre

Et le cri qu'ils ont en tombant
Est celui qu'attendait l'aurore

15 Il la délivre

  This poem was written in 1943 and published, under the pseudonym Rémy Walter, by the illegal Editions de Minuit in *L'Honneur des poètes II. Europe*, in 1944. (I shall refer to this anthology simply as *Europe*.) The title is a primitive battle-cry. The words 'nos ennemis' immediately introduce France as a theme. The plural 'ennemis' ensures that it is no abstract, generalised enemy that is envisaged, but flesh-and-blood individuals. Similarly, sticking a knife into someone is an unsophisticated way of killing, and involves physical contact: the enemy cannot remain a remote cipher, as might be the case with shooting or planting a bomb. Right from the start, then, the text is dealing in the primitive, concrete and down-to-earth. The first line expresses an uncompromising readiness to kill the enemies, even if it means stabbing them in the back. The use of 'pour' implies that there is something teleologically right about stabbing these backs: they exist in order to be stabbed. That something so conventionally base should be presented as natural and, by implication, self-evidently right, is the first of the paradoxes that constitute the poem. The essential feature of these enemies is indeed that they are an inversion of an implied natural humanity: they have eyes in order not to see; they turn their backs and ignore the sufferings of others (the structural parallelism of the three propositions in the first stanza implies that all three qualities are equally unnatural); and the little bit of life in them is anti-life, so that only death can make sense of their inadequate gestures and language.

The enemies' other characteristics are by implication also unnatural inversions of humanity. Nothing springs up into being when the enemies speak. Here, one might have expected the verb *susciter*, or even *évoquer*, in a phrase like 'leurs paroles ne suscitent rien'. With *se lever*, 'personne' would have been a more likely subject than 'rien'. Consequently, *se lever* here implies movement, action (getting up and getting on) and respect (rising when someone speaks to you); and eventually, when the reader comes to the image of dawn (line 14), it acquires the added implication of light, as in *le jour se lève*. Marcenac's line conveys a picture of a world which has been left motionless, dark and lifeless by a crippled, paralytic abuse of language (cf. line 6). If this is the unnatural inversion, then the implication is that a properly human use of language should be supple, dynamic and creative, calling new things into being. This idea is essential to the poem, as we shall see. First, however, there is more to say about line 5. The enemies' world was, of course, one built on hierarchy and authority, supported by copious, unending and strident propaganda, both spoken and written. It was a world in which one was expected to spring to respectful attention when spoken to, or shouted at. This was especially true metaphorically, the propaganda being a mobilising and a chastening force; but it was also literally true, in the eternal *appels* of the camps, which the escaped POW Marcenac had known at first hand. It was also a world in which right hands and arms were forever rising in Nazi salutes. Line 5, then, in baldly contradicting these concrete facts, is in effect saying '*rien d'essentiel* ne se lève quand ils parlent' — even if I stand up when a fascist shouts at me, he is commanding no assent from my values or my conscience. Line 5 is therefore more than just a metaphorical statement that fascism is death-oriented: in denying fascism any moral worth, it is itself an act of refusal and disrespect.

Developing the image of speech and anticipating lines 8-9, 'Leur souffle' is not the breath of life or of communication. It is used unnaturally, to tarnish mirrors and therefore isolate us in ourselves. In Marcenac's wartime poetry, the mirror is an image not of narcissism, but of the dynamic, fruitful and essential interdependence of self and others. This is a dialectical view of humanity. The implication here is that it is natural and essential for us to project ourselves in images and to see ourselves in others — that is, to realise ourselves in communication. Our enemies do not even use their eyes (line 2), and their breath is destructive or at least distortive, in that it dulls the mirror and imprisons us in a dualist, sterile, inhuman isolation from one another, tarnishing our image. Again, Marcenac does not quite use the word one would have expected, *embuer*. *Ternir* implies dirt, like the soot of smoke. It can apply metaphorically, as *tarnish* can in English, to someone's reputation or memory. In other words, we are all publicly soiled by our enemies' poisonous breath. Their talk is vicious; their life is our death.[5]

The inversion continues in the image of dawn. This takes up the two images of darkness – eyes that do not see, tarnished mirrors – and creates for 'Rien ne se lève' the added implication of continuing darkness. Not surprisingly, the dawn is a stock-in-trade of the writing of *les années noires*. However, Marcenac's treatment of it prevents its becoming a cliché. It is not a question of the wheel finally coming full circle, which would imply *attentisme* at best, and fatalism at worst: we have to make dawn come, through an act. This act is the culminating instance of the inversion which informs the whole poem: killing revives life, and the enemies' cry of death is our cry of life. Their words have caused nothing to rise into life – indeed, they themselves have risen against life. Now our stab with a knife puts a cry into their mouths which causes the sun to rise as they fall. Like their crippled words and inadequate 'signes', their cry is inarticulate. The final inversion is that their last utterance, which is not even a word, is supremely meaningful for us, the key to unlock the dawn.

The poem begins as a very down-to-earth incitement to kill, but ends by suggesting, through sustained metaphor and paradox, that language is in some way inseparable from the conflict: a death-dealing abuse of language characterises fascism, a life-giving use of language characterises resistance to fascism. But the poem does more than just suggest this. It is itself so unconventional an act of language that it attracts the reader's attention. The old cliché of dawn is transformed and brought to life. At key points, expected words are replaced by less expected ones ('rien' and 'ternit'). The octosyllables, in which the pronounced mute 'e' highlights certain key words (notably 'lève', 'élevé', 'signes' and 'elle seule'), set the militant text apart from primitive prose; but the degree of conventional formality which this confers on the text is restricted by the unconventional absence of end-rhyme; and this absence of rhyme is enough to underline the crucial opposition between death-dealing language and life-giving language in 'mort' and 'aurore', because these are the only end-rhymes in the piece ('misère' and 'faire' being surely too far apart to have much impact).

In other words, the poem is an example of the supple, creative, resuscitative use of language of which, it is suggested, fascism is incapable. In its own way, it gives new life to the French language (at least in preventing its ossification), and that is by implication analogous to giving new life to France. The text is itself an act of hostility to the enemies, and as such, a cry to help unlock the dawn. If the act of stabbing is metaphorically an act of language, this particular act of language is metaphorically an act of stabbing. In its skilful combination of the primitive and the sophisticated, Marcenac's articulate text *is* the enemies' virtual, as yet unuttered, inarticulate cry.

L'agent de liaison

Le cœur dur La tête en armes
Il échappe à l'ennemi
Son pas efface les rides
Son feu pur sèche les larmes
5 Et son éclat rend le sien
Au visage de la vie

Le cœur dur La tête en armes
Il traverse le pays

Les sauvages chasseurs d'étoiles
10 Sans méfiance Laissent passer
Ce voyageur sans bagages
Qui porte leur défaite et leur mort dans la tête.

'L'agent de liaison' was written in 1944 and published, under the pseudonym Paul-Louis Valentin, in the clandestine *Étoiles du Lot* in the same year. Like 'Mort à nos ennemis', it depends on paradox and inversion. The protagonist is hard-hearted, so 'La tête en armes' makes him sound like one of the enemy, some kind of unfeeling militarist, aggressive in both heart and mind. In line 2, however, this supposition is reversed: he evades the enemy, so he must be one of us. Again, the notion of enemy implies the notion of France. Yet his hard aggressiveness in heart and mind is repeated in line 7. So the effect he has on other people is unexpected. When they hear him coming, their faces lose their lines; he has a 'tête en armes', but his firepower is a metaphorical purifying fire, and, far from being cold-hearted, he has a comforting warmth which dries peoples' tears. He has an infectious brilliant vivacity ('éclat'), which restores the sparkle to life. The image of the 'visage de la vie' takes up that of lined faces, and brings to the surface its implied metaphor of a face lighting up (*illuminer* and *éclairer* are regularly used in this sense in French, and a lined face is also a *visage sombre*). The image of the enemy hunting down the stars confirms that the messenger is on the side of light. Finally, in the last two lines, the central paradox is repeated for the last time: he deals in death, but this is to restore light and life.

If he deals in death, how does he do this? He has no luggage, and his weapons are in his head. So this explosive purifying firepower must be ideas — not only doctrines, but values, beliefs, hopes and feelings. But how do you fire such guns? By utterance. The protagonist is an ***agent de liaison***, carrying messages to link together otherwise isolated units. Underlying the whole text, in fact, is the implied metaphor of words as loaded guns. A central theme is that language is essential to militant action. This is so banal that it would in itself make the reader ask why Marcenac has bothered to say it. But of course, the way in which he has said it is not at all banal — the language is even more unconventional than in 'Mort à nos ennemis'. Consequently, the language of the text is as much to the forefront of the reader's attention as the themes of language and resistance.

The most obvious peculiarity of the expression is that the banal truism should be accorded the dignity of verse. Yet the verse is significantly unorthodox. If the text were read as prose, many of the lines would be half thrown away. The effect would be one of thin-lipped, terse, almost staccato vindictiveness — and of course there would be nothing surprising about that. However, even the simple fact of pronouncing the mute 'e' means that some words receive more stress than in prose; the pace is slowed down, and the reader's attention drawn firmly to ideas and images which might otherwise go relatively unnoticed. Some examples are 'efface', 'sèche', 'visage' and 'traverse'. The text is denser and more reflective (without losing any of its tough combativeness). Nevertheless, while pronouncing the mute 'e' confers a certain stylisation and traditional dignity on the text, it also means that all but three of the lines have an unorthodox seven syllables. In other words, observing convention gives an unconventional result, and keeps the danger of pompous rhetoric at bay. Similarly, rhyme is a conventional device, but Marcenac's rhyme-scheme is unconventional. This twofold tension between orthodox and unorthodox form is one way in which the reader's attention is drawn to the text as language as well as to what it denotes.

This is done in more substantial ways as well. For example, the sustained metaphors of resistance as light, life and weaponry depend to a great extent on the fact that the context generates multiple meanings and connotations for 'feu' and 'éclat'. The initial reference to weapons means that 'feu pur' is gunfire as well as a pure flame. The moral connotation of 'pur' suggests that the fire is also a purifying one, a passionate moral commitment (cf. *avoir le feu sacré*) to cleansing the country of evil. Given the context of weaponry, 'éclat' connotes explosion and shrapnel, so that the light is a brilliant flash. Because the fire is 'pur', there is a suggestion that the brilliance of 'éclat' is diamond-like (and adamantine – cf. 'dur'). And because the messenger's 'éclat' causes anxious faces to light up, there is a connotation of sudden laughter (cf. *éclats de rire*) and youthful vitality (cf. *l'éclat de la jeunesse*). The combination of these multiple connotations of 'feu' and 'éclat' reinforces the role of 'étoiles' as part of the sustained metaphor of light. To any reader in 1944, of course, the hunted stars are also an allusion to the star of David worn by Jews, and perhaps also the red star of communism. So the bringer of light is an agent of a political struggle which is associated with the heavens as something self-evidently natural and right. The effect of the associations, connotations and multiple meanings is that the several attributes of the messenger are bound together into one complex overall image, as many-faceted as the implied diamond.

However, the main feature which forces the language of the poem on to the reader's attention is the dominance of certain sounds in key words. An example is the internal rhyme of 'dur – pur – dur', occurring in the same rhythmical position each time. This coincidence of stress and rhyme does two things. Initially, it underlines how paradoxical it is that the bringer of life should be hard-hearted, the hardness being that of concrete militant action to defend intangible light (that is, values); but then it helps to combine the light and the hardness into the single implied image of the diamond. Still more striking is the chain of assonance and internal rhyme in 'échappe – pas – efface – éclat'. All are important words, and all are stressed ('efface' largely because its pronounced mute 'e' confers greater weight on the tonic syllable). The dominant [a] recurs in two other chains. The first is 'visage – sauvages – bagages', a series of internal rhymes. Here again, 'visage' and 'sauvages' receive particular stress because of the mute 'e'. Along with 'voyageur', these two words prepare the way for 'bagages', which is also prominent because it is at the end of the line: a paradoxical traveller, this, with no luggage – and a lucky (or a canny) one, in a country where travellers' suitcases were searched without warning. The third chain in [a], 'voyageur – chasseur – passeur', overlaps with the second through the [aʒ] in 'voyageur'. This chain is less prominent, because the [a] is not tonic, but the words are associated through phonetic concatenation. The

216   *France, Soil and Language*

three chains together have two effects: vital ideas are highlighted through their coincidence with [a] (as well as through the mute 'e'), and they are bound together by sound as well as by association, connotation and meaning. Add the terminal rhyme and assonance of 'armes – larmes – étoiles' to 'bagages' etc. and it is legitimate to speak of a significantly dominant tonality in the text. This dominant [a] is in counterpoint with the terminal, and therefore stressed, rhyme and assonance in 'ennemi – rides – vie – pays': the contrast makes each more prominent, with a consequent highlighting of the words in which the sounds occur. This interplay of rhyme and assonance is very noticeable, but does not have a regular pattern: as we have seen, this is one way in which orthodoxy and unorthodoxy are put into fruitful tension with one another.

The tension bears its fruit in the last line, where the paradoxes come to a climax. The messenger has no suitcase, but he is carrying death and victory in his head – momentous luggage indeed. Formally, this line stands out boldly, because it is the only alexandrine in the poem.[6] It stands out still more, because orthodox treatment of the mute 'e' has meant that the unorthodox heptasyllabic line has dominated throughout. Marcenac further exploits this line's prominence through his use of verbal sound:

Qui *po*rte leur dé*faite*/et leur *mort*/dans la *tête*.

The phonetic parallelism in the four stressed syllables makes these climactic words stand out all the more. And so, of course, does the fact that they are exceptional, not being part of the chains of dominant [a] or of its counterpoint in [i]. They are a new mini-chain in themselves. The effect of this very striking climax is to emphasise that the victory is as yet virtual. A value and an ideal, 'dans la tête', as intangible as the diamond's light, it is something to be fervently wished for, implacably willed, and above all worked for, through concrete action and effective communication, as tangible as the diamond's substance. Just as 'Mort à nos ennemis' is a metaphorical act of stabbing, so the notably, and noticeably, condensed, stylised and efficient language of 'L'agent de liaison' is itself an example of one sort of linguistic gun worth firing in the struggle.

Each of the poems I have looked at has language as one of its themes. In the first, it is associated with the soil and the indestructibility of France, and in the other two with an implicit statement about the ontological and moral attributes of humanity. In all three, it is presented as inseparable from militant action in defence of humanity and

France, Soil and Language

France.

While language is not an essential theme in Resistance poetry, it is a very common one. One reason for this is that the French language was one of the few things left to the French by the Germans. The reference to 'Les signes qu'ils essaient de faire' in 'Mort à nos ennemis' is no doubt in part a scornful dismissal of German attempts at speaking French. One attraction of poetry was, as Jacques Gaucheron has said, that it was an extension of this malicious pleasure:

> Il est certain que la langue fait office de bien national. Parler français en présence d'Allemands qui ne comprennent rien est un plaisir. La communauté de langage est un élément, non suffisant certes, d'une complicité des cœurs. Il suffit d'aller un peu plus loin dans le jeu de mots, dans le langage à double sens, pour que cette complicité devienne joyeuse. Il suffit d'aller jusqu'au langage poétique, au point où ce qu'il y a de plus riche dans la langue n'est pas susceptible d'apprentissage, pour que l'expression poétique soit ressentie comme une parcelle de patrie, comme quelque chose d'absolument inaliénable.[7]

Another reason why language is so often a theme is that the poetry is conceived as a defence of the language against a perceived abuse in fascist propaganda. As Aragon wrote at the start of his anonymous preface to *Europe*:

> De tous temps, ce fut la mission des poètes . . . que de *Donner un sens plus pur aux mots de la tribu*. Il est bien que les poètes français aient su le faire . . . quand précisément le langage était détourné de son cours, les mots étaient dénaturés, pervertis par ces usurpateurs qui s'étaient emparés du vocable France lui-même . . .

The urge to speak out against a vicious language is a moral manifestation of the ontological need for self-projection in language. The silence imposed by political censorship is doubly sinister, because ultimately language is the means by which human beings realise themselves. Pierre Emmanuel puts this succinctly: 'Ce régime ne pouvait vivre qu'en pervertissant les mots: mais qui blesse le langage, blesse l'homme.'[8]

As with humanity, so with France. In Aragon's 'Le conscrit des cent villages',[9] the France of rivers, wheat and dwellings is seen as being *essentially* a set of words used in a certain way, and the poem ends with a wish for the enchanting 'music' of these words to be launched on the wind (cf. Bérimont's 'étendard de vent'). To clarify the relation between the themes of language and France, let us look briefly at the first two lines of another of Marcenac's poems, also in *Europe*, 'Les traîtres se trahissent':

Ceux de nos ennemis qui parlent notre langue
Et qui sont nés sur notre sol . . .

This coupling of soil and language is emblematic of Resistance poetry. One might have expected a reference to race rather than to language. One thinks, for example, of the racialism of Vichy and especially the Paris collaborationists, exemplified in the slogan of the Union française de défense de la race: 'Nous avons tout perdu. La seule richesse qui nous reste est désormais notre race.'[10] This attitude is typically expressed in a review of Maurice Fombeure's volume of poems, *A dos d'oiseau*: 'Je retrouve, intactes, toutes les cordes de la voix de notre *race* dans celle de la lyre de Fombeure' (my italics).[11] Contrast this with the typical Resistance thinker's view as represented by Aragon, writing of Resistance poetry in his preface to *Europe*: 'Dans cette musique qui ne s'est pas tue, le monde, étonné, retrouve la France, et il la reconnaît grande à la hauteur de sont chant: harmonieux résumé de l'expérience humaine, creuset des espoirs humains, entraînante, exemplaire.' France is envisaged not in itself, but as a 'musical' (*sc.* poetic – cf. 'Le conscrit des cent villages') expression of humanity.

It would perhaps be misleading to make of these poets existentialists or proto-existentialists, but the poems I have looked at are certainly anti-essentialist. In this they resemble *Pilote de guerre*.[12] Humanity is not a total of people, nor France a total of land. Neither is a substantial entity, to be taken or left. For Saint-Exupéry, 'l'homme n'est qu'un nœud de relations' (pp. 89, 154). Similarly, 'l'étendue véritable n'est pas pour l'œil, elle n'est accordée qu'à l'esprit. Elle vaut ce que vaut le langage, car c'est le langage qui noue les choses' (p. 93). The bird's-eye view in *Pilote de guerre* is a metaphor for the *esprit*, which considers the relations between phenomena ('le sens qui les noue entre eux', p. 23); it is contrasted with the view on the ground, that of the *intelligence*, which only considers the phenomena themselves. Saint-Exupéry's France is that of Bérimont and Marcenac; it is that of Guéhenno ('la patrie qu'on n'envahit pas') or Cassou ('une France idéale, moins une terre qu'un ciel, faite non pour des morts, mais pour des vivants').[13]

The argument of *Pilote de guerre* is conducted far more by metaphor than discursively. One reason for this is that the unity invoked is something ideal or virtual, expressible only analogically, in extended metaphor. (Similarly, the temporal dislocation is a structural analogy for the process by which the *esprit* discerns the links which give sense to the *pagaille* on the ground.) Nevertheless, for Saint-Exupéry – as for Bérimont and Marcenac – while language is essential to the realisation of relations between phenomena, it is not on its own sufficient: 'On ne fonde en soi l'Etre (*sc. nœud de relations* – in this case, France) dont on se réclame que par des actes. Un Etre n'est pas de l'empire du langage, mais de celui des actes' (p. 207). There is, however, a big difference between the poems and *Pilote de guerre*. The poems accord more militant value to the act of language than Saint-Exupéry does. While affirming the necessity for military action, they show that the world is a function of the way we utter it – in this particular case, that France, like humanity, is a relation between circumstances and the way we talk about them. And they show this not only thematically, but also though forcing on to our attention the relation between *signifiant* and *signifié*, or expression and content. It may indeed be this that specifically makes them into poetry. At all events, they typify what I am sure were two of the main attractions of Resistance poetry, and a major impetus to the *renouveau poétique* of those years: first, they are examples of unity in diversity; and second, they are creative denials of the *status quo*. Marcenac's fragmentary images and Bérimont's seething mixed metaphors derive their force from the fact that they interact contextually to make of each poem a single complex unit, in which every element is necessary and justified. To use Saint-Exupéry's terms, each poem is manifestly a *nœud de relations*, appealing to the *esprit* rather than the *intelligence*. At the same time, each poem manifestly embodies an 'ideal', 'mythical' France which is not that of Vichy. In this, each is fundamentally a negation of the given, and therefore also of the contemptible brand of political 'realism' exemplified by collaboration. With the country never more divided, these poems are themselves the *domaine français* which the maquisard protects with guns.

Notes

*I should like to thank Ann Longwell and Peter Read, who read this chapter in draft and made many helpful suggestions.

1. *Contrebande* is poetry which is published legally, and has therefore to be acceptable to the censor, but which, under the surface, has a subversive

meaning clear to the sympathetic reader.

Luc Bérimont (1915-1984) served in the army in Lorraine in 1939-40. After demobilisation, he lived for a while in Lyon, where he was an intimate of the Resistance-minded editorial team of *Le Progrès*. Thereafter, he settled in a remote village near Rochefort-sur-Loire, where he lived in semi-hiding with his Jewish wife. He worked for a Resistance network, and was a co-founder of the 'Ecole de Rochefort', a group of poets who had in common a dislike of dogma and abstraction in poetry.

Jean Marcenac (1913-1984) escaped from Stalag VIIA in September 1941, and made his way back to France. He reorganised the Quercy region of the Communist Party, and helped set up both the FTP and the Front National's committees of intellectuals in the Southern Zone. He printed many Resistance tracts in Figeac, and fought with the FTP in the liberation of Cahors and Toulouse.

2. Published at Niort by Les Amis de Rochefort. The suite of verse pieces is sandwiched between two sections of prose, narrative-descriptive versions of the verse section. The whole work is conceived as a single text. The text given here is the definitive one, as printed in P. Chaulot, *Luc Bérimont* (Paris, Seghers, 1966). Note that the title 'Pour les otages de Châteaubriant', given to the poem in P. Seghers, *La Résistance et ses poètes* (Paris, Seghers, 1974), p. 419, is not Bérimont's, but was added by Seghers.

3. A total of 27 hostages from Châteaubriant and 21 from Nantes were executed on 22 October 1941. These rapidly became legendary Resistance martyrs. Many poems were inspired by the episode, notably by Pierre Emmanuel, Loys Masson and Pierre Seghers. See I. Higgins (ed.), *Anthology of Second World War French Poetry* (London, Methuen, 1982). (It should be noted that the poets, editor and reader of this anthology are ill-served by the many misprints which disfigure it. Anyone using it is invited to write to the editor for a list of errata.)

4. In this, it is absolutely typical of Resistance poetry, and reminiscent in particular of Seghers' poem 'Octobre 41', also on the Châteaubriant executions, where the 'new Jeanne' – that is, a revitalised and resistant France – is born in and as the minds of schoolchildren, as it were by language out of events. The poem can be found in the Methuen anthology, 1982. See my article 'Pierre Seghers: une poésie à hauteur d'homme' in *La littérature française sous l'Occupation* (Actes du Colloque international de Reims), PU, Reims 1984.

5. Cf.Jean-Paul Sartre, 'La République du silence', written immediately after the Liberation and published in *Situations, III* (Paris, Gallimard, 1949), pp. 11-14: 'Nous avions perdu tous nos droits et d'abord celui de parler; on nous insultait en face chaque jour et il fallait nous taire ... partout sur les murs, dans les journaux, sur l'écran, nous retrouvions cet immonde et fade visage que nos oppresseurs voulaient nous donner de nous-mêmes.' (p. 11)

6. The alexandrine has twelve syllables, and is the staple line of traditional French verse, culturally equivalent to the iambic pentameter in English. For an introduction to French versification, see the Methuen anthology, 1982, pp. 31-44.

7. J. Gaucheron, *La Poésie, la Résistance* (Paris, Les Editeurs Français Réunis, 1979), p. 122.

8. P. Emmanuel, *Qui est cet homme?* (Paris, Egloff, 1947), p. 318.

9. In *La Diane française* (Paris, Seghers, 1965). It is noteworthy that this poem first appeared in *Domaine français* (Geneva, Editions des Trois Collines, 1943). The 'domaine' in question is emphatically not the soil of France, but French culture. The volume, in effect a special issue of Jean Lescure's review *Messages*, is a collection of texts by many writers, too inflammatory to be published in France.

10. Quoted in P. Ory, *Les Collaborateurs, 1940-1945* (Paris, Editions du Seuil, 1976), p. 157. Cf. the beginning of the march of the Ligue française: 'A l'appel sacré de la race/Debout, ligueurs, debout, les Francs' (quoted in S. Marchetti,

Images d'une certaine France (Lausanne, Edita, 1982).

11. M. Richard, in *La Révolution nationale*, 19 décembre 1942. Fombeure was, of course, in no sense a collaborationist poet.

12. A. de Saint-Exupéry, *Pilote de guerre* (Paris, Gallimard, coll. Folio).

13. J. Guéhenno, *Journal des années noires* (Paris, Gallimard, coll. Folio), pp. 18. 20ff; J. Cassou, 'Corps mystique de la France' in *Domaine français*, pp. 87-92.

14 LES CAHIERS DU SILENCE
Ethel Tolansky

A publication in French appeared in London in 1943 called *Les Cahiers du Silence*. It was to produce five cahiers from 1943-5. These small slim volumes, making their entry into an already varied French political and cultural scene, could be said to represent and tell the story of much that was going on in and outside France during those war years. The books were copies for the most part of a selection published by the clandestine publishing house *Les Editions de Minuit*. They shared the same objectives and ideals and this London based edition could be considered as yet another, but small and effective, contribution in the fight against the Nazi Occupation of France.

On the derelict walls of some bombed out buildings in London, on the walls of French restaurants and shops one could read: 'La France a perdu une bataille! Mais la France n'a pas perdu la guerre!'[1] The French exiles in London with de Gaulle and the Free French were continuing the battle militarily and politically. There was, however, another aspect to this battle and that was on the propaganda front in order to counteract the falsehoods emanating from Germany and Vichy France. There were news-sheets, among them *le Journal Officiel de la France Combattante* and a monthly magazine written in English, *La Lettre de la France Libre*, which carried news of France, the Resistance, Free French activities and the state of the war and the enemy. On the cultural scene there was the monthly *La France Libre* which, according to Jean Oberlé, bolstered the French cultural image: 'Elle était remarquable à la fois par son style et par son ton.'[2] At the same time literature was being smuggled into England through various underground organisations and their contacts in London. Reproducing the news-sheets of the underground press was part of this activity as well as underlining the courage, daring initiative and spirit of sacrifice that was involved in this clandestine resistance activity, as a reviewer in England wrote at the time:

> the book comes from the underground — where the printing of the simplest tract is nothing less than a desperate problem, and where every scrap of paper, every stick of type, carries with it a death sentence.[3]

Les Cahiers du Silence

The book in question came from *Les Editions de Minuit* set up in 1941 through the initiative of Pierre Lescure and Vercors. Its first publication in 1942 was the popular *Le Silence de la Mer* which included its manifesto. It stated the aims of the enterprise with its fervent desire not to comply in any way with the enemy through the censor and to be a means for the expression of freedom of thought that was being constantly stifled and would eventually perish. In spite of the conditions for printing in France the books were to be well produced as presentation and content would both be effective weapons against Nazi propaganda and an encouragement to resisters and waverers:

> Ces volumes il faudrait qu'ils fussent bien faits. Elégants même, si possible. Leur effet, leur puissance de choc (surtout à l'Etranger – et c'est à l'Etranger qu'il faut prouver que l'Esprit vit encore en France), dépendra beaucoup de leur aspect.[4]

When *Le Silence de la Mer* arrived in England it was an immediate success; other volumes followed and their impact coud be summed up by Maurice Schumann speaking to France from London:

> Au coeur même du pays occupé s'imprime une collection clandestine dont le titre: *Les Editions de Minuit* . . . et qui a l'insolence d'être un modèle en même temps qu'un miracle; et qui, sur du beau papier et en beaux caractères, et avec une belle mise en pages, continue comme si de rien n'étaient l'occupant et ses serfs . . . Audace et grâce à la fois . . . l'ennemi reçoit un double soufflet deux fois signé par la France.[5]

Here was a tremendous weapon, voices had risen phoenix-like from that silence. What better instrument in the war of persuasion and example than these clandestine publications produced in relative safety and with no real difficulty in printing them! And so it was that the series *Les Cahiers du Silence* was founded in 1943 with the express wish and encouragement of de Gaulle and the Free French, financed initially by Philippe de Rothschild and distributed by Hachette. Only five of the original collection of 24 were published from 1943-5 and only the first one, *Le Silence de la Mer*, appeared before the Liberation of France. It included, like its original, a preface stating the aims of the series by Maurice Druon. He, in turn, explained the silence of France, so difficult to understand from the outside. With this publication and other clandestine literature France had not abandoned her cultural role in the world, she had regained her honour and dignity:

> Ah non! ce n'est pas un peuple diminué, ce n'est pas un peuple absent, celui où à toutes les hauteurs de la société des hommes sont capables d'offrir leur liberté et leur vie pour la chose écrite. Que personne ne dise du mal d'un pays où le sang coule pour la primauté de l'esprit.
>
> La France n'abdique pas; et les grandeurs qu'elle semblait avoir perdues, elle les retrouve.[6]

Les Cahiers du Silence wanted to reproduce as far as it was possible the originals in format as well as in objectives; they were small, slim books effective for eventual clandestine distribution, with good quality paper and print with a cream cover and red and blue lettering and design. The three fictional titles have the same wording inside as the originals: *Le Silence de la Mer*: 'Ce volume publié aux dépens d'un patriote, a été achevé d'imprimer sous l'occupation Nazie le 20 Février 1942' or *Le Temps Mort*: 'Ce volume publié aux dépens de quelques lettrés patriotes a été achevé d'imprimer sous l'oppression à Paris le 1er, Juin 1944.' In all cases *Les Editions de Minuit* were mentioned on the inside pages.

Only five of the original collection were printed and they did not follow the original order. What determined the choice of these five texts? *Le Silence de la Mer* because it was the first of the series in France and had such an impact? And the others? Possibly because they were by authors who were well known in both countries or because they were known to the de Gaulle entourage? Or because these five were among the best? Or could it have been that they expressed different facets of the struggle in France, enhanced her image, showed the obvious commitment of her writers? I suggest that it was for these reasons and their perceptible message that they were chosen.

Le Silence de la Mer with its enigmatic title and German officer has been variously interpreted and misunderstood especially during the war period. Vercors has been criticised for not making his anti-Nazi message clearer and for making his German officer too sympathetic. The narrator and his niece have a German officer billeted on them during the early days of the Occupation. To refuse would mean possible death. There is no open revolt on their part except for constant silence when he tries to make conversation with them. The officer, Werner von Ebrennac, talks or rather monologues at length on his love and appreciation for France, for its culture and civilising influence. He does

Les Cahiers du Silence 225

not view the Occupation of France as the suppression of the people or their culture but the way to the eventual marriage of these two countries in equal partnership and recognising the virtues and defects of each one. His naïve interpretation of Germany's intentions are shattered when he meets some of his friends while on leave in Paris. It is their revelations about Germany's real intentions that Vercors wishes to draw to the attention of every Frenchman:

> nous avons l'occasion de détruire la France, elle le sera. Pas seulement sa puissance: son âme aussi. Son âme surtout. Son âme est le plus grand danger. C'est notre travail en ce moment: ne vous y trompez pas, mon cher. Nous la pourrirons par nos sourires et nos ménagements. Nous en ferons une chienne rampante.[7]

Disillusioned he volunteers for the Eastern Front with almost certain death if not of body, certainly of spirit. The mutism of the uncle and the niece day after day in whatever circumstance is a form of negation of the existence of the other presence and it humiliates as they are, and have been, humiliated. This appears to have no effect on von Ebrennac until the end when he is also humiliated by his fellow countrymen. The niece fights any attraction that she feels for him and her 'Adieu' as he leaves them, the only word she says to him throughout the story, is recognition of the fact that silence can be a weapon and can only be broken when the aggressor is in the losing position. The story emphasises the fact that no one should be taken in by the charm, good looks, culture and politeness of any German who falls in with the Nazi regime or pays lip service to it.

Vercors' next book *La Marche à l'Étoile*, though less controversial is more bitter and more disillusioned with the state of France and those who are helping the Nazis to do their work of eliminating people. It is 1943 and the struggle is bitter and intense. What Vercors shows in this story is not positive response to a situation but to reveal to the French and others the evil they are perpetrating. It serves as a warning that France could become as barbarous as her occupiers, and also what, in fact, the Resistance has to face: two enemies; France and Germany. The story, partly autobiographical of Vercors' own family, is the story of an old man who has made France his home and whose son gave his life for her in the last war; he in turn, will die, not as a sacrifice for his country but as a reprisal for an act against the enemy by the Resistance, and at the hand of a Frenchman whom he had known in the past. Muritz is also a naturalised Jew – hence the heavy symbolism of the title, which is based on a case that Vercors had read about: 'Ainsi était mort le vieux Berheim, ainsi finissait mon héros, livré par les Français qu'il avait tant aimés.'[8] The story, besides focusing on Muritz's own drama, shows how the French have become as cruel as the aggressor. It poses the inevitable question of how will one Frenchman be able to face another when that one has been found guilty of atrocities? 'Pourquoi m'en punissez-vous dans la limpidité de mon amour pour ma patrie? Car je sais bien, je sens bien qu'il y a quelque chose d'altéré dans cet amour'.[9]

Le Temps Mort also tells of atrocities, this time against a group of women prisoners who in some way or other have put themselves in danger in order to help the Resistance. They come from all sorts of backgrounds and are united in their plight and in helping each other not to collapse and give in to the enemy. It has been called a story about love or perhaps one could say charity, *agape*, in the help so generously given in such atrocious conditions and situations. It is also, in the case of Clémence, her love for her fiancé that strengthens her resolve not to weaken. It describes life in Fresnes, different forms of torture, the exploits and self-sacrifice of the women prisoners and the journey of deportation. It is with great economy of style and restraint that Aveline makes us share the experiences of his heroines. Both Vercors and Debû-Bridel thought that it was the best manuscript that had been submitted to *Les Editions de Minuit*: '*Le Temps mort*, un des plus remarquables récits de la vie des prisons de femmes, celles arrêtées par la Gestapo, est sans doute un des romans les mieux composés des *Editions de Minuit*.'[10] These women will try to fight to the end, the enemy will not vanquish their spirit and their will even if their bodies collapse '"Non, Clémence, non, nous ne mourrons pas, tu verras, ma jolie. C'est eux que nous verrons mourir, c'est eux." A l'aube du troisième jour, nous sommes arrivées ICI.'[11]

These very ordinary women committed themselves to help in the way they could, to fight against the oppressor, and besides the poignant drama of each one which is a message in itself we are left with a more heroic picture of France and what Frenchwomen are capable of, and an increased hatred of the enemy. To read about the plight of these women written in a semi-documentary style could have encouraged others to fight harder for the liberation of France and the destruction of the enemy.

The articles *Le Cahier Noir* and *Angleterre* are clearer and much more direct in their message, their intention is to rouse people, to educate and to convince them. These two volumes have additions by

Charles Morgan and Robert Speaight; they are meant to lend weight and other dimensions to the subjects of the articles. Speaight translated Mauriac's article for the series. Morgan and Speaight both loved France very much, both were at the forefront of the English cultural scene, although Morgan was on the decline, both were engaged in the war effort in their work. Speaight was a successful actor and a novelist who was also published in France. He was a Catholic and very much in touch with French Catholic writers. His short essay *The Christian Spirit in the Culture of Modern France* is a defence of those Catholics and Christians in France who were resisting the Nazi onslaught. The letter Charles Morgan addresses to the writer meant even more to the French than Speaight's contribution. Here was an author very much admired and appreciated in France, even though he was now considered in England as being too high-minded, and out of date, and out of sympathy with the then current English literary scene. He had been a success before the war here but was still very much in fashion in France. He was held in high esteem by all those involved in the Resistance on both sides of the Channel. He had readily jumped to the defence of France with his pen. He wrote an article in the *Spectator* in July 1941, 'Du Génie français' which subsequently found its way to Geneva and eventually to *Les Editions de Minuit*. He had also written an *Ode to France* which was translated and published by *Les Editions de Minuit*. His letter is an explanation and apology, mainly for English readers, for the harshness of Mauriac's article on the French.

Mauriac's contribution to *Les Editions de Minuit* and reprinted by *Les Cahiers du Silence* was written in 1941 as part of a journal he was keeping under the Occupation. It is the most polemic and forceful piece of writing published by *Les Cahiers du Silence*; the pseudonym, the risks and dangers in writing in France at that time, possible death, all incited Mauriac to be very direct in his attacks and aggressive in his tone and attitudes to the French in general. Mauriac saw the occupation of France by the Nazis not only in terms of a prison situation but also something much more sinister for mankind in general, and that was the spreading of evil over Europe and the destruction of the dignity of man. Through the biting sarcasm aimed at most categories of French society: the bourgeoisie, the capitalists, the Catholics, writers and profiteers, Mauriac is admonishing the French not to succumb to the propaganda of the enemy. One of the tactics of the Occupant was to reduce the French to a state of inactivity and paralysis; the method was to make them feel ashamed at their defeat, to stress their moral weaknesses, their cowardice and thus to despise themselves and so despair.

Where there is no hope there will be no resistance. Mauriac saw the dangers of this psychological warfare and so in his article he urges them to react, to fight and he cajoles, bludgeons them, encourages them and frightens them.

> quel géant nous couvre de son ombre et presse la petite France entre ses deux paumes ... pour lui tenir tête, ne nous condamne-t-il pas à devenir semblable à lui?[12]

He emphasises the value of man and whatever their past, any Frenchman can turn away from the enemy, safety and comfort to fight for something more valuable:

> Hé bien, non: nous croyons en l'homme; nous croyons avec tous nos moralistes que l'homme peut être convaincu et persuadé: même ces bourgeois qui enfouissent des cassettes dans leurs massifs de bégonias – oui, même ces intermédiaires pour la ventre de toute denrée consommable ...[13]

It was imperative to react to the contagious passivity that was suffocating France, to the contempt that was being encouraged towards themselves:

> Mais d'abord s'arracher à l'empreinte du géant, écarter ses mains de notre gorge, son genou de notre poitrine ... Il sera temps alors d'apprendre comment un peuple libre peut devenir un peuple fort – et un peuple fort demeurer un peuple juste.[14]

Morgan in his letter, though addressed to Mauriac, does well to remind the English reader of this, the only one of the five publications of the series to be published simultaneously in English, that the France that Mauriac is writing about is unknown to them:

> Therefore, I hope that my own countrymen, while first reading your book, will suspend, as far as possible, all agreement or disagreement with it, and even all decisive mental comment upon it, and then will read it again as news of a world unknown to them and almost unimaginable by them.[15]

The second non-fictional work to be published by *Les Cahiers du Silence* also deals with a characteristic element of the Nazi propaganda effort in France in order to isolate them in their fight for freedom and to denigrate their source of help — England: 'Germany is no enemy of France. France has but one adversary, an adversary of all time — England.'[16] It was to counteract this campaign that Jacques Debû-Bridel wrote his long essay *Angleterre (d'Alcuin à Huxley)* and to show the closeness of the relationship between the two countries from time immemorial. The two countries owed a lot to one another, they complemented each other, they could go on helping one another and indeed England and the BBC were saving France from total submersion in the Nazi campaign. For the English, the essay could be taken as a great compliment, an appreciation of her culture, spirit, and generosity and to the French reading it, an antidote to Nazi lies and poison and an admonition to ally themselves to England and not to Germany.

The author examines the records of both countries reaching far back into history to show that this alliance is not something new for the occasion. History is telescoped and thus greatly oversimplified but is a helpful way of looking at the common past of two countries which have fought against each other frequently. Conflict and quarrels have become merely civil disagreements or fratricidal arguments, which I suppose, if one bears in mind William the Conqueror, could seem very plausible in the circumstances:

> Justement, ces guerres séculaires de la France et de l'Angleterre dont l'histoire parle tant sont apparence plus que réalité. A bien y regarder, ces guerres furent surtout des guerres civiles et non des guerres nationales.[17]

Alcuin, of the title, was a venerable Anglo-Saxon monk whom Charlemagne asked to cross the sea and teach the French of the day how to read, and cultural exchanges have continued ever since. Both countries have served as places of refuge from persecutions in the past, and England is doing so again to loyal Frenchmen, and not only can she offer safety, but she can by her resilience and courage help and be an example to the Western world: 'Juin 1940 . . . Tout n'est pas perdu. L'Angleterre tient . . . L'Angleterre qui, seule continue la lutte . . . L'Angleterre tient. L'Angleterre tiendra.'[18] What was true in 1940 was still the case in the France of 1943 when the essay was originally published and even more so in 1944 as France was about to be liberated. The debt to England is immense according to Debû-Bridel, and to acknowledge it so openly and persuasively would not only be a help for the present but also for the future. When asked why he had chosen such a subject which could appear as a cultural and historical résumé of two countries, he replied in a letter dated 1 March 1984 as follows:

> à cette époque l'Angleterre et l'Angleterre seule faisait face à Hitler et qu'elle était pour nous le suprême espoir . . . Tous les résistants français prenaient à cette époque avec angoisse les émissions de la B.B.C. Les hommes de mon âge ne l'ont pas oublié.[19]

The role of *Les Cahiers du Silence* in the ideological struggle engaged in by the Resistance was clearly alluded to in the inside title page of the first issue, which said that the collection was dedicated 'aux écrivains qui, sur le sol de la France prisonnière livrent le combat de l'esprit'.[20] They had their place and played their part through the organisation of the Free French in the war effort of countering Nazi propaganda in France itself. How far it was successful is difficult to measure as with any literary war efforts, though we do know that the RAF dropped hundreds of thousands of miniaturised copies of *Le Silence de la Mer*.[21] When, in 1945, Vercors recalled the purpose of *Les Editions de Minuit* it was its role in defence of what he called 'la pensée française' which he emphasised . . .

> Et ce que je veux vous montrer, c'est que cette littérature clandestine n'a pas seulement été un certain nombre, un nombre plus ou moins grand, de ces oeuvres de la pensée interdites par l'ennemi, mais un véritable mouvement spirituel, un moment de l'histoire de l'esprit, et plus précisément, de la pensée française.[22]

This ideological struggle to preserve and sustain a certain way of thinking, a certain way of being, was just as vital a part of the Resistance as its military activities.

Notes

1. J. Oberlé, *Jean Oberlé vous parle* (Paris, La Jeune Parque, 1945), p. 95.
2. Ibid., p. 102
3. I.T. Bergeret, *Tricolore*. vol. IV, no. 3 (London, 1944), p. 60.
4. J. Debû-Bridel, *Les Editions de Minuit* (Paris, Minuit, 1945), pp. 22-3.
5. M. Schumann, *La voix du couvre-feu* (Paris, Plon, 1964), p. 70.
6. M. Druon, 'Préface', *Les Cahiers du Silence*, no. 1 (London, 1943), p. 5.
7. Vercors, *Le Silence de la Mer* (London, Les Cahiers du Silence, 1943), p. 39.

8. Vercors, *La bataille du silence* (Paris, Presses Cité, 1967), p. 296.
9. Vercors, *La marche à l'étoile* (Paris, LGF, 1956), p. 250.
10. J. Debû-Bridel, *Les Editions de Minuit*, p. 70.
11. Minervois, *Le temps mort* (Paris, Les Editions de Minuit, 1945), p. 75.
12. Forez, *Le cahier noir* (London, *Les Cahiers du Silence*, 1944), p. 24.
13. Ibid., pp. 19-20.
14. Ibid., p. 25.
15. Ibid., p. 28.
16. I.T. Bergeret (quoted by him in I.T. Bergeret, *Tricolore*, p. 60.)
17. Argonne, *Angleterre* (London, *Les Cahiers du Silence*, 1944), p. 9.
18. Ibid., p. 1.
19. J. Debû-Bridel, letter to E. Tolansky, Paris, 1 March 1984.
20. Inside title page of *Les Cahiers du Silence*, no. 1.
21. H. Michel, *Paris résistant* (Paris, Albin Michel, 1982), p. 133.
22. Vercors. 'Permanence de la Pensée Française', *Revue de Paris*, Décembre 1945, no. 9, p. 16.

Les Cahiers du Silence. 1943-5.
In order of publication in London.
　1. Vercors, *Le Silence de la Mer*. Preface by Maurice Druon. (London 1943) (*Les Editions de Minuit*, first text, received Oct. 1941, published 20 Feb. 1942. Second edition 25 July 1943)
　2. Forez (François Mauriac), *Le Cahier Noir* (London 1944). This volume includes two further essays: Charles Morgan, *Lettre à l'auteur du Cahier Noir*, and Robert Speaight, *Le Christ dans la Pensée Française d'Aujourd'hui*. All three are accompanied by English translations. (*Le Cahier Noir* was the 10th text to be received by *Les Editions de Minuit*, June 1943, and the 4th to be published, 15 Aug. 1943)
　3. Argonne (Jacques Debû-Bridel), *Angleterre (D'Alcuin à Huxley)* (London 1944). Preface by Charles Morgan, *Du Génie Français*, first published in *The Spectator*, 19 July 1941. (*Les Editions de Minuit*, 12th text to be received, Aug. 1943, and sixth to be published, 22 Sept. 1943)
　4. Minervois (Claude Aveline), *Le Temps Mort* (London 1945). (*Les Editions de Minuit*, 33rd text to be received, March 1944, and 16th to be published, 1st June 1944)
　5. Vercors, *La Marche à l'Etoile* (London 1945). (*Les Editions de Minuit*, 18th text to be received, and 10th to be published, 25 Dec. 1943)
There were two other wartime editions in England of *Le Silence de la Mer*: one edited with notes and a vocabulary by Thomas Mark, with a preface based on the one by Maurice Druon (Macmillan, 1944), and a translation by Cyril Connolly with the title *Put Out the Light* (Macmillan, 1944).

15 THE MAQUIS AND THE CULTURE OF THE OUTLAW (With Particular Reference to the Cévennes)

Roderick Kedward

For many years after the Liberation the history of the Maquis was left to the maquisards. The source material was thought to be composed mainly of anecdotes, semi-fictional accounts and exaggerated claims to actions for which there are no other records. Historians who wanted to be known as serious were discouraged from investigating the Maquis both by this impenetrability of the sources, but also by an absence of methodology, and the difficulty of finding a conceptual framework within which the highly diffuse material could be shaped into a rigorous general history. Some of the same difficulties existed in writing the history of *any* aspect of the Resistance, but these were confronted quickly where Gaullist Resistance and the Mouvements Unis de la Résistance (MUR) were concerned, since this was the Resistance which dominated the power structures after the Liberation, and history was one way among others of authenticating that power. Resistance in the provinces was investigated where it flowed into the mainstream of what soon became almost official history, which could be negatively defined by its suspicion towards Communist Resistance, whose sources were deemed to be the prey of a doctrinaire ideology, and its condescension towards the Maquis. Where the two came together in the Maquis units of the Francs-Tireurs et Partisans Français (FTPF) the blockage was almost total. No serious general history of the FTPF by a non-communist historian was thought to be either possible or worthwhile.[1]

Locally the situation has been much improved in the last ten years. Younger historians have begun to shake themselves free of the established guidelines, encouraged by the surge of interest in rural and regional history, and as doctoral projects mushroom in the provincial universities the mass of local detail produced by maquisards, who have not themselves been overawed by official neglect, is now being sifted and analysed with sensitivity and rigour. The self-confidence of these local studies testifies to the shift in intellectual aspirations, which, perhaps for the first time in modern French history, do not focus on Paris as the only serious goal of academic attainment, nor on national history as the ultimate test of understanding and relevance. The work of Pierre Laborie on the Lot, for example, is full of perception, and the way he handles his material is both original and stimulating. It tells us more about life in Vichy France than a dozen books of apparently wider scope.[2] The study of the Maquis in the Morvan by Jacques Canaud also has a core of insight which enlightens the general history of the occupation, and his method of working with ex-maquisards in a workshop situation yields impressive results.[3]

Not least among the products of recent local research is a wealth of statistics separating those who were purely réfractaires in refusing to go to Germany under the Service du Travail Obligatoire (STO) from those who were maquisards, a separation which undermines the view that STO is the main *point de départ* for a history of the Maquis, and warns against the practice of using the terms réfractaire and maquisard interchangeably. The separation has deep roots in the accounts by the maquisards themselves, and is now a norm of interpretation for local histories of the period following STO.[4]

Very few Maquis groups date from the period before STO. Resistance movements of 1940-2 were urban-based with urban values, and the idea of guerrilla warfare in the countryside or even a tactical retreat into the hills had hardly been discussed. The Resisters who operated in rural France before 1943 were mostly individual *passeurs* on the demarcation line or on the Spanish and Swiss borders, and they had undeservedly gained a reputation in the towns for the kind of financial calculation and horse-trading which the urban French traditionally impute to the peasantry. Henri Cordesse, a primary school teacher in the Lozère, who came to lead the Resistance in the *département* and has since written its history with elegance and perception, said that the first generation of Resisters in the town of Marvejols either dismissed the idea of setting up groups in the hills as madness or rejected it as an impossibility.[5] STO, he said, forced their hands, but forced them initially not so much to constitute what were later known as Maquis, but rather to find farms and villages where réfractaires could be hidden, fed and provided with work, and to extend the production of false papers so that increasing numbers of réfractaires could remain eligible for ration cards as well as escape detection. 'Le S.T.O.', agrees Pierre Laborie, 'a joué un rôle déterminant dans la Résistance en obligeant les mouvements à élargir leur champ d'action, à secouer une certaine passivité, à préparer des structures d'accueil . . . à prendre conscience d'une stratégie à long terme.'[6]

A thesis on the Ariège estimates that réfractaires made up only 35-40 per cent of the Maquis in the *département*,[7] and from the *Bulletins du Comité d'Histoire de la Deuxième Guerre Mondiale* it emerges that only 19 per cent of réfractaires in the Tarn joined a Maquis, and no more than 27 per cent in the Isère, although in the Hautes-Alpes the percentage was closer to 50 per cent.[8] In the Ocupied Zone Jacques Canaud found 106 réfractaires out of 161 maquisards in one Maquis in the hills of the Auxois, and his detailed study suggests that STO was generally important as a recruiting ground in the Morvan. But even in his estimation there was a major distinction between groups in hiding and groups involved in combat and sabotage, and in the South only the combat groups consistently qualify in local Resistance history as the Maquis.[9]

In his booklet on the Maquis des Corsaires, Georges Gillier, the Protestant pastor at Mandagout in the Cévennes, begins his history on 28 July 1943, which he describes as a hot, heavy Sunday with a storm circling the hills, when two workers deserted from compulsory labour with the Todt Organisation at Le Vigan and made their way towards his presbytery. Alerted by a local youth, he had to make an instant decision: 'Je réfléchis quelques instants, puis décide de les accueillir; ils arriveront cette nuit même. Le Maquis de Mandagout était créé.'[10] The style is one shared by many memoirs of the Maquis, but the claim would be disputed as premature. For months Gillier's band of réfractaires continued to grow, posing every problem of security, cover and food, but in no military sense was it a Maquis until January 1944 when the arrival of an instructor sent by the Organisation de Résistance de l'Armée (ORA) changed the life of the camp from one of boredom, frustration and inaction into one of preparation for active combat.

The head of the Renseignements Généraux in the Lozère, Rispoli, wrote to the Prefect in that same month, January 1944, announcing a total of 47 réfractaires who had given themselves up and who had talked, whether willingly or under duress, about the life they had led. All had gone to parts of the countryside where they had relatives, and although, in his words, they had become an easy prey to recruiting agents for clandestine organisations, they had not become involved.[11] Even later, in June 1944, it is possible to find descriptions of potential Maquis groups which never got started as combat units, such as the group of réfractaires from Capestang in the Hérault who loaded food and clothing on to two requisitioned lorries in the town, but met a German convoy as they left for the hills, resulting in the death of 5 killed on the side of the road, 18 taken prisoner and shot at Béziers, and 300 men from Capestang arrested for deportation.[12] The tragedy echoes that of Aire de Côte in the Massif de l'Aigoual a full year earlier where a badly organised camp of the first réfractaires in the area broke

The Maquis and the Culture of the Outlaw

up in the Spring of 1943, but not without antagonising one of the members who later betrayed the second camp in the same location to the Germans. The Germans attacked on 1 July 1943, and afterwards one of the réfractaires who escaped was discovered by the Vichy police sent from Nîmes to investigate the area. The evidence he gave was abundant, including information on the numbers and names of réfractaires who had gone into hiding. Escaping STO was an easy process, he stated, and he claimed that thousands were lying hidden in the Massif. The whole tone of his statement suggests a lack of serious planning or motivation by the réfractaires and a total ignorance of any Maquis organisation.[13]

Some maquisards in oral evidence have dismissed the réfractaires as no more than an expensive irrelevance to their history, diverting food and supplies from the active combatants, whom they portray as largely made up of committed anti-fascists and foreigners on the run from the Vichy organisation of Main d'Oeuvre Etrangère (MOE).[14] After the Liberation the Groupement National des Réfractaires was faced with endless problems in persuading the Resistance authorities in power to give those who had refused STO the same financial rights as those who had gone to Germany,[15] and at the present point in Resistance research the réfractaires look like being given a separate history of their own, as the hunt for réfractaires who took to the woods but did not become maquisards begins to use the same documentation as was used by the police at the time in order to discover names, jobs, home addresses and the farms and villages in which they took refuge. Who were they, and why did some become maquisards and not others, are the questions to which we will soon have detailed answers.

While recognising with admiration the scholarly drive of this research, and responding readily to the new areas for exploration which it has discovered, I want to try and show in this chapter its conceptual limitations for a history of the Maquis, and in so doing would like to suggest that we are still a long way from understanding the structures within which the Maquis operated. The foremost of these was a positive culture of the outlaw, barely conceptualised at the time and obscured by Vichy propaganda, which also made a distinction between réfractaire and maquisard for opportunistic ends, whose importance for the continuance of Vichy's *raison d'être* I wish to emphasise. To do this, and to establish the perspectives for the points I want to make about the Maquis, we must look at the predicament of Vichy at the crucial turning point in its history between 1942 and 1943. It was during that year that its dramatic decline from its high point in 1940-1 became the all-pervading message of prefects' reports and ministerial awareness, and it was during that year that the maquisards made their entry into the history of the period. What was the relationship between Vichy decline and these almost mythical figures on the run, these men, to quote one of the best maquisard historians, Aimé Vielzeuf, 'qu'on appelait les bandits'?[16]

It could reasonably be argued that the Vichy regime lost its *raison d'être* in the events of November 1942. In less than a month it lost its territorial identity when the Germans occupied the Southern Zone, it lost its North African Empire when first Darlan and then Giraud accepted the Allied invasion of Algeria, it lost its Armistice Army and surrendered most of the arms it had hoarded in scattered depots throughout the South, and before that, on the morning of 27 November, it sent its fleet to the bottom of the harbour in Toulon. The pride and honour which Pétain claimed had been rescued from the defeat of 1940 by the Armistice and by the authority of his government, were surely now no more than a nostalgic memory for the promises of the National Revolution and the illusions of Montoire.

Certainly, November was seen as the end of Vichy by several of the Vichy Ministers, including Jean Borotra, Pétain's young Minister of Sport, who had already been forced to resign when Laval returned to power in the Spring of 1942. Not only did Borotra, and Lamirand the Minister for Youth, try to persuade Pétain to leave France in November, but he also tried to leave himself. Both moves were unsuccessful. Pétain preferred to stay, and saw himself as already a kind of sacrificial prisoner of the Occupation, and Borotra, arrested at the station on his way to Spain, became an actual prisoner and a deportee. In fact Pétain was not subjected to any personal humiliation by the Germans until August 1944, and Borotra was moved from a certain death at Sachsenhausen to the relative privilege of Château Itter, after the personal intervention of the King of Sweden who wrote to Goering impressing on him the stature of Borotra as a great tennis player. In such ways the favoured status of Pétainism within Nazi-Occupied Europe limped on until the Allied invasions of 1944.

Such a view highlights the personality of Pétain and equates Vichy with Pétainism. It is attractive but misleading. A careful interpretation of the administrative archives shows that if anything the role of Vichy was not lost but intensified by the events of November 1942. This requires a shift of focus from Pétain to Laval, whose personality and political background were always unacceptable to the Pétainists, but whose philosophy of Vichy's role in the altered world of 1942 was never repudiated by them. If anything Pétain himself grasped it as a lifeline and it has been extensively used in the defence of Vichy by apologists ever since. No historian wishing to be judicious can afford to ignore it, though its full complexity will remain hidden all the while the Vichy papers are only made selectively available to research.

The first philosophy of Vichy in 1940 was essentially a combination of moral and spiritual revivalism and a negotiated position of favoured nation within the New Europe. The tone of the philosophy was optimistic and expansive. In 1942 it was gradually replaced by the 'shield philosophy' which was defensive and pessimistic, and many would say realistic, though realism was also widely used as a justification for the hopes and policies of 1940. Shielding the French people from a possible Gauleiter and from more extreme exactions and depredations was firmly established by the end of 1942 as the new *raison d'être* for Vichy and the main criterion of action. The Relève scheme and Laval's notorious speech of 22 June 1942 occur in the transition period between optimism and pessimism, assertiveness and defence, but by August and September the deportation by Vichy of immigrant and refugee Jews from the Southern Zone demonstrated the new thinking behind Laval's adaptation to German demands. His callousness towards the fate of these Jewish men, women and particularly children, conveyed in his response to Pastor Boegner,[17] can be ascribed not just to a level of inhumanity within Laval's personal value-system, but also to the clarity and conviction with which the new shield philosophy had been conceived. The corollary of Laval's decision that all *foreign* Jews should go, appeared to be that all *French* Jews should stay, but the more significant implication was that other 'expendable' groups in French society should also be used as bargaining counters in the statistical barter between Vichy and the Germans. This is exactly what is revealed by the instructions received by the regional prefects during November and December 1942.

In a flurry of despatches following the occupation of the Southern Zone, Laval and his ministers stressed how vital it was to preserve the independence of the French administration in the new situation. In his first circular after 11 November, Laval told the prefects that the presence of the Germans in the previously Unoccupied Zone was not on the same basis as their occupation of the North and that their forces should be known as *troupes d'opérations* and not *troupes d'occupation*.[18] He followed this on 27 November with a firm instruction that on no account should the German military authorities be allowed to 's'immiscer dans l'Administration civile en zone libre',[19] and officially the Vichy Zone continued to be called the 'zone libre' despite the German presence. But the other side of Vichy's policy in November and December was to make preparations for the inevitable bargaining that was to come. To this end all foreigners, marginals, suspects and other groups less easily categorised but potentially just as expendable were to be listed, supervised or collected together in camps, workplaces and known residences. A coded telegram from the Ministry of the Interior on 18 November 1942 told prefects to proceed at once to the arrest of all foreigners 'vous paraissant suspects au point de vue politique et susceptible troubler de quelque manière que ce soit ordre public'.[20] The regional prefect in Montpellier sent it directly to the prefects in his region and demanded an urgent reply listing the measures they had taken. These replies give figures and names of Spanish, Italians, Austrians, Germans, Poles, Russians, Ukrainians, Greeks, Dutch and Hungarians and many other refugees or immigrants who had been rounded up, and the lists were sent on immediately to Vichy.[21]

The importance that the Government attached to these measures against the immigrant groups can be seen by a letter from Vichy to the regional prefect in Montpellier accusing him of being too lenient,[22] and a continuous stream of telegrams extending and refining the process of supervision and internment. On 27 November the two aspects of Vichy policy, negotiations with the Germans on the one hand and administrative independence on the other, were explicitly revealed in two secret telegrams, the first permitting the lists of all Germans, Austrians, Poles and Czechs to be communicated on demand to the German police, and the second telling the French administrators that the German authorities were to be given no access to the prisons and supervised residences in which the foreigners had been located.[23] A further telegram on 1 December extended the list of immigrants whose names could be communicated to the Germans to include people from all countries occupied by Germany, leaving only Spanish, Italians and British effectively outside the bargaining process.[24]

The whole operation could be seen as merely one of law and order by an increasingly fascist-style administration, particularly since the new measures of supervision were to include Communists who had been released from prisons in Algeria following the Allied invasion, and who had returned to the mainland. Two sets of the most wanted Communists, anarchists, and others suspected of subversive activity, had been given code names S and S^1, and those listed were to be arrested immediately there was any threat of disturbance. Consequently one major aspect of Vichy police activity was the constant updating of the lists with current information and addresses.[25] In mid-December Henri Cado, Directeur adjoint au Secrétaire général à la Police, sent a 34-page booklet to the police in the South listing all those who had been imprisoned in Algeria. It contained seventeen pages of French names, but also five pages of Spanish names and over four pages of Polish internees, most of whom had fought in the International Brigades in Spain.[26] When added to the extensive files that the police had already prepared on Communists and anarchists in their area this new information on potentially active opponents of the regime made up an exhaustive dossier. The detailed information it contained confirms that Vichy's prime police obsession from 1940 onwards was the location and supervision of known Communists, and in that sense the instructions of 1942 were far from a new departure.

But the tabulation and surveillance of people seen as 'outsiders' either by nationality or by politics or both, was clearly more than an internal measure of security, since throughout 1943 and the first six months of 1944 Vichy at all levels held these people in readiness for a deal of some sort with the Germans, in exactly the same way that the foreign Jews had been used in the summer of 1942. The administrative area under discussion here, Hérault, Lozère and Gard, produced three prefects who were shot at the Liberation for extreme acts of collaboration, and already in December 1942 one of them, the prefect of the Lozère, is asking whether he can release lists of *all* foreigners to the Germans at Mende.[27]

This same prefect sent a report to the Minister of the Interior in March 1943 in which he showed satisfaction at the local round-up of Jews which he had promoted, and in February 1944 the police section of the Ministry of the Interior allowed him to hand over the complete list of local Jews, whether of foreign or French nationality, to the Milice, an act tantamount to delivering the names indirectly to the Germans but preserving the semblance of French responsibility.[28] Letters mailed in the Lozère in the first three months of 1943 and intercepted by the Contrôle postal have several strong expressions of disgust and horror at the treatment of the Jews, which the prefect passes on to Vichy but ignores in practice.[29] Throughout the region there was a high success rate in the arrest of foreigners who deserted from supervised work places,[30] and in February 1944 Boyez at the Vichy Ministry of Labour reiterates the offer, frequently made to the Germans in 1943, of placing the maximum number of foreigners at Germany's disposal.[31]

This was the 'shield philosophy' at work, in which the interests of people considered by Vichy to be marginal were traded for those considered to be central, and in its own terms this was successful until February 1943 when Laval was forced to introduce a fully rigorous STO and thereby directly affect the work and lives of hundreds of thousands of French people who could not be considered marginal to the Vichy state but were, on the contrary, central to the French economy. With the first reactions of public opinion to the forced departures, and the first figures of réfractaires, Vichy was faced with the dilemma from which it never escaped in the rest of its existence. Should the category of 'marginal' or 'outsider' be extended to cover those who refused to be sent to Germany, a refusal which could, even within Vichy's philosophy, be seen as legitimate and patriotic self-protection?

The dilemma confronted the prefect of the Lozère at once. Letters written on, or soon after, 12 March 1943 and extensively sampled by the Contrôle postal, describe the departure scene at Mende station when the first contingent of forced labour left for Germany. Insults, eggs and bottled fruit were hurled at the French and German authorities, and the prefect, who had come with a speech to speed the train on its way, was forced by public hostility to keep silent.[32] Other letters relayed events at Clermont-Ferrand, where The Internationale had been vociferously sung, and at Saint-Etienne where women had lain down on the tracks. The letters contained a proliferation of adjectives describing the departures as cruel, deplorable, sad and terrible. 'Tout le monde pleurait', wrote Mlle Bonicel from Mende, 'car chacun avait un fils, un frère, un mari, un fiancé, un ami . . . '[33] Quite apart from the damage done to local public relations, these reactions were a severe warning that Vichy's trilogy of protected virtues – travail, patrie and particularly famille – were seen to have been betrayed by Vichy officials themselves.

The extension of STO during 1943 and 1944 to include groups initially excluded, youth from the Chantiers de la Jeunesse, students, and finally certain categories of agricultural workers, put an ever increasing strain on Vichy's original philosophy, and once women were also included for service within France, and married men with families became liable for service in Germany, the collapse was almost total. But did the shield philosophy collapse at the same time? Not entirely. But it survived only because Laval adapted to the failures of his own system.

Initially after the promulgation of STO Laval ordered the strictest pursuit of any réfractaire in the belief that he could break any working-class solidarity by police methods. In a circular of 23 February 1943 he instructed the police to search for every absentee and to take each one physically to a closely guarded centre at which they would be submitted to a medical examination and then, if fit, transported immediately to Germany.[34] Three weeks later, Henri Cado demanded the full lists of défaillants so that he could circulate them and co-ordinate a police hunt across the whole of the old Unoccupied Zone.[35] In June fines up to 100,000 francs were decreed for anyone, even a parent, aiding a worker to become a réfractaire, and prefects were told to convert hotels or police buildings into secure centres from which recruits for STO could not escape once they had passed the medical.[36] Finally in the same year German doctors were substituted for French ones at the examinations, as one means of lowering the very high number of exemptions.[37]

None of these measures was as effective as the Vichy Government hoped, and in the latter half of 1943 Laval adapted to the circumstances and significantly changed his attitude towards réfractaires. After October he proposed a limited amnesty under which no police charges would be preferred against réfractaires if they regularised their position before the end of December. Still more attractively they would be given a job inside France and would not be sent to Germany. As December approached the deadline was stretched to January 1944 and eventually to 1 April, and the Vichy authorities adhered to the terms of the amnesty despite protests of injustice from the parents of those who had fulfilled the requirements of STO and had been duly sent to Germany.[38]

Laval was forced into these concessions, not just by the numbers who failed to report, but by the fact that the police were unable to carry out the necessary work involved in getting all the required workers to Germany. The administration of STO included a census of the eligible population, the notification of those picked to attend the medical, a complicated system of exemptions and suspensions for which government regulations changed almost monthly, the search for défaillants and the supervision of the departures. The amount of paper work involved was out of all proportion to the capacities of a local mairie, and the number of searches quite beyond the powers of the local gendarmerie. Even if the population had been in favour of STO it would have been difficult to administer quickly and efficiently, but with public opposition almost total it was impossible, without recourse to the kind of draconian measures from which Vichy was supposed to be protecting the French. Laval's answer to this was increasingly to accept the réfractaires as misguided youths who could be helped to see the folly of their ways. He denied that there was any invariable path from réfractaire to maquisard and he directed on to the Maquis the maximum force of police repression, public outrage and German reprisals. The maquisard as outlaw, in the Vichy sense, was a necessity of the Vichy shield philosophy. Foreigners, Jews, 'nomades' and those referred to as 'oisifs', were inadequate as bargaining counters in 1943: their numbers were not sufficient to buy off German demands, whether ideological or economic. Unable to defend the workforce against compulsory labour in Germany, Laval might have abandoned the shield philosophy altogether. But by making concessions to the réfractaires on the one hand, and stigmatising the Maquis as bandits, terrorists and outlaws on the other, he secured the survival of at least part of the philosophy. In a series of agreements with the Germans, police activity against the Maquis became the gauge of collaboration offered by Laval in return for the continued existence of Vichy. All the FTPF Maquis were deemed expendable from the start, and in the Spring of 1944 Vichy finally offered up the Gaullist Maquis as well.[39] Internally, after October 1943, Laval reaffirmed the shield philosophy with detailed self-justifications to the prefects,[40] and a propaganda offensive through Philippe Henriot. The new perspective was that Vichy was not only shielding the French from the Germans, but also protecting the French, including the réfractaires, from the Maquis. But by October it was too late.

Quite clearly the distinction made by Laval between réfractaires and maquisards had an entirely different motivation from the one made by local historians today, but they have in common an underestimation of the structural impact of STO on French society, particularly the crucial significance of Vichy's official condemnation and pursuit of the réfractaires in the months between February and October 1943.

It is abundantly clear from the cabinet archives of the regional and departmental prefects in Languedoc that the primary effect of STO as administered in its first seven months, was the alienation from Vichy of vast sectors of public opinion which had previously been cautious, even suspicious of Vichy, but not rebellious. It provoked a widespread sympathy for those on the run, or in hiding, without which no Maquis implantation would have been successful. This sympathy acted as a dissolvent of normative attitudes to law and order on which all authoritarian societies, whatever their precise ideology, depend. Whether or not a Maquis group was composed of réfractaires as a majority or

The Maquis and the Culture of the Outlaw

minority, it thrived on the tolerance increasingly expressed for those in dispute with the law, a tolerance which dissolved in particular the professional cohesion and institutional loyalty of the gendarmerie, the first major sign that Vichy as an authoritarian state was disintegrating.

A letter from Mende on 23 May 1943 described an STO departure by bus, which turned into absurdity due to the complicity of the gendarmes:

> Mercredi dernier a eu lieu un autre départ de travailleurs. Mais c'est assez rigolo, voici comment ça s'est passé. Il devait en partir 83. Lorsque le car a été là pour les prendre il y en a eu 17. Le car est tombé en panne avant d'arriver au Monastier. Du temps qu'ils réparaient, les autres se sont camouflés sauf deux. Arrivés à Séverac les deux ont fait de même. Ainsi les Lozériens seront nombreux cette fois! [41]

The complicity was normally les blatant. Gendarmes developed skilful approaches to défaillants which resulted in pages and pages of detailed reports on searches which led nowhere, or involved endless interviewing of witnesses who had nothing to say. The regional prefect in Montpellier was himself capable of giving an implicit approval to time wasting, and if the search for a défaillant extended from one *département* to another, the administrative delays could be extended for weeks, at the very time when Laval was demanding almost daily reports on progress in producing the required number of departures.[42]

The reaction of the collaborationist prefects, Dutruch in the Lozère and Chiappe in the Gard, was to establish close links with the Milice and to urge Vichy to send in more of the dependable mobile police units, the GMR, to track down anyone defying the law, and if they did not explicitly indict the gendarmerie for subversion it was because the gendarmes who were sympathetic to those in hiding covered their tolerance for réfractaires with their declamatory show of efficiency. Literal and excessive bureaucracy can subvert an institution as much as neglect, which was one reason why the branch of Resistance called Noyautage des Administrations publiques (NAP) was increasingly insistent that Resistance sympathisers in the administration should stay at their posts. In January 1944 at St Pons in the Hérault a tract was found flyposted on the Monument aux Morts promising vengeance against collaborators, prompting two gendarmes to find seven local witnesses who had seen nothing and to detail their answers over six pages of tightly written reports. As each witness declared at length a complete ignorance of everything, the researcher can only wonder what else was going on in the area while this elaborate enquiry was proceeding.[43]

While the covert defection of individuals in the gendarmerie should not be exaggerated during 1943, the extent of the cover this provided for acts of illegality was powerfully reassuring to the normally law-abiding citizens who found themselves either actively or passively defying the law. It was one of the main ingredients which made potentially isolated acts of rebellion by réfractaires and their friends or family into a structural alternative to Vichy legality, a veritable culture of the outlaw. Such a culture, wherever it has positively existed in history, embodies the conviction that the established law has exceeded its rights and has itself become illegal, so that real authority, real justice and legitimacy, now lie with those who have technically become outlaws. The dissolution of the gendarmes' corporate loyalty to Vichy was a symptom of this culture; and one of the most interesting features of local behaviour in response to STO was to put pressure on other authority figures to pronounce on the justice of the departures, notably the schoolteacher, the curé and the pasteur. Invariably these authority figures were taken to embody a sense of higher legality which transcended the vagaries of government policies and created a link between citizens and the essence of either republican or religious justice. Under this pressure, in the area under discussion in this chapter, many local curés, almost all the local pasteurs, and the vast majority of schoolteachers at primary level, provided the réfractaires and their families with a sense of moral rightness and legitimacy.[44]

When historians of the Jewish persecution ask why, from March 1942 to August 1944 85 convoys deporting 75,000 human beings by rail were allowed to leave France without a single major act of derailment or sabotage to interrupt their passage, the damaging answer is that although many people felt the Jewish deportations were morally indefensible, there were not enough people who felt their own lives and freedoms threatened by the deportations to produce an effective outlaw response. With STO it was different. In the eyes of a majority, Vichy's collaboration in the departures broke the limits of legality. Illegal defiance was therefore a positive defence of justice, acceptable on civic and patriotic grounds.

Recourse to the superior justice embodied in the curé, pasteur and schoolteacher was part of a wider cultural reference which mobilised myth, folklore and regional tradition to sanctify acts of rebellion. At the Protestant veillées in the Cévennes the history and legends of the Camisards had been kept alive over 200 years. Leaving the village or town to take to the hills had a resonance which few Protesant réfractaires could miss. 'Vers les Déserts, ou les Maquis, peu importe,' wrote Jean-Pierre Chabrol, maquisard and novelist of the Cévennes, 'mais être monté vers les sommets, vers le ciel, avoir cherché refuge au sein de sa montagne . . . Quand on couche vraiment à même la terre, ça change tout, on sent le pays qui vous pousse dans les reins, "La terre est mon lit," hurlait le Camisard. "Le ciel ma couverture," répondait la sentinelle du Désert.'[45] The collaborationist prefect of the Lozère also likened the Maquis to the Camisards, and said that since the local population continued to remember the fight against the Royalists they would continue to indulge in actions which would provoke German reprisals.[46]

What also appears in Cévennol memoirs and oral evidence of the Maquis period, but is rarely dealt with in histories, is the more nebulous cultural concept of purity, freedom and virtue which the earth and the open air were thought to bestow on those who left the compromises and artificiality of the towns. It was a similar, but alternative, concept to the 'retour à la terre' which Vichy had put at the centre of its National Revolution; it had distant echoes of 'les Purs' at the time of the Cathars, and recent undertones of rural anarchism. There was even some cultural recuperation of the Vichy ideology itself in a region where the peasantry had been voting to the Left since the 1870s and resented the assumption that they were by nature the pillars of an anti-Dreyfusard, Maurrassian France. Grasping such an idea of open-air freedom may present problems for both the cultural and political historian but there can be no doubt of its structural importance for the outlaw world which the réfractaires and their sympathisers inhabited after February 1943. From Gabriel Valouer at Marvejols in the Gévaudan came a letter in October 1943, fully quoted by the Contrôle postal, saying, 'Je t'écris cette petite lettre pour te dire que je vais bientôt quitter la ville pour aller dans le maquis, vie de grand aventurier, car je ne veux pas partir en Allemagne . . .'[47] It speaks for thousands of others, romantic and illusory as the expressions may have been. It comes as no surprise to find the Liberation newspaper *Le Volontaire*, the regional weekly of the Forces Françaises de l'Intérieur (FFI) in Montpellier, reviewing the film *Tarzan trouve un fils* with the headline 'Tarzan, héros populaire'.[48]

The conclusion to which this is leading is that the contribution the réfractaires made to the history of the Resistance in terms of action and manpower may be low, or high, depending on variables in the locality, but far more important for the history of the Maquis is the fact that the refusal to leave for Germany and the protracted defiance of the law which this involved, was the formative act in creating an alternative legality and culture within which the Maquis could operate, with relative safety and with the moral assertiveness of those who uphold a natural right or a popular tradition. In the Limousin, Georges Guingouin the rebel Communist who orchestrated the Maquis round Limoges into what he called 'une révolte occitane', formalised his alternative authority and legality with the title 'Préfet du Maquis'.[49] In the Maquis Bernard in the Auxois, money was raised in a distorting mirror of established legality by levying taxes on the population on a sliding scale from known collaborators at the top down to *attentistes* at the bottom, leaving Resisters untaxed.[50] In the Ain, Romans Petit assumed a kind of constitutional authority for the Maquis in all local matters of civil contention, and throughout the Maquis of the Cévennes there operated a Maquis police, punishing acts of gratuitous pillage by individual maquisards, and informing the population of the existence of false maquisards who were exposed as *blousons noirs* on the rampage, an inevitable social product of a desperate and disintegrating authoritarian regime.[51] François Rouan, one of the leaders of the Maquis in the Lozère, described, as many others have done, the seizing of goods and food by the Maquis from Vichy depots and its redistribution not only among neighbouring Maquis units, but among the peasant population as well. Frequently, livestock earmarked for requisition by the German army would be liberated and returned at a safe interval to their owners or producers, measures by which the Maquis could be seen as protecting the rural economy more effectively than Vichy.[52]

It is within this perspective of an alternative culture that the exactions and raids carried out by the Maquis, as well as the consequences of their military actions, have to be set. Without the complicity of the urban working population the réfractaires would not have escaped from STO in the first place. Without the complicity of the rural population who sheltered and fed the réfractaires the Maquis might have been created, but would not have survived. This chain of complicity in the outlaw culture was not easily broken by a sudden attack of conscience or second thoughts when the Maquis staged a rural ambush which led to a series of brutal German reprisals, or when they descended on a town to requisition money from a bank, or on a village to take food from a store and cigarettes from a dépôt de tabac. On 10 January 1944 the mairie of Durfort in the Gard was raided and ration books stolen, one of literally hundreds of such raids which escalated in a spiralling graph until the Liberation, and were all noted and investigated by the scrupulous gendarmerie. The local inhabitants might well go short as a result of the raid, but the mayor was reported by an informer as saying 'Il faut bien que ces jeunes gens mangent.' It was a simple expression of the outlaw culture, and the Renseignements Généraux did not think it was worth their time to try and discredit it.[53]

Away from the Cévennes in the Haute Lozère, which was conservative where the Cévennes were radical, and clerical and deferential where the Cévennes were Protestant and rebellious, condemnation of the Maquis, in Laval's or Henriot's terms, was commonplace, but there the Church, led by the Bishop of Mende, had advised those who were called for STO to 'do their duty and go to Germany'.[54] The culture of the outlaw never took root in that area, nor in many others in France, but it did so in enough regions, some as small as a valley, others wider than a *département*, to bring about the dissolution of the authority of Vichy several months before the invasions of June and August 1944 accelerated its collapse.

The full history of the Maquis is the history of this culture, this alternative structure, of which the history of the réfractaires is an integral part. But the revolt lay not just in those who went to the hills, whether purely to hide or actively to fight, but also in those who received, supported or covered them. The history of the Maquis is not just a history of the men in the woods, it is just as much the history of the women who stayed behind. This has vital implications for research into women and the Resistance. The strategies and tactics of being an outlaw *at home* have not yet been researched. The history also involves those who suffered from German reprisals but kept faith with the culture of the outlaw: it is the history of whole communities who were both within, and yet outside, Vichy France.

In his novel, *Un Homme de Trop*, set in the Cévennes, Jean-Pierre Chabrol describes the descent of the maquisards into the village of La Martinette. The passage should be seen not so much as a picturesque *event* in the story of the local Maquis, but as a *tableau* in which most of the characters in the full history of the Maquis are presented: the hills, the village itself, the maquisards, the women cooking the soup, the younger and older miners who come to the door, and the starry-eyed boy who followed the maquisards down the road imploring them to take him too.[55] The history of the recruitment of soldiers at the outbreak of the First World War reveals the same sort of family and community structure, from those who volunteered to those who stayed behind and those who wanted to go but were too young. In a long interview Chabrol described the sense of isolation which maquisards experienced, particularly when they looked down into the valleys and saw the village life they had left carrying on without them. But when asked whether there was resentment or enmity or a conflict of interests between the local Maquis and the population in that part of the Cévennes just northwest of Alès, he reiterated the scene he had described as fiction at La Martinette, the Maquis returning to their own people, the villagers welcoming 'les jeunes', their own.[56] The flavour and strength of this communal bond may be culture-specific to the Cévennes, but subject to many local variables it was also specific to the culture of the outlaw wherever it obtained throughout France. It is true that in certain areas the Maquis were outsiders to the local population in exactly the way Philippe Henriot asserted in his skilful and highly effective radio attacks on the Maquis. There is therefore an outlaw history of the Maquis in which no positive outlaw culture existed in the surrounding countryside to bind communities and maquisards together, and *that* history will draw heavily on the distinctions and conflicts which historians can easily perceive, and which at the time Laval and Vichy were determined to promote.

Finally, there could have been no positive outlaw culture in any area without a cohesion between town and country which signalled yet another major strategic failure of the Vichy regime. Such cohesion between the mining town of Alès-la Grande Combe and the surrounding Cévennes posed very few problems. The extended families of the close-knit mining community with its Protestant religion and Camisard tradition bridged the divisions of urban and rural life. But it was not a situation which existed everywhere. In an exceptional article in *Le Volontaire* just after the Liberation, headed 'Paysans et Maquisards', reference was made to experience from the Ariège across Languedoc to Provence. It argued that the maquisard had to deal with the effects of a Pétainist ideology which had attempted to divide the town from the country, first by the rural idealism of the 'retour à la terre', secondly by the Relève scheme by which peasants would benefit by the return of prisoners of war, and when both failed by an 'appel à la jalousie' by which workers were presented as 'fainéants, grassement payés, avides de plaisir, prétentieux' and peasants as 'comblés de ravitaillement, faisant un honteux marché noir, avares et cupides, sans idéal, sans autre souci que celui de gagner de l'argent'. But with STO 'les ouvriers partirent à la campagne. Et ils firent connaissance avec les paysans. Non pas comme autrefois au temps des congés payés pour une quinzaine de jours, mais pour des mois, des années même' The first contacts were

The Maquis and the Culture of the Outlaw 249

delicate. 'Beaucoup de maquisards commirent des erreurs, même des injustices, et il ya a eut des heurts, des incompréhensions. Mais on peut dire que dans l'ensemble les campagnes de France se sont beaucoup rapprochées des citadins.'[57]

It is an ironic comment that after Vichy had sedulously cultivated the peasantry in the first two years of its existence, it should be the Resistance which could finally claim the allegiance of so many of the rural areas; ironic too that Prefect Chiappe should propose a separate region of the Cévennes, distinct from Languedoc and Provence, with himself as regional Prefect, and yet be unable to set foot in a Cévennol village after February 1943. Such ironies were not noted by Charles Maurras, who, even after the Liberation, believed he was still the defender of rural and regional France. Writing from prison in his bitter attack on the Resistance called *Votre Bel Aujourd'hui*, he referred yet again to what he believed were the 'real freedoms' of the countryside. 'Tenons compte seulement,' he wrote, 'de l'abondance des libertés.'[58] It could have been written by any maquisard. If, as I have argued elsewhere,[59] Vichy in 1940 appropriated many of the words and sentiments which had traditionally been the property of the Left, by 1944 the Resistance was referring to 'libertés anciennes' and 'le pays des ancêtres' as if the concept of 'le pays réel' had been invented by the Maquis, and not by the Nationalist Right. The masthead of the Vichy Corporation Paysanne carried the words 'La Terre, elle ne ment pas.' Later, the Resister and artist, Chancel, painted a picture of a field of wheat, from which rifles jut out like stalks of brown corn pointing towards a convoy of German tanks on the road skirting the field. It is called 'Produits du sol'.[60]

Appropriation is the luxury of the dominant culture. In the Cévennes, at least, the culture of the outlaw dominated for a year and a half. Its power base was not the towns, nor the country, but a *rapprochement* of the two. Not all Resisters by any means were part of this culture, and many were suspicious of its unorthodox nature and revolutionary potential. It would need a further chapter to describe how the outlaw culture was destructured at the Liberation and rendered harmless, and such is the encouragement of some historians to see the Maquis experience purely in terms of unsubstantiated anecdotes, that we might easily doubt that the culture had ever existed at all. Such a view would deprive many French communities of their history, and there are few injustices, in any culture, greater than this.

Notes

1. The main work on the FTPF is still the book by Charles Tillon: *Les F.T.P.* (Julliard, 1962), written when Tillon was still a member of the Communist Party. For an interesting essay on the class-based concept of 'serious' writing, see Allon White 'The Dismal Sacred Word. Academic Language and the Reproduction of Seriousness', in *Journal of Literature, Teaching and Politics*, no. 2, 1983.
2. Pierre Laborie, *Résistants, Vichyssois et autres: l'évolution de l'opinion et des comportements dans le Lot de 1939 à 1944*, (CNRS, 1980).
3. Jacques Canaud, *Les Maquis du Morvan* (Académie du Morvan, Château-Chinon, 1981).
4. See the bibliographical article by Henry Rousso, 'La Résistance entre la légende et l'oubli' in *L'Histoire*, no. 41, janvier, 1982.
5. Henri Cordesse, *Histoire de la Résistance en Lozère 1940-44* (Cordesse, 1974), p. 52.
6. Quoted by Henry Rousso, 'La Résistance', p. 104.
7. Laborie, *Résistants, Vichyssois et autres*, p. 302.
8. Rousso 'La Résistance', p. 104.
9. Canaud *Les Maquis*, pp. 39-68. Cf. Lucien Maury, *Le Maquis de Picaussel* (Maury, 1980), ch. 4.
10. Georges Gillier, *Les Corsaires*, no publisher, no date, no pagination.
11. Archives Départementales (hereafter AD) Lozère R. 5902.
12. AD Hérault 18 W 15.
13. AD Gard CA 763.
14. Oral evidence from François Rouan, Jean-Pierre Chabrol, Lucien Maury.
15. AD Hérault 136 W 22.
16. Aimé Vielzeuf, *On les appelait 'les Bandits'* (Crémille, Genève, 1967). Vielzeuf, himself an ex-maquisard, has written exhaustively and rigorously on every aspect of Maquis activity in the Gard and Cévennes.
17. Boegner reported Laval as saying 'Je fais de la prophylaxie'. See H.R. Kedward, *Resistance in Vichy France* (Oxford University Press, 1978), p. 182.
18. AD Hérault 18 W 19.
19. Ibid.
20. AD Hérault 18 W 8.
21. Ibid.
22. Ibid.
23. AD Hérault 18 W 19 and 18 W 8.
24. AD Hérault 18 W 19.
25. Ibid.
26. AD Hérault 18 W 14.
27. AD Hérault 18 W 19.
28. Archives Nationales (hereafter AN) FIC III 1165 Lozère; and AD Hérault 18 W 14.
29. AN FIC III 1165 Lozère; and A.D. Lozère VI M.2.19.
30. AD Hérault 18 W 65.
31. AD Hérault 18 W 15.
32. AD Lozère VI M.2.23.
33. Ibid.
34. AD Hérault 161 W 69.
35. Ibid.
36. AD Hérault 18 W 64.
37. AD Hérault 161 W 69.
38. AD Lozère VI M.2.23.
39. AD Gard CA 367.

40. AD Hérault 17 W 10.
41. AD Lozère VI M. 2.23.
42. AD Hérault 16 W 51.
43. AD Hérault 172 W 35.
44. Oral evidence from Henri Cordesse, Maurice et Berthe Pouget, François Rouan, Gilbert de Chambrun.
45. Jean-Pierre Chabrol in Aimé Vielzeuf... *et la Cévenne s'embrasa* (Editions le Camariguo, 1981), Préface, p. 17.
46. AN FIC III 1165 Lozère. Report 8 July 1943.
47. AD Lozère VI M. 2.23.
48. AD Hérault 397. 29 October 1944.
49. Georges Guingouin, *Quatre ans de lutte sur le sol Limousin* (Hachette, 1974), p. 106.
50. *La vie d'un Maquis d'Auxois*, Assciation du Souvenir de la Résistance, n.d.
51. H. Romans-Petit, *Les Maquis de l'Ain* (Hachette, 1974).
52. Oral evidence from François Rouan.
53. AD Gard CA 662.
54. AN FIC III 1165 Lozère. Prefect's report of 8 July 1943.
55. Jean-Pierre Chabrol, *Un Homme de Trop* (Gallimard, 1958), p. 78.
56. Oral evidence from Jean-Pierre Chabrol.
57. AD Hérault 397, 29 October 1944.
58. Charles Maurras, *Votre Bel Aujourd'hui* (Fayard, 1953), pp. 281-94. See H.R. Kedward, 'Charles Maurras and the True France' in R. Bullen, H. Pogge von Strandman and A. Polonsky, (eds) *Ideas into Politics* (Croom Helm, 1984), p. 127.
59. H.R. Kedward, 'Patriots and Patriotism in Vichy France', *Transactions of the Royal Historical Society*, 5th Series, vol. 32, 1982, pp. 175-92.
60. Reproduced in *Histoire Vécue de la Résistance*, Document no. 111, no publisher, no date.

OUTLINES

16 COLLABORATION AND LITERARY CRITICISM: RAMON FERNANDEZ'S *BARRES*

Bill Kidd

The subject of this short chapter is not Ramon Fernandez's critical theories, nor his political career, both of which I have dealt with elsewhere. My aim in the space available is to show, very briefly, how Fernandez presented Barrès to the reading public of the 1930s as a right-wing nationalist figure, and after 1940 as a symbol of Franco-German reconciliation. As in S. Beynon John's chapter on *Pilote de guerre*, or Gabriel Jacobs's on Joan of Arc, we are dealing with literature, or the critical reaction to it, as a vehicle for ideological manipulation and, some would say, of propaganda.

Like Péguy before him, but without the aureole of martyrdom, Barrès's reputation declined considerably between 1918 and his death in 1923. 'La revanche' was no longer an issue, and the 'lost provinces' had been recovered, although at what cost. Moreover, the writer had been too closely associated with wartime 'bourrage de crâne' for his moral and esthetic values not to appear old-fashioned and doctrinaire beside those of his more subtly emancipated contemporaries, Proust and Gide, while younger figures upon whom he had a discernible, indeed acknowledged influence, evolved towards fascism (Drieu la Rochelle) or surrealism followed by communism (Aragon), respectively. Even Montherlant affirmed: 'Barrès s'éloigne'.[1] The 1920s were a most un-Barrésian decade. In 1929, however, the posthumous publication of *Mes Cahiers* (11 vols. by 1938) and a new study by François Duhourcau,[2] began a process of rediscovery which events accelerated. The 6 February 1934, the remilitarisation of the Rhineland, the electoral victory of Léon Blum's Popular Front, the Spanish Civil War, and finally, in 1938, Munich, put writers like Barrès and Péguy back on the literary-political map, as figures to be enlisted by different groups, a traditionally French phenomenon whose ambiguities were well summed-up in René Lalou's phrase: 'un guide ou un otage?'[3]

Ramon Fernandez, highly sensitive to the changing ideological temper of his times, reflects this process. His earliest 'maîtres à penser' were Proust, Bergson and Gide, the latter a major touchstone for his political position until 1933-4. The few references to Barrès in Fernandez's writings before then were generally unfavourable; he sided with Gide,

255

for example, in dismissing the idea of 'enracinement' as botanically and psychologically unsound,[4] and attacked his thought as a 'sophistique et stérile construction'.[5] But reviewing two of the 'Cahiers' prompted a reappraisal: like Duhourcau, he found Barrès more intimate, more poetic and more ideologically complex than he had remembered in the immediate post-war years.[6] And when after a period of militancy on the left, Fernandez moved to the right, joining Doriot's PPF (Parti Populaire Français) in 1937, he produced a series of major articles on Barrès which, with minimal editorial amendment, were incorporated into the book published in February 1944.[7] The evolution in emphasis which occurred between these dates is a measure of Fernandez's growing involvement in the subject, and of the changed ideological context in which he was writing. Comparison of the pre- and post-armistice view reveals how the very elements which made Barrès a traditional right-wing nationalist reference contained an alternative, collaborationist interpretation. Summarised very schematically, the pre-1939 Barrès is presented as follows:

1. With his cult of the dead ancestors, and his successive immersion in family, province and nation, the author of *Les Déracinés* was driven to seek emotional no less than ideological completion behind 'des murs de plus en plus espacés, mais de plus en plus solides' (*Barrès*, p. 70). As such, he was an archetypal nationalist reference, available to different shades of right-wing opinion including some, it should be said, who after 1940 supported Vichy ('le chêne du maréchal' is a Barrésian symbol), or the Resistance (Jean Touchard has identified Barrésian material in Malraux's work).[8]

2. The Barrès of *Leurs Figures* was an anti-parliamentary but still republican reference, as was the catholic Péguy (*Barrès*, pp. 45-50), and hence a useful banner for Doriotism which, while seeking a more authoritarian and ultimately totalitarian political system, still professed attachment to certain republican, indeed 'revolutionary' ideals. To this extent, Barrès marked off the republican right from the monarchist Maurras (ibid., p. 45), although the latter's influence, perhaps because of some loss of doctrinal specificity, was extremely pervasive, and extended to members of the PPF, including Fernandez himself.[9]

3. Finally, in spite of the contradictions revealed in the French right by Munich, the author of *Colette Baudoche* and the 'Watch on the Rhine' remained a fundamentally anti-German reference for those whose patriotism was 'tourné vers l'Est' (*Barrès*, p. 59). Barrès, as Fernandez would later remind us, had experienced as a child of eight

'le trauma de 1870' (*Barrès*, p. 19), had been forced as a 'lycéen' to ingest the alien philosophy of Kant, and in 1914, seen France nearly succumb once more.

In extrapolating and contextualising these points, I have of necessity simplified Fernandez's analysis very considerably. Mention must be made of the fact that the critic already saw in Barrès's 'virile' nationalism a precursor of fascism (*Barrès*, 64-6), and gave a Freudian dimension to his analysis in suggesting that the writer was driven unconsciously to closer identification with the mother in order to be reconciled with the father (*Barrès*, p. 92). Both of these factors are germane to the manner in which he arrived at the subsequent supranationalist, totalitarian and collaborationist position, which may be schematised once again, as follows:

1. Thibaudet (whose death in 1936 placed him above suspicion of 'collaborationist' sympathies), had pointed out as early as 1921 that the creator of Bouteiller had misunderstood Kantism;[10] nor indeed did that particular antipathy neutralise the more favourable impression left by other German thinkers such as Hartmann, Fichte or Schelling (*Barrès*, p. 25). His underlying attitude was not hostile but fundamentally, ambivalent: Germany was 'à la fois un pôle d'attraction et un pôle de répulsion' (*Barrès*, p. 13). There were not only 'bad' Germanies but 'good' ones; and within the emotional geo-politics which equated the Wilhelmine Reich with 'le mal prussien' (militarists, professors of philosophy), the Moselle and Rhineland-Palatinate represented a more meridional civilisation, amenable to French influence and perhaps capable, so Barrès seems to have imagined in his last years, of achieving autonomy (*Barrès*, pp. 19-21).

2. Barrès's mother's family originated in the Palatinate (his father was 'auvergnat'); mixed ancestry made of him 'un homme-frontière' (*Barrès*, p. 13). And since frontiers unite as well as divide, the affective, psychological and cultural divide within Barrès was the meeting place and symbol of certain Franco-German antitheses – rational/sentimental, classical/romantic, paternal/maternal – which his work was an attempt to overcome. By amalgamating pre- and post-armistice ideas in this way, and giving greater prominence to 'traumatic' influences on the author's personality, Fernandez comes close to suggesting, without stating outright, that Barrès's developing preoccupation with Germany may also have derived from oedipal dynamics.

3. Finally, Barrès himself had claimed before 1914 that the trilogy

of family-province-nation might ultimately lead him to catholicism as the spiritual terminus of the progression, a kind of supranational transcendence. For critics of Fernandez's ideological persuasion, there existed a supranationalism which remained firmly terrestrial and indeed territorial: the 'New Europe' being created from the Franco-German collaboration implicit in the writer's own heredity. It was but a short step to make of 'l'homme-frontière' a kindred spirit of Charlemagne and Goethe, Kleist and Novalis, whose inspiration had presided over the 'Congrès des Ecrivains européens' at Weimar in 1941 and 1942.

Fernandez's politics notwithstanding, his *Barrès* echoes other works written before and after 1940;[11] although not above criticism, its relative neglect has perhaps owed as much to the opprobrium incurred by its author as to its intrinsic qualities. In any case, Fernandez was too shrewd to suggest that Barrès himself, had he lived, would have championed collaboration (*Barrès*, 10-12). He claimed merely, to have identified tendencies in his work which events and Barrès's successors were already bringing to fruition (ibid.). And if the critic's neo-Freudianism begs more questions than it answers,[12] he was on stronger ground in suggesting that aspects of Barrésian nationalism herald developments in the 1930s and 1940s, a point subsequently endorsed by Robert Soucy[13] and Zeev Sternhell.[14] Indeed, this pre-fascism, combined with the psycho-affective evaluation of Barrès's attitude to the 'two Germanies', appears to provide additional ideological corroboration: 'Europeanism' marks the successful passage from a 'partial' to a 'total' and indeed *totalitarian* Germany . . .

Two final points: it was impossible to divest Barrès entirely of his previous status as a representative of Alsace-Lorraine, now re-annexed by Germany; except among the most committed partisans of collaboration, there was therefore an undoubted limit to his appeal, and unlike Joan of Arc, that other 'Lorraine' so assiduously cultivated by the PPF, he had little to offer those whose principal motivation was hatred of 'l'Albion perfide'. Nor did Fernandez exploit as one might have expected the anti-Semitism of the caricaturist of *Leurs Figures* and the opponent of Dreyfus. In fact, although he endorsed his party's wartime 'aryanism', his eulogistic obituary of Bergson in 1941,[15] and a major study of Proust in 1943, which angered Céline and others of like mind,[16] reveal an ambivalence which may say something about the critic himself, and ultimately about the ambiguous nature of literary activity during the occupation as a whole.

Notes

(Works published in Paris unless otherwise indicated.)

1. On 'les dettes barrèsiennes de la génération de 1895', see Marius-François Guyard's article in *Maurice Barrès: actes du colloque organisé par la Faculté des Lettres et des sciences humaines de l'Université de Nancy* (22-25 octobre 1962), Nancy, 1963, pp. 299-308.
2. *La voix intérieure de Maurice Barrès d'après ses 'Cahiers'*, (Grasset 1929).
3. *Maurice Barrès* (Hachette, 1950), p. 145 *et seq.*
4. *André Gide* (Corréa, 1931), pp. 39-40.
5. *Marianne*, 26 April 1933, p. 4.
6. Ibid., 24 January and 3 October 1934, p. 4.
7. Ramon Fernandez, *Barrès*, Editions du livre moderne, 1944. Fernandez's articles were as follows: 'Maurice Barrès', *Revue de Paris*, 1938 (IV), pp. 833-59; 'Double France: les Mères et les Maîtres', *Revue de Paris*, 1939 (V) pp. 143-66; 'Sur Maurice Barrès', *Nouvelle Revue Française*, LVIII (1943), pp. 732-43; 'Barrès et l'Allemagne', *Deutschland-Frankreich*, 2es Jahr, no. 5 (1943), pp. 10-22; 'Maurice Barrès et "l'Appel au soldat"', *Revue du Monde*, no. 2, January 1944, pp. 173-82.
8. 'Le nationalisme de Barrès' in *Actes du colloque de Nancy, 161-73*, p. 165.
9. 'Maurras ou le désintéressement', *La Revue Universelle*, LXVIII, 1937 pp. 58-60.
10. *La Vie de Maurice Barrès* (Gallimard, 1921); cf. R. Fernandez, pp. 17-19.
11. See, among others: Sylvia King, *Maurice Barrès, la pensée allemande et le problème du Rhin* (Champion, 1933); Henri Clouard, *Bilan de Barrès* (Sequana, 1943); Jean-Marie Domenach, *Barrès par lui-même*, Editions du Seuil, 1954); Pierre de Boisdeffre, *Barrès parmi nous* (Plon, 1969).
12. I discuss this and other aspects of Fernandez's critical practice in my PhD thesis, *Ramon Fernandez et la quête du père*, University of Stirling, 1981 (on Barrès, see esp. pp. 463-95).
13. Zeev Sternhell, *Fascism in France. The case of Maurice Barrès* (Berkeley, University of California Press, 1972), pp. 283-4.
14. *Maurice Barrès et le nationalisme français* (Cahiers de la Fondation nationale des Sciences politiques, no. 182, Armand Colin, 1972), pp. 360-4.
15. 'Henri Bergson', *Nouvelle Revue Française*, LIV (1941), pp. 470-3.
16. Letters to Lucien Combelle of *La Révolution nationale*, reprinted in *Les Cahiers de l'Herne*, 1972, pp. 105-6.

17 WRITING UNDER VICHY: AMBIGUITY AND LITERARY IMAGINATION IN THE NON-OCCUPIED ZONE

Robert Pickering

Writing published in the Non-Occupied Zone during the Second World War constitutes a very rich field of study in terms of the exploration of forms of ambiguity, ambivalence and intellectual integrity. Writers operating officially rather than clandestinely under Vichy control, without overtly espousing either the collaborationist ethos or the call to arms of the Resistance, constitute a large 'limbo' group, overshadowed since the war by those whose personal persuasion either reflected the general evolution of political events, or whose considerable literary talent can be appreciated despite the strident advocacy of official tenets. To characterise this intermediary group as subscribing by definition to a kind of poor man's collaboration (since publication would tend to imply adherence to official doctrine), or to shelve them as being of dubious literary merit, is to sidestep certain important issues which their situation in Vichy France raises. Those issues arise essentially from the relationship between literary creativity and the pressure exerted by certain strictures, associated with the material and ideological dominance of a foreign power.

Hence a dual approach to methodology; the definition, firstly, of the kinds of repressive strictures under which such writers are functioning. The delimiting of this canon of constraints includes two major directions: the *repressive* code arising from censorship directives, to be circumscribed by reference to the proscription of certain obvious political and moral themes; and the *assertive* code, based on the directions of Vichy propaganda, and of German propaganda disseminated through Vichy in the Non-Occupied Zone. Major aspects of this assertive code include the ideological content of the National Revolution and a study of the dominant modes of German propaganda in France (such as they are regularly expounded in, for example, the journal *Signal* (*Berliner Illustrierte Zeitung*)), circumscribing dominant literary themes and imagery, levels of discourse and specific directions of the German ethos advanced. It is only through such definition that a canon of legitimacy can be established, leading to the second step in the overall methodology: the establishment of a list of writers who carry out their activities as a function of the above, representative therefore of this intermediary group, with particular reference to writing published in the Non-Occupied Zone (Gerhard Heller's *Un Allemand à Paris* has adumbrated some of the parameters of literary repression operative in the Occupied Zone).

How does the literary imagination cope with such strictures? The many works published in the Non-Occupied Zone testify to the fact that there is no simple capitulation, no literary sterility consequent upon the imposition of the canon of legitimacy. The neglect into which this flowering has fallen may or may not be a trustworthy reflection of its literary worth; be that as it may, what is of particular value in approaching such works is to follow through the intellectual vicissitudes which inform them, as they attempt to cope with a new orthodoxy. In effect, the two codes of influence (repressive and assertive) operate both externally in the form of official censorship and internally on the literary imagination, engendering a complex and sometimes sophisticated system of self-censorship and correction, but at the same time favouring an atmosphere of ambivalence which in some cases comes close to deviation from the enforced norm.

The writer is thus faced with the problem of the respect or circumvention of a defined series of taboo themes, all the more powerful in their potential appeal since arising from first-hand experience in a national crisis of traumatic proportion. In Freudian terms, creative energies are often channelled in alternative directions. The theme of defeat, ideologically loaded, can be channelled in directions of morality and the betterment of humanity, since the search for the most fruitful means whereby national and personal inadequacy, perceived as an underlying reason for defeat and occupation, can be expiated, is at one and the same time an attempt to come to terms with a situation of radical subservience and foreign imposition. The use of imagery, similarly, echoes such tendencies. Images associated with division, intersection, or break of continuity (nostalgia for home and loved ones, etc.) articulate a deeper awareness of rupture, that devolving from divided political and ideological loyalties and from the specifically physical image of a dividing line demarcating Occupied and Non-Occupied France. Such imagery can foster an atmosphere conducive to ambivalence in attitude towards the German occupier, a tendency which can perhaps be imputed to a certain nostalgia for reunification, for continuity re-established. This vision of reunification and renewal is a highly problematic one because of parallels elsewhere, in particular points of contact and of contamination with the Hitlerian 'New Europe'.

The 'escapist' tendencies in writing of the time also contribute to the creation of a climate of ambivalence, since the repressed stratum of proscribed themes and attitudes is powerfully suggested in its very absence. Ambivalence is frequently aided and abetted by censorship itself, which dictates the increasing resort to literary techniques of allegory and allusion. In such a context the literary message is characterised by its polyvalent and polysemantic nature: hence the frequency of the use of myth in works of this period (*Les Mouches* and *Antigone* are well-known examples of this tendency).

It is scarcely surprising, therefore, that the ambivalence frequently present in writing of this kind allows of illuminating points of contact with tendencies in both collaborationist and Resistance literature. In relation to collaborationist writing, themes appropriate to the Vichy orthodoxy are often apparent: the trinity of *Travail, Famille, Patrie*; themes based on the establishment of a corporate identity, and on the benefit of the collectivity; the return to the land; the virtues of obedience and patience in education; pro-clericalism; and the ethos of the sporting outdoor life. In comparison with resistance writing there are obvious points of divergence, particularly apparent in the thematic orientation towards self-recrimination and the need for spiritual and material salvation, as opposed to resistance themes of reaffirmation of pride in self and in cultural and social heritage. But certain themes can also be shared: a conceptual parallel sometimes binds the generalized desire for renewal, for return to the freshness and virtue of simple things or ways of life (Resistance), to themes exploited by writers legitimised under Vichy censorship (the backward glance to the greatness of times past, or the prospect of rejuvenating society and re-establishing meaningful human relationships). A complex process of transposition and contamination can be seen to be at work, and helps us to define the relative degrees of freedom or of constraint encountered by writers actively publishing in the Non-Occupied Zone, under Vichy censorship directives.

A noteworthy example of writing in which degrees of ambivalence can be measured according to the methodology outlined above is the case of François Reuter, and his novel entitled *Le Chemin du stalag* (Jean Vigneau, Marseille, 1943). The novel is a case in point, in as much as it is centred on the experience of defeat in May 1940 and on its immediate and long-term consequences. The repressive code is carefully respected: there is an absence of overt reference to internal division of the wider French-speaking community (including the Walloons); absence of reference to the possibility of struggle against the German invader after the collapse of May 1940; and despite very occasional reference to the German invader as 'L'ennemi', an absence of comments based on the depiction of German 'otherness', peculiarity or difference. The assertive code is similarly apparent in at least three respects: (i) criticism of the lack of preparedness and of lack of training in the French Army in 1940; (ii) criticism of demagogic politicians ignorant of, and unconcerned with, what is happening to the ordinary soldier at the front; (iii) the inevitability of defeat in such circumstances: feelings arising from the sense of abandonment; the highlighting of certain principles (for example, respect of his duty by the ordinary French soldier); the constant suggestion of equality between French and German soldiery, including hints of fraternalisation, of the breakdown of established frontiers and traditional differences, and the creation of a uniformity of European manhood – hints also of the parallelisms of the military experience ('Nous sommes là parce qu'ils y sont, et eux parce que nous y sommes'), of mutual esteem or of pity; the theme of the death of hope, and the advocacy of resignation, of fatalism; the theme of national contrition: the prisoner-of-war experience as bringing out the best in Man, showing the falsity of the thin veneer of civilisation and pointing to a return to the solid moral values of fraternity and solidarity; respect of the family ethos in recurrent allusions to wife and family; elements of a stolid kind of nationalism (for example, fear on the part of the ordinary soldier that the destruction of Paris would destroy a crucial component of his national heritage).

But the sources of ambivalence in this novel are no less striking. There is emphasis in the early stages on the power of will, but later we note its progressive eclipse: in this way the values of determination and of perseverance are both asserted and constantly undermined. Ambivalence surrounds the central image of the road, and of the soldier's relationship to it ('Il faut savoir poursuivre sa route, même si le but vient à se trouver derrière soi'); the end of the road, the 'Stalag', promises an experience both of subjugation yet of solidarity and self-understanding, and hence becomes the focus for a cluster of opposing feelings (determination, courage, yet also of a certain dehumanisation, of the reduction of self to the level of automaton). Perhaps most surprisingly, the dominant tone of the writing throughout is situated on the level of questioning and of uncertainty. Such questioning is directed towards a wide range of differing preoccupations: the course of military events; self-questioning (the limits of bravery, principles of honour, coolness under fire); the meaning of war and of self-sacrifice, in the face of political demagogy and selfishness in the higher military command;

doubts expressed regarding both immediate destinations during the forced march, and more long-range perspectives (the path towards national recovery). The novel thus articulates a discourse which on one level is situated firmly in the *status quo*, in the acceptance of a dominant mode of thinking but which on another level is constantly subverting the authority of its own message by reflection, retrospective wondering, doubts and questioning, providing a typical instance of the problematic middle ground in equivocal writing of this nature.

18 THE CULT OF JOAN OF ARC IN FRENCH SCHOOLS, 1940-1944

Nick Atkin

Of the many ways by which those in charge of education under Vichy sought to remedy the weaknesses and decadence of French youth, one of the most effective means was considered the exaltation of national figures. Through the study of great men in schools, Church and State endeavoured to inculcate a respect for the Catholic and National Revolution values of discipline, order and obedience among the young. Consequently a whole array of national figures felt to embrace such ideals were paraded before French youth as examples for inspiration and emulation. Foremost, of course, came Pétain himself, revered as some kind of demi-god, accompanied by such other luminaries as Péguy, Berard and Saint-Louis; significantly not one a hero of the 1789 Revolution.[1] But, after Pétain, of those selected, it was probably the figure of Joan of Arc whose message was considered by both Church and State to be of most significance for the young.

It is not very difficult to perceive why Joan was to be valued so highly. As a symbol of national integrity, youthful piety, morality, courage and sacrifice, few of the other heroes adopted under Vichy embodied quite so many of the values Church and State were so eager to engender within French schools. But to discuss in this brief contribution all of the various means by which these virtues were to be invoked would, I feel, be an impossibility. Therefore, concentrating primarily on her cult in schools of the southern zone, I have chosen to look at three of the commonest and most consistent ways by which Joan would be presented to children: as a symbol of patriotism; as a figure of reconciliation between Church and State; and as an example of the obedience owed towards *le chef*. These I regard as important, not just because they reflect much of what Church and State hoped to achieve overall through the promotion of her cult, but because they also illustrate so vividly many of the differing types of problem that would arise from the choice of Joan as an instrument of ideological propaganda.

It is, of course, as a symbol of patriotism that we most commonly associate difficulties with her cult under Vichy. For the duration of the war children would be taught how well Joan had loved her country, and how she had been prepared to give everything for its sake, only to die in the hands of the English. Her example of sacrifice was a lesson for all. But this was as far as either Church or State schools were prepared to tell her story. In order to avoid awakening any militant form of aggressive, nationalistic patriotism directed against Germany, they neglected to add that it had also been her love of France that had driven her to expel a foreign invader and liberate French soil. Even from children, however, it was impossible to conceal this aspect of her life, especially from those of the occupied zone for whom it had a special significance. Subsequently, as early as May 1941, there would be reports, albeit few of them, of children of both zones displaying anti-German sentiments in the ceremonies commemorating Joan's feast day. Undaunted, Church and State still continued to use Joan as a symbol of patriotism, yet greater precautions would be taken in future to suppress the ambiguity of her message. These would be evident in the meticulous detail of the official instructions for the celebration of her festival day in 1942, which were clearly designed to leave nothing to chance or open interpretation.[2] How successful such precautions were to be is impossible to say, especially as many children may well have participated in official ceremonies with the secret intention of paying homage to Joan as the patriotic Resister. This was certainly the view of one observer who wrote to complain to Bonnard, in August 1942, that the only reason why the Vichy government was able to achieve unity on Joan of Arc day was because she had the support of the Gaullists.[3] But towards the close of the war, with the occupation of all France, even this sort of unity would become harder to maintain, with more and more people openly looking to Joan as a symbol of deliverance for their country.

Likewise, as the war progressed, the evocation of Joan as a symbol of reconciliation of Church and State would not be without its problems. To reflect the new harmony that prevailed between the old adversaries at the start of Vichy, children were to be taught how in the fifteenth centuries these two bodies had stood in opposition, yet how Joan, much in the same way as Pétain, had still been able to bring them together. This new-found unity was to be further emphasised on Joan's feast day, with children of Catholic and State schools marching together side by side. But I consider this image of Joan as the reconciler was to be damaged in two different ways. First, I cannot help feeling that despite official encouragement many secular instituteurs must have displayed a deep reluctance at the prospect of teaching about Joan as a unifier of Church and State, and chose instead to concentrate on the less 'contentious' aspects of her life. Secondly, with the return of

Laval, the stepping up of measures against the Jews, and the introduction of *Service Travail Obligatoire*, no longer were relations between the two to be so cordial in any case. In turn, these developments could well have undermined the credibility of Joan as a symbol of such unity, and have dented the confidence and enthusiasm of those members of the government, clergy and teaching profession who were anxious to promote her in this way.

In slight contrast, the use of Joan as an example of obedience towards *le chef* appears to have been more effective, although, ultimately, it too would have its share of difficulties. To emphasise the natural respect commanded by Pétain, children learnt how in Joan's day France had lain prostrate, wracked by misfortune and internal division, but how nevertheless Joan had emerged, a figure of hope and natural leadership around which the nation had been able to unite and take solace. Now once again France faced adversity, but as before she had a saviour, this time in the figure of Pétain. Children were therefore urged to rally round the Marshal as they had done Joan, and pay respect to legitimate authority. Speaking to children and youth groups at Lyon on Joan of Arc day, 1942, Lamirand would proclaim, 'Nous le suivrons fermement avec une confiance totale comme le peuple de France suivit l'étendard de Jeanne'.[4] Even in the uncertain atmosphere of 1944, frequent allusions would still be drawn between the two leaders, and this may be one of the many reasons why the cult of Pétain, sustained by that of Joan, was to retain its popularity with children until the Liberation. At the same time, however, Joan's success in this sphere should not be exaggerated. By the end of the war, with the growth of the Resistance, it is possible to detect a certain tinge of desperation in the rallying calls around Joan and Pétain. Henriot, for instance, would use the occasion of Joan's feast day in 1944 to urge his youthful audience in Lyon to unite around Pétain in the face of a possible allied *débarquement*.[5] But, furthermore, it may be that Church and State overplayed the similarities between the two heroes, and that the young had begun to tire of the continuous comparisons being made.

This points to what is one of the perennial problems associated with the cult for heroes under Vichy. As Dr Halls has recently remarked, although hero worship may well lead to emulation and imitation, too much eventually stultifies action.[6] This appears to a large extent to have been the case with Joan. At first she had been presented as a figure of dynamism and effort, in contrast to the lethargic ways of the old Republic. But after a while it became clear that she too could achieve little. By continuing to use her example Church and State merely helped to underline her ineffectiveness. However, to the various groups and factions that were in charge of education at the start of Vichy this development could not have been foreseen. For them Joan appeared as an ideal hero for children, and had busily set about devising ways by which her numerous values could be invoked. If any one overall theme would emerge, it would be that of Joan as a symbol of unity. This we have seen in the three examples I have chosen: unity between Church and State; unity around *la patrie*; unity around *le chef*. It was the umbrella theme underneath which her many other values would be invoked. But because Joan embodied so many causes Church and State would soon stumble across yet another problem with her cult: that of ambiguity, especially as a symbol of patriotism. Subsequently, as the war dragged on, ambiguity of this kind would become more and more difficult to contain, and would slowly eat away at the fragile unity Church and State had been so desperate to preserve through the figure of Joan.

Notes

1. For a much fuller discussion of the type of heroes selected under Vichy, cf. W.D. Halls, *The Youth of Vichy France* (Clarendon Press, Oxford, 1981), p. 167.
2. *Instructions pour l'organisation de la manifestation JEUNESSE FOI VOLONTE à l'occasion de la fête JEANNE D'ARC. 10 Mai 1942* (Edition du Ministère de l'Information, Vichy, 1942).
3. Archives Nationales F17 13336. Letter to Bonnard from the ex-commandant de l'infanterie de la Garde de Paris, 6 August 1942.
4. Lamirand quoted in *Les Jeunes Fêtent Jeanne d'Arc* (Imprimerie Commerciale, Lyon, 1942), p. 3.
5. Henriot quoted in *La Croix*, 16 mai 1944.
6. Halls, *The Youth of Vichy France*, pp. 226-7.

19 ROBERT BRASILLACH: THE MACHISMO OF IMPOTENCE

John Coombes

Written in the winter of 1939-40, during the last months of the Republic, Brasillach's provisional autobiography *Notre Avant-guerre* was published in the early months of the Vichy regime, at the outset of the scabrous flowering of that career of journalistic vituperation and denunciation which was to lead, in 1945, to conversion to the lachrymose religiosity of the *Poèmes de Fresnes*, and, eventually, to that definitive exclusion – by firing-squad – from the human community, which Brasillach had himself so vigorously sought for the Jews.

Though Brasillach was more politically committed, in a formal sense, than his contemporaries among writers of the extreme Right (with the possible exception of Rebatet), his text appears relatively free of the obsessive anti-Semitism which saturates, say, *Les Décombres*, or more particularly Céline's *Bagatelles pour un Massacre*. That the distinction is more apparent than real, however, becomes clear when we observe the gradual, sinuous heightening of Brasillach's anti-Semitic discourse across the text as a whole: when, early on, the idyllic semi-poverty of life as a *tapir* (private tutor) is evoked with rueful nostalgia, the concomitant anti-Semitism is articulated upon it so casually as to appear relatively insignificant, inoffensive even: 'J'ai donné des|leçons à de jeunes juifs qui disposaient sur leur table de travail, pour m'éblouir, les notes de leurs relieurs . . . '[1] Yet later, as the point of writing is approached and institutional politics is conflictually formulated with the rise of the Front Populaire, the tone rises rapidly from one of a 'liberalism' of dubious ritual disavowal to that of polemical frenzy:

Le Francais est antisémite d'instinct, *bien entendu*, mais il n'aime pas *avoir l'air* de persécuter des innocents pour de vagues histoires de peau. (p. 244, my emphasis)

Le cinéma fermait pratiquement ses portes aux aryens. La radio avait l'accent yiddish. Les plus paisibles commençaient à regarder de travers les cheveux crépus, les nez courbes, qui abondaient singulièrement. Tout cela n'est pas de la polémique, c'est de l'histoire. (p. 245)

The rhetorical brutality – in effect self-defeating – of the final assertion may (together with the earlier self-betraying 'bien entendu') be taken as a characteristic moment of the discourse of fascism: the sudden disruptive appeal to a mendaciously constituted external totality, to whose dictates writing and reading subject are alike, then, 'destined' to submit.

Such a submission of the self is, moreover, implicit in the range of significant, indeed determinant, absences of this autobiographical text. It begins with an account of the writer's entry into the *classes terminales* of the Lycée Louis le Grand; previous years of crucial experience – of parents, of family, throughout childhood and early adolescence – are totally omitted. Nor, perhaps even more significantly, is there any overt mention of sexual experience, with the revelatory exception of Brasillach's obituary evaluation of his relationship with his friend Annie Jamet (from whose surname it is indeed difficult to resist drawing a sub-Derridian pun):

> Pour moi qui n'ai peut-être pas eu d'amitié vraie, d'amitié que j'ai envie d'appeler amitié virile, pour aucune autre femme sinon pour elle . . . je ne puis croire encore aujourd'hui qu'elle ne soit plus. (p. 295)

Notable, here, is the way in which the generalised plangency of homosexual exclusion is overriden by the aggressive assimilation of woman into a norm of dominant maleness ('amitié virile');[2] yet more striking is the descent, in the subsequent phrase, into the utmost banality.

From these silences – and from the half-utterances which, as we have seen, confirm them – we read the general absence of any sense of a negotiation with, any productive appropriation of, the world. Thus, necessarily, fascism makes its appearance in the text, not as a position worked towards through a process of individual and political discovery, but as an unquestionable, pre-constituted bloc.

Refusal of any consideration of interpersonal relationships and of their political structuration; the subjugation of the self to a certain determined vision of the world: all of this means that the text becomes elaborated as a series of refuges.

Most evident of these is the perennial articulation of pathological nostalgia – whether for the numbers of defunct Paris bus routes or for the obsessively recalled details of lycée syllabus and organisation. Particularly revelatory, in this connection, is the initial governing characterisation of the past as 'un abri tellement profond que le reste de l'univers semble avoir disparu' (p. 8): seldom can the death-wish which accompanies the lust to power have been more graphically articulated!

From the generalised haze of fugitive nostalgia, there none the less emerge, by contrast, in Brasillach's construction of the past, moments of supreme and acute ecstasy.[3] The objects of this ecstasy (significantly the writer constantly declares himself 'ravi' by his key experiences) are certainly heterogeneous, evidence at first sight of a mad-dog eclecticism. Yet these moments, in their sinister succession – from the theatre of the Pitoëffs and the *renouveau idéaliste* of post-war French drama, through the amalgam of populism and surrealism effected by René Clair, to the master-race carnival of the Nuremberg rally – have as a perennial condition of operation the absorption into their discursive practices of a spectator at once highly sensitised and totally passive.[4]

At a more mundane level, willed absorption of the self into a range of spurious collectivities results in the presentation of a series of *images d'Epinal*: the lost world of the classroom, indulgently recalled, gives rise to elegiac expressions of the values of political toleration which are radically at odds with the fascist project of the writing subject: ' . . . nous discutions avec passion et avec amitié, et avec une sympathie intellectuelle, une sorte d'honnêteté que je n'ai jamais plus recontrée par la suite' (p. 41).

Such adolescent amiabilities – the fruits, so the writer asserts, of 'un peu de confusion d'esprit . . . et quelque penchant foncier pour l'anarchie . . . ' (p. 46) – have, none the less, their institutional sites. Particularly instructive in this respect, and for the way in which fantasy is located within ideology, is the writer's characterisation of the Ecole Normale Supérieure (on the occasion of his first – unsuccessful – attempt to gain admission to it): 'Quant à moi, cette première notion de l'anarchie légale où vit l'illustre communauté universitaire me laissa rêveur' (pp. 74-5).

The sentence represents a whole intellectual autobiography in itself: youthful 'anarchy' is defused, incorporated into established modes of authority ('l'anarchie légale'): from this process emerges a dominant structure ('l'illustre communauté') with which the subject feels no longer free to engage, but can only admire passively ('rêveur').

It is in this context that the given history of Brasillach's intellectual transactions needs to be viewed: reading is not seen as an active process of production of new meanings, but as evidence of consecration into an established élite-group: 'Car nous n'étions pas loin de penser que la littérature n'a de valeur que pour fournir des mots de passe' (p. 127).

This infantile exclusivism of the group (the work most frequently referred to in the autobiography is Jules Romains' anodine unanimist fable *Les Copains*) is subsequently projected into an unctuous evocation of the writer's fascist activities: we learn little of the *function* of *Je Suis partout* (the fascist weekly for which Brasillach wrote) but much about its supposed *nature* as a location of male camaraderie, of 'le sentiment de former une bande, et . . . pour choquer les bourgeois, le sens du gang' (p. 286). Where fascist activity is referred to, willed immersion in a fantasy of unquestioned social cohesion can result in the ludicrous: the assertion, for instance, that the fascists and the Front Populaire had the cult of youth in common; or the narration of a sense of 'fraternity' with left-wing militants in 1936: 'Et pourtant, si, aux quêteurs de juillet 36, on répondait: 'Non, camarade, je suis fasciste,' nul n'insistait' (p. 239)

Moments of ecstasy, *images d'Epinal* and the consistent repression of the conflictual and the problematic (whether psychological or political) – a repression effected as deviously in the text as it was brutally in fascist political practice – all of these discursive elements are, climactically, covered and ratified by the ideological assertion of 'la joie fasciste':

> Joie qu'on peut critiquer, joie qu'on peut même déclarer abominable et infernale, si cela vous chante, mais joie . . . je sais que rien n'empêchera la joie fasciste d'avoir été . . . (p. 362)[5]

In this assertion of what is presented, in its turn, as an unquestionable and self-ratifying principle, we discern both the scriptive paucity and the intellectual impotence of the fascist writer. A *motif* – recurrent to the point of dominance – in Brasillach's discourse is that of the *lapalissade*, the statement of such self-confirming banality as to appear incontrovertible. Its banality can reassure the dilettante aesthete, the tourist: 'Mais aujourd'hui pour moi . . . Venise reste toujours Venise . . . ' (p. 273) – just as its nullity can be deployed to cover a fascist life-project whose vicious energies derived from its manifest contradictions; notably passive internal acceptance of the collective movement vs. exacerbated aggression towards the sexual and social other: 'Ce qui a été ne sera plus, dans la paix ou dans la guerre.' (p. 8) 'Quel que soit l'avenir, il n'offrira plus désormais, ni pour nous ni pour autrui, le même visage.' (p. 442)

We are tempted to ask, with Julien Sorel, 'n'était-ce que cela?' In its ultimate articulation of nullity, Brasillach's discourse – of totalitarian collective – may be seen as the obverse to Céline's –that of exacerbated solitude. Both, in their different ways, demonstrate an attempted, but futile, refusal: of mediation between self and world, of historical process. A refusal of central importance for a characterisation of *homo fascistus*.

Notes

1. Robert Brasillach, *Notre avant-guerre. Mémoires* (Livre de Poche/Plon, 1973), p. 91 (all subsequent page references are to this edition).

2. The term 'amitié virile' recalls, of course, the 'fraternité virile' often supposed to be at the ideological centre of Malraux' novels. Yet in the case of Malraux, the relationship is structured as problematic, whether on the 'personal' level (Claude/Perken in *La Voie Royale*) or on the 'political' level (Kyo and Katow/the masses in *La Condition humaine*); whereas in Brasillach's text, assent is demanded to its simple homogeneity, its lack of difference.

3. The mentality which the text presents to us at this point has much in common with the essentialism of Annie and her 'situations privilégiées' in Sartre's *La Nausée*.

4. We have not space here to do more than note, in passing, the implications of the ease of the transition effected, in the text, from bourgeois to fascist aesthetics.

5. Jean Giono's novel *Que ma joie demeure* (1935) treats the problematic and contradictory nature of just such an abstract principle of 'joy', and of the problems which its dissemination engenders between leader/innovator (Bobi) and the masses (the peasant group). The contast between the novel and Brasillach's text is not so much one of *form* (novel vs. autobiography) or even one of *politics* (Left vs. Right: Giono's ideological vacillation brings other problems), so much as one between an investigative and a dominated consciousness.

NOTES ON CONTRIBUTORS

Louis Allen, Reader in French in the University of Durham. Current research: Japanese intelligence schools and agencies. Author of *Burma – The Longest War 1941-1945* (Dent, 1985) and other publications.

Roger Austin, Lecturer in Education (History), the University of Ulster, Coleraine. Has written 'Propaganda and Public Opinion in Vichy France: The Department of Hérault, 1940-44', *European Studies Review*, 1983, and other publications. Currently working on political surveillance in Vichy France as part of a wider study of persuasion and dissent in wartime France.

Nicholas Atkin, Graduate student, Bedford College, London University. Current Research: 'The French Catholic Church and Education during Vichy France, 1940-1944', London PhD.

John Coombes, Lecturer in Literature, University of Essex. Current Research: on narratives of the left in the 1930s; and on the literary discourses of fascism. Publication, 'British Intellectuals and the Popular Front' in F. Gloversmith (ed.), *Class, Culture and Social Change*, (Harvester, 1980), pp. 70-100, and other publications.

Brian Darling, Principal Lecturer at North East London Polytechnic. Current research on the École des Cadres d'Uriage; has contributed regularly to the Paris monthly *Esprit* and elsewhere.

John Dixon, Head of History, Tewkesbury Comprehensive School, Gloucestershire. Studying the impact of the National Revolution of Marshal Pétain on the City of Limoges 1940-4 for M.Phil. at the University of Warwick.

Hilary Footitt, Senior Lecturer in French/French History and *John Simmonds*, Senior Lecturer in European History both work at the Cambridgeshire College of Arts and Technology. They are currently writing: 'The Politics of Liberation: France' (forthcoming, Leicester University Press).

Notes on Contributors

W.D. Halls, University Lecturer, Department of Education, Oxford University. Current Research: The Church in Vichy France. Publication: *The Youth of Vichy France* (Oxford University Press, 1981) and other books and articles.

Ian Higgins, Senior Lecturer in French at St Andrews University. Currently writing a book on the poet Guillevic. Author of an *Anthology of Second World War French Poetry* (Methuen, 1982) and other publications.

Gabriel Jacobs, Lecturer in French at University College, Swansea. Currently researching on the language of propaganda in occupied France. Author of 'The Antigone of the *Resistance*' (AUMLA) and other publications.

S. Beynon John, Honorary Reader in French, University of Sussex. Current Research: Book on 'Vichy France and the Literary Imagination'. Author of: *Anouilh: L'Alouette and Pauvre Bitos* (1984) and other publications.

H.R. Kedward, Reader in History, University of Sussex. Currently preparing a book on the Maquis and the end of Vichy France. Author of *Resistance in Vichy France* (Oxford University Press, 1978) and other books and articles.

William Kidd, Lecturer in French, University of Stirling. Main research interests are ideological and psychological approaches to French literature 1919-1945. Publications on Vichy France and Ramon Fernandez, including a presentation of his correspondence with Jacques Rivière (in *Bulletin des Amis de Jacques Rivière et Alain-Fournier*, no. 14, 1979, pp. 9-51).

Robert Pickering, Professor of French, University College, Cork. Publications include *Paul Valéry, poète en prose*. Currently working on censorship and literary imagination in France during the Second World War.

Miranda Pollard, Postgraduate student of Modern History, Trinity College, Dublin. Working on Images of Women in the Policy and Propaganda of the Vichy Government, 1940-4.

Notes on Contributors

Derek Robbins, Principal Lecturer in the School for Independent Study at North-East London Polytechnic. Co-author of a contribution to *Towards the Community University* (1982), edited by D.C.B. Teather, and writes frequently for *Higher Education Review*.

Jeanie Semple, Senior Lecturer in French, Polytechnic of the South Bank. Current research for PhD on the French cinema during the Occupation.

Ethel Tolansky, Senior Lecturer in French, Senior Tutor, Polytechnic of Central London. Current Research: M.Phil. Westfield College, London: The Search for the Self in the early novels of Jean Cayrol. Other Research: The war writings of Vercors. Les Editions de Minuit.

John Wright, Principal Lecturer in French Studies, Department of Language Studies, Coventry (Lanchester) Polytechnic. Current research includes Mounier, Péguy, ideological developments in France 1930-50. Has written 'La vision des hommes et du monde: Péguy et Mounier' and other publications.

CHRONOLOGY

1939
July	28	Promulgation of the *Code de la Famille* by Daladier's Government.
August	23	Nazi-Soviet pact.
	27	Censorship mechanisms established in France.
September	1	Germans invade Poland.
	3	Great Britain and France declare war on Nazi Germany.
	17	Soviet army invades Poland.
	26	Parti Communiste Français (PCF) dissolved by Daladier's Government.
October	8	French Communist Deputies arrested.
During Oct.		*L'Humanité* reappears clandestinely.
November	30	Soviet army invades Finland.

1940
March	20	Daladier resigns. New Government formed by Reynaud.
March-April		Trial and conviction of French Communist Deputies.
May	10	Beginning of German offensive against the West.
	13	Germans break through at Sedan and cross the Meuse.
	18	Marshal Pétain brought into Reynaud's Government.
	19	Weygand appointed to take over from Gamelin as Commander-in-Chief of the French army.
	27	King Leopold orders the Belgian troops to surrender.
End of May-June	4	Evacuation of British and French troops at Dunkirk.
	5	Charles de Gaulle nominated as Under-Secretary of State in the Ministry of War.
	10	Fascist Italy declares war on France.
	10	French Government leaves Paris.
	14	German army enters Paris.
	16	Reynaud resigns. New Government formed by Marshal Pétain.
	17	Pétain calls for a cease-fire and announces that France is seeking an Armistice.

	17	De Gaulle reaches London.
	17	Acts of protest against the Armistice by Michelet in Brive and Moulin in Chartres.
	18	De Gaulle broadcasts an Appeal for resistance from Broadcasting House, London.
	21	A group of French politicians embark on the *Massilia* for North Africa. They are arrested on Pétain's orders on arrival.
	22	Armistice between Germany and France signed at Rethondes.
	23	Laval enters the Pétain Government.
	25	Armistice takes effect.
	28	British Government recognises de Gaulle as 'Chef des Français libres'.
	29	Pétain's Government leaves Bordeaux for Clermont-Ferrand and, later, Vichy.
July	3	British attack the French fleet anchored at Mers el-Kébir, near Oran.
	10	National Assembly at Vichy votes full powers to Pétain by 569 votes to 80.
	11	Pétain becomes Chef de l'Etat.
	12	Pétain appoints Laval effectively as Prime Minister (Vice-Président du Conseil des Ministres)
	22	Vichy law reviewing naturalisations aimed against Jews.
	30	Creation of the Chantiers de la Jeunesse by the Vichy Government.
end of July-early August		Henri Frenay envisages his Resistance Movement which eventually becomes Combat.
July-August		Clandestine publication of the Communist appeal 'Peuple de France', sometimes known as the 'Appel du 10 juillet'.
July-August		First secret agents arrive in France from London.
August	3	Abetz appointed as German Ambassador in Paris.
	7	Alsace and Lorraine incorporated into the German Reich.
	13-19	Vichy dissolves Freemasonry, and Trade Unions at National level.
	26-29	The French Cameroons and most of French Equatorial Africa rally to de Gaulle.

Chronology 279

	29	Vichy establishes the Légion française des Combattants.
September	16	First stagiaires arrive at Vichy's École des Cadres (at la Faulconnière)
	23-25	De Gaulle and a combined French and British fleet fail to take Dakar in French Senegal.
October	3	Vichy enacts its first *Statut des Juifs.*
	11	Vichy law regulating women's employment in the public sector.
	24	Pétain meets Hitler at Montoire.
	30	Pétain's broadcast on Montoire with the phrase 'J'entre aujourd'hui dans la voie de la collaboration'.
During Oct.		Widespread arrests of Communists in both zones, by Germans and by Vichy.
		De Gaulle establishes Brazzaville as the African headquarters of the Free French. Loustaunau-Lacau creates basis of network Alliance.
November	3	De Brinon appointed as French Ambassador in Paris.
	4	First stagiaires at Uriage, new location of Vichy's École des Cadres.
	11	Demonstration against the Occupiers by students and schoolchildren in Paris.
	25	First number of the clandestine *Liberté*, edited by François de Menthon.
November 1940-Aug. 1941		*Esprit* relaunched in ten monthly issues.
December 1940		First number of clandestine *Libération-Nord*, produced by Christian Pineau.
	13	Laval sacked and arrested by Pétain (later released after German intervention).
	15	First number of clandestine *Résistance*, produced by group from the Musée de l'Homme.
During Dec.		Translation of Shaw's *Saint Joan* put on in Paris.

1941

January	22	Arrest of the French agent d'Estienne d'Orves by the Germans.
February	1	Marcel Déat creates the Rassemblement National Populaire (RNP).
	9-10	Admiral Darlan appointed by Pétain as Vice-Prési-

		dent du Conseil des Ministres, and designated successor to Pétain.
	11	Arrest of members of Resistance organisation Musée de l'Homme.
March	29	Xavier Vallat nominated as Commissaire aux Questions Juives.
During March		Free French agent Rémy gathers isolated groups together into the network Confrérie Notre-Dame (CND).
May	11	First Vichy fête of Jeanne d'Arc.
	11-13	Darlan meets and negotiates with Hitler in Germany, leading to proposals for military collaboration 'Les Protocoles de Paris' which Vichy Government refuses to ratify.
	26	Start of Miners' strike in the Nord and Pas-de-Calais.
During May		Communists create basis of Le Front National (FN).
June	2	Vichy's second *Statut des Juifs*.
	22	Nazi Germany invades the Soviet Union.
	23	Péguy's *Jeanne d'Arc* opens in Paris.
July	7-18	Creation of the Légion des Volontaires français contre le Bolchévisme (LVF).
	7	First number of clandestine *Libération-Sud*, animated by Emmanuel d'Astier.
	26	Assassination of Marx Dormoy at Montélimar.
August	21	Fabien shoots German officer cadet at the Métro Barbès.
	29	Execution of d'Estienne d'Orves.
During August		Mounier excluded from all Vichy youth organisations. Last number of *Esprit*.
Sept.-October		Sequence of individual shootings of German Officers in Paris, Nantes and Bordeaux, followed by the execution of French hostages (98 executions, including 27 at Châteaubriant, on 22-23 October).
October	4	Vichy promulgates its *Charte du Travail*.
November		First number of the clandestine *Cahiers du Témoignage Chrétien*.
December		First numbers of clandestine *Combat* and *Franc-Tireur*.
	5	Execution of Gabriel Péri.
	14	100 hostages shot in Paris.
	31	Jean Moulin leaves London for his first mission to France.

Chronology

1942

January	10	Vermorel's *Jeanne avec Nous* opens in Paris.
February		Creation of Service d'Ordre Légionnaire (SOL) which later becomes the Milice, led by Joseph Darnand.
	15	Vichy makes abortion a crime 'against the race'.
	19	Vichy opens the Riom trial against Léon Blum, Daladier and others.
	20	First clandestine number of *Les Editions de Minuit*, the novel by Vercors, *Le Silence de la Mer* (English publication a year later).
	25	Execution of seven members of the Resistance organisation, Musée de l'Homme.
Feb.-April		First appearance of St Exupéry's *Pilote de Guerre* (English translation in *The Atlantic Monthly*, New York).
March		Creation of Francs-Tireurs et Partisans (FTP).
	18	Vichy makes 'enseignement ménager' compulsory for girls.
	27	First deportation of Jews from France to concentration camps.
April 18		Laval returns to power as head of the Vichy Government.
May		First number of clandestine *Le Populaire*.
	6	Darquier de Pellepoix becomes Commissaire général aux Questions Juives.
June	16	Meeting of Laval and Sauckel. Idea of the *Relève* accepted.
	22	Laval announces the *Relève* and uses words 'Je souhaite la victoire de l'Allemagne ...'
During June		De Gaulle's message to the internal Resistance, linking Liberation and Revolution, published by the clandestine Press.
July	16-17	Massive round-up of Jews in Paris ('rafle du Vel' d'Hiver').
August		Vichy hands over foreign Jews in the Southern Zone for deportation.
	18	Failure of Anglo-Canadian Dieppe raid.
	23	Episcopal letter from Mgr Saliège protesting against the persecution of the Jews.
September		First number of clandestine *Lettres françaises*.

November	8	Beginning of Allied invasion of North Africa (Operation Torch) leading to deal with Darlan.
	11	Germans occupy the Southern Zone.
	27	French fleet scuttled at Toulon
December	24	Assassination of Darlan.
End of December		Closure of the École des Cadres at Uriage.

1943

During year		Gradual implantation of Maquis units throughout France.
January		Fusion of Combat, Libération-Sud and Franc-Tireur into Mouvements Unis de la Résistance (MUR).
	30	Creation of the Milice.
February	15-16	Elaboration of the *Service du Travail Obligatoire* (STO).
May	27	Creation of the Conseil National de la Résistance (CNR).
	30	De Gaulle arrives in Algeria, leading to creation of the Comité Français de Libération Nationale (CFLN) led by de Gaulle and Giraud.
June	21	Jean Moulin arrested at Caluire, leading to his torture and death in early July.
July	14	*L'Honneur des Poètes* (poems assembled by Eluard) published clandestinely by *Les Editions de Minuit*.
September	5	Liberation of Corsica by the internal Resistance.
November	11	Biggest popular demonstrations throughout France since demonstrations began in 1941 on traditional French holidays.
December		St Exupéry's *Pilote de Guerre* published clandestinely in Lille.

1944

January		Arrest and deportation of leader of the Chantiers de la Jeunesse, General de la Porte du Theil, after suppression of the Chantiers.
	1	Darnand brought into Vichy Government as head of the police.
	6	Philippe Henriot becomes head of Vichy propaganda.
February		Anouilh's *Antigone* opens in Paris.
		First showing of Jean Grémillon's film *Le Ciel est à vous*.

Chronology

March	23	Consultative Assembly in Algeria supports votes for women.
	26	Battle on the plateau of Glières and defeat of the Maquis.
April	21	Women gain right to vote in CFLN Order for post-Liberation France.
	26	Pétain visits Paris.
May	1	*L'Honneur des Poètes. Vol. II Europe* published by *Les Editions de Minuit*.
May-June		Mobilisation of Maquisards throughout France.
June	2	CFLN becomes the Provisional Government of the French Republic.
	6	Jour-J (D-Day) Start of Operation Overlord in Normandy.
	9-10	SS Division *Das Reich* carries out hangings at Tuile and massacre at Oradour-sur-Glane.
	16-20	Battle of Mont-Mouchet. Maquisards disperse in the Massif.
	28	Assassination of Philippe Henriot.
July	7	Murder of Georges Mandel.
	21-23	Battle of the Vercors. Defeat and destruction of the Maquis, followed by massacres in the area by Miliciens and Germans.
	31	Disappearance of St-Exupéry on aerial photo-mission over the south of France.
August	15	Landing of French and Allied forces in Provence.
August-September		Progressive Liberation of France by the Allies, the French armies and the internal Resistance (Forces Françaises de l'Intérieur – FFI).
August	20	Pétain forced to leave Vichy and taken eventually to Sigmaringen with rump of Vichy Government and Paris Collaborators.
	19-25	Liberation of Paris.
	25-26	De Gaulle fêted in Paris.

1945

July	Trial of Pétain. Death sentence commuted to life imprisonment on the Ile d'Yeu. Died 1951.
October	Trial of Laval. Death sentence carried out, after his attempted suicide.

INDEX

Abetz, Otto 141
abortion 44
Actes de la Recherche en Sciences Sociales 150
Action Française 3, 49, 63, 64, 66, 68, 92
'agent de liaison' *see* Marcenac, Jean
agricultural workers 240
Ain 246
Aire de Côte 234-5
Aix-en-Provence 91
Albrecht, Bertie 203
Alcuin 229
Alès 18, 30, 248
Algeria 95, 236, 238, 239
Alias, Commandant 100
Alibert, Raphael 134, 135, 141
Allemand à Paris, Un 261
Alliance Nationale contre la Dépopulation 37
allies 140, 143
Alpes-Maritimes 13, 15, 16, 30
Alsace-Lorraine 220, 258
Alter, André 121
Amants d'Avignon, Les 194, 197
Ambrière, Francis 121
America, South 50
Amitié Chrétienne 78
Amitié Judéo-Chrétienne 81
anarchists 238, 248
Angers 209
Angleterre (d'Alcuin à Huxley) 226, 229
anglophobia 106, 109-10, 116
Anjou 209
Annales 196
Annunzio, Gabriele d' 63
Anouilh, Jean 108, 118, 194
anti-fascism 235
anti-feminism 40, 45
Antigone 194, 262
anti-Semitism 73-8, 82-5, 134, 136, 142, 258, 269
Aragon, Louis 107, 194, 197, 217, 218, 255
Arbellot, Simon 52, 69
Ardèche 13, 15, 17, 19-24, 27, 29, 30, 51

Ariège 233, 248
Armistice 53, 95, 101, 103, 108, 181, 236
Armistice army 208, 236
Armory 110, 113
Army, French 73, 76, 77
Aron, Raymond 84-5, 174
Aron, Robert 82
Arras 96, 99, 101, 137
Assembly of Cardinals and Archbishops 140, 142, 143, 144
assertive code 260, 261, 263
Association Catholique de la Jeunesse Française (ACJF) 135, 143
Association des Anciens d'Uriage 161, 162
Association Nationale des Anciens Combattants de la Résistance (ANACR) 202
Association Nationale des Combattants Voltonaires de la Résistance 202
Association pour la Création d'un Musée de la Résistance (Ivry) 202
Atlantic Monthly 92
attentisme 7, 208, 212, 246
Au Bon Beurre 8
Aubenas 1, 21
Aude 13, 17
Augustine, St. 76
Auvergne 59
Auvity, Mgr. 139, 140
Auxois 234, 246
Aveline, Claude 226
Aveyron 13, 15, 16, 27, 30
Azéma, J-P 77

Bagatelles pour un Massacre 269
Bailleul, Roger 143
Bailyn, B. 196
Barbier, Pierre 108
Barrès 255-8
Barrès, Maurice 74, 155
Baudéan, Jean 121
Baudrillart, Cardinal 138, 143
Beaussart, Mgr. 138, 139
Beauvoir, Simone de 115
Beigbeder, Marc 113, 116, 172, 186

284

Belloc, Hilaire 74
Benjamin, René 42
Bérard, Léon 75, 76, 266
Bergery, Gaston 92
Bergson, Henri 135, 185, 255, 258
Bérimont, Luc 206-9, 218, 219, 220
   Huche à pain, La 207, 209
   'Temps du beau plaisir, Le' 207-9
Berland, Jacques 113, 118
Bernheim 226
Beuve-Méry, Hubert 148-9, 154
Béziers 234
Bibliothèque de Documentation Internationale Contemporaine 202
Bibliothèque Nationale 202
Bichelonne, Jean 2
Blache, V. de la 164
Blankaert, Louis 137
Blondel, Charles 181
Blum, Léon 68, 77, 95, 255
Blum, Robert 77
Boegner, Pastor Marc 75, 237
Boltanski, L.150-1
Bonnard, Abel 32, 137, 138, 139, 265
Bonnet, Georges 55
Book of the Month Club 93
Borne, E.176, 180, 183
Borotra, Jean 236
Boterf, Hervé le 121
Bouhélier, Saint-Georges de 119
Bourdieu, P.150-1
Bourdin, J. 147, 150, 156, 159, 168, 169
Boutellier, Paul 257
Boutmy, E 166
Brasillach, Robert 61, 111, 126, 269-73
Brazil 108
Britain 55, 56, 58, 65, 66, 101
British Academy 169
British Broadcasting Corporation (BBC) 108, 229, 230
British Museum 202
Brun, G. 80
Bruyez, René 119, 122

Cado, Henri 239, 241
Cahier Noir, Le 226
Cahiers du Silence, Les 222-30
Cahiers du Témoignage Chrétien 142
Cahors 220
Caillot, Mgr. 140, 143
Calvet, Mgr. 138

Camisards 244-5, 248
Camus, Albert 194, 197
Canaud, Jacques 233, 234
Capestang 234
Carcopino, Jérome 15, 26
Casanova, Danièle 203
Casérès, Benigno 149
Cassou, Jean 218, 221
Castelot, André 116
'Castri Conubii' 40
Cathars 245
Catholic Church and Catholicism 20, 107, 133-44, 171-89 *passim*, 197, 227, 247
   and education 20,21, 31, 50, 265-8
   and Jews 73, 74, 75-6, 77-85
   hierarchy 75, 76, 78, 82, 133, 134, 136, 138, 140, 141-4
Céline, L-F. 258, 269, 273
censorship 48-59, 67, 68, 115-16, 118-19, 122, 260, 261, 262
Centre de Documentation Juive Contemporaine 73
Centre National de la Recherche Scientifique (CNRS) 169
Cévennes 234, 244-9 *passim*
Chabrol, Jean-Pierre 245, 247, 248
Chagrin et la Pitié, Le 4
Chambe, General 102
Champion, Pierre 119
Chantiers de la Jeunesse 108, 112, 148, 159, 160, 173, 181, 182, 240
Charlemagne 229, 258
Châteaubriant 209, 220
Chateaubriant, Alphonse de 138
Châteauroux 57
Chaulot, P. 220
Chautemps, C.52, 93
chef de la famille 42, 45
Chemin du Stalag, Le 262
Chevalier, Jacques 134, 135, 185
Chevallier, J-J.159, 165-8, 170
Chollet, Archbishop 134
Chombart de Lauwe, P-H.148, 159, 164-5, 169
Chrysostom, St. John 76
Ciel est à vous, Le 123-31
cinema 123-31 *passim*, 271
Clair, René 271
clandestine literature 222-4
Clark, T.N.170
Claude, Georges 56, 70
Claudel, Paul 114

Clermont Ferrand 187, 240
Cocteau, Jean 113
Code de la Famille 36
Cogniat, R.116
Colditz 77, 81
Colette Baudoche 256
Combat 149, 176, 187, 195, 198
Combes laws 73
Comeau 112
Comédie Française 111, 114, 121
Comité d'Action de la Résistance 202
Comité d'Histoire de la Deuxième Guerre Mondiale 202, 233-4
Comité de Libération du Cinéma Français 123
Comité d'Organisation de l'Industrie Cinématographique 128, 132
Comité d'Organisation des Entreprises de Spectacle 118
Comité Femmes de Prisonniers 203
Comité National des Ecrivains 198
Comité populaire de Femmes de Marseille 203
Comités cantonaux de Libération 30
Comité Populaire de Femmes de Marseilles 203
Comités Cantonaux de Libération 30
Juives (CGQJ) 76, 77, 136
Communism and Communist Party, 7, 14-15, 19, 20, 22, 60, 66, 196, 198, 238-9, 246, 255
Compagnons de France 173, 182, 183
Comte, Auguste 163
Comte, Bernard 176, 177
Congrès des Evrivains européens 258
Connoisseur 55
Conseil National 94, 141
Conseils à l'Occupé 199
Continental 128, 129, 131
contrôle postal and contrôle technique 17, 18, 19, 20, 28, 32, 239, 240, 245
Copains, Les 272
Cordesse, Henri 233
Corporation paysanne 249
Courbe, Mgr. 143
Courrier de Centre, Le 52, 53, 60, 70
Cousteau, P-A.95
Cri d'Alarme, Le 204
Croix de Feu 66, 72
Croix, La 50, 51, 52, 53, 57, 69, 95

Crommelynck, F. 113
Cross of Lorraine 107

D'Abord la France 102
Daladier, E.55
Dannecker, SS Hauptsturmführer 136
Dante 65
Darlan, Admiral 17, 53, 236
Darnand, Joseph 94, 48, 156
Darquier de Pellepoix, L.74
David, star of 215
Déat, Marcel 115, 138, 156
Debray, R 152
Debû-Bridel, Jacques 200, 202, 226, 229
Décombres, Les 269
Delarue, Maurice 115
Delay, Mgr. 140
Délégation de la France Libre 94
Démann, Fr. Paul 80
dénatalité 37-8
Denizot, Gaston 119
denunciations 20-3
Déracinés, Les 256
Dernier Métro, Le 7
Diebolt, Mme. 203
Dieulefit 171, 178
Domaine Français 219, 220, 221
Domenach, J-M.143, 147, 149-50, 176
Doncoeur, Paul 120
Doriot, Jacques 156, 256
Dreyfus, Alfred 49, 73, 80, 144, 245, 258
Drieu la Rochelle, Pierre 155, 255
Drôle de Jeu 194
Drôme 28
Dru, Gilbert 143
Drumont, E.74
Druon, Maurice 223
Ducruy, F. 159, 160
Dufour, Jean 69
Duhourcau, F. 255, 256
Dumazedier, J.148-9, 162
Dunkirk 66, 102, 106
Dunoyer de Segonzac, H.135, 148-9, 159, 172, 183
Duquesne, J.73
Durfort 246
Durkheim, E.163, 164
Duthoit, E.137
Dutoit, Mgr. 137, 138, 140

Eastern front 225

Index

Ecole des Cadres d'Uriage 7, 135, 136, 147-70, 173, 176, 178, 182, 183, 187
école normale 27
Ecole Normale Supérieure 271
école publique 27
Ecrivains Combattants 114
Editions de la Maison Française (New York) 92
Editions de Minuit 222-30
education 13-35, 133, 134, 135
    Ministry of 13, 15, 24, 25, 30, 94,
    and women 41-2
    see also Catholic Church and education
Eluard, Paul 107, 194
Emmanuel Mounier 176
Emmanuel Mounier and the New Catholic Left 172-4
Emmanuel Mounier, Pioneer of the Catholic Revival 176
Emmanuel, Pierre 217, 220
employment, women 42-3
enseignement ménager 41-2
épuration 15, 59, 60
Equipe Nationale d'Uriage (ENU) 161, 162
équipes sociales 135
Esprit 147-8, 155, 171-89 *passim*
Ethiopia 65, 66
Etoiles du Lot 213
Eveil du XXe Arrondissement, L' 204
Evolution de l'Empire Britannique, L' 166
Excelsior, L' 49, 52, 55, 58
Express, L' 152
exode 98, 102, 103

Faber, Juliette 111
Fabre-Luce, A. 85
fall of France 95, 101, 171, 236
familialism 36-9
famille 21, 23, 36, 123, 240, 244
familles nombreuses 39
Farnier, Me. René 49, 59-72
fascism 2, 8, 173, 211-12, 238, 255, 258, 270, 271
    and women 36, 40
Fay, Bernard 135
Faye, J-P. 199
Félibrige 59, 62, 63, 64, 67, 71
feminism 7

'Femme au foyer' 36, 40, 41, 45
Femmes Comtoises 203
Femmes Françaises 203
Femmes Patriotes 203
Ferguson, Stuart 120
Ferry, Gilles 147, 156, 159
fête des mères 43
Fichte 257
Figaro, Le 59
Film, Le 125, 131
Finaly brothers 80, 81
Flight to Arras 92, 93
Florisoone, M. 116
folklore 244
Footitt, Hilary 206
Fombeure, Maurice 218, 221
    A dos d'oiseau 218
Forces Françaises de l'Intérieur (FFI) 62, 245
Foreign Office, French 52, 93
Forestier, Père 143
Forêts de la Nuit, Les 8
France-Amérique 94
France, Anatole 107
France Forever Association 94
France Libre *see* Free French
France Libre, La 222
Franco, General 106
Franc-Tireur 194
Francs-Tireurs et Partisans Français (FTPF) 206, 220, 232, 242
Free French 7, 101, 222, 223, 230
    see also Gaullism
freemasonry 20, 133, 134, 135, 139
Frenay, Henri 149, 172, 187
Fresnes 226, 269
Freud, S. 257, 258
Friedländer, S. 79, 81
Front National 220
Frossard, L-O. 52
Fumet, S. 187
Furet, F. 84-5

Gadoffre, Gilbert 156, 159
Gaillard, Pol 114, 117
Gandilhon 59
Gard 13, 17-19, 23, 27, 30, 239, 246
Garric, Robert 135
Gaucheron, Jacques 217, 220
Gaulle, General Charles de, and Gaullism 4, 7, 67, 74, 92, 93, 94, 95, 108, 111, 117, 138, 139, 140, 141, 143, 195, 197, 198, 222,

288 *Index*

223, 224, 232, 242, 266
gender, and National Revolution 36, 39-45
Geneva 227
Gerbe, La 138
Gerlier, Cardinal 77, 86n5, 134, 135, 138, 140, 141-2
Gestapo 226
Gévaudan 245
Gex, Didier 113
Gide, André 255
Gillier, Georges 234
Giono, J. 273n5
Giraud, General 93, 95, 236
Giraudoux, J. 52, 113
Glasberg, Abbé 78,142
Glorieux, Chanoine P. 106
Goering, H. 236
Goethe 258
Gortais, Albert 143
Grégory, Georges 121
Grémillon, Jean 123-31 *passim*
Grenoble 28, 148, 160, 168
Groupe Collaboration 56, 70-1, 138
Guéhenno, Jean 218, 221
Guerlac, François 195
Guerry, Mgr. 137, 148
Guilhaumou, J. 200
Guillemin, Henri 120
Guingouin, Georges 54, 61, 246
Guitton, Jean 81
Gurs 77, 141
Gurvitch, G. 170

Hachette 223
Halls, W.D. 121, 177
Hamon, Auguste and Henriette 109
Harris, André 83, 84, 85
Hartmann, Ed. von 257
Harzcouet, Mgr. 139
Hébert, J.R. 200
Hébertot, Jacques 111, 113-14
Heller, G. 261
Hellman, J. 150, 153, 154, 172, 173, 174, 176
Henriot, Philippe 52, 54, 58, 68, 140, 242, 247, 248, 267
Henry-Haye, G. 93
Hérault 13, 27-8, 48, 50, 234, 239, 243
heroes, cult of 265-8
High Command, French 103
Himmler, H. 154
Hitler, A. 230
holocaust 82, 83

Holt, Jany 109
homosexuality 270
Honegger, Arthur 114, 119, 122
Honneur des Poètes, L', vols I and II 206, 210, 217, 218
Humanité, L' 194
  Edition féminine 203

Idealism, in theatre 271
Imperial War Museum 202
Information and Propaganda, Ministry of 50, 52,54, 57, 58
inspecteurs de l'Académie, 17, 19, 24-9, 32
Institut Charles de Gaulle 202
instituteurs, institutrices 233, 244, 266
  see also teachers
Instituts Catholiques, Lyon 137, Lille 137, Angers 137, Paris 138
Interior, Ministry of 13, 14, 15, 16, 17, 52, 67, 238, 239
International Brigades 239
internment camps 54, 60, 77, 78
  see also Gurs
Irish Free State 40
Isaac, Jules 82
Isère 234
Israel 74, 81, 82, 84
Italy 58, 65, 66

Jacobins 200
Jacobs, Gabriel 255
Jacoby, Jean 107
Jamet, Annie 270
Jean-Faure, André 55
Jeanneret, René 107
Je suis partout 49, 95, 125, 272
Jesuits 92
Jeunes Filles de France 203
Jeunesse-France 159, 160, 169
Jewish Chronicle, The 79
Jews 7, 19, 55, 66, 76-85, 133-42, 237, 239, 242, 244
  see also Catholic Church and Jews
Joan of Arc 6, 106-22, 203, 220, 258, 265-8
Jocistes 142, 143
John, S.B. 206, 255
Josse, R. 147, 156, 159, 169
Journal Officiel de la France Combattante 222
Juvenal, Bertrand de 155

Index

Kant 257
Kedward, H.R.182, 202, 206
Kelly, M.176
Kemp, Robert 121
Kérillis, H. de 93
Kernan, Thomas 14
'Kinder, Kirche, Küche' 40
King, J.200
Kleist, Heinrich von 258
Krug von Nidda 69

Laborie, Pierre 232, 233
Labour, Ministry of 239
Lacombe Lucien 9
Lacroix, Jean 148, 149, 174, 179, 180, 186
Lalou, René 255
Lamirand, Georges 135, 236, 267
Lamour, Philippe 153
Languedoc 242, 248, 249
Laubreaux, Alain 117-18
Laval, Pierre 9, 31, 48, 57, 62, 69, 70, 137, 140, 144, 198, 236, 237, 240, 241-2, 243, 247, 248, 267
Lebesque, Norvan 117
Leenhardt, R.172
Léger, A see Saint-John Perse
Légion d'Honneur 49, 50, 59
Légion des Voltonaires Français contre le Bolchévisme (LVF) 138
Légion Française des Combattants 14, 22-3, 27, 29, 30, 32, 49, 54, 56, 59-62, 64, 66, 70
Lemoine, Marcel 54
Lesaunier 74-5
Lescure, Pierre 223
Lesourd, Paul 138
Lettres Françaises 194, 198
Leurs Figures 256, 258
Lévi-Strauss, C.164, 170
Lévy, B-H.150-3, 169, 170, 172, 173
Lévy, J-P. 203
Libération 194, 195, 198
Liberation 59, 62, 136, 223, 235, 245, 246, 248, 249, 267
Liénart, Cardinal 137, 138, 140, 141, 142-4
Lille 95, 143
Limagne, Pierre 50, 51, 53, 55, 57
Limoges and Limousin 48-72, 92, 246
Lisbon 93
Loire 209
Loisy, Jean 119

London 108, 110, 222, 223
Longwell, Ann 219
Lot 206
Louis le Grand,Lycée 270
Louix XIV 17
Lozère 13, 15-16, 18-19, 21, 24-30, 233, 234, 239, 240, 243, 245, 246, 247
Lubac, R.P.Henri de 148
Lumière d'Eté 128, 132
Lustiger, Cardinal 73
Lyon 6, 15, 50, 94, 108, 141, 143, 171, 176, 181, 187, 220, 267

Main d'Oeuvre Etrangère (MOE) 235
Maison Française d'Oxford 204
Malle, Louis 9
Malraux, André 256, 273n2
Mandagout 234
Mandel, Georges 95
Man, Henri de 155
maquis 5, 6, 9, 114, 232-4, 242-9
Marc, Alexandre 112
Marcel, Gabriel 121
Marcenac, Jean 206, 209-16, 218, 219, 220
 'L'agent de liaison,' 213-16
 'Mort à nos ennemis' 209-13
 'Traîtres se trahissent, Les' 218
Marche à l'Etoile, La 225
Marchetti, S.220-1
Marianists 92
Maritain, Jacques 174
Marquet, Mary 119
Marrou, Henri 80-1
Marrus, M.7, 73
Marseillaise, La 4, 200
Marseille 108
Marsh, Patrick 118, 121, 122
Marvejols 233, 245
Marwick, Arthur 195
Massif de l'Aigoual 234, 235
Massis, Henri 187
Masson, Joseph 52
Masson, Loys 220
Matignon agreement 24
Mauchemps, Jacques 115
Maulnier, Thierry 115, 121, 155
Mauriac, François 227, 228
Mauriette, Marcelle 122
Maurras, Charles 49, 58, 63, 72, 74, 92, 245, 249, 256
Maydieu, Père 148
Mayer, Daniel 77
Memmi, Albert 83-4

Ménagère 203
Mende 18, 28, 239, 240, 243, 247
Merlat, Mme. 203
Mermoz, J. 92
Mers el-Kébir 66, 106
Mes Cahiers 255, 256
Messages 220
Michelet, Edmond 70
Midi 13-35 *passim*
Milice 6, 48, 55, 61, 118, 149, 152, 239, 243
miners 247, 248
Mistral, F. 62, 63, 65, 67
Monde, Le 149
Montauban 136
Montefiore, Sir Moses 80
Montherlant, Henry de 255
Montini, Mgr. 75
Montoire 2, 137, 236
Montpellier 28, 238, 243, 245
Montuclard, M. 188
Moore, W.E. 170
Morgan, Charles 227, 228
Mortara Case 80
Morvan 233, 234
Moscow 92
Mossé, Robert 148
motherhood 39-44
Mouches, Les 262
Mounier, Emmanuel 7, 147-50, 153-6, 171-89
Mouvements Unis de la Résistance (MUR) 232
Munich 58, 65, 178, 255
Murinet, Château de 149
Musée de l'Histoire vivante (Montreuil) 202
Musée de la Résistance (Lyon) 202
Mussolini, B. 58, 63, 65
myths 244

Nantes 209, 220
nationalism 110, 111
National Revolution 1-3, 4, 16-18, 23-4, 27, 32, 55, 56, 66, 68, 95, 113, 117, 162, 163, 165, 173, 174, 175, 177, 180, 182, 185, 186, 221, 236, 245, 260, 265
and women 36-45
naturalisations 134
Naurois, Abbé René de 148
Nazism 58, 76, 81, 84, 101, 133, 138, 175, 198, 199, 223, 227, 228, 229, 230

Nazi-Soviet Pact 4, 7, 196
'New Europe' 237
New Testament 82
New York 93
Nice 15
Ni Droite ni Gauche 154, 174, 175
Nîmes 27, 50, 53, 235
Niort 220
Nizan, Paul 153, 157
Noé, camp at 78
Nora, Simon 149
North Africa 93, 95, 236
  see also Algeria
nostalgia 271
Notre Avant-Guerre 269-73
Notre Jeunesse 172
Nouvelliste, Le 138
Novalis, Friedrich von 258
Noyautage des Administrations publiques (NAP) 243
Nuffield Foundation 200
Nuremberg racial laws 141
Nuremberg rallies 271

Oberlé, Jean 222
Occitan 63, 246
occupied zone 73, 74, 79, 86, 95, 133, 136, 184, 186, 209, 234
Ode to France 227
Old Testament 82
'Opération vert printanier' 77
Oradour-sur-Glane 72
oral history 61, 245, 248
Ordre viril et l'efficacité dans l'action, L' 167-8
Organisation de Résistance de l'Armée (ORA) 234
Orléans 108, 121, 122
Ory, Pascal 220
outlaw 244-9

Palais de Chaillot 119
Palais de la Mutualité 111
Palatinate 257
Papal Nuncio 134
Paris sous l'occupation 194, 197
Parrot, Louis 107
Parti Démocrate Populaire 137
Parti Populaire Français (PPF) 56, 66, 67, 257
Parti Social Français (PSF) 66
Pascal 68
passeurs 233
Passeur, Stève 113

Index

paternalism 36, 42, 45
patrie 21, 23, 25
Patriote parisienne 203
Paxton, R.O. 7, 73, 85, 150, 156
Paÿs, Marcel 48-59, 60, 66, 67, 68
Pearl Harbour 93
peasantry 232-49 *passim*
Péguy, Charles 6, 109, 111-14, 150, 157, 172, 255, 265
Péguy, Marcel 112
Père Duchesne, Le 200
Périgord 92
personalism 171-89 *passim*
Peste, La 194, 197
Pétain, Marshal Philippe and Pétainism 3, 4, 7, 16, 18, 22, 23, 25, 26, 28, 30, 32, 37, 38, 42, 45, 48, 49, 58, 61, 62, 63, 65, 66, 67, 68, 74, 76, 79, 81, 85, 92, 93, 94, 95, 96, 101, 106, 107, 111, 115, 118, 134, 137, 139, 140, 141, 143, 148, 153, 160, 163, 182, 198, 236, 237, 248, 265, 266, 267
Peuple et Culture 149
Peyre, Commandant Henri 51, 52
Peyrouton, Marcel 67
philistines 209
phoney war 15, 17
Pierrard, Pierre 73, 76
Pilote de Guerre 91-104, 206, 218-19, 221, 255
Pioch, Georges 116
Pitoëffs 109, 271
Pius XI 40
Play, F. Le 37, 163, 168
Poèmes de Fresnes 269
poetry, *contrebande* 206, 208-9, 219-20
Resistance 206-21
police, French including Gendarmerie 17-20, 22-3, 29, 30, 52, 67, 235, 239, 241, 242, 243, 246
German 238
Populaire du Centre, Le 71
Popular Front 4, 49, 68, 107, 117, 123, 124, 255, 269, 272
Porché, François 119
Porte du Theil, General de la 135, 159
posters 120
Poulantzas, N. 2
Pour la Victoire 93, 94
Pour retrouver la France. Enquêtes sociales en équipes 164-5
Préaux 20
prefects 14-19, 21-4, 28-9, 32, 52-5, 60, 67, 236-48 *passim*
Prélude choral et fugue 172, 183
primary schools 13-35 *passim*
Privas 28
procreation 40, 44
Progrès, Le 220
Prominente 77
pronatalism 36-9
propaganda 13, 16, 23, 36, 37, 40, 45, 222, 223, 230, 237-8, 242
Propaganda Abteilung 95
Protestants 234, 244-5, 247, 248
Proudhon, Pierre-Joseph 74
Proust, Marcel 255, 258
Provence 248, 249
Pugey, T 107
Puy-en-Velay, Le 50
Pyrénées-Orientales 13, 17

Que ma joie demeure 273n5
Qu'est-ce qu'un collaborateur 194
Quercy 220
Quinel, Charles 116

racialism 39-40, *see also* anti-Semitism
radio, Vichy 248
ralliement 144
Raknem, Ingvald 110
Read, Peter 219
Rebatet, Lucien *see* Vinneul, François
Récébédou 78
Reconnaissance Group 2/33 99
réfractaires 233-5, 240, 241-2, 244, 245, 246
regionalism 61, 62, 64, 67, 68
Relève 237, 248
Renaud, Madeleine 129, 130, 131
rénovation 36-7, 261-2
Renseignements généraux 17, 19, 29, 56, 234, 247
repressive code 260, 261, 262
Reuter 262
Revel, J-F. 172
Révolution Nationale *see* National Revolution
Reynaud, P. 95
Rhineland 103, 255
Rhodain, Mgr. 141
Richard, M. 221
Rideau des Jeunes, theatrical company 111, 116
Rieucros 19
Rivesaltes 77

292 *Index*

Robin, Régine 199
Rochefort-sur-Loire 209, 220
Rodez 15
Romains, Jules 272
Romans-Petit, H.246
Roque, Colonel de la 92
Rostand, Maurice 112
Rothschild, Elie de 77
Rothschild, Philippe de 223
Rouan, François 246
Roubaix 142
Rouen 120
Rougemont, Denis de 153, 173, 174
Rouleau, R.109
Roux, François de 115
Royal Air Force 102, 230

Sachsenhausen 236
Sadouo, Georges 125, 128, 131, 132
St. Etienne 240
Saint-Exupéry, Antoine de 91-9, 101-4, 218-19
St. Jean de Muzols 23
Saint-John Perse (Léger, A.) 93
St. Junien 62
Saint Louis 265
Saliège, Mgr. 78, 79, 136, 138, 142, 144
Salle Pleyel 119
Salut National, Le 63
Samson 209
Sarraut, Albert 52
Sarreau, Henri de 107
Sartre, Jean-Paul 108, 115, 118, 194, 197, 220
Sauvenay, Jean 116
Savoy 63
Schaeffer, P.108, 172, 183
Schelling, F. 257
Schiller, F. von 119
Schumann, Maurice 120, 223
Schwarz-Bart, André 79
scouts 135, 143
Secours National 135
Sedouy, Alain 83, 84, 85
Seghers, Pierre 220
Service d'Ordre Légionnaire (SOL) 62
Service du Travail Obligatoire (STO) 28, 31, 55, 57, 60, 136, 142, 143, 144, 152, 233-48 *passim*, 267
sexuality, female 36, 43, 45
Shakespeare, W.110
Shaw, G.B. 109-11

Shaw, G.B: 109-11
Siegfried, A. 164
Sigmaringen 2
Signal 260
Silence de la Mer, Le 194, 199, 223, 224, 230
Simmonds, J.C.206
soil of France 206-21 *passim*, 245, 249
Solages, Mgr. 136, 148
Sorel, Georges 155
Sorokin, P.163, 170
Soucy, Robert 258
Spaak, Charles 128, 129, 131
Spain 106, 239
Spanish Civil War 255
Speaight, Robert 227
Special Operations Executive (SOE) 6
Spectator, The 227
Speer, Albert 2
Spencer, H.163
sport 236
Stalag VIIA 220
Statut des Juifs 75, 76, 77, 85, 183
Sternhell, Z.154-5, 174, 175, 258
students 240
Suhard, Cardinal 134, 138, 139, 141
surveillance 13-35, 239
Sweden, King of 236
Switzerland 107
Syndicat National des Instituteurs 15

Tardini, Mgr. 75
Tarn 234
Tarzan 245
teachers 13-32, *see also* instituteurs
Témoignage Chrétien 142, 187, 195, 197
'Temps du beau plaisir, Le' *see* Bériment, Luc
Temps Mort, Le 224, 226
Texcier, Jean 198, 199
Theas, Mgr. 78
theatre 106-20
theatres, Paris 108-19
Thibaud, P. 172
Thibaudet, Albert 257
Third Republic 32, 49, 63, 64, 68, 93, 134, 139, 175, 179, 185
Tillon, Germaine 203
Tissen, Berthe 114
Tixier, A.94
Todt Organisation 234

Index 293

Torrès, H. 94
Touchard, Jean 256
Toulon 236
Toulouse 220
Toulouse-Lautrec 56
trade unions 2, 133, 142
'Traîtres se trahissent, Les' *see* Marcenac, Jean
travail 21, 23, 37, 262 *see also* famille, patrie
tricolour 209
Triolet, Elsa 194, 197, 203
Troyes 27
    treaty of 108
Truffaut, F. 7, 8

Union française de défense de la race 218
Union nationale des associations des déportés, internés et familles de disparus 202
Uriage, *see* Ecole des Cadres
USA 92, 94, 95, 101
USSR 101, 209

Vailland, Roger 194
Valentin, François 41, 135
Vallat, Xavier 74, 76, 77, 136
Vallery-Radot, R. 135
Van des Esch, J. 115
Variot, Jean 112
Vatican 134
    Second Council 74, 82, 83, 84
Vélodrome d'Hiver 77, 78
Vercors (Jean Bruller) 194, 199, 223, 224, 225
Véré, Claude 113
Vermorel, Claude 109, 114-19, 121
Vers le Style du XXe Siècle 149, 159
Vielzeuf, Aimé 236
Vigan, Le 234
Villerabel, Mgr. 139
Villier, André 119
Vinneul, François (Lucien Rebatet) 125, 131
Vioux, Marcel 106
virility 167
Vivarais 91
Voix des Femmes, La 203
Voix françaises 138
Volontaire, Le 245, 248
Voltaire 74

Wagner, Mme. 203
Weil, Simone 76
Weimar 258

Weisz, G. 170
Winock, M. 176, 178
World War I 55, 56, 60, 61, 62, 64, 65, 68, 247

Youth, Minister of 236

Zérapha, G. 183

For Product Safety Concerns and Information please contact our EU representative GPSR@taylorandfrancis.com
Taylor & Francis Verlag GmbH, Kaufingerstraße 24, 80331 München, Germany

www.ingramcontent.com/pod-product-compliance
Lightning Source LLC
Chambersburg PA
CBHW071346290426
44108CB00014B/1458